FASHION

ENTREPRENEURSHIP

FASHION

ENTREPRENEURSHIP

■ RETAIL BUSINESS PLANNING ■

MICHELE GRANGER

Southwest Missouri State University, Springfield, Missouri

. . . .

TINA STERLING

TC Strategies, Inc., Columbia, Missouri
Stephens College, Columbia, Missouri

FAIRCHILD PUBLICATIONS, INC., NEW YORK

Executive Editor: Olga T. Kontzias

Assistant Acquisitions Editor: Carolyn Purcell

Editor: Joann Muscolo

Assistant Production Editor: Amy Zarkos

Art Director: Adam B. Bohannon

Production Manager: Priscilla Taguer

Editorial Assistant: Suzette Lam

Copy Editor: Roberta Mantus

Interior Design: Carla Bolte

Cover Design: Adam B. Bohannon

Chapter 6: Becoming an E-trepreneur authored by Jana Hawley, University of Missouri

Library of Congress Catalog Card Number: 2002103886

ISBN: 1-56367- 233-2

GST R 133004424

Printed in the United States of America

3 RESEARCHING THE INDUSTRY AND THE MARKET   53

Extended Contents

Contents

Preface

This text has been written for those college students, practitioners, or new entrepreneurs who desire to start their own retail businesses in the fashion industry. It has also been developed for those fashion retailers who are already in business and want to examine and strengthen their entrepreneurial skills. While there are hundreds of books available to the entrepreneur who is starting a business, there is very little information available to the entrepreneur who is interested in starting a fashion retail operation. Why is the retailing of apparel, home furnishings, accessories, and soft goods unique? The fashion industry operates on a distinct seasonal calendar with merchandise provided through vendors operating in specific channels purchased by customers of varying target markets in an industry of intense competition. This text is distinctive in that it focuses on the fashion retail business from the development of a concept to the construction of a business plan that can be used to solicit funding and guide the business to a growth or exit point. It is significant to note that this text is directed to fashion retailing rather than manufacturing. While this text examines fashion retailing from a broad perspective that includes service businesses and Internet sales, it also provides an in-depth analysis of the retail business from defining the target market, clarifying product selection, and selecting a location to operational issues related to merchandising, personnel, and control.

In Chapter 1, the prospective fashion entrepreneur begins by developing an understanding of entrepreneurship. The prospective entrepreneur is guided to conduct a self-analysis of his or her entrepreneurial mindset and skills. Defining and knowing traits possessed by successful entrepreneurs increases the chances of prosperity for new entrepreneurs. Next, timing and funding availability are examined as they play a crucial role in determining whether or not to act upon the desire to start a business. The prospective entrepreneur then begins to clarify the business concept. The business concept takes the idea for a business venture and tests it against industry, financial, political, and economic environments before beginning construction of the actual business plan. Finally, in Chapter 1, the prospective entrepreneur will look at the importance of developing a comprehensive business plan.

In Chapter 2, the entrepreneur's concept for the potential fashion business in terms of product is examined. Entrepreneurs have the option of creating a new product or marketing an existing product. Frequency of purchase, availability of the product and its lifespan, and product alternatives are all factors that impact the entrepreneur's choice of merchandise for the business. One of the challenges in choosing a merchandise selection for a business is determining the position of a product or product lines on the product life cycle. Two factors often distinguish a fashion entrepreneur's merchandise from that of competitors: service and branding. Branding is a dominant trend in the apparel and soft goods industry. Today's consumer, more than ever before, is selecting a brand that corresponds with his or her personality and values. Product differentiation and company image are central to the success of an entrepreneurial endeavor.

Chapter 3 focuses on the techniques commonly used to obtain information needed to objectively analyze the industry and determine the potential of a specific target market. Emphasis is placed on how to analyze market data and information for the purpose of developing a comprehensive marketing strategy through a market feasibility study. The market feasibility study includes an exploration of the fashion industry's current trends, norms, and standards. To be successful in a new business, the entrepreneur needs to know two things. First, he or she needs to know what the business really is and to which businesses it is connected. Second, he or she needs to know where this business lies in the broad scope of the industry. This exploration begins with a global perspective that filters down to a regional viewpoint.

Chapter 4 will use the market feasibility study to decide the best way in which to enter the market, whether one is starting a new business from the ground up, purchasing a franchise operation, or acquiring an existing business. Equally important to the entrepreneur is determining the way in which the entrepreneur will exit the business when it is time. Chapter 4 guides the potential entrepreneur through the process of determining the value of the business, selecting the best method to determine the value of the company, and, finally, structuring and implementing the sale.

The business concept begins to move toward reality in Chapter 5, in which finding a location for the business is discussed. Every entrepreneur has heard it: "The three most important keys to a successful business are location, location, and location." While the most important key to a profitable business is likely a top-notch business plan, location certainly can play a significant role in the success of a company. Location in Chapter 5 is examined from the perspective of a physical site that requires deciding whether to build, buy, or lease a facility. Exterior and interior characteristics are discussed as they relate to effective selling space. Chapter 6 expands upon location by focusing on the Internet as a business site and E-commerce as a vehicle of operation for the prospective business. A background for E-commerce, related computer technology, and Internet trends in fashion retailing are presented in this chapter.

Chapter 7 provides an examination of strategies the entrepreneur may implement to penetrate the defined market. A marketing strategy is developed by differentiating and analyzing the interrelationships of the product, place, price, and promotional aspects of the proposed business. Additionally, customer service is explored as a significant part of the marketing strategy. Good management and effective employees are necessary to provide positive customer service.

In Chapter 8, the importance of a management team is discussed in terms of leadership and organizational structure. Organizational culture and effective communication are examined with an emphasis on creating an intrapreneurial environment. Recruiting, interviewing, hiring, training, and motivating employees successfully are explored as keys to effective management. Conducting job analyses and constructing job specifications are discussed, as these activities may significantly impact the quality of personnel hired for positions.

In Chapters 1 through 8, the entrepreneur views the prospective business from a company, or holistic, perspective. The market potential of the company, its prospective customer and the product, marketing approaches that will service this customer, strategies for locating the company, and the development of a management team are explored in terms of the business as a whole. In Chapter 9, a specific area of the business is examined. The entrepreneur is now ready to begin examining the business from an operational perspective—merchandising. Merchandising is the key area of difference between a retail store of almost any product line and a fashion retail store. Fashion goods require unique policies and procedures in merchandising that other product classifications do not. The reasons for a specific focus on fashion merchandising are diverse; however, they primarily include the following: seasonality of goods, limitations and localization of resources, and diversity of product life cycles. Often, it is the merchandise selection that generates success or failure of the fashion retail business. It is the retail buyer's responsibility to locate, secure, price, and promote the merchandise assortment. Whether the entrepreneur takes on the role of the buyer or assigns it to an employee, it is one of the most significant decisions within the fashion business.

When forming a new venture, the entrepreneur must also make an informed decision about the type of ownership under which the business will operate. Chapter 10 explores the criteria for selecting a business entity. Choosing a form of ownership involves reviewing tax considerations, liability issues, costs of forming the legal entity, control of the business, and ease with which ownership can be transferred and capital can be accessed. The forms of ownership that are examined include a sole proprietorship, partnership, corporation, s-corporation, and limited liability corporation.

Chapter 11 presents a foundation for understanding and constructing basic financial statements, and it identifies which variables in a business affect the numbers in those statements. Key ratios are examined, as these are the tools used to determine how well the business is doing. Chapter 11 also illustrates how to calculate the break-even point for the business, how cash flow affects the business, and how to access capital. The financial plan is one of the most critical elements of the business plan. Most entrepreneurs also find it one of the most frightening. It will help determine the amount of financing that will be needed to make the plan feasible, what type of financing will be needed, and the time frame in which to obtain the financing.

In Chapter 12, the procedures and policies that need to be developed and implemented for merchandising and management functions to succeed are discussed. These are referred to as operations and control. Operations are the procedures put in place to actually run the business, while control refers to the points in the strategic planning process where results are compared to the goals and objectives. In this chapter, operations and control plans are explored as they relate to the facility, merchandise, employees, customers, inventory, and the computer. Additionally, the research and development needs of an entrepreneurial business are examined. A good operations and control plan facilitates a number of goals for the organization, and acts as a monitoring tool by providing continuity and summarizing information about the organization's infrastructure. It communicates and coordinates the activities that allow the business to grow.

Chapter 13 focuses on the entrepreneur's role in planning the business's growth. Strategies for facing new competition, becoming a market leader, and creating a market niche are explored. As a separate growth strategy, options in the global retail market are examined from using the World Wide Web and exporting to establishing international locations and foreign licensing. The importance of identifying capital and personnel requirements in growth planning is discussed and steps to growth planning are specified.

The primary purpose of Chapters 1 through 13 is to provide guidance and the framework necessary to understand and develop the business plan. Throughout the text, the key components that must be addressed in a well-written business plan are reviewed, and information needed to construct the different sections of the business plan is provided. Chapter 14 illustrates the key elements and format preferred to present a well-written plan. It specifies how the business plan may be assessed by investors, funders, and key management personnel within the company. At the end of Chapter 14, a sample business plan for a fashion retail operation is provided.

Entrepreneurship is a discipline like no other. It is an opportunity to act on dreams, to become one's own boss, secure financial freedom, and share a passion with others. Some people are cut out to be entrepreneurs and do what it takes to learn the skills necessary to succeed, while others are not. Owning a business requires an analysis of both personal and professional traits, and planning is critical to a successful business. The entrepreneur must analyze the business from a variety of angles, looking for its strengths, while seeking out its weaknesses with equal vigor. The challenges of business ownership are immense, but the rewards can surpass even the boldest dreams.

ACKNOWLEDGMENTS

- Writing a book can be a lonely process.
- Being an entrepreneur means striking out on your own, communicating your vision, and selling the idea.
- Fashion and business are often perceived as direct opposites.

This project found the best in all of these assumptions. Writing was not solitary, thanks to a partnership and the encouragement of family and friends. The entrepreneurial spirit was shining as we created this business called a book. Fashion merged with business in a fascinating, pragmatic, and unique manner.

Michele:
I am most grateful to my daughter, Annie, for surviving one more book. She continues to amaze and delight me, and is my soulmate of substance even at age 14. Daily, she brings truth, beauty, joy, and pride into my life. Her skills as a cheerleader and a comedian were put to the test throughout this project; she passed with flying colors. I wish for her the independence, self-satisfaction, and excitement that an entrepreneurial life can elicit. I would also like to express special thanks to the wonderful women of The Cool Girl Club—Marci, LaRaine, Debbie, Linda, Patty, Karla, Randee, Leann, and Mary—for their love and support. To Kirsty and Sarah, you are lifelines only a phone call away. At Southwest Missouri State University, I am fortunate to work with Sandy, the ideal colleague and friend, and students who share my enthusiasm for the fashion industry and inspire me to do and be my best. I thank my loving parents for nurturing an entrepreneurial spirit, one that can be found in all three of their children and the work they have chosen. To my brother, sister, and grandmother, you are always in my heart. I acknowledge with deep affection our precious Chewy. She is so missed and loved. To my co-author Tina, I have learned to appreciate friendship, patience, and perspective, the rewards of sincere collaboration.

Tina:
I wish to thank my wonderful daughter, Sierra, for her incredible support and love throughout this project. Even at the young age of 15, she inspires and encourages me to grow as a mother, an entrepreneur, and an individual. She's a wonderful, giving, and

compassionate person, and I am so very proud to be her mother. I also want to thank my husband, Peter, for all the computer help (we needed a lot!), washing the dishes, feeding the cat, and doing the laundry. I want to thank him most of all for encouraging me every step of the way and for the opportunity to pursue my entrepreneurial dreams. To my mom, my late father, sister (who, by the way, wants a copy of the book, but laughingly says she'll never read it), and my brother, for their love and understanding. I want to thank my friend, Ron, for being by my side, for being there when I needed a shoulder to lean on, and for pushing me forward when I needed an extra push. I wish to thank Kelly and David for their friendship, for pursuing their entrepreneurial dreams (you go my friends!), and for their undying support and encouragement as I pursued my own entrepreneurial venture. I am grateful to Davy and Kim for being such great friends and for their wonderful sense of humor. Thank you to Stephens College, its faculty and students, for the opportunity to teach entrepreneurship. Finally, I wish to thank all of my friends at the Kauffman Center for Entrepreneurial Leadership at the Ewing Marion Kauffman Foundation. It was through the Kauffman Center that I found the inspiration and knowledge to open the business I had always dreamed of. Thank you, Stefanie, for believing in me. Michele, thank you for your friendship, understanding, and patience as we pursued this wonderful venture.

Michele and Tina wish to thank Jana Hawley, Ph.D., University of Missouri, Department of Textile and Apparel Management for her contribution of Chapter 6: E-Commerce; Greg Bier, Ph.D., of Stephens College for his review of Chapter 8: Management, and Bogdan A. Susan, Attorney at Law of the law firm, Davis, Susan, and Holder, LLC for his review of Chapter 10: Legal Entities. We also wish to thank Ron Mueller of the Small Business Development Center in St. Charles, Missouri for his input in Chapter 11. A special thank you to Kathleen Hayes for all her help with the glossary and getting the manuscript to New York. To Jessica LaMonda, Bridget Abraham, and Shannon Lawson for allowing us to use their class business plans as a resource for Chapter 14. To the Kauffman Center for Entrepreneurial Leadership for allowing us to use their business plan format and include their Business Mentor CD-ROM. For their insightful comments, we acknowledge those who reviewed the manuscript: Jo-Ann Rolle, Kathleen Colussy, Jeanne C. King, Nancy Stanforth, Terry W. Noel, Dr. Luann Gashill, Dr. Yue He Harps-Logan, JoAnn Boric, and Debi Forse. Finally, to Olga Kontzias, Mary McGarry, and Joann Muscolo of Fairchild Publications, thank you for the opportunity and belief in this project.

Chapter 1

TAKING THE ROAD TO ENTREPRENEURSHIP

INTRODUCTION

In this chapter, you, the prospective fashion retail entrepreneur, begin by developing an understanding of entrepreneurship. Then you conduct a self-analysis of your entrepreneurial mindset and skills. Defining and knowing the traits possessed by already successful entrepreneurs increases the chances of success for new entrepreneurs. Next, timing and funding availability are examined. Timing and funding play crucial roles in the process of determining whether or not to start a business. The prospective entrepreneur then begins developing the business concept. The business concept takes the idea for a business and tests it against social, political, financial, and economic realities before the actual business plan is begun. Finally, the prospective entrepreneur looks at the importance of developing a comprehensive business plan.

UNDERSTANDING ENTREPRENEURSHIP: THE AGE OF THE ENTREPRENEUR

Never before has there been a more exciting time to enter the world of entrepreneurship. Entrepreneurship is challenging and ever changing. Each new day brings a new set of rewards and obstacles. Through this barrage emerge some of the most successful businesswomen and men in the world. Understanding entrepreneurship, owning a business, knowing how that business works, planning a business carefully, and knowing one's personal qualities will differentiate those who succeed from those who fail.

Millions of small businesses contribute to local economies, provide jobs, pay taxes, and generate a comfortable living for their owners. Today's economic climate and lifestyle preferences, as well as education and business trends, encourage and nurture entrepreneurship. Hundreds of thousands of college graduates, corporate executives, retirees, and individuals interested in career changes are striking out on their own. It has been the key to survival for individuals affected by corporate downsizing, outsourcing, and restructuring. Outsourcing refers to contracting for services, such as accounting and marketing, with individuals or businesses outside the company. Because of downsizing, outsourcing, and restructuring, many very skilled people are entering the world of entrepreneurship. The *age of the entrepreneur* provides opportunities for individuals from every imaginable background and category: male, female; young, old; rich, poor; college educated or not. It provides an abundance of economic opportunities for the fashion retailer.

Entrepreneurship is in an upward trend both nationally and internationally. With the growth of e-commerce, the number of "virtual companies" (companies offering goods and services on the Internet) has increased the opportunity for small businesses to increase sales and tap into global markets. Technology has made it possible for companies to accomplish more and reach more markets with fewer employees. Thanks to entrepreneurs, the technology boom is driving much of the world's economic growth. The apparel and footwear industry accounted for $249 million worth of Internet purchases in August 2000, according to the National Retail Federation and Forrests Research. Research has projected that small companies can respond quickly to change, thus creating a competitive advantage over larger companies. Entrepreneurs play a key role in our economy from a macroeconomic perspective, because of their role in the growth of the Internet.

The economic future of the United States rests in great part on the creation and growth of the small business. Small business is the backbone of the U.S. economy. According to the U.S. Small Business Administration (SBA), small businesses with fewer than 500 workers employ 53 percent of the private nonfarm workforce, contribute 47 percent of all sales in the country, and are responsible for 51 percent of the private gross domestic product. Industries dominated by small firms contributed a major share of the 3.1 million new jobs created in 1998. Between 1990 and 1995, small firms with fewer than 500 employees created 76 percent of new jobs. The SBA also reports that the number of firms with at least one employee but with fewer than 500 increased by 10.6 percent, from 4.95 million in 1988 to 5.48 million in 1996. About 21 million Americans, 17 percent of all U.S. nonagricultural workers, are engaged in some entrepreneurial activity, including both full-time and part-time entrepreneurship.[1]

"A study by the Entrepreneurial Research Consortium found that more than 35 million U.S. households, 37 percent of the U.S. total, have an intimate involvement in a new or small business. Approximately 18 million of those households include someone currently running a business, and another 6.8 million include someone trying to start a business."[2] In an article entitled "Dream Job" published by *Entrepreneur* (January 1997), author Lynn Beresford states that in a study conducted by the George H. Gallup International Institute, college students are leaning toward entrepreneurship rather than preferring to join the corporate world. In a survey of college seniors, 49 percent of men and 31 percent of women said they were interested in pursuing entrepreneurship after graduation.

To the fashion retail student, the study of entrepreneurship can play an important role in future career opportunities. Change is constant. Being conditioned to change will better prepare the student to succeed in the business world. Studying the field of entrepreneurship provides the opportunity to deal with change on a daily basis, to study all aspects of the business, and to become familiar with entrepreneurs throughout the world. Even those seeking traditional business careers will require knowledge of various aspects of business in order to be successful. Many companies are encouraging their employees to have an entrepreneurial mindset.

FASHION TRENDS LEAD TO ENTREPRENEURIAL OPPORTUNITIES

What is the future of the fashion industry? What trends and issues are having an impact on the direction of entrepreneurial business in apparel and soft goods? Teri Agins, author of *The End of Fashion: The Mass Marketing of the Clothing Business* (1999), states, "The fashion industry powers at the head of the class prevail because they swear by retailing's golden rule: The consumer is king."[3] She continues, "In today's competitive marketplace, those who will survive . . . will reinvent themselves enough times and with enough flexibility and resources to anticipate, not manipulate, the twenty-first-century customer. There's just no other way."

The monetary opportunity is there. In 1999 alone, retail sales in apparel and accessories in the U.S. surpassed $135 billion, an increase over the $127 billion reported in 1998.[4] With total retail sales for 1999 at $3 trillion, the slice of the pie taken by apparel and accessories sales is a healthy serving. The entrepreneur who not only recognizes, but also anticipates, consumer needs and wants has the greatest chance of reaping the rewards.

Following over 140 personal interviews and extensive research of the fashion industry and its consumer through secondary sources, Agins summarizes the changes in consumer behavior that have affected fashion over the past decades. She indicates, "Rich people don't care to wear their affluence on their sleeves; women aren't fixated with chasing the trends; intrinsic value often trumps designer logos; nobody's dressing up; and everybody loves a bargain."[5] Consumer trend-watching has become as important as fashion trend-watching in this industry. Casual dressing in the workplace, a lack of interest and/or knowledge of apparel quality, the resistance by manufacturers to gamble on fashion chances—these issues influence the apparel and soft goods industry. They will surely cause the death of some companies, while at the same time they will provide opportunities for new firms. The successful entrepreneur identifies the trends and then translates them into business opportunities.

THE ENTREPRENEURIAL PROFILE

What is an entrepreneur? What distinguishes an entrepreneur from a business owner? Many views exist on the definition of an entrepreneur. In an article entitled, "What Is an Entrepreneur," published on www.about.com, Dr. Judith Kautz explores differing views on the definition or description of an entrepreneur. She quotes the following definitions from Hypertext Online Webster. An entrepreneur is "one who creates a product on his own account." Kautz points out that this definition raises the following questions: "Does just creating a product make you an entrepreneurial if you never do anything with it? What if you take someone's product and make it a success?" "Investorwords," a set of definitions of financial terms, defines an entrepreneur as "an individual who starts his/her own business." But limiting the definition to someone *starting* a business implies that once a business is no longer in the start-up phase, it would not be entrepreneurial.

The International Society of Entrepreneurs defines an entrepreneur as "a person who organizes and manages a business undertaking, assuming all the risk for the sake of profit."[6] This may suggest that the motivation for *starting* a business is purely profit. Although profit is at the top of the list for most entrepreneurs, businesses are started for many reasons. Some people create businesses out of necessity after they lose their job.

Others start companies because they feel excitement in creating a new method of retailing for the market. Kautz quotes entrepreneur Daile Tucker's article "Are You an Entrepreneur?" definition of an entrepreneur as "A person who has decided to take control of his future and become self-employed whether by creating his own unique business or working as a member of a team, as in multi-level marketing." Tucker identifies work ethics and several character traits of successful entrepreneurs: "Entrepreneurs compete with themselves and believe that success or failure lies within their personal control or influence."

None of the above definitions is wrong. As the entrepreneurial alternative becomes more prevalent, the definition will evolve. Entrepreneurship may be more clearly defined by people's traits, strengths, and weaknesses, and by comparisons of many definitions and views. Jeffrey A. Timmons, one of the pioneers in the development of entrepreneurship education and research in the United States, defines an entrepreneur and entrepreneurship in the following terms, "Entrepreneurship is a way of thinking, reasoning, and acting that is opportunity obsessed, holistic in approach, and leadership balanced."[7]

Entrepreneurs recognize an opportunity. They size up its value as well as the resources necessary to make that opportunity a success. They are visionaries. They have a vision of how the business will grow, and they have the drive to make it happen. Entrepreneurs are always looking for better and innovative ways to find new markets, to add to an existing product line, and to tap into larger geographic territories. They move with the times or, more often than not, before the times. They are futurists in that they anticipate and embrace change. They see "outside the box." E-commerce, for example, becomes a welcome challenge, not something to be feared and rejected. Entrepreneurs persevere and are not easily defeated. They thrive in a challenging environment and have a tremendous need to be in control. They will take calculated risks and welcome responsibility. They are absolutely passionate about what they do.

DO YOU HAVE WHAT IT TAKES?

Why are some fashion retail entrepreneurs successful while others fail? Who is cut out for owning a fashion retail business? The retail industry requires that businesses be both people-oriented and service-oriented. This entails juggling both satisfied and dissatisfied customers, maintaining merchandise that sells, and keeping an eye on costs and prices. Retail success requires the effective combination of attractive layout and design, great customer service, and attention to detail. It requires a flair for selecting appealing merchandise at the right time and that is priced for the right market. Most importantly, retail success is predicated on an understanding of what the customers need and want in order to create an atmosphere that will sell, sell, sell.

Retailing can provide an opportunity to meet new people, develop a successful business team, travel for business, and contribute to one's community as an economic entity. Most importantly, it can provide the opportunity for financial success and independence from working for someone else. Not everyone, however, is a candidate for the entrepreneurial route. Entrepreneurship requires an open-minded, in-depth self-analysis as a first step. The prospective entrepreneur must identify strengths and weaknesses, both personally and professionally, and recognize and take action in those areas that need to change.

BHC Inc, is a company based in New York City that helps women, minorities, and middle-class consumers make informed financial decisions. Melissa Bradley, founder and president of BHC Inc. (Bradleyml@yahoo.com), also teaches a marketing course at City College, part of the City University of New York. Previously, she founded the Entrepreneurial Development Institute, a nonprofit in Washington, D.C., that trained young people to develop small businesses. She also served as a financial regulatory affairs fellow with the U.S. Department of Treasury and as a marketing specialist at the Student Loan Marketing Association. Ms Bradley offers the following advice to entrepreneurs of start-up companies:

Don't start a business unless you have enough money to invest in the business yourself and enough money to live on for a year. You're not going to be profitable for at least that long. How are you going to pay your rent in the meantime? And when you do take money from other people, be selective. So many entrepreneurs come to me and say, "It's no longer the business that I started." That's because they lost control. Control doesn't come with the title of CEO; control comes with cash.

You don't need to have a million dollars in the bank. Be creative, and understand how to get money. For the venture that I'm involved in now, we held a series of fund-raisers 6 months before we launched the company and raised $50,000 just to get things going. For example, we teamed up with a local theater, charged double the ticket price, and held a reception afterward. If we had taken $1 million from an outside investor, we would have lost more than half the company.

In the beginning, venture capitalists didn't want us. After all, being a financial educator for the poor isn't very sexy. Now they see that we have something to offer. But we feel that they would sell out our target market, and we don't want to become McStreet. Here are my tips for starting a business.

Make your idea your idea—legally. Get the paperwork done for patents and trademarks. Know your market. And don't just focus on traditional demographics, such as white males, ages 35 to 45. Dig deeper: What are the buying habits of your customers? What are their families like? Getting that kind of information takes time and money. So partner with universities to do market research.

Develop an exit strategy from the get-go. Go beyond strictly financial considerations. What is your personal exit strategy? You're not going to want to run the company forever. Step aside when the mission has to change or when the market need shifts to involve something that you know nothing about. Otherwise, you're going to run your company into the ground.

Balu, R., "Unit One of One: Starting Your Startup," Fastcompany.com.

Traits of Successful Entrepreneurs

Although the need exists to understand the competitive, economic, and cultural climates in the retail industry, it is just as important to assess and understand one's personal skills and needs. Entrepreneurship requires a particular way of thinking and acting. By observing both successful and unsuccessful entrepreneurs, you will find a wide range of personalities. While special talent and self-discipline come naturally to some, to others, these attributes must be learned.

Numerous studies have been conducted to analyze the differences in traits between successful and not-so-successful entrepreneurs. In the challenging world of the entrepreneur, chances of success increase dramatically if the prospective entrepreneur begins by understanding who he or she is. The following discussion covers some of the traits that research has shown are possessed by successful entrepreneurs.

Passion/Desire   Perhaps the most important of all traits successful entrepreneurs possess is passion. Unquestionably, the successful entrepreneur has the passion to be one. The entrepreneur also relishes sharing that passion and desire with others. Entrepreneurs are driven to succeed. Many have determined that they cannot work for others. They want to be their own boss. When one is passionate about what he or she is doing, tasks seem relatively timeless and effortless. Launching a new venture requires long hours and many challenges.

Determination/Perseverance   Entrepreneurs are determined. They want to succeed and do not give up easily, even when it may be wise to do so. Determination is a key factor in a winning attitude. The role of the entrepreneur requires the ability to persevere in the toughest of times. Successful entrepreneurs will figure out the path they need to take to reach their goals and challenge all obstacles blocking those paths. Establishing a successful business takes time. Most entrepreneurs acknowledge that it takes 4 to 5 years before the money starts rolling in and the hours decrease to a manageable level.

Responsibility   Many entrepreneurs say that they believe that one of the keys to their success was their willingness to take responsibility for themselves, their employees, and their businesses. Owning a business provides entrepreneurs with the freedom to make decisions independently, to make things happen, and to influence and determine outcomes. An entrepreneur who manufactures and sells an apparel line through his own stores, as well as distributes the line to retailers throughout the country, has said that, on a recent delivery to a retail operation, it was discovered that the top-of-the-line golf jacket was misticketed. Through an incorrect style number, the ticket priced the jacket at $20 less than the wholesale price should have been. The entrepreneur learned that 200 units of this jacket were priced incorrectly. Clearly, this would greatly affect the bottom line. The owner explained that several things might have happened as a result of the mistake.

The employee who put the wrong price tickets on the jackets could have been fired. The jackets could have been relabeled, increasing the price to the point it should have been. The owners of the stores receiving the jackets could have been asked to send them back to the factory. Firing the employee was not the answer. The entrepreneur had just spent several hundred dollars training him. To have reticketed the jackets would have stopped the production line, affecting not only the price of the mislabeled style, but affecting profits by holding up production. Asking the owners of the stores receiving the misticketed jackets to send them back would have been an inconvenience for the retailers, not to mention an indication of poor service on the part of the manufacturer. The owner of the golf wear company chose to take responsibility for the mistake and allowed the jackets to be sold below market value. The employee was grateful; the retailers were happy; and production continued. The owner said, "Always take responsibility for your business and yourself."

Health and Energy   Starting a business requires a tremendous amount of energy, and good health has a great deal to do with the amount of energy one has to expend. Entrepreneurs are motivated and driven to build thriving, healthy companies, but ironically, when it comes to their own health, some prospective entrepreneurs are not as diligent as they could be in achieving success. As the energy level goes down, so does the tolerance level and the ability to keep up with the pace required to make that business successful. Studies conducted by various health-care professionals indicate a direct correlation between good health and energy levels. Health affects one's ability to think clearly and to handle situations in a controlled manner. Customers and employees need to know that the entrepreneur has the stamina and skills to handle any situation that may arise. Health does not simply refer to diet and exercise. It also refers to balancing one's life, to making time for one's self.

Ability to Work Independently   Employees of large corporations may have a team of assistants, accountants, marketing departments, researchers, and financial analysts to help them with the daily activities and overall planning of the company. When a new business is started, more often than not the entrepreneur is the company and all its departments. In the beginning, entrepreneurs generally have little support. The funds are simply not available. Entrepreneurs start out as janitor, secretary, bookkeeper, and strategic planner. They have only themselves to rely on to do the work that may be unfamiliar or unpalatable. Recognizing the necessity to do whatever it takes to get the job done to ultimately make the business a success is crucial.

Respect for Money   It is easy to get caught up in the glamour of owning a business. Many businesses get into financial trouble because they spend far too much money on items that have very little to do with the success of the business. Successful entrepreneurs are conservative and careful with their money. They spend what is necessary and save the rest. Successful entrepreneurs do not typically judge themselves based on what they spend or can afford to buy. Satisfaction is obtained through achieving their own internal goals and objectives.

Ability to Manage Time Wisely   Getting a business started is extremely time consuming. Because entrepreneurs are working with little or no staff and limited budgets, the ability to plan and to prioritize effectively is crucial. It is not uncommon for entrepreneurs to work 70 to 80 hours per week in the initial stages of a business and still leave the office with many tasks unfinished. The inability to manage time efficiently will lead to poor performance. Poor performance reflects on the company. In the initial stage of the business, entrepreneurs are guilty of trying to perform too many tasks on their own. Good entrepreneurs will utilize the personnel they do employ to their best advantage. They will learn to delegate duties and responsibility and enable employees to fulfill their duties.

Dependability   It is important to follow through on commitments that have been made. Storefront retail businesses need to open the doors when the sign on the front of the door says they will open. E-commerce businesses need to deliver goods within the time frame indicated. Lack of dependability can lead to disaster for fashion retail businesses. Consumers have come to expect excellent service.

Flexibility   Successful entrepreneurs must be able to adapt to the changing demands of customers and their businesses. The world has become a fast-paced, ever-changing place. The tastes, wants, and needs of the consumer are also ever changing. The ability of the entrepreneur to adapt to these changes will increase the opportunity for success.

Less Successful Traits of Entrepreneurs

The personality traits in the following discussion have been identified as negative qualities for the entrepreneur as they relate to success. Note that negative characteristics can be changed. It requires effort. If the prospective entrepreneur has the determination, self-discipline, and objectivity to identify and rectify possible problem areas, the potential for entrepreneurial success increases.

Dishonesty   The fastest way to creating an unsuccessful business is to be dishonest with one's self, customers, suppliers, or funders—any of the people and businesses with whom the entrepreneur deals. People want and need to trust business associates. Once that trust had been broken, it is difficult to reestablish. Credibility is crucial to the success of any business.

Impatience   It is true that disasters follow entrepreneurs who lack patience. Impatience sometimes leads to hiring the wrong people, targeting the wrong market, pricing inventory too low to make a profit (just to get it sold), and opening a business at the wrong time. People who are impatient believe that the business absolutely has to be open now or the market will disappear or go elsewhere. This does not hold true for most industries. Only after careful planning and research should a business be staffed, stocked, and opened.

Reluctance to Ask for Help   There is a misconception among potential entrepreneurs that asking questions about how to run the business suggests that they lack the skills and information needed. Entrepreneurs cannot be experts in all areas of a business. All business owners need help and support. More often than not, unsuccessful entrepreneurs waited until it was too late to ask questions about issues critical to their business. There are a number of organizations across the United States whose mission is to champion the entrepreneur. They provide education and resources to help small businesses succeed. (A list of these support organizations is provided in the Appendix).

Lack of Interpersonal Skills   Successful fashion retailing begins with making the customer feel comfortable, welcome, and valued. If someone has a low tolerance for people, retail business ownership is not the career path to pursue. Envision trying to shop in a favorite store with the "out of control child" screaming in the background and destroying merchandise as the mother pursues her search for the perfect dress. Picture a disgruntled employee complaining to customers about the business operation. The successful entrepreneur must be able to pacify discontented customers, motivate sales associates, and negotiate with suppliers. Successful businesses provide excellent customer service. Successful entrepreneurs recognize the people skills needed to provide this service.

Assessing Yourself: Traits and Skills

Entrepreneurs have to know their strengths and weaknesses, both on a personal level and on a business level. Additionally, entrepreneurs must compensate in some way for the areas in which they are not especially proficient. The business is a reflection of the person running it. By conducting a self-analysis before going into business, the prospective entrepreneur will develop an inventory of his or her personal needs in the areas of motivation, skills, and talents. Self-analysis also clarifies the entrepreneur's values in terms of money, power, fun, independence, and security. The prospective entrepreneur should compare personal qualities and preferences with those of entrepreneurs who succeed and those who have been less fortunate. The analysis should examine the following: (1) How the prospective entrepreneur gets things done, (2) how the entrepreneur interacts with people, and (3) how the entrepreneur goes about making decisions. Many successful entrepreneurs constantly assess themselves and solicit feedback from friends, family, peers, and employees. The process of continual self-assessment becomes a habit for many successful business developers.

Figure 1.1 is a personal assessment evaluation form that can be used to score and assess individuals who are considering becoming entrepreneurs. Assessment instruments

Figure 1.1 Personal Assessment Form

(1 = strongly disagree, 2 = disagree, 3 = agree, 4 = strongly agree)

STATEMENT	SCORE
I attend the organizational meetings I have scheduled.	4
I show up for classes and other events on time.	4
I take responsibility for my college courses and assignments.	4
I prioritize my "list of things to do."	3
I finish my assignments on time.	3
I know how much time I spend on each activity and/or class per week.	3
I manage my time well in college.	3
I am excited when new opportunities and projects present themselves.	3
I have the ability to make decisions quickly.	2
I make good decisions.	3
I like working on numerous tasks at the same time.	3
I enjoy competition.	3
I set goals for myself and meet those goals.	2
I am responsible with my finances.	3
I am happiest when I am responsible for myself and my own decisions.	3
I prefer to work in a group setting on a class project rather than alone.	2
I have the ability to motivate others.	3
I volunteer to take on leadership roles. I enjoy being the one responsible for organizing a project and keeping the project on schedule.	2
I enjoy new challenges.	3
I am talented at finding new ways to do things.	2
I am intuitive.	3
I enjoy staying busy. I don't like to sit around.	4
I am self-motivated.	4
I enjoy public speaking and/or speaking in class.	2
I look for ways to acquire new skills that will enable me to grow both as a person and as a student.	4
I welcome change. I find it exciting.	4
I can adapt easily to change.	4
I am not timid about speaking in class and asking questions.	2
I recognize that my health is important, and I take the steps necessary to maintain my health.	3
I can work on projects independently.	4
I am able to get along and work well with other students.	4
TOTAL POINTS	92

are used in many different industries and come in many different forms. This assessment tool was developed simply to help prospective entrepreneurs identify areas in which they are weak and those in which their strengths lie. It is recommended that the prospective entrepreneur complete it independently and then ask someone, such as a professor or colleague, to fill out the evaluation about the prospective entrepreneur. The personal assessment is most helpful when the participants are open-minded and willing to receive feedback.

The prospective entrepreneur should read each statement and enter a score in the right-hand column, using a scale of 1 to 4. When completed, the score is calculated by adding all points in the score column.

A score of between 31 and 80 points is in the mid to low range. Starting a business requires a commitment by the entrepreneur to focus significant amounts of time and energy on the business. A mid to low score could mean that the prospective entrepreneur may need to spend more time developing confidence, skills, and abilities in certain areas before committing time and funding to a new venture.

A score between 81 and 124 points is in the mid to upper range. It indicates that the prospective entrepreneur possesses many of the key habits and skills needed to become successful. A high score indicates that prospective entrepreneur will welcome challenges, set goals, and implement the steps necessary in achieving those goals.

Assessing Your Business Skills

Many successful entrepreneurs believe that they learned much of what they know through the "school of hard knocks." Because the business climate changes much more rapidly now than it did 10 or even 5 years ago, the school of hard knocks may not provide the education it once did. Technological, social, and economic trends have resulted in increased levels and speed of communication and product life cycles. Globalization is part of today's business world. Entrepreneurs cannot be everywhere at once. They cannot possibly experience firsthand all the skills needed to successfully grow a business. Time and resources are limited for new companies. Entrepreneurs can, however, compensate for these limitations. How? By hiring personnel or forming an advisory team with strengths in their areas of weakness. The business failure rate is high for those who go into it without the skills and knowledge as well as a good support system in place to know how to deal with the issues of today and tomorrow.

Good entrepreneurs assemble a management team or advisory team to take care of areas in which they lack knowledge and experience. For example, the prospective entrepreneur may retain the services of a law firm or an accounting service, in anticipation of opening the business. It should be pointed out that there are businesses that have succeeded where the owner lacked any firsthand experience in the industry, but brought on a management team or advisory team that did.

On a daily basis, the entrepreneur must make decisions that require a basic knowledge of business. The entrepreneur is the person responsible for the strategic planning and growth of the company. Often, he or she is the person who will develop a marketing plan for the organization based on an evaluation of the general industry and competition. The entrepreneur is also likely to be the person who identifies the target market, how to reach it, and where it is located in numbers large enough to sustain the business.

In addition to analyzing the customer, the entrepreneur will have to know how to read and understand financial statements and how to access money. Often because of the lack of a financial background, the entrepreneur does not initially know what the business needs in order to operate and grow. Many times, insufficient research has been done to determine all the start-up capital needed. For example, retail stores in most states are required to post a sales tax bond based on projected sales. A sales tax bond is essentially a deposit held by the state to offset any unpaid sales tax incurred in the business. For a business projecting large sales, the amount of the bond can be significant. Entrepreneurs may also struggle because they do not understand financial information. What happens when inventory does not turn over as anticipated? Should more inventory be added? How often should the inventory turn over? Good market and financial research will provide answers to these questions.

The entrepreneur will have to analyze trends and personnel requirements as well as how to strategically plan for growth. He or she will be required to negotiate the lease agreement for securing a piece of real estate or determine the cost of producing and distributing a catalog or the terms for developing and managing a Web site. Entrepreneurs in many areas of fashion retailing must purchase and manage inventory. The entrepreneur will need to ensure that procedures are in place to turn inventory the fastest way possible and limit the amount of inventory to reduce storage, stocking, and maintenance costs. Without the education and knowledge needed to address these issues, the chances are high that a new business will not succeed.

Funders, such as bankers, will always look at whether or not the entrepreneur has experience in the industry in which he or she wants to start the business or is associated with an individual(s) who has experience in the industry. Funders are individuals or institutions and organizations that loan or grant money to the business. They believe, and rightly so, that unless a person has worked in retailing, he or she will not have the knowledge and practical skills needed to run a retail operation. Many prospective entrepreneurs establish a career plan designed to enable them to gain as much experience as possible in the area or field in which they want to establish a business.

As an entrepreneur, one has to have a basic understanding of all aspects of the business. There are a number of internship programs available that provide an opportunity to work in the fashion retail industry. Small businesses are a wonderful place to learn about the world of the entrepreneur since the entrepreneurs and employees wear many hats. Business knowledge should come from academic training and textbooks, work experience, and networking with entrepreneurs. It is important to seek out those who have been successful, as well as those entrepreneurs who have failed. Most entrepreneurs are eager to share their knowledge, as long as the prospective entrepreneur will not be in direct competition with them.

TIMING AND FUNDING AVAILABILITY

Several factors come into play when determining the right time to start a business and whether or not the capital is available to do so. There are several reasons why it may not be a good time to start a new business venture. First, the venture may demand too much of the entrepreneur's time. Second, the business will not provide the entrepreneur with the lifestyle he or she had anticipated it would. Finally, it may take more money than the entrepreneur has available or can secure.

Assessing where the entrepreneur is in his or her life is important. Careful planning, as well as articulation and revision of goals, will help the entrepreneur to know when to start the new venture. It is important to address one's life priorities. The pursuit of a higher educational degree, lack of experience in the field, more money in the bank, the need for more time with fewer responsibilities, development of a stronger support system—these are all life choices that may cause someone to postpone entrepreneurial endeavors. The ability to measure where one is and what one wants in life at this stage of the game is significant to entrepreneurial success. Entrepreneurs begin by defining what is most important to them in life. For example, "I want to be surrounded by beautiful clothes," "I want to make lots of money," "I want to live on the East Coast," "My friends and family will come first in my life," "I want to complete a doctorate program." After determining what is most important and most motivational, the entrepreneur will want to analyze how the business will allow him or her to accomplish those goals. If one lives in an extremely warm climate year round, sells swimwear, and has a desire to relocate to a climate that is very cold, then selling swimwear in the new location may not be a good choice. If the prospective entrepreneur has determined that earning a doctorate is at the top of his or her list of immediate goals, then he or she may want to consider waiting until that goal is met before opening a business.

Above all, balance in life is critical. The burnout rate is high among entrepreneurs who do not take time for themselves, friends, or family. Numerous entrepreneurs burn out within the first 2 years simply because they have no balance in their lives. Successful entrepreneurs recognize the importance of balance.

COMMON MYTHS ABOUT ENTREPRENEURS

There are several myths about entrepreneurs. These misconceptions and myths can influence whether someone has the desire and attitude to pursue the entrepreneurial dream. It is important, then, to distinguish between myth and reality. Following are some commonly held myths and misconceptions:

1. *A person is either born to be an entrepreneur or is not.* Entrepreneurship can be learned. If you want something badly enough, you have the ability to do what it takes and learn what is needed to make it happen.
2. *Entrepreneurs are their own bosses.* This is true to a degree. Practically speaking, entrepreneurs work for many people. To succeed in the fashion retail business, the boss must work hard to please employees, customers, the bank, and others.
3. *Entrepreneurs have to be big risk takers.* Entrepreneurs do take risks, but good entrepreneurs take calculated risks. Careful consideration must be given to the timing of the venture, the funding needed, and long-range planning.
4. *The entrepreneur will make money fast.* Developing a new business takes time. Many entrepreneurs say that it takes 5 years before the business actually starts providing a good return. Entrepreneurship requires patience, determination, and hard work. Add to this the responsibility for generating a paycheck for the entrepreneur and others. It takes time to make money. Very few entrepreneurs make it big overnight.[8]

WHY SOME BUSINESSES FAIL WHILE OTHERS SUCCEED

The personal traits or characteristics of an entrepreneur have been examined. This section addresses issues relating directly to the proposed business. Among the top reasons for a business's failure are lack of good initial research of the concept, lack of sufficient capital for the start-up phase, lack of a solid business plan, poor management by the entrepreneur, and lack of a good exit strategy. Seeking and forming a market niche, understanding the competition, knowing the market, and providing great customer service are some of the factors needed to make a business successful. A more detailed discussion of the reasons new businesses fail or succeed will help identify the pitfalls to avoid.

A *well-researched concept* is critical to any entrepreneur. Furthermore, theory should be measured against reality. Successful entrepreneurs research customers, product, competition, personal goals, and timing and funding availability before moving forward. Entrepreneurs who are not successful often have not taken the time to evaluate and test their concept.

Sufficient capital is a must. More often than not, entrepreneurs open their doors without sufficient capital to sustain the business through the start-up phase. Researching other fashion retail businesses will provide hard data on the approximate amount of capital needed. It is important to remember that every business will be different and that some adjustments will need to be made to the financials to fit a specific business.

In addition to sufficient capital, it is also necessary to understand the *financial statements* of the business. The financial statements serve as a management tool. They show the condition of the business and provide information necessary to make good financial decisions. The decisions to increase inventory, to seek additional financing, and to hire new employees rest on the financial health of the business.

A business will fail due to a *lack of planning.* Some prospective entrepreneurs believe that they do not have time to work on a business plan. This can be the kiss of death. The *business plan* provides direction. It allows the entrepreneur to look at the business as a whole, in its entirety. The business plan is used to carefully analyze any challenges that may arise as the venture is started. A business plan addresses both the strengths and the weaknesses of the venture. A good business plan will increase chances of success dramat-

Seven Serious Retail Mistakes

David Ellis, the chief operating officer of a corporate evaluation and crisis management firm, has spent 15 years providing retailers with advice on issues related to business turnaround plans (how to take a bleeding business and turn it around to a successful business) and liquidations (selling everything in the business). From his experience, he has compiled seven serious mistakes that a retailer can make:

1. Having an unclear business plan.
2. Operating in unprofitable locations.
3. Giving marginal merchandise prime space.
4. Neglecting true costs.
5. Ignoring the competition.
6. Clinging to old habits.
7. Having a pack-rat mentality.

Young, Kristin, "Seven Ways to Get Stuck," *ApparelNews.Net.* http://www.apparelnews.net/News/newsfeat.html

ically. How could it not? Through development of an effective business plan, the entrepreneur addresses the business from a variety of angles. The business plan is discussed in greater detail throughout this text. At this point, it is important to recognize the significant role this plan plays in the overall success of a business.

Poor management can be the greatest single cause of business failure. Management of a business encompasses planning, organizing, controlling, directing, and communicating. It is important to hire the right people, to properly train the employees, and to motivate them. Effective management requires good leadership skills. *Leadership* is the art of persuading and inducing, guiding, and motivating. An effective manager will encourage productivity and guide the employees through the business rather than simply dictate what tasks need to be done.

Entrepreneurs should determine how they will *exit the business* before the business is started. Planning can afford the entrepreneur the opportunity to create value in the company so that it can be sold sometime in the future. Closing the doors without a plan can sometimes leave unpaid obligations, employees without jobs, unsold inventory, and a broken lease. Exit strategies involve determining what the business is worth and how this is to be calculated. It also involves knowing the time frame in which the entrepreneur plans to exit the business.

Those entrepreneurs who have succeeded generally acknowledge that *perseverance* is at the top of the list of success factors. They did not give up. They recognized that continually monitoring the industry and market and maintaining the willingness to change with that industry and market kept them going. *Flexibility* is important in their ever-changing environment. Entrepreneurs also know that to succeed in the fashion retail business, they must be able to establish loyalty with their customers. Good business owners will make their customers the number one priority. They will provide service beyond the expectation of the consumer. In the words of Benjamin Franklin, "I have not failed. I have found 10,000 ways that don't work." Entrepreneurs do not set out to fail. Careful planning and knowledge of the industry and markets increase the chances of finding the one way that works.

DEVELOPMENT OF THE BUSINESS CONCEPT: WHAT WILL THE COMPANY BE?

If, after careful assessment of both personal and business skills, the prospective entrepreneur determines that he or she has what it takes to open a new business or buy an existing business, then it is time to develop the business concept. The concept begins with an idea. It often arises out of a consumer need that is not currently being satisfied. The entrepreneur has looked outside of the box and created an opportunity for a new product. Although the concept is not an actual part of the written business plan, it is crucial to the planning process. To be successful, the business concept must meet four requirements:

1. There must be a group of customers willing to prurchase the product or product lines featured by the business at the price offered.
2. The market must be large enough to support the business and generate a profit.
3. The entrepreneur must be able to differentiate his or her business from that of the competition.
4. The entrepreneur must be able to finance the business—either personally or through funding sources.

With these requirements taken care of, the entrepreneur is ready to contemplate business ownership.

Picture yourself totally lost. Then someone gives you a map. You need two other things. You need to know where you are and where you are going. The concept and business plan revolve around a mission statement, which addresses what business the company is in, and a vision statement, which addresses what the owner stands for and believes in. The mission statement defines the purpose and reason for being. The vision statement helps guide the business by defining a desired future. Formulating mission and vision statements and committing those statements to writing establish a sense of direction for the company. Mission statements might include: "Our mission is to create an atmosphere that puts the needs of our customers and employees first," or, "Our mission is to provide a line of clothing that addresses the needs of the physically challenged." The concept and business plan for the company should define and agree with the entrepreneur's belief system. Committing a mission and vision statement to writing enables the prospective entrepreneur to stay on track. Business goals may include creating a new Web-based fashion retail business or achieving a certain new profit within a certain time period. Personal goals may include selling the business within 5 years, helping children who are physically challenged, or donating five outfits to a local charity each year. The following box asks key questions that entrepreneurs and their employees should respond

Questions a Mission Statement Should Answer

- What are the basic beliefs and values of the company? What does the company stand for?

- What is the company's target market?

- What are the company's basic products and services? What customer needs and wants do they satisfy?

- How can the company better satisfy those needs and wants?

- Why should customers do business with this company rather than with the competition?

- What constitutes value to the customer? How can this company offer the customer better value?

- What is the company's competitive advantage? What is the source of this advantage?

- In which markets (or market segments) will the company choose to compete?

- Who are the key stakeholders in the company, and what effect do they have on it?

- What benefits should be provided to the company's customers 5 years from now?

- What business does the company want to be in 5 years from now?

Adapted from Norman Scarborough and Thomas Zimmerer, *Effective Small Business Management: An Entrepreneurial Approach,* 6th ed. (Upper Saddle River, New Jersey: Prentice-Hall, 2000, p. 42–43) to as the company mission statement and vision statement are developed. Figure 1.2 illustrates an example of a mission and objective statement for Garland Stores.

By addressing these questions and defining a clear mission for the company, the entrepreneur will have a much clearer picture of what the business concept is and what it will be. It is essential that the mission and vision statements be communicated to employees, who in turn will communicate them to customers. It must become a natural part of the culture of the company. In the process of creating the concept, entrepreneurs should also explore and list both personal and business goals.

An example of a business concept that reflects a personal mission is that of Wishing Wells, a line of special clothing for special people. Although many know her as Mary Ann of Gilligan's Island, Dawn Wells is also an author, speaker, philanthropist, and entrepreneur. Dawn created the company Wishing Wells, a line of apparel designed for the elderly and physically challenged. Wells believes that giving someone special clothes can make all the difference. She says, "I know what if feels like to take care of someone you love, to care for them, dress them, and even spend hours trying to rip a bathrobe down the back to make dressing easier. I know what it feels like because I had a grandmother we took care of at home."[9] Easy-on, easy-off clothing became the concept for her entrepreneurial venture. The market was there to support the idea.

Once the personal and business mission statements have been developed, they will become the foundation on which the business will be based and the grounds on which the direction and feasibility of the concept will be explored. Mission statements may change as research begins. There is nothing wrong with that, as long as the personal and business mission statements, as well as the business plan, complement one another. As the concept is developed, the entrepreneur will want to look closely at what matters most to him or her. The concept may be defined and redefined many times.

The reason for researching and developing the concept for the business is to test it against economic, financial, and political realities. This development process helps determine whether or not efforts should go forward and additional resources should be committed to the concept. It is important to develop a business concept and business plan from an objective perspective. The prospective entrepreneur must be willing to revise the original concept if the need arises.

Researching the Concept

A tremendous amount of research should go into the business concept before large amounts of time, money, and energy are put into the business. It is important to think through and identify ways in which the business will distinguish itself in the market. Some competitors may do some things well; others may not. The entrepreneur should seek new or better ways to offer a unique and competitive advantage over the other businesses in the marketplace. Also, the prospective entrepreneur will encounter some companies that have not changed with the industry and kept up with e-commerce. Such businesses may provide an excellent opportunity.

It is critical for the entrepreneur to look at the economic trends, technological advances, and demographic shifts in order to assess the impact these elements will have on the fashion retail industry. For example, the ripple effect of the terrorist attack of September 11, 2001, in the United States affected small businesses in New York City and across the nation. "A report assessing the economic impact of September 11 that was prepared

Figure 1.2 Sample Mission and Objective Statements

GARLAND STORES
Mission and Objectives Statement

Garland Stores mission is to be the premier quality department store in all our locations and to be the fashion leader for our target customers. To be the first store that our customer thinks of and goes to when shopping and to offer our customer the finest quality fashion merchandise in the upper-moderate to better price range. Our longest term goal is to achieve not only more profit, but to be the number one fashion department store in the United States. To achieve these ends, our objectives include such factors as: target customers, positioning merchandise, value, service, promotion, and expansion. These factors are outlined below:

Target Customers
Garland Stores target customers are middle, upper-middle, and upper-level income consumers who shop for fashionable, well-made apparel, accessories, and home furnishings. Our focus is on consumers who want fashionable, well-made lifestyle merchandise of identifiable worth.

Positioning
We want our target customers to perceive Garland Stores as having the most timely and competitive selections of fashionable, quality merchandise. We believe that one of the keys to our future growth is the consumer between the ages of 18 and 55, who shops for fashionable, updated merchandise; therefore, our focus will be on an appropriate balance of updated and traditional merchandise, with an emphasis on updated, fashionable apparel, accessories, soft goods, and home furnishings of recognizable worth and value.

Merchandise
Garland Stores' will present a balanced selection of fashion apparel, accessories, soft goods, and home furnishings in a variety of colors, fabrications, styles, and brands. Because our focus is on updated goods, fashion merchandise must be timely, offering the newest colors, styles, and fabrications that are just beginning to gain our target customer's acceptance. Our merchandise must be of the finest quality available, in the moderate to better price range.

To create a sustainable competitive advantage, the merchandise focus in most lines will be on Garland Stores private labels and on recognizable name brands of excellent quality. Consistency and longevity in the private labels will build brand acceptance, which will encourage repeat purchases, and thus will increase profits in both the short and long terms. In the fashion apparel lines, recognizable designer bridge and better lines will also be offered in limited quantities, but in sufficient numbers to satisfy our upper-end target consumer's needs. An adequate supply of these designer goods will not only augment our private labels, but will keep our fashion offerings on the cutting edge and will sustain our long-term goal of being the fashion leader in the United States.

Because Garland Stores buying offices are centralized, our merchandise is consistent from store to store (with regional and specific needs taken into account for each branch). We want our customers to know that when they enter a new or different Garland Store, they will be met with the same excellent quality, price, and service that they have received in any other Garland Store.

Value
While Garland Stores wishes to be the fashion leader, we also want to offer our customers the best available price on all offered goods. Because our buying offices are centralized, we have the opportunity to buy top-quality merchandise in large quantities, which will assist in keeping the prices in the moderate range. Our buyers have been instructed to purchase those goods that are not only fashionable, but also are well-made and of obvious value. Our private label merchandise will assist us in achieving this end as the majority of merchandise will be of a caliber that we can control, while the bridge and better designer lines will help us to achieve an important balance between the moderate and upper-end prices and consumers.

Service
In keeping with our overall goal of leadership, we wish to offer our customers the finest possible service available. Our sales staff must be courteous, caring, and knowledgeable about our merchandise and the current fashions. Above all, our sales staff must be available to our customers, and be willing to help our client achieve the look they want. To accomplish this, we require a regular updating of our computerized client profile lists, and we encourage all our sales staff, buyers, and department executives to actively call our listed clients to advise them of new merchandise shipments that would be of interest to those clients.

Also in keeping with this level of courteous, caring, knowledgeable, and comprehensive service are such other services as: a variety of low-cost gift wrap is available year-round (free Garland Stores logotype gift wrap is available during the Holidays); free home delivery on purchases over $200; low-cost alterations; layaway; mail-order; Garland Stores credit cards. Our credit accounts are one of our most important services, as it not only encourages more sales by offering our customers an easy way to shop with easy payments, but it also garners profit for the store through the interest payments.

Promotion
To reach our target customer, to gain new clients, and to promote our image as a fashion leader, Garland Stores will continue to pre-sent our merchandise in a variety of formats and locations. In addition to our semi-annual fashion shows (Fall and Spring), we sponsor several fashion design contests and bridge trunk shows that are presented in Garland Stores locations throughout the United States. We actively seek cooperative advertising agreements with major brands and designer bridge lines, while at the same time presenting frequent television, radio, and print media ads for our private label brands. Our nationally advertised quarterly sales (Fall, Winter, Spring, and Summer) and our monthly one-day sales also help us to gain new, value-minded customers, while also keeping our merchandise stock fresh and updated. Because Garland Stores strives to remain open to all new merchandising promotion avenues, we are currently pursuing a Garland Stores home shopping club, a CDRom catalog, and selling on the Internet and the Web. Our long-term, highly profitable billing inserts will also be continued, as this is one way to definitely reach our established, credit clients with our best merchandise and values.

Expansion
In our overall goal of being the number one fashion leader in the United States, Garland Stores is actively pursuing new locations and new markets. While the concentration of the majority of our stores is in the Midwest and Southeast, last year's opening of two new branches in the Northeast and three branches on the West Coast has made Garland Stores an up-and-coming force in these two all-important markets. Next year, the further expansion into these two markets will ensure our overall growing leadership in the United States.

Michele Granger, *Case Studies in Merchandising Apparel and Soft Goods* (New York, New York: Fairchild Publications, 1996, p. 107–108) for the New York City Partnership, by KPMG and SRI International, another consulting firm, predicted that for the two years, small businesses' sales would continue to fall short of what was expected before the trade center attack. Employment among small businesses will continue to fall through the first quarter of next year, the report said. On West Eight Street in Greenwich Village, shoe salesmen stand forlornly on the sidewalk in front of Leather & Shoes.com, smoking cigarettes and staring blankly into the distance, wondering where all the customers have gone."[10]

During economic downturns, the sales in the better clothing market may take a turn downward. Technological advances may provide new channels of distribution through the Internet, linked Web sites, and video catalogs. Demographic shifts in the population may indicate more disposable income for teen customers. A comprehensive survey of environmental factors often identifies trends that may offer new business niches.

In 1985, Nicholas Graham revolutionized the world of men's underwear by adding signature wit and humor to boxer shorts. Today, Joe Boxer has evolved into a global lifestyle brand of apparel, accessories, and home furnishings for men, women, and children. The product is currently distributed throughout the United States in over 4,000 better department stores and catalogs. In 1999, Joe Boxer added an innovative way to retail its product when it launched "Underwear to Go!" the underwear vending machine that talks. The vending machine is outfitted with a motion sensor. When triggered, it speaks to passers-by with such messages as, "Psst. . . wanna buy some underwear?" With the swipe of a major credit card, people can purchase Joe Boxer products, each retailing between $14 and $18 and vacuum packaged in aluminum cans. The vending technology of the "Underwear to Go!" program allows the company to collect demographic data as well as instantly track sales and inventory. Joe Boxer continues to research its market, experiment with new channels of distribution, and reconceptualize its product.

What makes the Joe Boxer concept exceptional? Creating a new market for an old product? Locating a product in an unexpected place? Packaging with a twist? Retail sales without the overhead of a store and staff? All these factors provide entrepreneurial inspirations, from the original concept to the new concepts that keep the company growing (www.joeboxer.com).

Researching an entrepreneurial venture involves more than library research. It encompasses seeking the advice of friends, bankers, other entrepreneurs, business advisers, and professors. As advice and information is offered, the entrepreneur must listen and keep an open mind. Entrepreneurs should not expect people to simply confirm what they are thinking. They should give information sources the freedom to be honest. Entrepreneurs should acknowledge the importance and value of the perceptions and opinions of others. The prospective entrepreneur will want to know whether or not a product will sell and whether or not financing will be available. The entrepreneur must remain objective in studying and evaluating information.

SWOT Analysis

A SWOT Analysis is used to determine whether or not a business idea will work in the "real world." The use of a SWOT (strengths, weaknesses, opportunities, and threats) analysis can help determine the strengths, weaknesses, opportunities, and threats to both the entrepreneur and the business by considering both internal and external factors. In the following paragraphs, condensed descriptions of this business analysis model provides further details.

A SWOT analysis contains the following four steps:

- *S—identify our strengths.* Factors such as imagination, the ability to sell yourself and your ideas, persistence, confidence, and expertise in a particular industry, as well as personal and business potential, are just some of the areas to consider.
- *W—identify weaknesses.* In what areas do personal and business weaknesses lie? Is there a time limitation, a health issue, no management experience, lack of financial stability, or lack of people skills? Regarding human resource issues, look at diversity, employee education and experience levels, hiring practices, job design, turnover/retention rates, and wages and benefits. In a SWOT analysis, competitive advantages, marketing, human resources, finance, corporate culture, corporate structure, operations, information technology, innovation, and strategies in terms of growth, direction, quality management, and international capabilities should all be considered.
- *O—identify opportunities.* What opportunities exist? Is there an opportunity for an internship prior to opening the business, to establish a network of resources, or to take courses that will prepare the prospective entrepreneur for business ownership? Does the opportunity exist to improve on an existing service or product?
- *T—identify threats.* Consider such issues as health concerns, lack of financial stability, and personal or family issues.

An in-depth analysis will consider opportunities and threats in such areas as bargaining power of customers, buyer relationships, customer loyalty, distribution channels, e-commerce, and market demographics. As industry and market research are conducted, the answers to these questions will present themselves. Industry and market research are explored later in the text.

Writing the Concept Statement

A fully developed concept should contain the marketing strategy, financial strategy, distribution method, market penetration strategy, and an analysis of the competition. Since the concept does not appear in the final business plan, why is it necessary to write out the concept? First, the concept is used to determine whether or not the business idea is sound. Second, it is used to help the entrepreneur focus on what she or he wants the business to be and how it is going to get there. The concept should be concise and well thought out.

Note that concept statements should not be too general. A statement such as, "The business will provide good service," will mean different things to different people. Concept statements should not be too broad. "Fashion retail store" tells very little. "Fashion retail store featuring clothes designed for the physically challenged" is a more complete statement. Many concept statements are incomplete because they omit key elements needed to provide enough information to let readers know precisely what the business is going to be and do. The test for a well-defined concept statement is to let someone such as a funder read it and then relate precisely the business proposed. The business concept statement issues should not be more than one or two pages and should include the following information:

1. Discuss the nature of the business. (e.g., a fashion retail store specializing in women's apparel).
2. Give the address (if known) and/or location of the business.

3. Discuss any unique or proprietary aspects of the product. Proprietary refers to an ownership interest in the product or service. For example, Michael Graves for Target represents a proprietary brand. Target has a proprietary right to this brand.
4. Describe the position the concept occupies in the industry such as retailer, distributor, manufacturer, and so on.
5. Discuss both the demographics and psychographics of the customer. Establish the age group targeted, geographic location, consumer buying habits, and so on.
6. Describe the method used to move the product from the business to the consumer.
7. Determine the method of penetrating the market.
8. Describe where the product will come from in terms of suppliers and the like.
9. Determine the type of funding to be requested.[11]

Writing the concept will help the entrepreneur focus on key elements for creating a successful company. (Data may change as the market is analyzed further.)

WHY BUSINESS PLANNING IS IMPORTANT

The remainder of this text focuses on the development of the business plan itself. The importance of a comprehensive business plan cannot be overemphasized. A well-thought-out business plan provides direction for knowing what the company is or will be, defining what the company goals are, and determining how those goals will be reached. The business plan is critical for obtaining outside capital. It will provide information key to managing operations and finances. It will also provide a way to measure performance; it will detail a tactical plan for carrying out strategies and accomplishing goals. The process of developing the plan gives the entrepreneur the opportunity to evaluate the entire business. In addition, the business plan will allow the entrepreneur to take a proactive, rather than reactive, approach to the business.

Business plans are not measured by size, but by content. All business plans should be organized into distinct sections:

COMPONENT OF BUSINESS PLAN	RELATED CHAPTERS IN TEXT	BUSINESS MENTOR CD-ROM
■ Cover page	1	
■ Table of contents	1	
■ Executive summary	1	Executive Summary
■ Product/service plan	2	Product Plan
■ Management plan	4, 8	Management Plan
■ Marketing plan	3, 6, 7	Marketing Plan
■ Location	5	
■ Merchandising	9	
■ Financial plan	10, 11	Financial Plan
■ Operating and control systems	12	Operating and Control Systems
■ Growth plan	13	Growth Plan
■ Appendix		

In the content of the plan, funders look for experience in the industry, identification of a market niche, the ability to generate cash flow, and whether or not the entrepreneur has the necessary operating and control systems in place to manage the business. The business plan is intended as a management tool to be evaluated on a regular basis.

The plan is intended to provide a means to measure the direction the company is taking against the projected outcome. The plan will provide important information about the goals of the company, financial forecasts, market information, industry information, management strategies, and other information needed to lead the company to success. The plan should be visited often. Fashion trends change frequently. Both the internal and external environments can affect the business. The ability to analyze and adapt to change through a well-written plan eliminates unwanted surprises.

Another distinct function of the business plan is to attract capital. Lenders and investors will require a written business plan before they decide to fund the venture. The plan reflects the commitment of the entrepreneur. Funders will review the plan in an effort to determine whether or not the entrepreneur has addressed the weaknesses of the business, as well as the strengths. Addressing weaknesses within the plan is not a negative. In most cases, the potential entrepreneur can find ways to compensate for those weaknesses.

Although there are many organizations and consultants ready and willing to assist with writing business plans, the plan should be prepared by the entrepreneur. Lenders and investors will view this as an indication that the entrepreneur understands the business and the business plan. They will want to know that the entrepreneur is aware of the risks involved in creating the new venture and that measures have been taken to reduce those risks. The criteria used by lenders and investors in evaluating business plans are covered in Chapter 11, The Financial Plan.

Business plans should be used to evaluate the concept. It is considered a success if the potential entrepreneur researches the concept, writes the business plan, and then determines the potential business will not work. It is important to determine this prior to investing time and resources into a venture.

The value of the business plan lies in the process the entrepreneur goes through to develop the plan. The success of the venture depends on the entrepreneur's open-minded, analytical approach in developing the plan. The end of each chapter provides a section, Entering the World of the Entrepreneur, which is a compilation of activities designed for helping the student gather information crucial to understanding the world of the entrepreneur and developing a well-thought-out and well-written business plan.

CONCLUSION

"Success depends on acting on dreams."

—Estee Lauder, chairman of the board, Estee Lauder, NY, NY.

Understanding entrepreneurship, its rewards and challenges, is the first step. Entrepreneurship is a discipline like no other. It is an opportunity to act on dreams, to become one's own boss, to secure financial freedom, and to share a passion with others. Some people have the personal attributes needed to be entrepreneurs and do what it takes to learn the skills necessary to succeed; others do not. Developing a business requires an analysis of both personal and professional traits. It requires an examination of the traits that differentiate those who succeed in business from those who do not. Successful entrepreneurs persevere. They have a passion for what they want to do. They take responsibility for themselves and for their business. They learn the skills necessary to run a business.

Planning is critical to a successful business. The entrepreneur must analyze the business from a variety of angles, looking for its strengths and weaknesses with equal vigor. The challenges of business ownership are immense, but the greatest challenge may be the objective evaluation of oneself and one's ideas.

Begin with the end in mind.

KEY TERMS

business plan   sales tax bond
funder   SWOT
mission statement   vision statement
outsourcing

QUESTIONS

1. What are some of the factors that contribute to a successful retail operation?
2. What are the personal characteristics or traits common to the majority of successful entrepreneurs? Identify several entrepreneurs who exemplify these traits.
3. List personal areas of weakness that may affect the success of a prospective entrepreneur.
4. Conduct a self-analysis using the areas of strength and the areas of weakness discussed in questions 2 and 3 above.
5. Identify the top three reasons why a business might fail. Provide examples of actual businesses that succeeded, even though they would seemingly fit into one or more of the criteria for failure.
6. Although it is not included in the business plan, why is the development and evaluation of a business concept important?
7. Select an entrepreneurial company for which you can locate the business concept and/or mission statement. Then put yourself in the shoes of the entrepreneur, and write a personal mission statement that corresponds to the business concept and mission statement.
8. Discuss the advantages of the SWOT method of business analysis.
9. List six sources that could be used to research a business concept in the apparel and accessories industry.

REFERENCES

1. U.S. Small Business Administration, *Office of Advocacy—The Facts About Small Business* (1999)
2. Norman Scarborough and Thomas Zimmerer, *Effective Small Business Management: An Entrepreneurial Approach,* 6th ed. (Upper Saddle River, New Jersey: Prentice-Hall, 2000, p. 1–2)
3. Teri Agins, *The End of Fashion: The Mass Marketing of the Clothing Business* (Santa Ana, California: Harper Collins Publishers, 1999, p. 16)
4. Annual Benchmark Report for U.S. Trade, U.S. Department of Commerce, Census Bureau, June 2000
5. Agins, *The End of Fashion,* p. 280
6. Dr. Judith Kautz, "What Is an Entrepreneur," www.about.com, 1999
7. Jeffry Timmons, *New Venture Creation: Entrepreneurship for the 21st Century,* 5th ed. (Boston, Massachusetts: Irwin McGraw-Hill, 1999, p. 27)
8. Original authors Richard Buskirk, R. Mack Davis, and Courtney Price, *Planning and Growing a Business Venture: Venture Planning Field Guide* (Kansas City, Missouri: Kauffman Center for Entrepreneurial Leadership at the Ewing Marion Kauffman Foundation, 2001, p. 9. Used by permission.)
9. http://www.aawn+wells.com/Wishing_Wells/wishing_wells.html
10. Edward Wyatt, "Ripples of September 11 Widen in Retailing," *The New York Times,* December 10, 2001

11. Adapted from FastTrac, *New Venture: Making Your Entrepreneurial Dreams a Reality* (Kansas City, Missouri: Kauffman Center for Entrepreneurial Leadership at the Ewing Marion Kauffman Foundation, 1999, p. 39–41. Used by permission.)

SUGGESTED READINGS

Stanley Rich and David Guimpert, *Business Plans That Win: Lessons from the MIT Forum* (New York, New York: Harper & Row, 1985)

Michael Gerber, *The E Myth Revisited, Why Most Small Businesses Don't Work and What to Do About It* (New York, New York: Harper Collins, 1995)

Harvey Mackay, *Swim With the Sharks Without Being Eaten Alive: Outsell, Outmanage, Outmotivate, and Out-negotiate Your Competition* (New York, New York: Ivy Books, 1988)

CASE STUDY

What do analysts in the business world mean when they call a company a *gazelle?* The term refers to an emerging growth company that outruns the market. Who is the proud entrepreneur of a gazelle? Stephen Kahn is the man behind the gazelle, Delia's Inc. The company sells stylish clothes and accessories to teenagers (in age or in spirit), primarily girls and young women ages 10 to 24. In 7 years, Kahn's New York catalog company has stunned retail analysts with its sales performance. In 1999, profits were $5.5 million on annual revenues of $150 million, up from $150,000 in sales in 1995. To Stephen Kahn, the 34-year-old CEO (chief executive officer) of the company, it is a sweet victory. When venture capitalists were presented with his business plan, they scoffed. They believed teens were an elusive demographic group with no access to credit cards. The idea of funding a catalog company with teens as a target market was not appealing. With perseverance as his middle name, Kahn dished out $100,000 of his own savings and then solicited $1 million from family and friends. This provided him with the start-up capital needed to print and mass-mail catalogs. As he recalls, it was blind ambition. "The naysayers never dissuaded me. I was convinced this overlooked niche had potential."

How did Kahn get the idea for his hot company? It began when he decided to quit his job at Paine Webber and set up a retail business that sold clothing to young women on college campuses through a catalog distributed by a network of sales representatives. He enlisted his former-college roommate as a partner to help develop the catalog and a sales strategy. Their mission was to be the nation's leading direct marketer to teenage girls, a group of 28 million customers who spent $60 billion in 1999. Within 3 years, Kahn and his partner say they had cornered 100 percent of the direct-mail girls' teen market. Revenue growth began to slow as catalog competitors, such as Alloy, Wet Seal, and Just Nikki, entered the market. Rather than hitting a wall with a saturated customer base, Kahn and company explored new ways to reach their existing market and to expand their clientele.

Kahn began to add new ways of reaching new customers. In addition to his catalog business he built retail stores and developed a Web site on the Internet. To develop an Internet business for Delia's, Kahn bought an extensive on-line girl's community, www.gurl.com in 1997. It featured chat-room forums, home-page hosting, and e-mail services. His idea was to plug into the lifestyles and minds of his target market, to gain insight into their likes and dislikes, and to build brand awareness. In 1998, Kahn established five of his own sites on the Web, targeting different teen customers. These sites included a Delia's on-line boutique, a home furnishings store for kids, and a teenage boys' apparel store. A new market was tapped. Kahn had expanded the business by targeting the brothers of Delia's shoppers.

CASE STUDY QUESTIONS

Using the case study on Stephen Kahn, answer the following questions:

1. What do you believe are the personal characteristics that have made Stephen Kahn a successful entrepreneur?
2. What research steps did Kahn take to minimize risk while implementing growth strategies?
3. In your opinion, where should Stephen Kahn go from here with his entrepreneurial empire? Can you identify any additional target markets, product lines, or channels of distribution (the avenues selected for moving goods from producer to consumer, such as mail order, retail stores, or an Internet business) that are a good fit with his business strategy.

. . . .

ENTERING THE WORLD OF THE ENTREPRENEUR

. . . .

Taking the opporunity to interview an entrepreneur in the fashion industry can provide valuable information about the prospective business. It should be explained to the entrepreneur that the time will be used to conduct an interview. You should let the entrepreneur know how much time will be needed to conduct the interview when setting up the appointment.

1. Develop a set of specific questions you wish the entrepreneur to answer and the general areas you would like information on.
2. Conduct the interview with the entrepreneur.
3. Evaluate what you have learned.
4. Write a thank-you note.

The Interview

Tell me about yourself:

- Tell me about entrepreneurs you knew growing up and how they influenced your decision to start your own business.
- Were your parents, relatives, or close friends entrepreneurial? How so?
- Did you have role models?
- What was your education/work experience? In hindsight, was it helpful? In what specific ways?
- Were you self-employed during your youth?
- Did you have any sales or marketing experience? How important was it (or the lack of it) to starting your company?
- When, under what circumstances, and from whom did you become interested in entrepreneurship? Did you learn some of the critical lessons?

Describe how you decided not to take a job but to create a job by starting your own venture:

- How did you determine an opportunity existed?
- What were your goals? What were your lifestyle needs or other personal requirements? How did you fit your goals and your needs together?
- How did you evaluate the opportunity in terms of the critical elements for success? The competition? The market? Did you have specific criteria you wanted to meet?
- Did you find or have partners? What kind of planning did you do? What kind of financing did you have?
- Did you have a start-up business plan of any kind? Please tell me about it.
- How much time did it take from conception to the first day of business? How many hours a day did you spend working to get to the point of that first day?
- How much capital did it take? How long was it before you began to show a profit and make money? If you did not have enough money at the time, what were some ways in which you funded the venture (e.g., bartering, borrowing, and the like). Tell me about the pressures and crises during that early survival period.
- What outside help did you get? Did you have experienced advisers? Lawyers? Accountants? Tax experts? How did you establish these connections, and how long did it take?

- How did outside advisers make a difference in your company?
- What did you perceive to be the strengths of your venture? Weaknesses?
- What was your most triumphant moment? Your worst moment?
- Did you want to have partners or do it solo? Why?

Once the business was going:

- What were the most difficult gaps to fill and problems to resolve as you began to grow?
- When you looked for key people as partners, advisers, or managers, were there any personal attributes you were looking for because you knew they would mesh well with you and were important to success? How did you find them?
- Are there any attributes among partners and advisers that you would definitely try to avoid?
- Have things become more predictable? Or less?
- Do you spend more time, the same amount of time, or less time working now than in the early years?
- Do you feel more managerial and less entrepreneurial now?
- What are your plans for the future?
- In an ideal world, how many days a year would you want to work? Please explain.
- Have your goals changed? Have you met them?
- Has your family situation changed?
- What did you learn from success and failure?
- What were/are your most demanding conflicts or trade-offs (e.g., the business vs. personal hobbies, a relationship, or children)?
- Describe a time when you ran out of cash and what pressures this created for you, the business, and your family. What you did about it? What lessons did you learn?
- Can you describe a venture that did not work out for you and how it prepared you for your next venture?

Concluding the Interview

- What do you consider your most valuable asset—the thing that enabled you to make it?
- If you had it to do over again, would you do it again and in the same way?
- As you look back, what do you feel are the most critical concepts, skills, attitudes, and know-how you needed to get your company started and to the point where it is today? To what extent do you think any of these can be learned? What will be needed for the next 5 years?
- Some people say that being an entrepreneur is very stressful. What have you experienced? How would you say it compares with other "hot seat" jobs, such as being the head of a big company or a partner in a large law or accounting firm?
- What things do you find personally rewarding and satisfying as an entrepreneur? What have been the rewards, risks, and trade-offs?
- Who should try to be an entrepreneur? Who should not? Can you give me any ideas there?
- What advice would you give an aspiring entrepreneur? Could you suggest the three most important lessons you have learned? How can I learn them while minimizing the risk?

- Could you suggest any other entrepreneur I might be able to talk to?
- Are there any other questions you wished I had asked, from which you feel I could learn valuable lessons?
- What was the biggest surprise you had?

Jeffrey A. Timmons, *New Venture Creation* (New York, New York: Irwin/McGraw-Hill, 1999, p. 19–20.)

. . . .

ENTERPRISING ENTREPRENEUR

. . . .

There is probably no greater example of the effect of developing, communicating, and implementing a successful mission statement and vision statement than that of the Kauffman Center for Entrepreneurial Leadership at the Ewing Marion Kauffman Foundation in Kansas City, Missouri.

Ewing Marion Kauffman, or Mr. K as he is affectionately known, based the Kauffman Center on the following vision and mission statement:

Vision: Self-sufficient people in healthy communities. The Kauffman Center will be a center through which:

1. Emerging entrepreneurs learn how to grow their business, and successful entrepreneurs share their experience and give something back to society.
2. Educators learn how to teach young people the concepts, skills, values, and attitudes of entrepreneurship.
3. Researchers, educators, and entrepreneurs contribute to the "state of the art" and make it their mission to help entrepreneurs.

Mission: To research and identify the unfulfilled needs of society and to develop, implement, and/or fund breakthrough solutions that have a lasting impact and offer a choice and hope for the future.

The Kauffman Center will serve as a catalyst for:

1. Stimulating entrepreneurial leadership in both the for-profit and the not-for-profit sectors.
2. Researching, identifying, teaching, and disseminating the critical skills and values that enable entrepreneurs to succeed.
3. Introducing young people to the excitement and opportunity of entrepreneurship.
4. Encouraging others to support entrepreneurship.

Best known as owner of the Kansas City Royals (which he has given to the city), Mr. K founded Marion Laboratories, Inc., a pharmaceutical manufacturing firm, in 1950. He guided this Kansas City-based company from gross sales of $36,000 and a net profit of $1,000 in its first year to become a diversified health-care products company that exceeded $1 billion in annual sales. Referred to as "associates," rather than "employees," Marion Laboratories generated over 300 millionaires among its 3,400 associates. In 1989, Marion merged with Merrell Dow Pharmaceuticals to form Marion Merrell Dow, Inc., where Mr. K served as chairman emeritus until his death in 1993.

Mr. K started his company because of the treatment he received from the president of the company for which he worked. As a salesperson, working on straight commission without expenses or benefits, he reached pay higher than that of the president's salary. At that point, the president cut back his commission. The next year, Mr. K made more money than the president again, so he cut back Mr. K's territory. As a result, Mr. K started his own company in his basement, Marion Labs.

Mr. K grew his company on three principals: (1) Treat people as you would want to be treated, (2) Share the wealth with those who contribute to its creation, (3) Give back to the community that enabled your success.

Mr. K's most enduring gift was to establish a foundation to help others live self sufficiently in healthy communities. Created in the mid-1960s the Kauffman Foundation is now among the 15 largest foundations in the country, with nearly $2 billion in assets.

Kauffman Center for Entrepreneurial Leadership, *Overview Brochure* (2000, p. 1. Used with permission.)

Chapter 2

ANALYZING THE PRODUCT

INTRODUCTION

There are two main types of retail entrepreneurs: those who create the product they sell and those who sell an existing product. The product is often the source of inspiration for the prospective entrepreneur. It can begin with one of those lightbulb moments. An apparel designer, expecting her first baby, realizes that attractive and fashionable maternity career apparel is virtually nonexistent. A lightbulb moment. While scanning fashion magazines, she notices that expectant celebrities are now showing off their pregnant bellies with pride, even posing for cover shots in the nude. Another lightbulb moment. She attends prenatal exercise classes with other hip mothers-to-be; all are wearing spandex leotards and leggings. The lightbulb moment strikes again. She decides that the world needs a fashion-forward, curve-hugging maternity clothing for today's woman. The product is born, possibly before the baby.

Another potential entrepreneur begins as a Wall Street executive on holiday in London. His feet hurt him as he tours the city. He stops into a shoe store and buys a pair of Campers, a division of Dr. Martens. In addition to a new glide to his stride, he receives a number of compliments on these comfortable, new shoes. Back in the United States, he begins to observe the shoe selections in retail stores, the shoes on the feet of passers-by on the street, and the shoes worn by his coworkers and friends. The lightbulb moment. He researches the market, determines that the data support his conclusion, and walks to the bank. The opening of a shoe store featuring Campers is his next step.

DEFINING THE PRODUCT

What is a product? A product is anything offered to a market for attention, acquisition, use, or consumption. A product can satisfy a customer's want or need and may be an object, a service, a place, an organization, or an idea. A product can be a maternity dress, a pair of shoes, an image makeover, a promotional plan, a trend forecast, a personal trainer, a fashion show production, and more. The product can be classified as intangible or tangible. Intangible products include those that cannot be touched or held, such as a service or an idea. Tangible products are divided into two primary classifications: nondurable goods and durable goods. Nondurable goods are those that are normally consumed in one or a few uses, such as shampoo. Durable goods are those that normally survive many uses. Apparel, shoes, home accessories, and fabrics are examples of durable goods. Service products refer to activities, benefits, or satisfactions that are offered for sale. Custom design work, alterations, and personal shopping are illustrations of fashion-related service products.

Another method of classifying products is through brand preference and frequency of use. Convenience goods are those that the customer purchases frequently and easily, usually with minimal comparison shopping and evaluating. Pantyhose and some beauty products are examples of convenience goods. Shopping goods, on the other hand, are those the customer often compares on the basis of price, quality, style, and other related factors. A sweater is an example. Specialty goods are those for which a significant group of buyers is habitually willing to make a special purchase effort. This merchandise has unique characteristics and/or specific brand identification, such as Polo Ralph Lauren sportswear. Merchants work to move their products into the specialty goods arenas, as this is where the devoted, repeat customer resides. Figure 2.1 illustrates the differences between convenience, shopping, and specialty goods in terms of price, frequency of purchase, type of shopping trip, and level of customer service.

The final category is unsought goods. The name says it all. Customers did not seek out the merchandise; they did not even know they needed or wanted it until it found them. Promotion is the key to selling unsought goods. An example is Topsy Tail®, created by Tomima Edmark. Topsy Tail® is a hairstyling tool that was marketed through television demonstrations and magazine advertisements showing how to use the product.

There are a number of other product terms that are commonly used in the fashion industry. Fashion goods refer to items that are popular for a given period of time. Staple or basic goods, in contrast, are those steadily in demand and rarely influenced by fashion changes. Hard goods refer to appliances, electronics, and home furnishings. Soft goods incorporate textile and apparel products, including accessories.

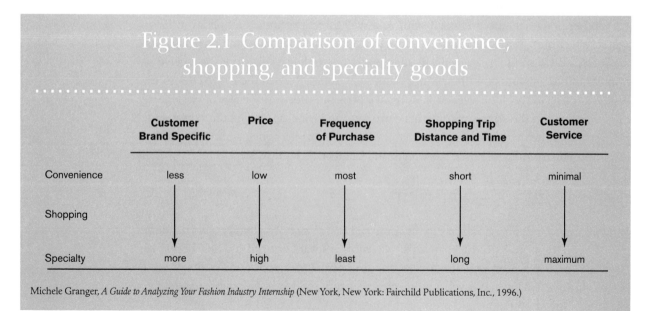

Figure 2.1 Comparison of convenience, shopping, and specialty goods

	Customer Brand Specific	Price	Frequency of Purchase	Shopping Trip Distance and Time	Customer Service
Convenience	less	low	most	short	minimal
Shopping					
Specialty	more	high	least	long	maximum

Michele Granger, *A Guide to Analyzing Your Fashion Industry Internship* (New York, New York: Fairchild Publications, Inc., 1996.)

Retailers also refer to merchandise in terms of pricing with high-end goods being at the top of the pricing scale, and low-end goods representing lower or budget priced merchandise. Types of merchandise assortments are also labeled in the fashion industry. A merchandise assortment refers to the selection of inventory a retailer carries or a manufacturer produces. It refers to the amount, type, size, color, and style representation in the inventory. Inventory refers to the merchandise selection carried by a retailer, to include fashion and/or basic goods, hard and/or soft goods. General line refers to a wide variety of merchandise, one that has great *breadth*. A department store that features women's, men's, and children's apparel, as well as home furnishings and home accessories, illustrates a retail organization featuring a general line of merchandise. A limited line represents the other end of the spectrum, a particular product category with *depth* of selection. A limited line retail operations, for example, may feature ladies' accessories including handbags, belts, jewelry, and millinery.

Why the lesson in fashion language? The entrepreneur in the fashion industry should be able to discuss the business concept in the terms of the trade when communicating with vendors, competitors, or bankers. The way you say what you think often adds credibility and persuasion to the message. Another reason for understanding product terminology is to allow for the examination of product alternatives. The prospective entrepreneur considering a fashion retail operation should explore price lines, assortment alternatives, frequency of purchases, and the amounts of fashion and basic merchandise within his or her entrepreneurial vision.

DISSECTING THE PRODUCT

One of the best ways to start analyzing a product is to divide it into parts. The three levels of all products are core, formal, and augmented. Core refers to the true product—the product's main benefit or service. If, for example, the entrepreneur intends to open a business that retails handbags, the core product is the handbag. The formal level includes the packaging (e.g., a fabric drawstring bag), the brand name (e.g., Coach Bags), the quality of the product, the styling of the handbag, and any other tangible features, such as the leather identification tag. The final level, augmented, refers to the product extras, such as advertising and promotion, warranty, and after-sale service. In this case, Coach Bags advertises in a number of national fashion consumer publications. The company will repair its handbags if there are any defects. Additionally, the customer can purchase a new shoulder strap or leather lotion for the bag. The advertising, warranty, and after-sale service are there—all parts of the augmented level of the product. Figure 2.2 illustrates the levels of a fashion product.

Whether creating the retail product or retailing an existing product, the prospective entrepreneur should consider the degree to which the merchandise will fill each of the three levels. In some cases, the augmented level may be minimal. Many customers will accept a low augmented level in exchange for a low price. For example, a consumer may elect to pay $30 for a fashion watch with an unknown brand name and a 1-year warranty, rather than buy an expensive, classic timepiece. In other cases, the extra features incorporated in the augmented level distinguish one business concept from another. One of the success stories that illustrates an entrepreneur's understanding of product line in the e-commerce channel of distribution is Bluefly.com.

After a frustrating day of outlet shopping, rummaging through bins of disorganized, two-season-old designer clothing, E. Kenneth Seiff knew there had to be a better way. An

Figure 2.2 Levels of the Fashion Product

Augmented Level:
National Advertisement,
Guaranteed Satisfaction

Formal Product:
The Brand Name,
the Styling

Core Product: The Handbag

entrepreneur before his Bluefly.com lightbulb moment, Seiff was the founder and CEO of a golf apparel firm, Pivot Rules. He says that he recognized that traditional outlet stores were not offering the kind of shopping experience that customers wanted. They were, in fact, viewing shopping as a chore. Seiff saw the solution in the Internet, which, at the time, was a significant untapped source for retailing designer off-price apparel and home furnishings. What differentiated his concept from others? Bluefly.com features a dynamic design, superior customer service, and advanced search technology. An exclusive "My Catalog" feature allows customers to target their own preferences in terms of brands, styles, and sizes. In essence, the customer can develop a personalized on-line catalog. Additionally, the Web site offers fashion features and new fashion tips, competitive flat-rate shipping, and a 90-day guarantee/return policy. How many outlet stores offer this level of augmented product?

THE PRODUCT LIFE CYCLE

Something old, something new . . . For the entrepreneur who will develop a new product, as well as the one who will work with an existing product, an understanding of the product life cycle is essential for determining the target market, pricing and promoting the product, and selecting a channel of distribution. The product life cycle is a model designed to identify the maturation stage of a particular product by approximating its level of customer acceptance. To effectively market the business concept, the entrepreneur should be able to objectively identify the product's stage in the life cycle.

Introductory Stage

The first stage of the product life cycle is the introductory stage, which is the time when innovative goods that appeal to fashion leaders, or trendsetters, are first offered. During the introductory stage, the focus is on marketing the new product to potential consumers. Effective advertising and promotion must be used to educate consumers about the new product and how it will satisfy their needs. The introduction of a new product into an existing market brings with it a unique set of challenges. The cost of introducing a new product can be high, while profitability is often low. The entrepreneur must continually monitor the external environment for changes in economic climate, changes in the original assumptions, and reactions by the competition.

Growth Stage

The next stage in the product life cycle is the growth stage. A product enters the growth stage when a larger number of consumers begin to accept and purchase it. The product typically generates its peak sales volume as it moves through the growth stage. Typically, profits increase as the demand for the product increases. Thus, the cash flow position of the company usually improves. In the fashion retail industry, styles change, and they change frequently. It is important to recognize that in order to continue reaping the success of a new product, consumers must believe this product is meeting their needs. Failure to meet their needs will result in a decline in sales. Successful entrepreneurs have found a number of ways to meet the needs of consumers in the fickle fashion market. Some modify the product to make it appear new. Others find new uses for existing products. Still others develop entirely new products and use the customer's comfort level with the company as an entry into the new product category.

Maturity

The next stage is the maturity stage. The product is either at a peak or plateau in sales, and it is mass-produced and mass-marketed. During a product's maturity stage, sales generally continue to increase, but typically at a slower rate than during the growth stage. The success of the product in the marketplace brings on the challenge of increased competition. Many times in order to compete, prices must be lowered to hold market share, thereby lowering profit margins. During the maturity stage, the entrepreneur must work diligently to differentiate the business's product from products of competitors. Often, this is the time when services are added to the product mix. The entrepreneur attempts to increase profits through competitive pricing, effective promotion, and service add-ons, such as delivery or gift wrapping. When the product enters the maturity stage, it becomes a test of marketing know-how.

Decline Stage

As consumers lose interest in the product, it enters the decline stage, the final stage of the product life cycle. At this point, the product is often found in discount stores and on markdown racks. Some entrepreneurs take advantage of this stage of the product life cycle by selling the discounted merchandise at clearance prices to the consumer. Some retail operations, such as T. J. Maxx and Gordman's, specialize in buying and reselling products in the early period of the decline stage. Sales continue to drop until profit margins become extremely low. The product is often a dead trend, unless or until someone develops a new twist, a new use, or a new image to revive its popularity. (See Figure 2.3 for an illustration of the fashion product life cycle.)

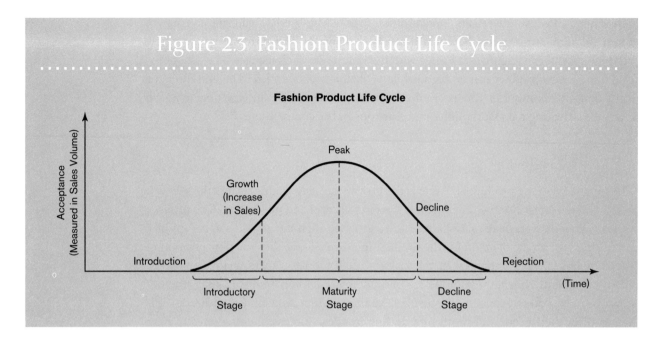

Figure 2.3 Fashion Product Life Cycle

Practical Application

As a product moves through its life cycle, entrepreneurs can measure opportunities for growth by analyzing life cycle stages. The entrepreneur can use this information to make decisions about whether or not to continue selling the product and when to introduce new follow-up products. It is important that fashion retailers recognize the life cycles of their products, as well as those of competitive products. There are a number of successful fashion companies that have survived decades of fashion changes by keeping an eye on the product life cycle. Jockey International, Inc., is an example of one of these companies. Today, it is in the process of burnishing its somewhat dulled image by repositioning its undergarment line.

In an article originally published by *Bobbin* and located on www.findarticles.com "Jockey Colors Its World" (February 1999), author Jules Abend states that the "Chief Operating Officer (COO) and his team are analyzing the essence of the Jockey brand—the innovations that made the company what it is today—and targeting the business to adapt to modern-day consumers." COO Edward Emma reports:

> [Today] consumers' product expectations are different; the marketplace is different. We have to be able to react to what the market is telling us. But the basic qualities don't change. They're just so core to our brand. Jockey's new fashion products and marketing approaches are aimed at attracting a younger audience while retaining the loyalty of its tried-and-true-customers . . . [we] did lose some market share, but the good news is we're gaining it all back.[1]

Jockey International, Inc., is looking for ways to boost sales. The company recognized the opportunity to enter the growth stage of the product life cycle based on the popularity of its unconstructed bras. With a new target market of young women to entice, Jockey began to do battle in a very competitive arena in April 2001, by selling a line of fully constructed bras for the first time. "Jockey is keeping in touch with its innovative past on the new products by offering women a unique product that the intimate apparel industry hasn't seen before," stated Steven Tolensky, Jockey's president.[2]

The product life cycle must be understood in order for the entrepreneur to determine if and when to introduce new products into the existing product lines and to revise existing ones. The time to introduce a new product into the market is during the early stages of the life cycle of the current product, when sales are strong and profit margins are high. To successfully launch a new product, the entrepreneur must be committed to the new product and be willing to adjust to changes in the environment. Adequate planning and knowledge of the market are important. The entrepreneur must understand how the different levels of the fashion industry interrelate and when new lines should be introduced. Figure 2.4 illustrates the timing sequence in the industry as it relates to the product life cycle for the designer/product developer, manufacturer, and retailer.

NEW USES OR IMAGES FOR OLD PRODUCTS

Something borrowed, something blue . . . another route for the entrepreneur is to develop new uses or images for existing products. Consider Joe Boxer, Kate Spade, and Earl Jeans. Was there anything new under the sun to do with undershorts, fabric totes, and blue jeans? Yes, and these companies found them. The influx of vintage clothing stores, as well as resale stores for sporting goods, children's apparel, and special occasion gowns, are examples of entrepreneurial ventures that put new faces on old products. Children's Orchard (www.childorch.com) has grown into a national franchise that features bargain-priced, "gently used" clothes, toys, and furniture for kids. The company prides itself on being "right in step with today's value conscious and environmentally concerned consumer."

AT YOUR SERVICE

For the entrepreneur whose business is a service, the examination of the product should focus on an intangible, the core service. This entrepreneur will determine how to augment the core service to make it as appealing to the consumer as possible. Examples of services as core products for businesses in the fashion industry include trend or color forecasting, image consulting, and fashion event production businesses. For the entrepreneur whose product is tangible, decisions need to be made about the types and levels of customer services the entrepreneur will offer to complement the actual product. Following is a discussion about service as both a product and a supplement to a tangible product.

When the Product Is a Service

For the entrepreneur interested in a service business, plans for the types and prices of services must be carefully developed. Customer relations are at the heart of a service business. If a woman purchases a dress from a retailer and is satisfied in terms of price, styling, and quality, she may forget that the salesperson was rude or that the dressing rooms were a mess. However, the customer buying a service has nothing to reflect upon except the service itself. It must be a pleasant reflection for the customer to return and to recommend the business to others.

Types of full-service operations within the retail fashion industry cover a wide range of businesses. For example, a designer opening a new apparel line may use a trend forecast-

Figure 2.4 Timing Calendar for Fashion Industry

	January	February	March	April	May	June
The Designer/Product Developer	Style early fall ———	Shop for fall fabrics Sample, design, and construct Refabricate —— summer promotions	Duplicate sample line ——— Research late fall and holiday colors and fabrics	First of month, early fall goes into showroom —— Style late fall and holiday	Duplicate samples	Shop and research spring and cruise seasons ——— Late fall and holiday lines go into showroom late, May or early June
		Paris couture shows, spring		Paris pret-a-porter shows, fall	Interstoff, international fabric show, Germany	
The Manufacturer	Sell summer line; goes into showroom right after New Year (Introduction) ———			Sell early fall (Introduction) ——— Sell summer promotions and —— reorders (Growth)		Sell late fall and holiday (Introduction) ——— Order fall fabric
	Order summer stock fabric	Manufacture and —— ship summer goods (Growth) Ship and produce —— spring clothes (reorders) (Growth)			Manufacture summer promotions and reorders (Decline) Manufacture early fall and ship (Growth)	
The Retailer		Receive and sell ——— early spring/cruise (Introduction) Rainwear important in coat department	First spring mark-downs (Growth)	Receive and sell early summer (Introduction) Easter promotions for children's wear	——— Major spring ——— mark-downs (Decline) Sell summer ——— (Growth)	Major summer mark-downs (Decline)
	After-Christmas sales of holiday and late fall garments (Decline) Swimwear opens (Introduction)	Swimwear promotions (Growth)			Wedding ——— promotions	Swimwear mark-downs (Decline)

(continued)

Figure 2.4 Timing Calendar for Fashion Industry *(continued)*

	July	August	September	October	November	December
The Designer/Product Developer	Style spring	Duplicate spring		Early October, spring goes into showroom		Research early fall colors and fabrics Duplicate samples
		summer colors Refabricate and do fall promotions	Research Style summer and trends sample fabric for summer			
					Interstoff international fabric show, Germany	
		Paris couture shows, fall		Paris pret-a-porter shows, spring		
The Manufacturer		Sell reorders and promotions	Sell spring cruise			
		Manufacture and ship late fall (Growth)				
			Order spring stock fabric	Manufacture cruise and spring. Ship in late Nov.-early Dec.		
	Order late fall and holiday fabrics			Ship holiday catalog merchandise		
		Manufacture and ship late fall and holiday				
The Retailer	Receive and sell early fall (Introduction)		Fall opens Sell fall (Growth)		First fall mark-downs (Decline) Children's party clothes	
		Coats important now Furs open				
	Summer clearance (Decline)		Early fall mark-downs (Decline)		Holiday fill-ins	Holiday promotions
		Back to school for young apparel (Introduction)		Holiday merchandise arrives (Introduction)	sells (Growth)	Mark down glittery/dressy before or around Dec. 25th (Decline)

(continued)

Figure 2.4 Timing Calendar for Fashion Industry *(continued)*

	January	February	March	April	May	June
The Designer/Product Developer	Style early fall	Shop for fall fabrics Sample, design, and construct	Duplicate sample line	First of month, early fall goes into showroom		Shop and research spring cruise
		Refabricate summer promotions	Research late fall and holiday colors and fabrics	Style late fall and holiday	Duplicate samples	Late fall and holiday, breaks late, May or early June
					Interstoff, international fabric show, Germany	
		Paris couture shows, spring		Paris pret-a-porter shows, fall		
The Manufacturer	Summer line goes into showroom right after New Year			Sell early fall		Sell late fall and holiday
				Sell summer promotions and reorders		
	Order summer stock fabric	Manufacture and ship, summer				Order fall fabric
					Manufacture summer promotions and reorders	
		Ship and produce spring clothes (reorders)			Manufacture early fall and ship	
The Retailer	Receive spring/cruise Sell spring Stores have new color story				Major spring mark-downs	
		Rainwear important in coat department	First spring mark-downs			
				Early summer–sell summer		
						Summer promotions
	After-Christmas sales of holiday and late fall garments			Easter promotions for children's wear		
					Wedding promotions	
				Swimwear opens		

(continued)

Figure 2.4 Timing Calendar for Fashion Industry *(continued)*

	July	August	September	October	November	December
The Designer/Product Developer	Style spring	Duplicate spring		Early October, spring goes into showroom		Research early fall colors and fabrics Duplicate samples
		Refabricate and do fall promotions	Research summer colors and trends, sample fabric for summer		Style summer	
		Paris couture shows, fall		Paris pret-a-porter shows, spring	Interstoff international fabric show, Germany	
The Manufacturer		Sell reorders and promotions	Sell spring cruise			
	Manufacture and ship, fall		Order spring stock fabric	Manufacture cruise and spring Ship in late Nov.-early Dec.		
	Order late fall and holiday fabrics			Set holiday catalog merchandise	Ship holiday catalog merchandise	
		Manufacture and ship late fall and holiday				
The Retailer	Early fall (Introduction)		Fall opens Sell fall (Growth)			First fall mark-downs
		Coats important now Furs open				Children's party clothes
	Summer clearance (Decline)		Early fall mark-downs (Decline)		Holiday fill-ins (Growth)	Holiday promotions
		Back to school for young apparel		Holiday merchandise arrives (Introduction)	sells	
			Swimwear sales			Mark down glittery/dressy before or around Dec. 25th

M Granger, *Case Studies in Merchandising Apparel & Soft Goods* (New York, New York: Fairchild Publications, 1996) ing company, such as Tobé, to determine color and style directions for a specific season. The designer may also visit a fiber representative, such as Cotton, Inc., to gather names of fabric sources. Once the line is developed, the designer hires a public relations firm to promote it. The public relations firm employs a special-event company to produce the fashion show debuting the designer's first collection. A glowing review in *Women's Wear Daily* and *Vogue,* and a star is born, with a range of service businesses helping to launch it.

If the product of the business is a service, then the entrepreneur must know how to articulate, price, and market the service. Types and levels of service need to be determined before prices can be established. The entrepreneur may decide that the business will offer a superior level of service. An illustration of high-level service is the wedding consulting firm in which the entrepreneur does everything for the bride and groom from locating the caterer to fluffing the bride's train before she walks down the aisle. In contrast, the entrepreneur may elect to open a no-fringe service business at below-competition prices.

How does the entrepreneur of a service business set prices for the services? It is a challenging and detailed process, one that must be continually monitored and reevaluated. First, the entrepreneur will want to calculate the costs of materials and equipment needed to provide each service. Labor costs must then be determined. Overhead expenses, including promotion of the business and its services, will be calculated and divided among an estimation of the frequency of service offerings. Additionally, the entrepreneur will want to examine the prices of services offered by competitors. What do businesses featuring similar services charge customers for their work?

An example is the entrepreneur, a woman who desired to establish a trend-forecasting business. Initially, she determined the types of services she would offer. In this case, the entrepreneur decided that she would develop four reports for each of the five fashion seasons. These reports would forecast color, fabric, silhouette, and designer trends for early fall, late fall, holiday, spring, and summer seasons. She would also offer consulting services as corporate or one-on-one presentations. The entrepreneur then investigated the costs of travel to Paris, London, Milan, and New York five times annually. She determined the costs of setting up an office, including a computer and software, a color copier and scanner, office furniture, a telephone system, and a lease. She calculated hourly wages for a part-time assistant. She comparison-shopped printers to produce the trend reports. Additionally, she developed a promotional plan to market the business and determined the associated costs. Armed with this stack of figures, the entrepreneur was able to estimate the cost of producing each report. Pricing intangible products can be more challenging than pricing tangible ones.

When the Product Is Tangible

If the product of the business is tangible, the entrepreneur still must make customer service and pricing decisions. In most cases, the price of the product relates directly to the level and types of customer services being offered. When merchandise carries a relatively high retail price, the customer usually expects relatively high levels and forms of service. For example, high-end fashion boutiques carrying expensive designer garments will often offer a wide range of customer services, from alterations to home delivery. On the other hand, discount retail operations, such as Sam's Wholesale Club, will provide fewer customer services as a means of keeping overhead and, subsequently, prices below those of its competitors. At Sam's Wholesale Club, for example, the customer is not provided with dressing rooms, packaging, or delivery. Instead, the customer is provided with a focused selection of merchandise at very competitive prices.

Types of Service   What types of services should the entrepreneur consider for the business? Customer services can be classified in two ways: prepurchase and postpurchase. *Prepurchase* services include special-order availability, exclusivity, lay-away, personal shopper assistance, and educational programs. *Postpurchase* services can include a replacement guarantee, delivery, alterations, ease of payment, gift wrap, and repeat purchase discounts. The list is ever-evolving as new entrepreneurs find more and better ways to service their customers. Nike, for example, offers a new form of customer service through its customized shoe program, which is available on-line. The customer can select the colors, symbols, and trim for a running shoe that is one of a kind.

Levels of Service   Levels of service, too, are often parallel with price. Payless Shoes, for example, offers a low level of customer service with its racks of boxed shoes and limited number of sales associates. What is the payoff for Payless? The company retails its products in volume at below-market prices. The price element may be enough for customers to overlook service and environment. T. J. Maxx is another example of an apparel and soft-goods retailer for which low prices offset a lower level of service.

There are a number of places in the development of a business plan in which the entrepreneur must consider types and level of customer service. How does service fit into the market niche? What are the customer service offerings of competitors? What are the target market's needs in terms of service? How much will customer services cost? Where will these costs be absorbed? How might payroll be affected? The bottom line is that the customer pays for the services offered by retailers in one of two ways: the services may be financed through higher prices, or the services may be sold as entities separate from the product, through fees for such extras as gift-wrapping or alterations. The entrepreneur must decide how types and level of services offered will affect the image of the company.

BRANDING

Branding has become an integral part of the fashion industry. When the prospective entrepreneur investigates potential products or product lines for the business, he or she must consider branding and how it will affect company image, customer identification with the business, and profit potential. What is a brand? A brand is a name, term, sign, design, or combination of these that is intended to identify the goods or services of one seller or group of sellers and to differentiate them from those of competitors. Branding is used as a means of distinguishing one product or service from another. It is used to create differentiation and image. "Branding is the process of attaching a name and a reputation to something or someone."[3] A brand name can be both that of the company or product owner and that of the particular product or product range.

There are brand names that immediately conjure up images in the consumer's mind. When customers think about Gucci, Calvin Klein, or Polo Ralph Lauren, they frequently envision a certain status. These brand names often transmit feelings of prestige, confidence, and success. This is exactly what the promotion department of these companies intended to do with their advertising efforts. Brands such as French Connection United Kingdom, Kenneth Cole, Benetton, and Moschino approach branding in a unconventional and, at the very least, rebellious manner. They want to be known as the "bad boys" of fashion imagery brands, looking to rebel against traditional brand imagery. They intentionally go against the grain to create a defined image. Today's fashion customers, more than ever before, are choosing a brand with which they can identify. Customers are choosing the brands that reflect their inner selves—who they want to be or believe they are. If customers perceive themselves to be rebels (or wish for the confidence to show a rebellious side), then Benetton may be the ideal brand badge. Brands provide customers with ways to identify products as part of their personalities.

In most cases, the entrepreneur must decide whether the firm will put a name, a logo, or an identifier on the organization's product. Even if the entrepreneur is not manufacturing a product and is, instead, retailing existing product lines, a name for the business must be determined. A store name is actually a brand name. Branding can add value to a product. For this reason, some entrepreneurs prefer to be affiliated with an established brand through licensing, franchising, or naming the business to bring a particular brand to customers' minds. In other cases, the entrepreneur may choose to create a brand and its related imagery. This can be extremely successful, now more than ever before, because businesses are able to reach huge numbers of people through the Internet.

Intellectual Property: Brand Names, Trademarks, and Copyrights

The brand is the visual identifier of the product or business. There are a number of brands that are identifiable by the model or even the typeface used in advertisements. An example is the cosmetic company that places a high-profile supermodel under contract to exclusively represent the product line in promotional efforts. Another example is the distinct typeface used by Calvin Klein in that company's billboards and advertisements in fashion magazines. The brand name is the part of the brand that can be vocalized, while the brand mark is the part of the brand that can be recognized but cannot be spoken.

Intellectual property is any product, service, or retail operation that is the result of a creative process and that has commercial value. Intellectual property can be protected through the use of trademarks, patents, and copyright. Protecting intellectual property can be critical to the success of a company. In December 1999, Spiegel Catalog, Inc., announced that it had signed a letter of intent with J. Crew to purchase the intellectual property of Clifford & Wills, a women's apparel catalog company. The intellectual property includes the Clifford & Wills name, its U.S. customer file, images, logos, trademarks, and its uniform resource locator (URL). According to John Irvin, president and chief executive officer of Spiegel Catalog, Inc., "While complementing our brand positioning, style and merchandise offer, acquiring the intellectual property of Clifford & Wills provides the opportunity to leverage our existing resources, including our merchandising and marketing expertise as well as our customer service and fulfillment operations." The company expected to build its customer base and drive incremental sales through this move.[4] Spiegel Catalog and J. Crew have since signed this agreement. As one of the nation's leading direct marketers via catalogs and Internet sites, Spiegel Catalog can benefit greatly from this agreement. The purchase of Clifford & Wills increases Spiegel Catalog's market share by adding the customer following of an established brand name. To J. Crew, the intellectual property rights of Clifford & Wills proved to be extremely marketable.

A trademark is a word, design, symbol, logo, shape, color, or a combination of these that a company uses to identify and distinguish itself from other companies. There are a number of trademarks that have become icons in the fashion industry. The word and the "swoosh" of Nike create a powerful trademark. Trademarks may be thought of as brands. The visual components of a trademark, when combined, are referred to as a trade dress. The unique combination of the word, design, symbol, logo, shape, and color is considered a company's trade dress. For trademark protection, trade dress must be unique to a company, and another company's use of that trade dress must be likely to confuse consumers.

The exclusive rights to reproduce, publish, or sell the trademark in the form of a literary, musical, or artistic work is referred to as a copyright. While the ability to copyright a brand name or brand mark is fairly cut and dried from a legal perspective, less clear is the right to protect the way an entrepreneur conducts business or the actual fashions created by a designer. These concepts are considered intellectual property—a topic of major discussion in the fashion industry. Can a dress design or a store concept be protected from copying? A.B.S. is a formal wear company that has generated tremendous profits from "knocking off" or copying the gowns worn by celebrities, particularly those worn at events such as the Oscars. These special-occasion dresses are available on the racks of retailers carrying the A.B.S. line within weeks after they appear on the superstars—with one big difference. The A.B.S. knock-off sells for $200, compared to the original which is on the original designer's line at $2,000. At this time, this is completely legal.

Similar questions can be asked in terms of the fashion retailer. Should, for example, a retail operation have the legal opportunity to reserve and protect the look of its merchandise assortment, the type of advertising it conducts, and the image it projects to its target market? This question was one of legal debate between two major retailers at the start of the new millennium. In June 1998, the fashion retail store Abercrombie & Fitch filed a lawsuit against American Eagle Outfitters "claiming trade dress infringement and unfair competition. American Eagle filed a motion with the courts, which argued that Abercrombie & Fitch 'has no rights, and cannot acquire rights, in the type of generic marketing devices which are described in the complaint.' American Eagle prevailed. The judge's decision concluded that the factors identified by Abercrombie & Fitch were both generic and descriptive, and to forbid other clothing retailers from adopting similar methods of advertising would be unduly anticompetitive. The judge referred to nine other retailers 'who use similar features in their advertising.' "[5] In this particular case, Abercrombie & Fitch was not able to prove that the trade dress of American Eagle would confuse customers and harm the sales of Abercrombie & Fitch.

Should a designer have the option of copyrighting an original design? How should "original" be defined? Should a copyright protect modification of styles? If so, where does the copyright option begin and end? Should the designer be able to copyright a collar, a sleeve, or a full garment? What if the style is today's version of a historical fashion? The dilemma is complex and lengthy. The jury is out on how the results of this debate will affect the fashion industry, but the ramifications could be tremendous.

Brand Sponsorship

The entrepreneur may need to make decisions about brand sponsorship. Brand sponsorship refers to the selection between three primary alternatives available to the fashion retailer: First, there is the manufacturer's brand, which is the most traditional type of brand sponsorship and is often referred to as a national brand. Manufacturer's brands are those brand names promoted by the producers, often advertised nationally. The manufacturer targets a broad range of retailers to purchase the line and sell it to consumers. Examples of manufacturer's brands are Liz Claiborne, Donna Karan, and Adidas. Second, there is the private brand, which may be referred to as the agent (intermediary) distributor, or dealer brand. Usually, a distributor sells and ships merchandise purchased from a variety of manufacturers under a brand name that is developed by the distributor. This branding technique helps create consistency among the distributor's product offerings. An example of a private brand usually is a jewelry wholesale company, such as Gerson, which purchases merchandise from jewelry manufacturers in New York and resells the goods to its retail account. Third, there is the branding choice of private label.

Private label represents a major trend in the fashion industry. Private label merchandise carries a brand name created for the retail operation. Decades ago, private label was only available to major retailers with the purchasing power to buy extremely large quantities of goods. Today, small retail operations have the opportunity to participate in private label branding due to lower minimum quantity requirements. Also, small retailers are able to secure private label goods by buying through resident buying offices or buying groups. The resident buying office collects purchase orders from several of its client stores then consolidates the orders to meet the quantity minimum required by the manufacturer for the production of private label merchandises. Private label goods are exclusive to the distributor. In most cases, a retailer determines the name and visual identity of a line (i.e., private label) in a specific merchandise classification (i.e., men's tailored apparel). The apparel manufacturer attaches the label and hangtag developed by the retailer to the selected garments prior to shipping. Illustrations of private label goods are the Strafford line of J. C. Penney and Real Clothes for Saks Fifth Avenue. Private label lines may also be referred to as proprietary brands. These lines are often represented by celebrity partners who add prestige and familiarity to the brand image. Kathie Lee for Wal-mart and Michael Graves for Target are examples of proprietary brands.

Why is there an influx of private label goods in fashion retailing? Most importantly, private label adds exclusivity goods to the retailer's merchandise assortment. Exclusivity refers to merchandise that is limited in distribution to specific retail operations. Exclusive goods aid in providing prestige and patronage motives for the consumer. Second, private label merchandise allows the retailer to get involved in the development of the product or product lines. This participation allows the retailer to tailor merchandise to specifically meet the needs, desires, and tastes of the clientele. The prospective entrepreneur may consider developing private labels to differentiate the merchandise assortment from that of competitive retailers. What is the downside of private label goods? The label may have little or no meaning to the customer. Worse, it may have a negative association for the customer. It often takes funding for promotion and time to create a desired image and appeal for a brand—to teach the brand to talk. In *Brand.New,* the author Jane Pavitt proposes that the idea of the brand also encompasses the associations that the name has for consumers. Pavitt states:

> The brand image, or brand value, results from the "dialogue" that takes place between producer or brand owner and the consumer or user. A brand's strength rests upon a close correlation between the image the brand creates through the process of branding, and the reception of that message by the consumer. Any distortions to that message tend to result in a weaker brand—for example, a brand that promotes itself as "cheap and cheerful" may actually be read as poor quality if the message is mismanaged.[6]

Three key concepts contribute to the message of any particular brand. Irrespective of the kind of target market or the nature of the product, most brands depend upon *trust, familiarity,* and *difference*. In fashion, Diesel is an example of a manufacturer that successfully sends a message of all three values. This Italian fashion and lifestyle brand projects an image that is international, innovative, and fun.[7] Diesel customers trust the company to bring them the newest fashions through quality clothing that allows consumers to express their personalities. The three values are there—trust, familiarity, and difference. Brand value is the articulation of one or more of these qualities.

Brand Value

What is brand value and how is it established? Brand value is the worth of the brand in terms of customer recognition, image, and potential sales volume. The invention of a new brand overnight with subsequent rapid sales is unlikely to occur. Brands with strong images are the result of a successful nurturing of the relationship between producer and consumer. They also require economic investment, marketing, and corporate support. The most recognizable brands tend to maintain their position by establishing loyalty and ubiquity, by becoming the market standard. In some cases, the brand name becomes the generic name for that product, such as Rollerblade or Levi's. The branded article, in these cases, has created a direct relationship between the consumer and the producer.

Creating a brand is not restricted to companies the size of Levi's. Brands can target narrowly identified market sectors, such as those start-up entrepreneurs would be likely to focus on. An image can be perpetuated through the use of a storefront, a catalog, or a Web site. Recent technological advances, and in particular the emergence of e-commerce, are changing the way in which businesses operate and consumers make their decisions and purchases. The markets serviced by e-commerce are without national boundaries and have unlimited information available to them. They are markets that are provided an almost limitless array of choices from which to select with a simple click of the mouse. Whether constructing a brick or click retail operation, the prospective entrepreneur will need to make branding decisions. A brick, or brick and mortar, operation refers to a traditional retail store with a facility in which the customer shops for merchandise. A click operation refers to an Internet-based retailer. Will the entrepreneur buy existing branded merchandise to play off an established reputation? Will he or she develop private branded goods to generate an exclusive, personalized image?

Licensing and Royalties

Licensing can be an effective and expedient way to establish brand value. Licensing is the practice of buying or selling the use of a brand name from one company to another. The brand name can be that of a celebrity (e.g., Mossimo, Kathie Lee, and Spike Lee), a designer (e.g., Donna Karan, Calvin Klein, and Chanel), a manufacturer (e.g., Nike, Fossil, and Dr. Martens), or a company (e.g., Harley Davidson, John Deere, and BCBG). Companies that own successful brands can expand the number of product lines carrying this name by licensing their brands to companies that make specialized products. Some companies manufacture licensed products for other companies, while licensing their names to others. Fossil, for example, produces watches for Donna Karan under her label. At the same time, Fossil licenses its name to handbag and belt companies that produce the leather goods under Fossil brand. Confusing? Possibly. Profitable? Definitely. Table 2.1 shows the licensees for the Donna Karan Company.

Nautica, Polo Ralph Lauren, Donna Karan, and Martha Stewart are masters of the licensing venture. These companies have built their names and trademarks into powerful marketing tools, ones that companies will pay large sums to use on their products. The designer (or brand house) receives a royalty for the merchandise manufactured by licen-

Table 2.1 Licensees for the Donna Karan Company

Product Type	Product	Licensee
Eyewear	DK/DKNY eyewear	Marchon
Hosiery	DK/DKYN women's hosiery	Hanes
	DK men's hosiery	Echo Lake
	DKNY men's hosiery	Mallory & Church
Neckwear	DKNY men's neckwear	Mallory & Church
	DK signature men's neckwear	Mantero
	DKNY scarves (Europe only)	
Intimates	DK women's intimates	Wacoal
	DKNY women's underwear	Wacoal
	DKNY men's underwear	
Tailored clothing	DKNY men's dress shirts	Phillips Van Heusen
	DKNY men's tailored clothing	Peerless
Jeans, activewear	DKNY jeans	Liz Claiborne
	DKNY activewear	
	DKNY juniors	
	DKNY city	
Coats	DK signature	Fairbrooke
	DKNY women's coats	
Children	DKNY kids	Oxford (N. America) CWF (Europe)
Beauty	DK/DKNY beauty	Estee Lauder
Accessories	DKNY belts, men's leather goods	Cipriani
	DKNY jewelry	Swank
Watches	DKNY watches	Fossil
Home	DK home	C. S. Brooks
Swimwear	DKNY women's and men's swimwear, DKNY active swimwear	Swimwear Anywhere

Donna Karan Co., 2000, New York, NY.

Licensing Show Breaks Records

The June Licensing 2001 Show broke all standing records of attendance, square footage and exhibitor presence. With more than 18,000 visitors, the mid-June event, which took place at the Jacob K. Javits center in New York, reported a five-percent increase in attendance. The 469 exhibitors spanned a space of over 355,000 square feet that represented over 5,000 properties. Another all-time high was reached with an international presence of 85 foreign exhibitors—a 49-percent increase from last year's show. There were 72 countries registered at the show, with more than 17 percent of the attendance from outside the United States.

"Licensing Show Breaks Records" *Earnshaw's* (September 2001, p. 24)

sors. A royalty is a payment that can vary in terms of amount, usually from 3 to 10 percent of wholesale, often with an established minimum amount. It is estimated that $5.5 billion in royalties were paid to licensers based on sales on licensed products in the United States and Canada in 1998. When the numbers are totaled, the sum indicates that the retail volume of licensed products in these two countries alone is about $100 billion annually. What does this mean to the prospective entrepreneur? Licensing is a way to get into business by using an established name that has a customer following. Perhaps the entrepreneur can spot a winner before the race is run by anticipating that a product is going to be successful. If this is the case, the entrepreneur may elect to license the brand name in exchange for an established royalty. In contrast, the entrepreneur may develop a new brand, intending to build it through a long-range plan of licensing to other companies in the future. *The Licensing Book,* published monthly by Adventure Publishing Group (2000), is a resource that provides the most current information on hot licensing properties. It has become a big business. Whether private label, national, or licensed, branding may, indeed, create the ties that bind.

CONCLUSION

Entrepreneurs have the option of creating a new product or marketing an existing product. Frequency of purchase, availability of the product, product lifespan, and product alternatives are all factors that affect the entrepreneur's choice of products for his or her business. One of the challenges in selecting merchandise for a business is determining its position in the product life cycle. To effectively market the business concept, the entrepreneur should be able to identify the product's life cycle stage.

Two factors distinguish an entrepreneur's product from that of competitors. The first is customer service. Service can actually be the product, or it can be a key tool for selling the product. The second is branding, a dominant trend in the apparel and soft goods industry. Today's consumer, more than ever before, is selecting a brand that corresponds to his or her personality and values. One of the fastest routes to branding is through licensing, the use of an established name to label and market a product. Product differentiation and company image are central to the success of entrepreneurial endeavors.

WRITING THE PLAN

Develop the Product Plan Section of the business plan using the following topics from chapter 14 as a guide:

SECTION	TOPIC
Product	Purpose of the product
	Unique features
	Proprietary properties
	Governmental approvals, if applicable
	Product limitations
	Product liability
	Related products
	Facilities
	Suppliers

Business Mentor™ CD-ROM—Business Plan—Product Plan

KEY TERMS

augmented product
brand
brand mark
brand name
brand sponsorship
brand value
branding
brick operation
click operation
convenience goods
copyright
core product
decline stage
durable goods
exclusivity goods
fashion goods
formal product
general line
growth stage
hard goods
high-end goods
intangible product
intellectual property
introductory stage

inventory
licensing
limited line
low-end goods
manufacturer's brand
merchandise assortments
national brand
nondurable goods
private brand
private label
product
product life style
proprietary brand
royalty
service products
shopping goods
soft goods
specialty goods
staple (basic) goods
tangible product
trade dress
trademark
unsought goods

QUESTIONS

1. Describe a type of fashion retail operation that would carry each of the following product classifications: intangible goods, convenience goods, shopping goods, and high-end goods.

2. Using a pair of Levi's 505 blue jeans as the illustration, describe the core, formal, and augmented levels of this particular product.
3. Identify a product and a retail operation that effectively represent each of the following stages of the product life cycle: introductory, growth, maturity, and decline.
4. Provide four examples of retailers developing new uses for old products. How have these companies created fresh images for their rejuvenated products?
5. What does the future of licensing look like to you? Have the sales of licensed products increased or decreased over the past decade?
6. Provide an example of a service business that can be found at each of the following levels of the apparel and soft goods industry: primary (e.g., fibers and fabrics), secondary (e.g., apparel manufacturing), auxiliary (e.g., supplementary to the primary, secondary, and retail levels), and retail (e.g., specialty operations).
7. What costs can be associated with customer service? Identify trends in customer service offerings by fashion retailers.
8. What methods do fashion retailers use to generate a strong brand identity?
9. How is selecting a business's name similar to a creating a brand for a product?

REFERENCES

1. Jules Abend, "Jockey Colors Its World," www.findarticles.com, February 1999
2. Jane Pavitt, *Brand New* (Princeton, New Jersey: Princeton University Press, 2000, p. 21)
3. Ibid., p. 21
4. Message posted to PR Newswire, December 21, 1999, "Spiegel Catalog, Inc., Signs Letter of Intent with J. Crew to Purchase Intellectual Property of Clifford & Wills," www.findarticles.com
5. Message posted to PR Newswire, July 15, 1999, "American Eagle Outfitters Wins Dismissal of Abercrombre & Fitch Lawsuit," www.findarticles.com
6. Pavitt, *Brand New*, p. 21
7. Ibid., p. 64

RESOURCE

Maurice Johnson and Evelyn C. Moore, *Apparel Product Development* (Upper Saddle River, New Jersey: Prentice Hall, 2001)

SUGGESTED READINGS

David F. D'Alessandro and Michele Owens, *Brand Warfare: 10 Rules for Building the Killer Brand* (Boston, Massachusetts: Harvard Business School Publishing, 2001)
Marc Gobe, *Emotional Branding: The New Paradigm for Connecting Brands and People* (New York, New York: Allworth Press, 2001)
Nancy Koehn, *Brand New: How Entrepreneurs Earned Consumers' Trust From Wedgwood to Dell* (Boston, Massachusetts: Harvard Business School Publishing, 2001)

CASE STUDY

St. John Knits, a better knitwear company, was conceived when Marie St. John, a model and television hostess, knitted a dress designed to impress her husband-to-be, Robert Gray. He was so impressed that he brought the dress to several department store buyers and returned home with 84 orders. That was nearly 40 years ago. Today, Mrs. Gray holds the position of vice chairman and chief designer, while Mr. Gray is the chairman of the board and chief executive officer of the company. Their daughter, Kelly Gray, has held the position of president since 1996.

Over the past 10 years, annual sales have grown from $36 million to $281 million, with 1998 third-quarter sales increasing by 24 percent of the previous year's sales for the same time period. The company also operates its own boutiques. These stores, too, have shown a double-digit annual increase in sales volume. Company lines include St. John Knits, St. John Sport, St. John Coat Collection, and Griffith & Gray, as well as licensed lines of accessories, eyewear, watches, and fragrances. St. John Knits have appeared on the *Forbes* list of 200 small best companies for 5 consecutive years.

In 1989, the Grays sold 80 percent of the company to Escada, a luxury apparel firm based in Germany. This relationship ended, however, in 1993, and the company went public. Net profits slipped 3 percent to $33 million for the first time in 6 years after St. John Knits went public. The proximate causes were varied and included poor investments, legal battles, and rapid growth, which resulted in production and styling errors, inconsistent quality, and increased markdowns by their own stores and those of retail accounts. A number of business analysts claim that the two most critical mistakes occurred when the Grays invested in product lines outside their known business niche. The first was outside the apparel sector. The second was intended to reach a new target market.

Initiated through a friendship Kelly Gray had with the owner, the Grays invested in a chain of home furnishing boutiques. The investment resulted in a lawsuit, a $9 million loss, and ownership of several failing home furnishing stores. A second investment error associated with St. John Knits occurred in 1997. The company decided to launch a line of lower-priced fashions, SJK, aimed at a younger customer. It quickly appeared that customers in this niche had allegiances to contemporary bridge lines and did not want to wear what their mothers were wearing. After only three seasons, St. Johns Knits discontinued the SJK line. The fallout continued well past a few seasons, as these product changes had significantly confused St. John Knits faithful customers and jeopardized their loyalty.

When asked about the company's decision to turn public and to diversify in product classifications, the Grays indicated that the company had been growing too fast. They discussed the need to turn the company private again. Mr. Gray stated, "It is in the company's best interest to slow the growth rate to about 10 percent per year and focus on what we do best—delivering the highest quality merchandise and service to our loyal customers." (www.forbes.com/articles)

CASE STUDY QUESTIONS

1. Conduct research using the Internet, as well as fashion and business trade publications, on the product lines that St. John Knits has developed. Describe each line, the intended target market for each, the success or failure rate of each.
2. Based on your analysis of St. John Knits product development efforts, suggest different product classifications with which you believe the company would have success. How would these lines be implemented? For example, would you recommend private label, a proprietary brand, and/or licensing? Describe the target market for each of these new classifications.
3. Place yourself in the position of business consultant for St. John Knits. Where did the company go wrong with previous efforts? What can St. John Knits do today to increase profits through product development for the future?

. . . .

ENTERING THE WORLD OF THE ENTREPRENEUR

. . . .

Select a product that you believe has significant potential in the fashion market. Interview a number of sources that may have helpful information for you about the market potential for this product. Consider interviewing the owners of retail operations and manufacturing firms, bankers, professors, business consultants, and representatives of business support organizations. Questions you may consider asking these sources include:

1. What is the life cycle stage of this product?
2. What is its position in terms of competitive products?
3. Are supply sources currently available and affordable? In the future?
4. What future opportunities exist with this particular product?
5. What criteria or research was used to determine the product mix?
6. What criteria did the store need to meet in order to carry its existing lines?

ENTERPRISING ENTREPRENEUR

Gap Inc. represents the entrepreneurial spirit, from its humble start to its present stature as a superstar in global retailing. This company was founded by two entrepreneurs, Don and Doris Fisher, who opened the first Gap store in San Francisco, California, in 1969. In 1983, another entrepreneur joined the ranks of Gap Inc. Millard Drexler was hired as president of the Gap division. In 1995, he was named chief executive officer of Gap Inc. A key to success of this company is its keen ability to continually develop innovative and timely product lines. Three years after Drexler took the helm, Gapkids opened its first store. Following its success, babyGap was born in 1990. Four years later, Old Navy was introduced as a shopping environment that offered both fun and affordable fashion. Old Navy was soon followed by the introduction of private branded lines of personal care products and GapScents.

Gap Inc.'s product development offices are located in New York City. It is there that designers, product managers, and graphic artists create the look and feel of each season's merchandise. The development of new product classifications is an ongoing mission for this staff. In 2000, the company announced the arrival of GapMaternity, a line of 16 classic Gap styles in comfortable, easy-to-wear shapes and fabrics made for pregnant women. Gap Inc. announced the arrival of its newest signature scent, So Pink, through a line of fragrances and bath and body products. Today, through more than 2,300 stores and 140,000 employees in the United States, Canada, the United Kingdom, Japan, Germany, and France, as well as the Internet, Gap, Inc. develops and sells constantly evolving lines of clothing, accessories, and personal care products for adults, children, and infants (www.gapinc.com).

RESEARCHING THE INDUSTRY AND THE MARKET

INTRODUCTION

In Chapter 1 the prospective fashion entrepreneur conducts a self-analysis of his or her entrepreneurial mind-set and skills. Next, the entrepreneur's concept for the potential fashion business is articulated, and the potential product is defined. This chapter focuses on the techniques commonly used to obtain information needed to objectively analyze the industry and a potential target market. Emphasis is placed on how to analyze market data and information for the purpose of developing a comprehensive marketing strategy. The market feasibility study includes an exploration of the fashion industry's current trends, norms, and standards.

Why look at the big picture? To be successful in a new business, the entrepreneur needs to know two things: First, he or she needs to know what the business will be and to which businesses it will be connected. Second, the entrepreneur needs to know where the business lies within the broad scope of the industry. This exploration begins with a global perspective that later filters down to a regional viewpoint. The effective market feasibility study starts with a definition of the industry in which the new business will be positioned.

MARKET RESEARCH DEFINED

Market research is the systematic, objective collection and analysis of data about both internal environments and external environments. Internal environments are those business activities that are under the direct control of management. Examples of internal environments are the merchandise assortment, personnel, financial procedures, and control systems for accounting and inventory. External environments are those variables that affect the firm's performance, but that are outside the direct control of management. They include competitive and economic environments, as well as natural, social, legal, and political environments. A diagram of external environments is presented as Figure 3.1. Following the process of market research, data are analyzed to create useful information to guide the entrepreneur in determining the business's potential to generate

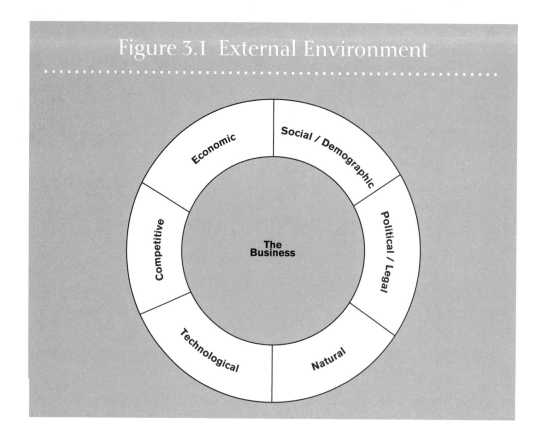

Figure 3.1 External Environment

sales and create a positive cash flow. This process is referred to as market analysis. Market analysis is defined as the study of the set of characteristics that define and influence a group of primary and secondary businesses supplying a related product or service.

Market research, market analysis, and market penetration are processes that encompass all aspects of a company. They affect all business decisions from hiring the best sales people to deciding which product will be sold. Internal service policies, pricing strategies, location, and promotional plans are also guided by market research and analysis. Market penetration refers to the strategies used to reach the company's target market. It includes promotional efforts, service offerings, and product choices. Every decision made within the company should be analyzed and compared to the marketing plan. Carefully constructed marketing plans provide an organized, cost-effective, results-oriented, profitable way to promote the product. Market research and analysis help define target markets, formulate clear product positioning, and provide detailed strategies for taking the product to market.

Market research looks at data from both primary sources and secondary sources. Primary sources include focus groups, current customers, employees, suppliers, and consultants. Secondary sources refer to data that are already there for the taking such as government census reports, information from news organizations, the Internet, commercial on-line services, and trade associations. Secondary sources evaluate and analyze both quantitative and qualitative data to explain the demographics, psychographics, and economics of an industry and its customers. Demographics refer to income levels, age, gender, race, nationality, profession, and geographic location of potential target markets in the industry. Psychographics refer to values, attitudes, and belief systems of these prospective target markets.

To conduct market research, the following ten-step process may be implemented:

1. Brainstorm the marketing idea and define the business opportunity. Analyze every possible element that may affect the outcome.
2. Formulate a hypothesis that will become the working assumption.
3. Identify the information needed by generating a list of questions that should be answered.
4. Research primary and secondary sources.
5. Check the information gathered against the hypothesis.
6. Analyze and interpret the data collected. These data will help identify trends such as market opportunities and consumer preferences.
7. Check the hypothesis again against the analyzed data.
8. Create a marketing plan.
9. Present the plan to the management team, funders, and others who may guide the company to success.
10. Devise the avenues through which the marketing plan will be implemented.

Market research should be analyzed as objectively as possible. Frequently, entrepreneurs do not read data objectively. They see what they want to see. Only through objective analysis can an entrepreneur clearly understand the data collected and determine whether or not the potential business can be successful.

DEFINING THE INDUSTRY

It is important to recognize that no company operates in a glass bubble. Every business is part of a larger, overall industry. The term industry, in this case, refers to all companies supplying similar or related products (which can include services). It also incorporates the supply and distribution organizations supporting such companies. Types of companies representing the fashion industry include, but are not limited to, soft goods and apparel manufacturers, manufacturers' representatives, trend forecasting services, fashion promotion companies, trade publications, and retail operations. A model of the types of businesses that comprise the fashion industry is shown in Figure 3.2.

The external factors that affect the general industry will likely affect the smaller businesses within it. The entrepreneur must be able to articulate how the prospective business will be similar to and different from those companies within the broader scope of the industry. Similarly, the entrepreneur must know where the industry is headed. The market feasibility study (at the end of this chapter) begins with development of an industry analysis that is broken down into the following sections: First, a description of the industry from an economic perspective, one of revenue and employment, is developed. Second, the industry is examined in terms of life cycle stage, economic conditions and cycles, seasonality of products, technological advances, and sources of supply and distribution. Third, financial patterns for the industry are examined to determine industry norms and standards. Next, competition in the industry is studied. Finally, the consumer for the industry is analyzed in terms of psychographic, demographic, and political trends. The key purposes of the market feasibility study are (a) to identify strategic opportunities that exist, present and future, (b) to understand why these opportunities exist, and (c) to identify how the company will capitalize on those opportunities.

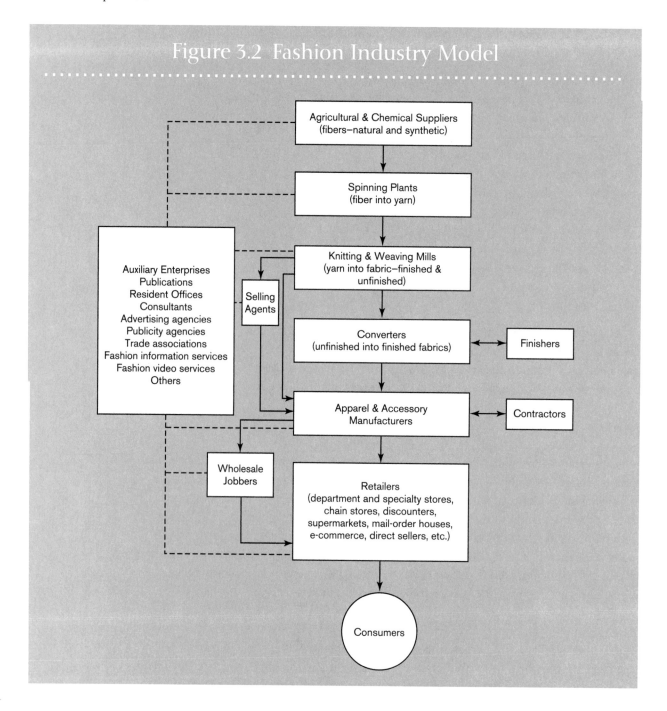

Figure 3.2 Fashion Industry Model

One of the major obstacles to the market feasibility study is the entrepreneur's desire to rush into the business as well as his or her disdain for research. However, realistic operating, marketing, and financial strategies cannot be developed without an understanding of the industry factors that will directly affect the company, Because the entrepreneur usually has limited funds and time, it is important to gather information from readily available sources. The information needs to be clear, pertinent, and timely. A listing of suggested resources (the Entrepreneur's Research Tool Kit), which may be used to research secondary data is included at the end of this chapter. There are numerous secondary sources available for researching the market. The goal is to narrow the choices to those that are most relevant to the needs of the particular analysis.

In addition to secondary sources of information, significant data can and should be obtained from primary sources. As stated earlier, primary sources would include group interviews or focus groups, mystery shoppers, as well as questionnaires and surveys. Focus groups are often conducted using small group discussion to learn the opinions of the participants. A mystery shopper refers to a person employed to shop at specific stores, then to report on findings related to customer service, merchandise assortments, store layout, and other topics. Focus groups can be a cost-effective way to gain more customer insight and to identify the future wants and needs of potential customers. This format is typically used at the beginning of the research process when the entrepreneur is not sure what is important to the consumer. Focus groups give the entrepreneur an opportunity to show concepts or prototypes to participants for feedback. Focus groups also allow for an in-depth discussion of reasons for the group members' opinions. The focus group should be conducted in an informal and relaxed setting, The moderator should ask open-ended questions that allow participants to answer freely while someone other than the moderator records the responses. In sophisticated versions of focus groups, marketing experts will recruit anywhere from 6 to 12 participants (usually by phone) from the general public, customer lists, or other sources. A discussion will be lead by a moderator according to a preplanned guide. The discussion will be audiotaped or videotaped. Later, the tapes will be transcribed, and an in-depth content analysis will be conducted.

Customer surveys are another means of gaining valuable information about the fashion retail industry. Surveys may be conducted in person, by mail, on-line, or by telephone. Through these surveys, questions are presented to a targeted group. The goal is to gather objective data, both qualitative and quantitative. The survey is usually conducted from a sample—a group randomly selected from the targeted population. The sample should include those individuals whose opinions, behavior, attitudes, and preferences will influence the marketing strategy.

Focus groups and customer surveys are only as good as the questions being asked. Participants should be informed that the moderator is looking for honest answers and that there are no negative consequences for unfavorable feedback. The questions listed on a survey should be well-thought-out and open-ended so as not to lead participants to answers that may not be their own choices.

DESCRIBING THE INDUSTRY

For the entrepreneur who is evaluating a potential company, the world in which the business will be situated resembles a pyramid turned over and balanced on its apex. First, the industry is examined. It is assessed from a global perspective with particular emphasis on economics, to include life cycle stage and technology. Next, the entrepreneur analyzes the specific product area in terms of opportunity. Following this, the entrepreneur may examine the business concept from a regional perspective. It is a filter-down process, moving from the broad perspective to a more detailed focus.

Economic Sectors of the Industry

The four general sectors of most industries, whether fashion or not, are service, manufacturing, retail, and distribution. Some businesses fall into one category, while others cross over into two or more. For example, the business concept may be to produce a line of apparel, sell it through the Internet, and ship it directly to the customer from the factory. This concept intersects the sectors of manufacturing, retail, and distribution. As a result, the three sectors must be examined in the industry analysis for this entrepreneurial enterprise.

Through analysis of business and trade publications, the entrepreneur should determine the past performance and growth trends in his business sectors. One of the first steps to beginning this research is to identify the North American Industry Classification System (NAICS) code. The NAICS code was formerly known as the Standard Industrial Classification Code (SIC code). The NAICS system classifies U.S. industries by type and then further divides the classification into subcomponents. For example, the classification for retailing may be divided into such subcomponents as women's apparel, men's apparel, or sporting goods. This system was developed to assure uniformity and comparability of the data collected and published by U.S. government agencies, state agencies, trade associations, and research organizations. A sample description from the directory of NAISC is included as Figure 3.3. The NAISC may also be retrieved from the Web site, www.ntis.gov/naics.

Some of the questions the entrepreneur should answer when compiling a description of the industry are:

- What is the economic sector and sector classification for this industry?
- How does the growth rate for the industry sector compare with the growth of the gross national product?
- What is the level of employment from past, present, and future perspectives?
- What is the total revenue for each sector from international and national views?
- What is the number of total units sold based on past and present data?

Figure 3.3 Sample of North American Industry Classification System

4481 Clothing StoresCAN
This industry group comprises establishments primarily engaged in retailing new clothing.
44811 Men's Clothing StoresCAN
See industry descriptions for 448110 below.
448110 Men's Clothing StoresCAN
This industry comprises establishments primarily engaged in retailing a general line of new men's and boy's clothing. These establishments may provide basic alterations, such as hemming, taking in or letting out seams, or lengthening or shortening sleeves.

Cross-References. Establishments primarily engaged in–

- Retailing men's and boys' clothing via electronic home shopping, mail-order, or direct sale–are classified in Subsector 454, Nonstore Retailers;
- Retailing custom men's clothing made on the premises–are classified in Industry Group 3152, Cut and Sew Apparel Manufacturing;
- Retailing new men's and boys' accessories–are classified in Industry 448150, Clothing Accessories Stores;
- Retailing specialized new apparel, such as raincoats, leather coats, fur apparel, and swimwear,–are classified in Industry 448190, Other Clothing Stores;
- Retailing new clothing for all genders and age groups–are classified in Industry 448140, Family Clothing Stores;
- Retailing secondhand clothes–are classified in Industry 453310, Used Merchandise Stores; and
- Providing clothing alterations and repair–are classified in Industry 811490, Other Personal and Household Goods Repair and Maintenance.

Extracted from the North American Industry Classification System, United States, and reproduced with the permission of Bernan Press, a division of the Kraus Organization Limited.

Industry Life Cycle

Industries can be classified in terms of maturation. Just as there is a product life cycle, there is a life cycle for trends in industries or markets. The four phases of the industry life cycle are new, expanding, stable, and declining. The new or emerging stage provides excellent opportunities for entrepreneurial businesses early in their development. Since small or start-up companies have the ability to respond to rapid changes in the industry, they often have an edge in emerging markets that established businessess do not. This stage of the life cycle provides entrepreneurs with opporunities for large profits. On the other hand, this is a period when acceptance by the market has not yet been established and is therefore risky.

The expanding stage is a growth stage and has the advantage of a rapidly increasing consumer base. As markets expand, they experience increased sales and profits and represent a lower investment risk. They can also experience more formidable competition. This phase of the industry life cycle also provides opportunities for entrepreneurs to enter the market. In contrast, expanding markets, unlike those in the growth stage, present the entrepreneur the challenge of possible inadequate staffing, the need for additional funding, and the inability to control costs.

The stable stage is a time when market increases have leveled off. Stable markets are often characterized by mature businesses with loyal customers; however, they are at a crossroads. They can either begin to cool off and decline, or they can regenerate growth through new products and services, thus making it difficult for new businesses to enter the industry. The declining stage for markets results from technological, social, economic, and demographic shifts in the external and internal environments of the businesses. Profits and cash flow are reduced because of the lack of demand for the product. To survive, the entrepreneur must create a new direction for the business. Obviously, a declining market is not where the entrepreneur wants to position a new business.

Economic Conditions and Cycles

Because the fashion industry is dependent on economics, both nationally and internationally, it is critical to understand the economic conditions and cycles that can (and likely will) affect its businesses. Retail businesses, such as discount children's clothing stores and resale apparel shops, perform relatively better in poor economic cycles than in strong ones. Luxury products, such as special occasion wear and expensive home furnishings, have a higher success rate when the economy is on an upswing.

If a business will be in a geographic location where the customer base is largely dependent on a specific employer, the impact economic cycles may have on that employer's business will be a critical factor. The entrepreneur will want to examine patterns in interest rates, employment levels, consumer confidence, and inflation levels. An analysis of the industry's sensitivity to economic cycles is an important part of the industry description within the market feasibility study. It is critical to look for evidence that key industry factors may be changing.

Seasonality of the Fashion Industry

Seasonal patterns refer to distinct changes in activity within a calendar year. Seasonal patterns include changes in climate that influence apparel needs and holidays and affect consumer spending trends. For many types of businesses in the fashion industry, certain times of the year produce higher sales than others, thus affecting sales, cash flow, and profits. While spring is the key season for prom and bridal gown manufacturers, the winter holiday months of November and December result in top revenues for many fashion retailers in other merchandise areas.

The geographic location of a retail operation also interrelates with the seasonality of merchandise. Retailers, for example, located in southern states with consistently warm climates will carry lightweight goods year round. The National Retail Federation produces reports by store type and merchandise classification, Merchandising and Operating Results (MOR), that promote information on retail sales for each month. Particularly in the fashion industry, these seasonal projections will drastically affect cash flow projections established in the business plan. As the owner of a new business, the entrepreneur may not have established the credit rating needed for vendors to offer credit on new merchandise. A credit rating indicates whether or not a company has paid its bills on time and in full. Instead, the business owner may be required to pay cash on delivery (COD) for goods. If the merchandise is not sold until December but must be paid for in November and may be obsolete in January then seasonal factors will have a strong impact on the business's income and expenses.

One of the most effective ways to anticipate seasonal factors is to develop an annual chart showing each month as a percent of sales based on the total year. Table 3.1 illustrates variances between two types of retail stores and their respective monthly revenue projections. These monthly sales projections are not firm or fixed for specialty stores within these two merchandise classifications. Two location factors—climate and community—strongly influence the seasonality of merchandise and services. These factors are examined later in this chapter when the market feasibility study at a regional level is introduced. For now, the focus is on industry trends.

Table 3.1 Monthly Sales Percent as a Portion of the Total Year

	WOMEN'S SPORTSWEAR (%)	SPECIAL OCCASION FORMALWEAR (%)
JANUARY	5	2
FEBRUARY	7	12
MARCH	10	20
APRIL	8	20
MAY	8	10
JUNE	5	5
JULY	5	2
AUGUST	7	3
SEPTEMBER	8	3
OCTOBER	9	5
NOVEMBER	10	8
DECEMBER	18	10
TOTAL	**100**	**100**

Both cyclical and seasonal patterns affect the fashion retail industry. Cyclical patterns are those recurring swings that move the business activity—its sales, cash flow, and profits—from a downslide to an upswing. The entrepreneur will want to compare industry cycles to those of the overall economy, using such indicators as the gross domestic product and personal disposable income. Then a determination can be made as to the extent to which industry sales and profits are sensitive to economic change. From seasonality in the fashion industry, the market feasibility study moves to technological changes and their impact on the industry.

The Impact of Technology

Is there an industry that is not affected by the rapid advances of technology in today's world? The raw materials from which fashion goods are produced, the methods used to manufacture the products, the speed with which they can be delivered, and the way information regarding the performance of these products is managed are some of the areas in which technology affects the fashion industry. Although it is difficult, if not impossible, to predict the future capabilities of technology, it is important to identify the trends of the past 5 to 10 years. In essence, the entrepreneur can create a mind-set that enables him or her to "think future" about technological capabilities by examining recent advances in technology.

Supply and Distribution Channels

The supply and distribution channels in an industry can greatly affect the opportunity for a business's entry into the field. In the fashion industry, limited supply can create demand. Supply channels are the companies that provide materials and equipment needed to manufacture the product, as well as the companies that actually produce the goods. Supply channels can dramatically influence the success or failure of a business. For example, a new fabrication may be expensive to produce and, therefore, may be available only in garments at higher prices. Limited supply can mean fewer sources, higher costs, and greater vulnerability to failure. It is important for the entrepreneur to explore the number and location of supply sources, as well as the availability of distribution channels.

Distribution channels are the routes taken to move the product to the consumer. They can include selling directly to a manufacturer, a retail operation, wholesale businesses, or to the ultimate consumer. They can include selling through a traditional retail store, the Internet, a catalog, or television. Analysis of the availability of distribution channels requires an examination of the different ways a business can deliver its product or service to its primary consumer. Some businesses target more than one customer market and elect to use more than one channel of distribution. Others, particularly in the start-up stage, focus on one target market and one channel of distribution. There are advantages and disadvantages to this approach.

For example, a contemporary dress manufacturer based in Dallas, Texas, targeted a major department store and was contracted to produce private label dresses designed exclusively for the department store and made to its specifications. The company shipped the dresses directly to the department store's central distribution warehouse in Dallas. Because the dress manufacturing company was a new business in its start-up stage, it did not have the resources to produce more than the department store ordered. One poor selling season for the entire department store resulted in a complete turnover in the buying staff. The consequence was that the new buyers brought in new resources, leaving the dress manufacturer to struggle with building a customer base and a channel of distribution almost overnight.

Financial Patterns

Financial patterns are the standards and norms used to determine pricing, to evaluate merchandise performance, and to specify billing terms within the fashion industry. This information is available through trade journals, academic texts, and the publications of industry trade organizations. Financial patterns not only vary by type of business, but also by merchandise classification. For example, a new business owner may expect to pay for merchandise on delivery, until a positive credit rating is established. For another business owner with a good credit rating and an approved loan from the bank, the term for merchandise payment may be an 8 percent discount, if the bill is paid within 30 days of the date of the invoice. Although there are no hard and fast rules, there are general industry standards that can be determined from a number of sources. Those who are already in the industry, as well as suppliers of the product lines, are excellent resources for industry standards. Additionally, information from the National Retail Federation will provide financial industry standards for apparel and accessory retailers. What types of financial standards does the entrepreneur need to know? This information is examined in greater detail in Chapter 11.

Knowledge of financial standards within the industry is critical so that the entrepreneur can accurately develop financial plans for the business. Start-up expenses, monthly budgets for inventory payment, and profit potential are all locked onto these industry financial standards. Knowing the general industry norms allows the entrepreneur to determine specifics for the business plan.

Competition

In the industry analysis section of the market feasibility study, the entrepreneur will examine sources and levels of competition from both national and international perspectives. The reviewer of the business plan will be very interested in the extent to which sales of the potential business's product will be affected by direct, indirect, and future competition. Through this analysis, the number of new businesses that entered the industry over the past 5 to 10 years will be investigated. The type of industry sector (e.g., manufacturing, service, retail, or distribution) will be explored within these statistics. The success and failure rates of new entries will also be examined. By looking at these data, the entrepreneur will have the opportunity to see whether new businesses enter and leave the field rapidly or slowly. Through this analysis, the entrepreneur will be determining whether the prospective business is in an open or closed competitive environment. An **open competitive environment** is one in which there is a low level of competition, while a **closed competitive environment** refers to one that is saturated with a high level of competition.

Competition should be examined by analyzing direct, indirect, and future competitors. **Direct competition** is the retailer's products or services that consumers view as acceptable alternatives to the entrepreneur's product. For example, Saks Fifth Avenue can be classified as a direct competitor of Neiman Marcus because they carry similar lines and cater to similar target markets. Indirect competition is the retailer's products or services that can be easily substituted for one another. For example, Wal-Mart may be an indirect competitor of Saks Fifth Avenue for the customer who purchases hosiery, beauty products, or other basic products. Future competition should not be overlooked. Entrepreneurs sometimes fail to anticipate new competitors and wait to adjust after a new business has entered the market. For example, ABC Fashion Store, a boutique already in existence, may not offer handbags until the owners see a new business selling handbags to its customers. What was not there as competition before, may soon become a factor.

Some of the questions the entrepreneur should answer when compiling information regarding the competition on a national and an international level include:

- Which are the major companies in the industry?
- How many new firms have entered this industry in the past 5 years?
- What new products have been introduced in this industry in the past 5 years?
- What is the basis for competition within the industry? Is it, for example, price, merchandise selection, or prestige?
- Historically, how difficult has it been for new businesses to enter the industry?
- Can you profile the intended customer based on national and international statistics?
- How is this segment of the market captured?

The Consumer

The final step to the market feasibility study is an examination of the external environment in which the industry operates. The environmental scan provides an overview of significant areas that include economic, technological, natural, social, demographic, and political trends. Population shifts, for example, are acknowledged in terms of demographics, psychographics, social, and political influences. In an environmental scan, the entrepreneur answers such questions as:

- What are the national and international demographics?
- What are the national and international birthrates?
- Where is the population currently located? Where is it moving?
- What types of jobs are most available? What are the salaries for these jobs?
- How are people spending their leisure time?
- Are there trends in gender roles? Are there trends in families?
- Are there political trends, influential leaders, or social causes affecting the population?
- Who has the most purchasing power? Where and on what are these people spending their disposable income?
- Are there opinion leaders, such as celebrities, influencing the population?
- Is the customer base stable or changing?
- Regarding the customer base for the industry, why as a member of this industry will the company be able to reach the consumer?

The purpose of the environmental scan is to identify population trends and to find business opportunities that result from these trends. For example, if the baby boomers are spending more time and money on physical fitness, then perhaps the entrepreneur wanting to sell active wear has a timely business concept. If people are entertaining at home more frequently than in the past, then maybe a home accessories retail operation with a catalog channel of distribution has a high chance of success. Sometimes, population trend information can be overlaid with economic data to identify a new market niche. For example, although birthrates are down, sales in children's apparel and children's home furnishings are showing a steady increase. A scan of the number of units sold at retail indicates that fewer units are being sold but that price per unit has dramatically increased. A scan of the demographic data of parents reveals that they are having children at a later age than previous generations' and both members of the household are now employed. Young couples are focusing on their careers and postponing starting families. When they do have children, they (and their parents) are spending much greater amounts of money on them. From the nursery décor to the infant's wardrobe, sales of higher-priced goods are fueling the children's apparel and accessories industry. The point of the environmental examination is to translate how a population trend will generate a trend in the fashion industry.

There are a number of resources that provide data on social, demographic, and political shifts in the world population. John Naisbitt, Patricia Aburdene, and Faith Popcorn are authors who identify population trends and project outcomes for these trends. Through its newsletters and Web site, www.fgi.org, the Fashion Group International, Inc., provides information on consumer trends and issues, and then applies this information to the fashion industry. Additionally, the British Web site, www.wgsn.com, features trend and business information for the fashion industry from a global perspective. There are also a number of journals that focus on population analysis, such as American Demographic magazine, Marketing Tools, and Sales and Marketing Management. More recently, there is an emerging market for private database vendors, companies that prepare custom demographic reports for a fee.

REGIONAL MARKET FEASIBILITY STUDY

Once the entrepreneur has a handle on industry statistics, trends, and issues through a general market feasibility study, it is time to construct a similar market feasibility study on a different level—the regional or community level. Most entrepreneurs are not seeking to open a business nationwide. With the exception of the Internet as a channel of distribution, it would take a tremendous amount of capital to promote a retail operation nationally, which the majority of new business owners do not have. As the saying goes, most new businesses must crawl before they walk (and later run). The majority of entrepreneurs are limited to specific locations for their businesses. If the business is a success in Springfield, Illinois, for example, the next steps may be to open several outlets in nearby towns and, later, a branch operation in Chicago. In fact, many people choose the entrepreneurial path to allow them to make a living in a specific location, perhaps one where employment opportunities are limited.

The point is that the data generated from the industry market feasibility study must then be overlaid or compared with new data developed from a regional market feasibility study. For example, a market feasibility study may reveal that the teen market for apparel and accessories is on an upswing. If an entrepreneur is planning to open a business in the town where he or she resides and it is a retirement community, the industry statistics are irrelevant. A market feasibility study of the regional customer will assist the entrepreneur in comparing national trends to local ones.

The Regional Consumer

A primary area of focus in the regional market feasibility study is the consumer. The *customer profile* is a description of the local population based on demographics, psychographics, buying behavior, and product usage. Regarding buying behavior, the regional target market should be examined in terms of customers' desires for comfort, security, adventure, and physical pleasures, among other attributes. One of the most important product usage characteristics is determined by the consumer's position in the product life cycle. For example, new and innovative products are often first purchased by people who think of themselves as open-minded and adventurous trendsetters.

Next, the regional target market should be examined in terms of buying behavior. When, where, what, how, and why do customers buy in this region? In other words, how do target customers behave when making purchasing decisions? What is the customer's "I don't care" zone? Customers within an industry will have an "I don't care" zone. For example, ABC Fashion Store is selling scarves via the Internet. Is the consumer willing to pay $15 extra to have the scarf delivered in a red box instead of a brown box? Chances are that the consumer is more interested in receiving the scarf in a timely manner. The packaging may be irrelevant.

Another common classification used for target market analysis is product usage. The entrepreneur should explore heavy users and light users within the potential regional target market. Think about evening gowns in contrast to T-shirts; then consider varying regional locations. The female customer in most suburban areas of the Midwest will purchase an evening gown once (twice or maybe three times) in a year. Yet she will buy more than three T-shirts in that same year. If the regional area is, however, a city in Texas with a high per capita income and a busy social scene, then the female customer may be a heavy user of evening gowns and a light user of T-shirts.

Another aspect of consumer analysis for the regional market feasibility study is user characteristics. Three categories of user traits should be examined. First, is the buyer the ultimate (or end) user, or is he or she purchasing the item for someone else? There are a number of children's wear stores that make their profits from targeting the children's grandmothers rather than their mothers. Children's apparel that appeal to grandmothers is often very different from that the mother is seeking. A certain style of clothing referred to as "grandma bait" may be more expensive and formal than the garments the child's mother would select. The child's mother may be more interested in washability, price, comfort, and fit. The second user characteristic asks, "What is the site of consumption; the at-home market or the away-from-home user?" The entrepreneur opening a swimsuit boutique may find that swimwear sold to local residents has a very different look from swimwear sold to resort customers. Finally, the third user characteristic asks, "What is the purpose of the use of the product?" As an illustration, boot-cut-leg jeans may be a fashion trend in some cities for a given period of time. In rural towns with a farming industry, the boot-cut jean may be a wardrobe staple for the local population.

Where can the prospective entrepreneur find regional market data? Many areas have Small Business Administration offices that offer regional statistics. Data from the U.S. Census Bureau can be segmented by regions. In most states, there is a department of economic development that includes a business assistance center which helps with regional market feasibility work. Many chamber of commerce offices provide local and regional reports on demographics, the numbers and types of new and existing businesses, geographic locations for businesses, as well as opportunities for city and state support of new businesses. Local colleges and universities often provide assistance to prospective entrepreneurs through educational programs that are linked to the community. Media sources within the region, such as television and radio stations, frequently supply regional market data to prospective entrepreneurs, potentially their future customers.

The Regional Location

Although there are a number of questions related to the viability of the business concept that can be addressed through consumer analysis, others relate more directly to the physical location of the business. Following is a list of questions about location that should be answered through the regional market feasibility study:

- Are there any environmental issues relating to the business?
- Does the product have any specific location needs?
- Do building type, traffic count, parking facilities, receiving requirements, and other business establishments play a significant role in the success of the business concept?
- Is the business concept suited for a particular type of trading area, such as downtown, urban, suburban, or rural?
- Can the area support a business similar to the one proposed?
- Are there any governmental restrictions and permit requirements in the region in which the business may be located?
- How important to the business concept are the following location criteria: accessibility, visibility, convenience, and population density?

Another factor to consider with respect to regional location is seasonality. As mentioned earlier in this chapter, seasonality and fashion merchandise go hand in hand. Seasonal changes in merchandise, resulting from either weather or fashion trends, create a need or desire within the customer that elicits him or her to buy. On the other hand, seasonality also generates costs, such as the costs of end-of -the-season markdowns, the expense of market trips, and the dollars needed to promote the items that will "spoil" if they do not sell quickly. Seasonality as a factor in merchandise assortments also demands cash flow. As mentioned, the entrepreneur of a new retail business may be required to pay cash for merchandise on delivery until a positive credit rating is established with the vendors. It may take a few months to sell stock at retail to recoup the investment. Meanwhile, when another fashion season, climate change, or merchandise trend hits, the entrepreneur must spend more funds on new inventory. The upside is that each one of these changes has the potential to generate sales. The down side is the constant need for cash flow, as well as the risk of additional markdowns.

Within the regional market feasibility study, entrepreneurs of fashion businesses will want to consider how often seasonality will affect the business concept. They should consider the merchandise classification (e.g., coats, suits, sportswear—men's or women's), the climate in which the business will be located (if a brick-and-mortar operation), and the number of fashion seasons for which the manufacturers in this particular industry produce lines. For example, in designer apparel, there are five to six seasons: fall I, fall II, holiday and/or cruise, spring, and summer. To the entrepreneur of a designer apparel operation, this may be translated as five seasons with the potential of having leftover goods to mark down, at least five times, during the year when new merchandise will need to be promoted, and a minimum of five market trips to buy merchandise.

The Regional Competition

A critical part of the regional market feasibility study is the analysis of the competition. The prospective entrepreneur must know who the competition is within a region. If competition exists, and it will in one form or another, this does not mean that the business concept should be abandoned. Instead, the entrepreneur should determine how the business concept measures up against the competition by answering the following key questions:

- What sets this business concept apart from the competitors?
- Will this business concept meet a need for an underserved market?
- Can a better job be done at meeting customer preferences through this business concept?

When measuring the business concept against competition, the entrepreneur should consider quality, price, and service as well as location. Additionally, at this point, the entrepreneur should examine how to communicate the unique qualities of the new business to the target market. Competition analysis is a tricky business. A lack of competition does not necessarily suggest a profitable business opportunity. The niche may not be filled because the niche may not be there. Consider the retirement community discussed earlier in this chapter. There are no maternity apparel stores in this area. This does not signify a business void; it is highly unlikely that a maternity apparel store would survive there. When examining competition, it is important to research not only direct competitors, but indirect and future ones as well. The entrepreneur will want to examine the discount and mass merchandise stores in the area, e-commerce retailers, and catalog operations. Today's customer is extremely value-oriented and is not above buying sandals for $16.99 at Wal-Mart to wear with a $400 Nicole Miller dress. Saving money has become very fashionable. The competition arena is boundless.

CONCLUSION

The key purpose of the market feasibility study is to identify strategic opportunities that exist—present and future—for a new business in the fashion industry. It provides an examination of the external and internal environments in which the business will operate. The resulting data and background information will either support or refute the business concept. In some cases, the prospective entrepreneur will scrap the plan and return to concept development when the market feasibility study does not support the original idea. Scrapping the plan is better to do sooner than later, after resources (including blood, sweat, and tears) have been poured into the new business.

After a market feasibility study of the industry is conducted, a regional study is implemented. An analysis of the consumer within the region where the business will be located is of particular importance. Demographics, psychographics, buying behavior, and product usage are among the categories examined in the regional consumer analysis. In addition to target market research, general location factors, to include numbers and types of competitors, are examined. The regional market feasibility study will further support or disprove the business concept for that particular region. The information obtained from both the industry analysis and the regional analysis is then used to make a realistic set of assumptions about the future of sales volume known as a *sales forecast*. At this point, the entrepreneur decides to proceed as planned, to toss out the business concept, to adjust it, or to investigate an alternative region in which to launch the business.

When the industry market feasibility study substantiates the business concept, a summary of the key supportive data is included in the business plan under the heading, Industry Analysis. Specific information from the regional market feasibility study may also be included in the location section of the business plan. The market feasibility study supports the business plan by illustrating the potential for growth opportunities in a particular market. These opportunities may be summarized in the growth plan section of the business plan. The research and planning required to develop the market feasibility study lessens the risk inherent in the start-up of any new business.

WRITING THE PLAN

Develop the Marketing Plan Section of the business plan by using the following topics from Chapter 14 as a guide.

SECTION	TOPIC
Marketing	Industry Profile: Current Size
	Industry Profile: Growth Potential
	Industry Profile: Geographic Locations
	Industry Profile: Industry Trends
	Industry Profile: Seasonal Factors
	Industry Profile: Profit Characteristics
	Industry Profile: Distribution Channels
	Industry Profile: Basis of Competition
	Competition Profile
	Customer Profile
	Target Market Profile

Business Mentor™ CD-Rom—Business Plan—Marketing Plan

KEY TERMS

closed competitive environment
customer surveys
cyclical patterns
declining stage
demographics
direct competition
environmental scan
expanding stage
external environments
financial patterns
focus groups
indirect competition
industry
internal environments
market analysis

market penetration
market research
Merchandising and Operating Results (MOR)
mystery shopper
new stage
North American Industry Classification System (NAICS)
open competitive environment
primary sources
psychographics
sample
seasonal patterns
secondary sources
stable stage
supply channels
user characteristics

QUESTIONS

1. What is meant by the term "industry" in respect to conducting a market feasibility study for a potential fashion business?
2. If you decided to open a brick-and-mortar apparel store, with which components of the fashion industry would you be connected? What would your connections be to other industries?
3. Describe a fashion business that fits in all three of the following industry sectors: service, retail, and distribution. Is there a difference between this firm and one that is vertically integrated?
4. Identify a well-known fashion business for each of the following industry life cycle stages: new, expanding, stable, and declining.
5. What are the five primary selling seasons for most manufacturers of fashion apparel?
6. List three fashion merchandise classifications that are strongly influenced by seasonality.
7. Envision a contemporary women's apparel store in a Texas college town. Then discuss how climate and community can influence the seasonality of merchandise.
8. When assessing technological advances over the past 5 years, which development do you believe had the greatest impact on the fashion industry?
9. Which types of businesses do you believe would be successful in your community that are currently not there? Why?
10. Is there a type of business in your community that is saturated in terms of competition? Describe the business type, list a number of the suppliers (or retailers), and explain why you believe there are so many businesses offering this product or service.

RESOURCE

Rhonda Abrams, *The Successful Business Plan: Secrets and Strategies* (Palo Alto, California: Running 'R' Media, 1999)

CASE STUDY

Body-scanning technology may make clothes shopping a new proposition. Apparel retailing may never be the same again. The largest scale national sizing survey to be undertaken in the United Kingdom since the 1950s is taking place now. Through this national project, the changing shape of the human body in men, women, and children will be electronically mapped in three-dimensional measurements. The resulting database of body metrics will then be used as a basis for launching customer clothing and virtual shopping services. It will be a unique and highly valuable resource for industry and research, and one that can be supplemented by future surveys and other industries, such as military services and the health-care arena. For the first time, body scanning will provide readily available, detailed, and complete information of human body sizes and shapes in a format that can be stored, manipulated, and processed by computer.

What is the impact of body scanning on apparel retailing? For apparel consumers, the primary benefit of three-dimensional body scanning is that no item of clothing need ever be a poor fit again. The customer will be able to scan in his or her body shape and view his or her image in made-to-measure fashions before making a purchase. For both the consumer and the retailer, this service will allow custom-ordered garments to be made at a fraction of the cost of today's personalized tailoring services and in a fraction of the time. This retail strategy also has the potential to save revenue lost by clothing catalog companies when customers return items because they have ordered the wrong size, or the style does not flatter the body.

Who are the players sponsoring this national survey? The Centre for 3D Electronic Commerce, the government of the United Kingdom, and a consortium of 27 organizations from education, manufacturing, and retailing have collaborated on this project. Partners from the retail apparel industry include GUS Home Shopping, Freemans, Littlewoods, John Lewis Partnership, New Look, and Oasis. The center's research is being coordinated by three international organizations: Nottingham Trent University, the Ministry of Defense's Department of Clothing and Textiles Agency, and University College London.

How will technology affect the way we buy clothes in the future? "No one really knows, but we can be sure the impact will be major," says Robin Crosher, project manager. "The Internet is making traditional geographical boundaries insignificant when purchasing goods. My son buys his specialist outdoor clothes over the Internet from a store in Vancouver, Canada. Why not purchase all clothes online once we can be measured and our sizes stored electronically?"

L. Nicole, "Made to Measure: Technology Information," *Computer Weekly* (March 29, 2001)

CASE STUDY QUESTIONS

1. In terms of the case study, what are the future prospects of body scanning as it relates to apparel retailing? What are the positive consequences? What are the potential problems?
2. What types of businesses would most benefit from the database being prepared by the United Kingdom?
3. What new types of businesses may result from the development of this research? How does this information support an industry analysis for these new business?

. . . .

ENTERING THE WORLD OF THE ENTREPRENEUR

. . . .

1. Ask an entrepreneur to discuss the obstacles he or she faced when entering the market.
2. Ask an entrepreneur to discuss what research told him or her about the market he or she was entering. Did it reveal a market niche?
3. Using the Entrepreneur's Research Tool Kit, construct an industry analysis for your business concept. Indicate the factors that support and disprove the potential of your concept; cite the sources from which you obtain your data. Develop a chart to illustrate product classification, target market, and external and internal environments—all from an industry perspective.

THE ENTREPRENEUR'S RESEARCH TOOL KIT: SOURCES OF INDUSTRY INFORMATION

Primary Sources

- *Observation*—watching what people buy, counting the number of customers making purchases in a store.
- *Interviews*—talking with business owners, professors, bankers, and prospective customers.
- *Self-directed survey or focus group*—constructing a survey to administer one-on-one or coordinating a group of people to discuss the proposed business.

Secondary Sources

- *Internet*—Web site addresses listed in the Appendixes.
- *Media agencies*—promotional agencies or media sources such as newspapers, radio, and television.
- *Census data*—available in print and on-line at www.census.gov.
- *Newspapers*—determining trends by scanning articles in periodicals such as *The Wall Street Journal* and *Women's Wear Daily*.
- *Magazines*—perusing consumer publications, such as *InStyle, People, House & Garden*, and *W*, to gain insight on trends, vendors, and retailers.
- *Fashion industry trade journals*—depending upon the sector of the industry and the merchandise classifications; some are *DNR* (men's wear), *Stores* magazine, *Accessories* magazine, *Footwear News*, and *VM & SD* (visual merchandising and store design).

- *Business journals—Inc., Entrepreneur, Business Week, Money,* and *Forbes,* to name a few.
- *Business periodicals and indexes—Standard & Poor's* and *Sheldon's Retail Directory,* as well as www.hoovers.com.
- *Competition information*—check *Standard & Poor's* profiles as well as *Dun & Bradstreet* and companies' annual reports.
- *Banks*—lending institutions often provide blind data on types of businesses funded and loan amounts.
- *Foundations*—Ewing Kauffman Foundation provides entrepreneurial support through its Web site (www.entreworld.org), educational programs, and publications.
- *Planning offices*—often employed by cities and counties.
- *Chambers of commerce*—often there is a person at the chamber of commerce assigned to small business development who will have industry data available.
- *Monthly catalog of U.S. government publications*—call, write, or e-mail the U.S. Government Printing Office (GPO). Also, contact the U.S. Department of Commerce online at www.doc.com. The catalog is a comprehensive index of available government documents. It can be accessed by subject, author, or title, and it contains a current list of publications issued by departments and bureaus of the U.S. government.
- *Reports*—from colleges and universities, including small business development centers.
- *Databases*—some are free; some are not. Some good ones include the Dow Jones News' Retrieval Service, Lexis/Nexis (available in many college libraries), and CompuServe.
- *Real estate firms*—major real estate companies have demographic data summaries that they make available to the public.
- *Small Business Administration (SBA)*—call, write, or locate on the Internet at www.sba.gov.
- *North American Industry Classification System Codes (NAICS)*—a system in which a number is assigned to almost every identifiable industry; these codes are contained in the North American Industry Classification System or SIC Manual, which is available in most libraries.
- *Trade associations and organizations*—Fashion Group International, Inc., International Textile and Apparel Association, and American Association of Apparel.

Other resources that can provide information for the actual business plan include display fixture companies, insurance agents, certified public accountants, attorneys, the local utility commission, and mall management.

ENTERPRISING ENTREPRENEUR

Les Wexner, chief executive officer of The Limited, Inc., is truly at the top of the enterprising entrepreneur chart. Since opening his first store in 1963, he has created a fashion retailing empire that supports his philosophy, "Better brands. Best brands. I don't believe bigger is better. I believe better is better" (www.limited.com). One of the secrets to Wexner's success is his ability to anticipate opportunities in the industry. In 1987, Wexner launched the Limited, Too concept after conducting an industry analysis and learning that there was a market niche for fashionable children's apparel. It began as a Limited, Too department within the existing specialty retailing stores. The product line was unique in that in featured European styled miniadult clothing for boys and girls. After incorporating as a division of The Limited, in 1993, Limited, Too expanded to include a line of baby merchandise. Wexner soon discovered that the baby apparel market was extremely saturated. As a result, the company decided to focus on an older target market, the 7- to 14-year-old girl. Limited, Too refers to this consumer as one who is in the "tween years" (www.jobsatto.com/abouttoo). From 1993 through 1995, Limited, Too stores expanded to 288 different retail locations. In 1996, a senior management team at Limited, Too was assigned to refocus the company's strategy to target fashion conscious girls. Today, Limited, Too has 380 locations nationwide. In 1999, Limited, Too spun off from The Limited, Inc., to become an independent company traded on the New York Stock Exchange. What is next for Wexner? The sky is the limit for The Limited, Inc.

Chapter 4

STRATEGIC PLANNING FROM ENTRY TO EXIT

INTRODUCTION

Chapter 3 of this text focuses on the techniques commonly used to obtain information needed to analyze the industry and to determine a potential target market. This chapter focuses on using that information to determine the best way in which to enter the market. There are three methods of entering the market: starting a new business from the ground up, purchasing a franchise operation, or acquiring an existing business.

Equally important to the entrepreneur is determining the way in which he or she will exit the business when it is time. This chapter guides the potential entrepreneur through selecting the best method(s) to use for determining the value of the company, and finally, the best way to exit the business. The entrepreneur may decide to sell the business, to close it completely, to pass it on to employees or family, or to retain a share of the business.

ENTRY STRATEGIES

The entry strategy an entrepreneur selects affects much of what will be needed to develop the business plan. The decision to start a business through the route of franchising sets into motion one set of activities. Deciding to purchase an existing business sets another set of activities in motion. Starting a business from scratch will result in yet another set of activities. With all entry strategies, costs and benefits must be carefully weighed.

Starting a Fashion Retail Store

- Gain experience by working in a fashion retail store.
- Find a niche or a unique specialty in the fashion retail industry.
- Create a realistic business plan. Make sure there is enough capital available to keep the store going for a year.

Opening a New Business

Starting a new business provides the entrepreneur with the opportunity to allow his or her imagination, passion, and effort to lead to financial rewards, pride of ownership, a sense of accomplishment, and control of his or her destiny. It carries with it positive and negative sides—a sense of freedom on the one hand, and the feeling of servitiude to the dream on the other. Ideas for a new business concept can come from many places: a hobby, expansion of a part-time activity, technical expertise, a spin-off of a current job, a new invention, observation of a market need, development of a home-based business, friends and family, personal preference, and, of course, desperation. There are illustrations in the fashion industry of all of these.

Surviving the Manhattan cold with little money, Norma Kamali constructed a down-filled coat from a sleeping bag—the coat was a new invention created out of desperation. Donna Karan determined that there was a market need for clothing that the fashion-forward, young woman with New York attitude would purchase. The result of her observation was the successful apparel line, DKNY. Technical expertise has led some entrepreneurs to develop computer-imaging businesses used by hair salons and cosmetic retailers to allow customers to "try on" makeup and hairstyles via the computer. Anthony Mark Hankins combined his childhood hobby of sewing original designs for family and friends with recognition of the need for designer clothing that appealed to the mass market. Anthony and his AMH line are featured on the Home Shopping Network, and the line is sold through retail stores across the nation. Genie, a successful manufacturer's representative company in Dallas, illustrates how multi-level marketing and spin-off endeavors can generate a new business concept. The company added line after apparel line until it needed to hire additional salespeople to work in order to service a growing list of retail accounts. The sales personnel sell to the retail buyers the lines Genie's owner has secured; the salespeople may be in their offices or in the showroom at the Dallas Apparel Mart. They receive a percent of the commission on their sales paid to Genie by the manufacturers. Other examples abound. Ideas for business can come from many places.

There are, however, several critical factors that are necessary to turn a great idea into a successful business. The great idea may not be new, and it may not come from the entrepreneur. It may be an idea upon which a franchise operation has based its business. It may be an idea that a successful entrepreneur has already executed. Regardless of whether the idea belongs to the entrepreneur or someone else, whether it has been done or not, the business concept must meet four requirements. First, there must be a group of customers willing to purchase the product or product lines featured by the business at the price that the products are offered. Second, the market must be large enough to support the business and generate a profit. Third, the entrepreneur must be able to differentiate his or her business from that of the competition. Fourth, the entrepreneur must be able to finance the business, either personally or through funding sources. With these requirements in place, the entrepreneur is ready to contemplate business ownership. Opening a new business from scratch, however, is just one route to entering the entrepreneurial world. Another route is through a franchise operation.

Purchasing a Franchise Operation

What is a franchise? A franchise refers to the right or license an individual or a group is granted to sell products or services in a specified manner within a given territory. A franchise typically enables the entrepreneur, the investor, or the franchisee, to operate a business. By paying a franchise fee, the entrepreneur is given a format or system developed by the company (franchisor), the right to use the franchisor's name for a limited time, and assistance in business operations. For example, the franchisor may help the entrepreneur find a location for the outlet; provide initial training and an operating manual; and provide advice on management, marketing, and/or personnel. Some franchisors offer ongoing support through such vehicles as a monthly newsletter, a toll-free telephone number for technical assistance, and periodic workshops or seminars. Although buying a franchise may reduce the investment risk by linking the prospective entrepreneur with an established company, it can be costly. The entrepreneur also may be required to relinquish significant control over the business due to contractual obligations required by the franchisor.

The purchase of a franchise will allow the entrepreneur to sell goods and services that have instant name recognition. The entrepreneur must, however, be cautious. Like any investment, purchasing a franchise is not a guarantee of success. Why would an entrepreneur choose a franchise operation? Many business owners have successfully entered the fashion industry by becoming a franchisee in a profitable system. The Small Business Administration has found that the chances of business success are higher with a franchise than with a typical start-up operation (1998). Data from the Department of Commerce (1998) indicates that 92 percent of all franchise companies formed during the last decade are still in business today.

While there are many advantages to becoming a franchisee in a successful organization, the greatest advantage is that the franchisor has done most of the work for the entrepreneur. The product is proven. The franchisor has already developed the company image, positive name recognition, an appealing visual identity, training techniques, and effective ways of operating the business. The franchisor benefits from company expansion through increased revenues, consumers, and visibility. Since it is in the franchisor's best interest for the franchisee to succeed, continued assistance as the business develops is usually provided. Much of the trial-and-error learning that comes with opening a new business has been experienced by the franchisor and is passed on to the entrepreneur so that pitfalls can be avoided. Most of the operation "bugs" have been worked out by the parent company. Depending on the franchisor, supplies and inventory may be bought in conjunction with the parent company to save money through quantity discounts. In general, the entrepreneur may have a lower level of risk when buying a franchise operation than when starting a business from scratch. The key to success is finding a good franchise operation.

A good franchise operation should offer three primary benefits. The first and most important is *experience and knowledge*. The franchisor should provide the entrepreneur with management training needed to effectively run the business. Second, the franchisor should offer a turnkey operation. This is a business that is completely assembled or set up to begin operation and is then leased or sold to an individual to manage. In most turnkey operations, the franchisor will guide the new entrepreneur through the early stages of the business to make certain it is successful. It is a partnership of sorts in which the franchisor's continued reputation and profitability is dependent upon the entrepreneur's success, and vice versa. The third benefit of an effective franchise is a *ready-made customer base*. Some franchisors, through strong promotional efforts and a clearly defined market niche, have created a demand for their products that will come to the entrepreneur once the business is opened. A ready-to-buy consumer base can be a significant result of a well-chosen and carefully negotiated franchise arrangement.

The key disadvantage of the franchise system relates to costs. The front-end cost or start-up cost refers to costs that are incurred by the entrepreneur to begin the operation of a business. It is often high and can be greater than what would be paid to open a business from the ground up. In addition, franchisees may pay a percent of revenues to the franchisor, lowering profit margins. Franchisees may have to purchase supplies, fixtures, and inventory from the franchisor. Additionally, the franchisee may be required to pay a monthly fee and a portion of the franchise's national advertising expenses. The franchisee may be committed to purchasing part of group inventory buys. Some successful franchise operations require monthly payments of up to 20 percent of gross sales to cover the franchise fee, marketing, royalties, and advertising. To avoid excessive monthly fees, the entrepreneur may elect to investigate getting in on the ground floor of new franchise operations for lower costs. There are low-cost franchises for apparel and soft-goods operations. While they are frequently high-risk propositions that may offer the franchisee little in experience as he or she learns the ins and outs of the business, the profit potential may make the risk and limited assistance worthwhile.

In exchange for obtaining the right to use the franchisor's name and its assistance, the entrepreneur may expect to pay some or all of the following fees:

- *Initial franchise fee and other expenses.* The initial franchise fee, which may be nonrefundable, may cost several thousand to several hundred thousand dollars. Significant costs may be incurred to rent, build, and equip an outlet and to purchase initial inventory. Other costs include operating licenses and insurance. The entrepreneur may also be required to pay a grand opening fee to the franchisor for promoting the new outlet.
- *Continuing royalty payments.* Franchisor royalties may be required based on a percentage of the weekly or monthly gross income. The entrepreneur often must pay royalties even if the outlet has not earned significant income. Even if the franchisor fails to provide promised support services, payments of royalties may have to be made for the duration of the franchise agreement.
- *Advertising fees.* The entrepreneur may have to make payments to an advertising fund. Some portion of the advertising fees may go for national advertising or to attract new franchise owners. The advertising is usually not directed at the entrepreneur's outlet. The entrepreneur's contribution to the advertising fund is often made without promising the entrepreneur a say in how these funds are used. The following questions can be used to help assess whether the franchisor's advertising will be of benefit to the entrepreneur and which costs will be involved:
  - How much of the advertising fund will be spent on administrative costs?
  - Are there other expenses that will be paid from the advertising fund?
  - Will the franchisee have any control over how the advertising dollars will be spent?
  - What advertising has the franchise already implemented?
  - What advertising will be implemented in the near future?
  - How much of the fund will be spent on national advertising?
  - How much of the fund will be spent on advertising in the entrepreneurs's prospective location?
  - Will all franchisees contribute equally to the advertising fund?
  - Will the entrepreneur need the franchishor's consent to conduct his or her own advertising?

- Will rebates or advertising contribution discounts exist for entrepreneurs who conduct their own advertising?
- Will franchisees benefit from such commissions or rebates, or will the franchisor profit from them?

It is important to note that costs in the franchise agreement with any single company may vary from one franchisee to another. Often, franchisors offer a sliding scale of fees based on the level of assistance the entrepreneur requires. For example, the entrepreneur who does not require assistance with personnel training, advertising, or store setup may negotiate lower monthly fees than the entrepreneur requiring full assistance in every aspect of establishing and running the business. To determine the true costs of a franchise agreement, the entrepreneur should recognize the business expenses that the franchisor may cover. If the franchisor selects, purchases, labels, and distributes the inventory, the entrepreneur may be able to eliminate the costs of market trips from the operational budget. If the franchisor provides a computerized sales and inventory system, the entrepreneur may be able to exclude the purchase price of this system from start-up costs. In summary, the entrepreneur should analyze costs generated by and eliminated by the franchise arrangement before making a decision about the financial investment for a franchise contract. Costs, however, are not the only potential disadvantage to this entry strategy.

Another significant disadvantage to the franchise entry strategy pertains to the entrepreneur's control (or lack of it) of the business. In some franchise agreements, the entrepreneur is required to forfeit control of the business. In many franchise arrangements, there is much less room to be creative and vary the product. The franchisee will be required to follow the policies and procedures of the overall franchise operation. In such cases, the franchisees may feel that they are not free to manage the business as they would like. As a result, entrepreneurs may feel as though they have purchased a job, rather than a business. The franchisor, on the other hand, has a motive in developing and maintaining such controls. They are developed and implemented to ensure uniformity among outlets. For the franchisor, these controls are often ways to safeguard quality. The following are typical examples of such controls:

- *Site approval.* Many franchisors require that they preapprove sites for outlets. This may increase the likelihood that the entrepreneur's outlet will attract customers. Franchisors may impose design or appearance standards to ensure that customers see a consistent image in every outlet. Some franchisors require periodic renovations or seasonal design changes. Complying with these standards may increase costs.
- *Restrictions on what is sold.* Franchisors may restrict the goods and services offered for sale. For example, the owner of an accessory store franchise may not be able to add inventory items not specified in the franchise agreement. Similarly, the franchisee may not be able to delete items noted in the agreement. From the franchisor's perspective, these limitations on goods and services can ensure that customers receive a uniform level of quality. For the entrepreneur, however, this might restrict merchandise assortment and services tailored to meet the regional customers' wants and needs.
- *Restrictions on method of operation.* Franchisors may require the entrepreneur to operate in a particular manner. For example, the franchisor may require the entrepreneur to operate during certain hours; use only preapproved signs, employee uniforms, and advertisements; or abide by certain accounting or bookkeeping procedures. These

restrictions may keep the entrepreneur from operating the outlet as he or she may deem best. The franchisor also may insist that the entrepreneur purchase supplies only from an approved supplier, even if supplies could be purchased elsewhere at a lower cost.

- *Restrictions on outlet locations.* Franchisors may limit the business to a specific territory. While these territorial restrictions may ensure that other franchisees will not compete for the same customers, they could impede the entrepreneur's ability to open additional outlets or move to a more profitable location.

Maintaining a positive image may be a disadvantage to a franchisee if the franchisor's reputation declines. If the franchisor loses market share for one reason or another, the entrepreneur's business may experience a similar decline. If the parent company receives negative publicity, customers may view all businesses under that name in a negative light. If this occurs, and the franchisee wants to get out of the business, it may be difficult to exit the franchise agreement. Most franchise contracts specify that the business cannot be sold to just anyone. Additionally, most franchise contracts require a long-term commitment. Franchise agreements typically run for 15 to 20 years; however, a 3- to 10-year term of agreement is not unheard. If the parent company collapses for one reason or another, the individual franchise may not be able to survive. The destinies of the parent company and its franchise operations are intertwined. A franchisor can end the franchise agreement, if, for example, the franchisee fails to pay royalties or abide by performance standards and sales restrictions. If the franchise is terminated, the entrepreneur may lose the investment.

Franchise agreements often do not provide guarantees that the contracts will be renewed. At the expiration of the contract, the franchisor may decline to renew the contract or decide to change the original terms and conditions. The franchisor may raise the royalty payments or impose new design standards and sales restrictions. The entrepreneur's previous territory may be reduced, possibly resulting in more competition from company-owned outlets or other franchisees.

In conclusion, it is important to note that choosing a franchise is a dream for some entrepreneurs and a nightmare for others. The franchise entry strategy appeals to the following people: (1) those who do not have the expertise or desire to build their own businesses from the bottom up, (2) those who desire a lower level of risk and/or a higher level of assistance, or (3) those who believe there is a large profit opportunity in a specific franchise system.

Acquiring an Existing Business

There can be many advantages to buying an existing business. The first may be location. Often, the only way an entrepreneur can obtain the location in which he or she wants to do business is to buy an existing business in that location. It is as though the entrepreneur is not buying a business, but is buying a place in which to conduct business. Second, there may be fewer start-up costs. It can take a start-up company 3 to 5 years to get to the point where the existing business already is. Buying an existing business may be a quick way to get to the point the entrepreneur wants to be. The entrepreneur acquiring an existing business may also acquire an existing clientele, an existing income stream, a positive business image, and business experience upon which to build.

In buying a business, the entrepreneur may find a low-cost source of financing—the seller. Sellers, in their eagerness to close the sale and possibly to sustain the businesses

Figure 4.1: Classified Advertisements of Businesses for Sale

Apparel Manufacturing Business for Sale

Est'd apparel mfr. since 1984 based in L.A. area. 1.5M yearly sales. Well maintained factory in a 22,000 sq. ft. bldg. All equipment and inventory included. Owner retiring. All serious offers considered. To request business prospectus, write to:

Business For Sale

JEWELRY WHOLESALE CO.

Highly reputable & well est'd designer jewelry whsle co. We design & sell sterling silver w/gemstones & gold. Exquisite designs, quality product. Strong repeat cust. base, great expansion pot'l.

BRA/SWIMWEAR
BUSINESS 4 SALE

Long established Mexican Mfg. Co. 600 machines. Strong brand I.D. in Mexico. Long established maquilla division for top U.S. houses.

they have built, often give buyers in whom they have confidence highly advantageous terms of sale. The ultimate financial deal is one that allows the business to buy itself. With this arrangement, the buyer pays the seller from the business's operating profits. If financing through the seller is not an option, financial institutions are more likely to fund a known entity, a business with a proven track record, rather than one without a history of success.

Price can prove to be a disadvantage with the entry strategy of buying an existing operation. Often, the business, with its location, fixtures, and inventory, may cost more money up front than the potential entrepreneur will have on hand. The entrepreneur may decide that, with a smaller and less expensive location, a lower inventory level, and used fixtures, the business could increase in size in the future, as time and money become available. Often, the owner of a successful business may include a charge for an intangible asset in the price of the business. This asset, called blue sky, refers to a dollar amount determined as a fee for the business's image or personality. Blue sky includes the business's existing customer base, its reputation, and possibly, its name. In other words, through blue sky, the seller seeks compensation for building the business into a viable entity.

Another disadvantage to buying an existing business is that the entrepreneur is buying its glory and its problems. It may be difficult to determine from the financial reports provided by the seller whether the business is on an upswing, maintaining, or declining. Relationships with vendors, customers, and the community will certainly affect future success, and such relationships are not spelled out in the documentation provided to assess the value of a business. When an existing business is purchased, the entrepreneur may be buying many unknowns. For example, what is the true reputation of the current owner? Did the business truly make a profit, or do the financial books gave a false impression of the business's true profitability? How current and how reliable are the inventory and equipment? Planning which questions to ask may prove to be more valuable than simply sifting through information provided by the seller.

In buying an existing business, the purchase price is a major issue. It is extremely difficult to make a profit on a business if the initial price is too high. Success using this entry strategy is dependent upon how economically the entrepreneur buys the business. Buying an existing business usually requires the assistance of outside professionals. The buyer of an existing business will need to have an attorney and/or a licensed accountant review all legal and accounting records for the previous 3 to 5 years at a minimum. Additionally, the buyer will need to arrange for a thorough inspection of the inventory, equipment, and supplies. An attorney should be hired to review all contracts. If the buyer will also be purchasing real estate as part of the transaction, a title search should be conducted. A title search assures there are no recorded claims or liens against the property. Finally, a purchase agreement will need to be drafted. The purchase agreement outlines the purchase price, terms of payment, and items involved such as fixtures, equipment, and inventory. While protection from future liabilities may be expensive and time-consuming upfront, failure to conduct a thorough investigation of the company may prove to be costly.

Typically, the best buys are businesses that are unsuccessful but for which the entrepreneur believes he or she has solutions to the problems. If the entrepreneur determines good reasons for a turnaround, then an unsuccessful business may be advantageous from a financial perspective. A turnaround refers to a business that is failing, but for which there are obvious changes that, when implemented, would make the business successful. These turnaround buys are also referred to as salvage investments. In some cases, the entrepreneur may not have to make an actual financial investment. Management expertise and product knowledge may be enough. For example, the owner of Jellybeans in Springfield, Missouri, began by taking over a small, failing children's wear store, improving the store image, and reversing the declining sales of the store. Jellybeans has grown in size from its original 800 square feet to 4,000 square feet with apparel, shoes, gifts, and home furnishing for infants and boys and girls to size 14.

EXIT STRATEGIES

Many fashion retailers have suffered great financial losses because they did not plan on how the business would eventually be sold or closed. Planning allows the entrepreneur to explore various alternatives to closing the entire business. Examples of such alternatives are mergers, acquisitions, initial public offerings, or a joint venture with another company. Venture managers are those who plan to take the business public once its size and profitability allow. Venture managers specialize in starting and increasing the size of a business to the point that it can be sold on the stock market. Martha Stewart's enterprise is an example of how an entrepreneur can maintain control of a business while making a fortune by selling shares in the company. St. John Knits, on the other hand, illustrates how the strategy of taking a business public may not be the best choice. The former owners of St. John Knits, the Gray family, negotiated to buy back the company because of lack of control over the business and declining sales. By developing and analyzing a clear set of objectives, knowing when to sell all or part of the business, recognizing the strengths and weaknesses of the business, and clarifying the bottom line, the risk of failure diminishes while the chances of success and financial reward increase dramatically.

The decision to sell all or part of a business is one of the most complex strategic and emotional decisions an entrepreneur can make. Sooner or later, it will happen. It will be time to exit the business. The business is a result of much hard work, sweat equity, and achievement. Various factors can affect the decision to sell; some good, some bad. In many cases, selling may have been the ultimate goal all along. It other cases, selling is a reaction to changes in the market, changes in personal circumstances, or changes in company strategies. Retirement, health problems, relocation, or a change in career are common reasons for selling. Some owners will sell when it becomes too difficult to manage the operation, or if they lack the necessary capital for expansion. Perhaps the demand for the product has lessened, thereby decreasing sales and profits. Perhaps the lease has expired and will not be renewed or can be renewed only with unfavorable terms. New competitors may be entering the marketplace, taking too great a share of the market.

On the upside, entrepreneurs often relish the excitement and risk of moving on and creating yet another new business. Selling an existing business can provide the capital necessary to begin another venture. The entrepreneur may find that by allowing an acquisition by another company, his or her personal and professional objectives may be met faster and at a lower cost. Larger companies will often have the resources, such as capital and people, to move the business forward at a faster rate and at a lower cost. If the entrepreneur's goal is to build the business and then to sell it at a profit, then selling it may accomplish that goal.

Whatever the reason, the decision to sell must be given careful consideration and planning. It is imperative to plan for the exit early, to make it the choice of the entrepreneur and not the choice of another. Selling wisely through careful planning can allow for greater profit and for the flexibility to pursue other opportunities. The maximum selling price will be achieved if the business is sold at some point during its growth stage. Waiting to sell once the company shows declining sales can lead to financial disaster. Trying to sell the business out of desperation or when profits turn downward can be challenging. It reduces the amount the entrepreneur may receive from the sale.

Careful assessment of the objectives, before making the decision to sell, can be accomplished by asking and answering the following questions:

- Is this the right time to sell?
- Where is the business in its industry cycle?
- Where is the company and what can it reasonably expect to accomplish in the next 5 to 10 years?
- Is the industry in the growth stage, is the industry declining, or has the business reached its maturity?
- Is the business keeping pace with or outpacing the industry as a whole?

To determine the best exit strategy, the entrepreneur must reevaluate the marketing plan, the product/service plan, and the financial position (present and future) of the company. The entrepreneur will begin by analyzing the company's products and its market position. Next, he or she will examine the company's current and potential market share, product strengths and weaknesses, and product development capabilities. Externally, the entrepreneur will investigate competing companies and their products, industry trends, and possible future technological changes. Each of the company's functions should also be analyzed. In marketing and sales, the entrepreneur will want to evaluate the current distribution and pricing strategies. He or she will want to assess the company's financial position and needs by estimating how much money will be needed in the future using cash forecasts, projections of funds needed to maintain and grow the business. Finally, the entrepreneur will want to calculate the company's current and future profitability.

Buyers will want to know that they can maintain the bulk of the customer base through a change of ownership. They will also want to be assured that the products and/or services delivered by the company will survive a change of ownership. It may be important to the sale of the business to make sure that key employees will remain with the company after the business changes ownership. Key employees may be part of critical customer relationships. The buyer may want to retain these employees to be sure that the business runs smoothly in the absence of the entrepreneur. The smooth transfer of ownership will directly affect the perception of the company's value.

Management Succession

If the business is to be sold or passed on, a plan for management succession is critical to its future success. Effective **management succession** is, in essence, a changing of the guard. It is an evolutionary process, and it is often a time of conflict. In some cases, the business has been such a focal point in the entrepreneur's life that he or she feels a loss of identity when turning it over to others. At the same time, the successor may desire autonomy. The new owner will be, after all, the future operator of the company. Succession planning helps reduce the stress and tension resulting from these issues.

What are the critical stages of a management succession plan? The first phase is a time for the entrepreneur and the successor to communicate. They may want to begin by examining the values they hold about running a business. The ways in which businesses operate reflect their owners' personal values about people, work, money, and power. Second, the entrepreneur should brief the successor about all critical documents. These would include, but are not limited to, insurance policies, financial statements, bank accounts, key contracts, corporate bylaws, and leases. The entrepreneur should not only provide a list of key suppliers and customers, but should also take the time to discuss how these key players should be treated to ensure a smooth transition. People within the business should also be identified and discussed in terms of their strengths, weaknesses, and contributions to the company.

In the second phase of the management succession plan, the entrepreneur focuses on teaching the successor how to run the business, while promoting an environment of trust and respect among the employees. This process may take months or years, depending upon the preferences of the entrepreneur and the successor. While most successors will want to implement a management succession plan, some will prefer a straight business sale in which the entrepreneur simply steps away and turns the reins of the company over to the new owner.

Selling the Business to Outsiders

While the techniques for valuing a business are examined later in the chapter, it is important to note that the value of a business can be greatly affected by the economic climate, the time constraints placed on the sale, and the terms under which the sale is negotiated. For example, the entrepreneur may decide to accept a 20 percent reduction in the value of the business for a 100 percent cash payment at closing. Some entrepreneurs prefer to maintain a portion of the business, while selling parts of the company. "Going public," selling stock in the business, is one way to provide this option. This alternative is available to entrepreneurs who are skillful enough to get the organization to grow to the point where it can be publicly held, when stock holdings can be sold to the public. Through this option, the privately held business that once held no real market for its stock can be transformed through an **initial public offering (IPO)**, selling publicly traded shares of stock in a corporation to investors. An initial public offering is the company's first sale of stock to the public. At this point, the entrepreneur can gradually liquidate personal equity in the business through the sale of publicly traded stock at market price. The fashion retail industry has seen a number of successful entrepreneurial companies take this route, among them Donna Karan, Martha Stewart, Gucci, Delia's, and Decorize.

Selling the Business to Insiders

Selling the business to employees is another route the entrepreneur may take when exiting the company. For the most part, the following options are available to the entrepreneur: (1) sale for cash plus a note, (2) a leveraged buyout, (3) an employee stock ownership plan. In the first alternative, **sale for cash plus a note**, a selling price for the company is established with one or more employees specified as the buyers. The seller holds a promissory note for a portion, large or small, of the business. With this option, the entrepreneur often takes a seat on a board of directors to help ensure that the business stays on track while the note is being paid. Through a **leveraged buyout**, employees borrow money from a financial intermediary and pay the owner the selling price at closing. The third option, an **employee stock ownership plan**, provides the entrepreneur with the opposite results. Instead of walking away from the sale with cash, the entrepreneur allows employees to purchase the business gradually. An employee stock ownership plan is a plan under federal law which allows employees to buy stock in the company with funds borrowed from a bank, with the principal repaid from an employee's profit-sharing plan. While it is a long-term exit strategy, it often benefits all involved. Employees become owners in the business they are building, while the entrepreneur has the time to transition smoothly out of the company.

Liquidating the Business

Finally, the entrepreneur may find it necessary to liquidate the business. **Liquidation** refers to the process of closing the business and converting everything to cash. In essence, a company will sell all its assets. While this may be the only option for an unsuccessful endeavor, there are other reasons for an entrepreneur to choose liquidation. Personal reasons, such as health or financial issues, may create the need for quick cash. Some entrepreneurs choose to close the businesses they have built rather than pass them on to new ownership. Regardless of the reason, liquidating a business is a business in itself.

The entrepreneur liquidating a business will want to minimize financial loses, or, in some cases, try to profit from the closing. Closing an operation at the end of the lease minimizes a cash loss generated from breaking a lease. Selling off the closing inventory, fixtures, and even the customer mailing list can generate cash. Some entrepreneurs will allocate promotional dollars for a liquidation sale. They will work with vendors and brokers of off-price goods to purchase closeout merchandise. While representing legitimate values, these goods can be sold at full markup and carry a clearance price. At the end of the liquidation sale, the entrepreneur may elect to donate any remaining goods to charity or to sell the lot off to an off-price broker.

Liquidation value represents the value of the company after all assets have been sold and all liabilities paid off. Liquidating assets is typically done in an auctionlike format. For fashion retail stores, the owner may choose to sell off as much inventory as possible and donate the remaining inventory to charity, which provides a tax deduction. Another option for the fashion retailer is to secure the assistance of a jobber. A jobber is a person or company representative who is paid a flat fee and/or a percentage of the liquidation sale (sales commission) to sell off inventory and dispose of the unsold stock. In some cases, the jobber may bring in additional inventory to increase the sales commission. Although liquidation is an alternative that is not often used, it is important know what the business may be worth in case a desperate situation arises.

When constructing the business plan, the entrepreneur must consider the worst-case scenario. What options are available if the business is unsuccessful? Will there be assets, such as property, fixtures, and inventory that can be sold to pay off business loans and other debts? While planning for failure is not a pleasant task, it is critical to let bankers and other funders know that there is a backup plan if it is needed.

THE PROCESS OF VALUATION

In order to sell or shut down a business, the entrepreneur must determine how much it is worth. First, the entrepreneur should realize that it is not possible to come up with a firm answer to the question of how much a business is worth by simply using financial ratios. Like many things in life, a business can be worth one price to one person and another amount to someone else. Often, personalities and emotions enter the picture. Why is it important to determine the value of a business? The entrepreneur may be buying an existing business. At some point in time, the entrepreneur may want to sell his or her business. While it might not seem of importance at this point, how to create value in a business must be evaluated from the onset. What should an effective valuation accomplish? Buyers will want the entrepreneur to be able to justify the asking price. A competent valuation meets two tests. First, it reaches a supportable fair market value conclusion. Second, it clearly and convincingly establishes how the conclusion was reached.

The first step in preparing to sell the business and in determining its value is to gather information and to know what is being sold. The following steps provide the necessary data:

1. Determine the assets held by the company. The assets will vary depending on whether or not the business is a fashion retail store or an internet or a service operation. The valuation procedures will vary according to the nature of those assets. It is much easier to place a value on physical assets than on intangible assets, such as customer lists or employee contracts. Physical assets may be valued by using replacement costs, where intangible assets may be valued by making comparisons to similar businesses. Replacement costs refer to the amount of money needed to purchase new items rather than resale or used values. Retail businesses have assets such as store fixtures, leases on the store premises, inventory, customer lists, licenses and franchise arrangements, contractual agreements with key employees (if any), and supplier contracts.
2. Collect all financial information for the previous 3 years and year-to-date financials; existing contracts with employees, customers, or suppliers; any patents, trademarks or copyrights; and 3 years of tax returns.

Next, it is critical to look at adjustments in financial data. Experienced entrepreneurs may legally adjust financial data so as to pay as little in taxes as possible. In doing so, they do not paint a true picture as to the value of the business. While this approach is done to minimize earnings for tax purposes, it is also underestimating the true value and earning potential of the business. The income statement may reflect everything from exaggerated travel expenses, commissions to employees and owners, to leased vehicles, and shrinkage. The numbers, adjusted for tax purposes, have to be brought back in line. Adjustments must be made in order to compare the performance of the business with the performance of other businesses in the industry. Just as consumers shop and compare prices on clothing and other items, potential buyers will often compare sales of one business to that of others.

What Is the Business Worth?

If one asks a banker, a business broker, the seller, the buyer, an attorney, or a certified public accountant how to come up with a value for a business, six different answers and methods will be presented. The perception of how much a business is worth depends on which side of the fence one sits on. Sellers typically see the value of the business as being much higher than the buyer will see the value of the same business. The seller will want to receive as much out of the company as he or she can. The buyer, on the other hand, will want to pay as little as possible. Both parties will use various methods for justifying the price.

There are numerous valuation methods that can be used to come up with the basis for the asking price or what a prospective buyer is willing to pay for the business. The assets of the company will determine, to some extent, the method for ascertaining its value.

Selecting the Valuation Method(s)

The concept of value and the techniques used to determine value can be viewed in the following three ways: fair market value, book value, and liquidation value. The Internal Revenue Service (IRS) defines fair market value as the price at which the property would change hands between a willing buyer and a willing seller when the seller is not under any compulsion to sell and both parties have reasonable knowledge of the relevant facts. The fair market value of a business is a result of internal and external factors. Internal factors include those that are unique to the particular business being sold. Internal factors for retail fashion businesses might include such things as the age and desirability of the inventory, name recognition, the quality of employees, the strength of the existing lease, and so on. External factors are typically outside the entrepreneur's immediate control and may include overall economy (including interest rates), competition, taxes and regulations, and interruption of accessibility to the location. Using the method of fair market value, the business is examined in terms of the amount of money it would bring if it was put on the block, in liquidation rather than book value (where the value of a company is determined by the value of assets as reflected in the company's books). Value may be added by using off-balance sheet valuations. Off-balance-sheet valuations refer to the values within a business that do not appear in the firm's financial reports. For example, these values would include such assets as customer lists, special licenses, and exclusive vendors.

One method used to arrive at fair market value applies comparable sales figures. This technique determines a company's value by comparing the company with a similar company or with recently sold businesses. Unlike selling residential real estate, each business brings its own unique features. When comparing the company to others, consideration must be given to whether the company is worth more or less than the comparable companies selected. Price adjustments should be considered on the basis of potential earnings, size comparison in terms of gross sales, and other criteria. Several databases and organizations compile and maintain data on reliable comparable business sale information for entrepreneurs. Data can be obtained through BIZCOMPS located in San Diego, California (www.bizcomps.com), the Institute of Business Appraisers, and business brokers.

If good financial records have been kept, book value can be the easiest method to apply. In its simplest terms, book value refers to the difference between a company's total liabilities and its total assets (Assets − Liabilities = Net worth). Book value is a reflection of historical information and can be severely affected by the accounting practices used at the company. For tax purposes, a business will accelerate the depreciation of its assets as quickly as possible. By doing so, the book value of the business is lowered. A comparison of accelerated depreciation to that of the adjusted balance sheet of ABC Custom Fashions reflecting standard depreciation is illustrated in Figure 4.2.

In this example, depreciation on the retail business is shown as standard and accelerated. As accelerated, the fixed assets were depreciated over the shortest time period allowed by generally accepted accounting principals. In the standard example, the useful life of the fixed assets was extended, resulting in the reduction of accumulated deprecia-

Figure 4.2 Balance Sheet

ABC Custom Fashions
As of December 31, 20–

Assets	Standard Depreciation	Accelerated Depreciation	Liabilities & Net Worth	Standard Depreciation	Accelerated Depreciation
Cash	$ 5726	$ 5726	Notes payable–bank	$ 0	$ 0
Accounts receivable	0	0	Notes payable–other	0	0
Inventory	50,000	50,000	Accounts payable	397	397
Prepaid expenses	0	0	Accruals	212	212
			Income tax payable	0	0
			Current portion of LTD	9736	9736
			Other current liabilities	0	0
Total Current Assets	**$ 55,726**	**$ 55,726**	**Total Current Liabilities**	**$ 10,345**	**$ 10,345**
Fixed assets	22,550	22,550	Long-term debt	39,508	39,508
Accumulated depreciation	−4,510	−11,275	Subordinate officer debt	0	0
Total Fixed Assets	18,040	11,275	**Total Liabilities**	49,853	49,853
Notes receivable	0	0	Common stock	18,000	18,000
Intangibles	0	0	Capital Surplus & Paid in Capital	0	0
Deposits	4,250	4,250	Retained earnings	10,163	3,398
Other Assets	0	0	(Less) Treasury Stock	0	0
Total Net Fixed Assets	22,290	15,525			
Total Assets	**$ 78,016**	**$ 71,251**	Total Net Worth	28,163	21,398
			Total Liabilities & Net Worth	**$ 78,016**	**$ 71,251**

tion in the amount of $6,765. The accounting entry has allowed an increase in the value of the business from $21,398 to $28,163 (refer to Total Net Worth on the Balance Sheet).

One of the disadvantages of using book value as a method of arriving at a selling price is that it does not take into account the value of the intangibles. Generally speaking, fashion companies can derive significant value from off-balance-sheet items such as a loyal customer base, exclusive supplier arrangements, a fashion or price image, and name recognition. These intangible benefits are referred to as blue sky or goodwill assets.

OFFERING MEMORANDUM

Once the value of the business has been determined, the entrepreneur can prepare an offering memorandum (or selling memorandum). A business broker often prepares this. The offering memorandum contains comprehensive information about the company. It will serve as a basis for the buyer's preliminary evaluation of the company. The more information provided, the more comfortable the buyer becomes.

For a fashion company, a typical offering memorandum would contain the following components:

- *Executive summary.* An executive summary in the business plan provides an overview of the business (i.e., highlights of the current stage of development of the company, management team, primary market, marketing plans, and financial summary). Similar to the executive summary in the business plan, it is constructed to gain the reader's attention. The executive summary in an offering memorandum explains that the company is being sold and summarizes the key elements contained in the document. The summary is intended to attract the buyer's attention.
- *Management employees.* The management section should list the key management positions and specify whether or not the people in those positions will remain with the company. It should describe the experience and skills of each these people; however, their compensation is not disclosed. The entrepreneur should discuss the number of employees and the manner in which the employees are compensated, as well as what benefits they receive.
- *Products/service.* Unique features of the product lines, such as cost, design, and quality, are described in this section. Licensing or royalty agreements associated with the products and plans for future agreements are also discussed. Any distribution rights that have been obtained are presented.
- *Marketing.* The marketing section of the memorandum should be as extensive as it is in the business plan. It should contain an industry profile and a description of competitors, including their strengths, weaknesses, and market share. The entrepreneur should describe existing and future marketing plans, as well as related pricing. The target market, market size, market trends, and growth potential, as well as user demographics and psychographics, should be presented.
- *Financial data.* The entrepreneur should include both historical and projected financial information for 3 to 5 years, including year-to-date information. Assumptions underlying the projections should be included.

Since this document is a reflection of the quality of the company, it should be as comprehensive as possible. Once the offering memorandum is in place, the seller can begin looking for buyers.

Looking for Buyers

Buyers are interested in purchasing businesses based on what they reasonably believe the company can accomplish down the road. They want a good return on their investment and/or they are very interested in the company's products and technology. A qualified purchaser has the following four characteristics: (1) an established desire to purchase a company, (2) the financial capability necessary to complete the transaction, (3) the qualifications and resources necessary to run the company, and (4) the willingness to move forward in a timely fashion. Prospective buyers may be found through a number of sources. Advertisements are often placed in the business opportunities sections of local and regional newspapers, in publications specific to the industry in which the business operates, and through business brokers. An existing business has relationships with a banker, accountant, lawyer, suppliers, and manufacturers. They can provide referrals for potential buyers. It is important to remember that it may be to the entrepreneur's advantage to be as discreet as possible in advertising the sale of the business. Employees and customers will begin to look elsewhere for employment and services if they are uncertain about the future of a company.

Often, the reason for selling the business is one of the first things a prospective purchaser will want to know. Earlier in this chapter, various reasons for selling the business are explored. The entrepreneur will need to decide which of these reasons will be presented to prospective buyers. Some buyers are not quick to purchase a business they believe is on its way down. Others see an opportunity to bring on different management teams with new skills and resources to turn the company around. Serious buyers will analyze the business. Withholding vital information may undermine the credibility of the entrepreneur and may be subject to legal penalties.

Structuring the Sale

Once a buyer is found, the structure of the sale becomes critical. The seller may be interested in how involved the current owner wants to remain in the company. The legal structure and whether or not the entrepreneur is willing to owner-finance will be important to the buyer. Owner-financing, a situation in which the business owner allows the purchaser to pay off the debt in installments, can be beneficial for two reasons. First, more often than not, buyers may not have 20 to 30 percent capital available for the down payment required by most lending institutions. Second, if the entrepreneur is willing to owner-finance and take less than 30 percent down, this constitutes a contract of sale and defers taxation obligations until the end of the note. The buyer, on the other hand, will be interested in structuring the sale to reduce the after-tax cost of acquiring the business. Structuring the sale with both parties in mind can lead to a win-win situation for all involved.

Negotiating the Sale

Successful negotiations are conducted when both parties know and understand the objectives, needs, strengths, and weaknesses of the sale and the business. Ideally, the goal is one of mutual satisfaction, one that gives both parties what they want from the arrangement.

A **letter of intent**, a letter addressed to a company stating the desire to conduct business, is typically drafted. The letter of intent usually indicates that the prospective buyer is serious and sets a timeline for negotiations. Upon signing, both parties will begin the process of negotiating in good faith, removing any obstacles to performing the tasks necessary for evaluating all operational and financial aspects of the business. Upon agreement of a price and other terms, the contract for sale is completed and signed, and the actual closing takes place. Throughout this process, it is important to note that attorneys and business brokers play key roles in the success and legal credibility of the sale.

CONCLUSION

Determining entry and exit strategies is critical to the success of a new company. Entrepreneurs can enter the market in one of three ways: starting a business from scratch, purchasing a franchise operation, or buying an existing business. Each strategy sets in motion a different set of activities. With all entry strategies, costs and benefits must be carefully weighed.

Entrepreneurs must also consider how they will exit the business. At some point, the entrepreneur will leave the business. Businesses can be liquidated or sold as an on-going business. Also, a portion of the business may be sold. When it comes time to sell, the value of a company must be established. Many valuation techniques exist for determining the value. Once the value is determined, the entrepreneur can begin looking for prospective buyers through advertisements, business brokers, or existing business relationships. Once found, the process of selling the business begins.

WRITING THE PLAN

Develop the business plan by using the following topics from Chapter 14 as a guide:

SECTION   **TOPIC**
Growth Plan   Exit Strategy

Business Mentor™ CD-ROM—Business Plan—Growth Plan Section. There is one question in the Growth Plan section on the Business Mentor CD-ROM that deals with exit strategies. This information should be entered here, if you are using the CD-ROM template.

KEY TERMS

accelerated depreciation
blue sky
book value
cash forecasts
employee stock ownership plan
fair market value
franchise
franchise fee
franchisee
franchisor
initial public offering (IPO)
jobber
letter of intent
leveraged buyout

liquidation
liquidation value
management succession
off-balancing sheet valuations
offering memorandum
purchase agreement
sale for cash plus a note
salvage investments
standard depreciation
start-up (front-end) costs
title search
turnaround
turnkey operation
venture managers

QUESTIONS

1. Compare the advantages and disadvantage of the three routes available for entering or starting a business.
2. Exit strategies must be given careful consideration. List 4 factors that should be considered in planning the exit strategy.
3. Why is it important to the funder that an exit strategy has been developed?
4. Explain why the services of a business broker, attorney, accountant, and banker would be valuable and should be utilized in selling the business.
5. List the steps taken in selling a business.

SUGGESTED READING

Ernest J. Honingman, *Buying and Selling a Small Business: A Complete Guide to a Successful Deal* (Riverwood, Illinois: Commerce Clearing House, 1999)

Ed Paulson, *Complete Idiot's Guide to Buying and Selling a Business* (New York, New York: Macmillan Publishing Company, 1998)

Lawrence W. Tuller, *The Small-Business Valuation Book* (Avon, Massachusetts: Adams Media Corporation, 1998)

Wilbur M. Yegge, *A Basic Guide for Buying and Selling a Company* (New York, New York: John Wiley and Sons, 1996)

CASE STUDY

Alina Roytberg, 40, and Lev Glazzman, 41, are two-faceted in the beauty product industry. One part of their company is in manufacturing, while the other sells the products to retailers and through its own stores. Their company, Fresh, was started in 1991 with a small store funded by a $10,000 loan. One decade later, the company's sales totalled $14 million. "Our first production sold out overnight," says Roytberg. "In 1994, we opened a larger store in Boston and filled our first retail order to Barney's New York." In describing the key to the company's success, Roytberg explains, "Our organic approach has inspired legions of devoted fans." The partners are always looking for new ideas. For example, while on holiday in Italy, they discovered an Umbrian clay that had been used for healing for centuries. The pair created a skin bar from the clay, one that treats everything from acne to diaper rash. Additionally, they used the clay to develop a toothpaste that whitens teeth without chemicals. The word about these natural products, which includes sugar bath and milk formula lines, spread quickly. A strategic plan was in place to take the company to soaring heights.

Through word of mouth, exclusive retailers, such as Colette in Paris and Liberty in London, were eager to buy the products. As global positioning was part of the strategic plan, Fresh was quickly shipped abroad. Next, additional channels of distribution were sought. In 1998, Fresh became one of the first upscale beauty brands to go on-line. As the New York brick-and-mortar business continued to grow, Roytberg and Glazzman opened a second Manhattan boutique in 1999. Where would they go from here? Louis Vuitton Moet Henessey (LVMH), the multinational giant in luxury products, stepped in and made an offer to buy the company. Fresh was suddenly at a critical point in its strategic plan, one that the partners had not anticipated.

P. Kooiman, "Almost Famous: Fresh, a New Face," *Entrepreneur* (January 2001, p. 288)

CASE STUDY QUESTIONS

1. What new opportunities are available to Fresh in order for the company to maintain growth and a competitive edge?
2. What are the advantages of and disadvantages of the LVMH offer?
3. What are the various strategies that Roytberg and Glazzman could take in response to the LVMH proposal?
4. Beginning with the LVMH offer, develop a step-by-step strategic plan for Fresh for the next 5 years.

ENTERING THE WORLD OF THE ENTREPRENEUR

1. Locate a fashion franchise in your area. Talk with the owner and ask about the franchise fees, why the entrepreneur chose to open a franchise instead of starting a business from scratch or buying an existing business. What assistance was given by the franchise operation? What type of assistance with marketing was received?

2. Visit the local library or the World Wide Web to find out how to contact the International Franchise Association. Write the association and ask for information on franchising.

3. Contact a local fashion entrepreneur who purchased an existing business. How was the value of the business determined? What documents did the buyer receive to validate that value? Did the entrepreneur pay full asking price? Were the financials accurate? How was this determination made? What was included in the purchase of the business: hard assets, customer base, and so on?

4. Contact a local business broker to determine how the sale of a business might be structured. What methods are used to determine the value of the business?

5. Contact a local banker and ask what documentation would be needed to (a) start a business from scratch, (b) buy a franchise operation, and (c) purchase an existing business.

6. Contact an attorney and ask about buying a business or franchise. What advice can the attorney give in terms of buying an existing business or negotiating a franchise agreement?

ENTERPRISING ENTREPRENEUR

As a young girl, entrepreneurship was the last thing on Anita Roddick's mind. She wanted to be an actress. Instead, she became a driving force in the skin- and hair-care industry. Most notably, Roddick redefined the face of cosmetics retailing by positioning her company as a firm based on environmental awareness and social responsibility. In 1976, Roddick opened her first store, The Body Shop, with 25 hand-mixed products. Today, The Body Shop offers more than 1,000 items and has generated sales in excess of $1 billion in 2000–2001. The 1,800 Body Shop stores are located in 49 countries. Roddick states, "My business was a response to the extravagance and waste of the cosmetics industry. I [felt] there were plenty of people like me hungry for an alternative." Strategic planning was the foundation for the success of this business. As part of its strategic plan, the company first offered franchise opportunities, and then went public in 1984. Global expansion was a key factor in the strategic plan. The greatest challenge to growth has been public cynicism. Roddick remarks, "People feel there has to be an ulterior motive to The Body Shop's activism, as though our principles are a marketing ploy."

What are Anita Roddick's perspectives on entrepreneurship? She defines entrepreneurs as "obsessive visionaries, pathological optimists, passionate storytellers, and outsiders by nature." She further explains, "I don't think being an entrepreneur is something you question. It's just something you are." She believes that entrepreneurs must be experimental so that they can retain the spirit that helped them conceive their businesses. Though she no longer sits on The Body Shop's executive committee, Roddick serves as cochair, sources new products, and keeps the company active in human rights, environmentalism, and animal protection issues. In terms of her legacy as an entrepreneur, Roddick states, "The future is being shaped by the forces of the global business, so I would hope that I've helped change the vocabulary and practice of business, and contributed to the awareness that it can and must be a force for social change."

A. P. Sherman, "The Idol Life," *Entrepreneur* (January 2002, p. 56)

Chapter 5

FINDING A LOCATION FOR THE BUSINESS

INTRODUCTION

In Chapter 2, the product is examined as it relates to the entrepreneur's business concept. In Chapter 3, this product or product line is evaluated through an industry analysis and then is further assessed in terms of its market feasibility on a regional level. Entry and exit strategies for the business are explored in Chapter 4. The *what* (the product), the *when* (the industry analysis and market feasibility study), and the *how* (the entry strategies) have been discussed. The business concept begins to move toward reality with the *where*, finding a location for the business.

Every entrepreneur has heard it: "The three most important keys to a successful business are location, location, location." While the most important key to a profitable business is likely a top-notch business plan, location certainly can play a significant role in the success of a company. The definition and significance of a business location has changed considerably over the past decade with the advent of e-commerce and the growth of mail-order sales. The definition of business location is no longer confined to the geographical site of the company's headquarters or its retail outlets. Business location can refer to the destinations to which catalogs are mailed. It can also refer to the company's Web site and/or Internet links. More traditionally, it refers to the site and facility where the business is physically situated.

Although location for today's fashion industry businesses can be interpreted in a wide variety of ways, location is always directly tied to target demographics. The demographics of the target market are the specific demographic subgroups in a given population that a retail business aims to attract. They include age, income, education, and family size, among other factors. It is believed that people with similar demographic characteristics within a given region will purchase a similar range of goods and services. Thus the entrepreneur must define the target market before determining a location for the business—no matter if the location houses a bricks, clicks, service, or catalog operation. Target demographics are intertwined with image. Who the customer is affects how other people see the business.

Whether the business is in a downtown location, part of a regional mall, or a free-standing store, the geographic location sets an image. Location as a convenience factor is also important, but convenience of location alone is not the major criterion for the success of a retail business. In enclosed malls, the name of the mall and the location of the business within that mall combine as image makers. In fact, shoppers often recall the name of a mall before they remember the name of the store.

Location is a multi-faceted factor in business planning. It has an entirely different meaning to e-commerce entrepreneurs. For this discussion, the location factors refer to tangible buildings, brick-and-mortar stores, storefronts, or warehouses. In Chapter 6 on e-commerce, location and visibility on the Internet are explored. In this chapter, the decisions the entrepreneur must make in terms of physical location for the business are explored. These decisions involve many factors, the geographic locale of the building, to the facility itself, and finally to the interior of the building.

In this chapter, business location is first examined in a traditional context—where to position the physical site of the company headquarters and/or retail outlet(s). Second, the information on how to evaluate the location in terms of the specific facility from which the consumer will procure the company's product is explored. Criteria for evaluating the visual impact of the building exterior is also covered as is the design of the building façade, logos and signing, approach, and windows. Finally, perspectives on the interior of the facility are examined—size and layout of the sales area, interior display elements, lighting, fitting rooms, and the checkout area.

THE LOCATION HIERARCHY: REGION TO STATE TO CITY TO SITE

The entrepreneur's ultimate objective in deciding where a business should be located is to position the business at a site that will maximize the likelihood of success. Choosing a location is a matter of selecting the best place that best serves the needs of the business's target market. Sometimes, the general location for the business may be limited to the area where the entrepreneur lives. If there are no such limitations, the location selection may begin with a broad regional search that is systematically narrowed down to a state, then a city, and then a specific site. Unfortunately, many entrepreneurs never consider locations beyond the places they reside. Choosing not to look beyond one's comfort zone may prevent the entrepreneur from discovering locations that might be better suited to the business and that would improve its potential for success. Assuming that the entrepreneur is open about the location, the first step is to explore different regions.

The Region

The entrepreneur should begin by analyzing which regions of the country (or the world, in some cases) have the greatest number of characteristics necessary for the business to succeed. An important characteristic is the growth of a particular population segment that fits the business's target market. Rising disposable incomes and a stable economic environment are also desirable qualities. Access to suppliers, low operating costs, as well as an adequate and affordable labor pool, are additional factors to investigate. The entrepreneur should look for a low level of competition from similar businesses in the region. In some cases, climate will affect the location decision. For example, if the entrepreneur is planning to open a custom-fit swimwear business, then the regional search may be limited to geographic areas with warm weather during as many months of the year as possible.

The State

Once the entrepreneur narrows in on a region, the next step is to select a state. Every state has a business development office that is designed to recruit new businesses to that state. While the information provided by these offices will likely have a bias toward the state, such offices are an excellent source of facts that the entrepreneur can assess objectively. Some of the key issues to examine are state laws, regulations, taxes, and any incentives or investment credits that the state offers to businesses locating there. The entrepreneur will want to evaluate the prospective workforce by looking into the quantity and quality of the labor supply, wage rates, and the union or nonunion status of the state. Proximity to suppliers, such as apparel, gift, or home furnishing market centers, as well as sales representatives for merchandise lines, will also be critical factors. Finally, the entrepreneur will want to evaluate the general business climate of the state.

The City

Once a state is selected, the next step is to identify a city for the location of the business. The entrepreneur will begin an assessment of a city as a location candidate by analyzing the city's population in terms of it psychographic and demographic characteristics. Psychographic characteristics include attitudes, beliefs, and values. Demographic characteristics include growth trends, family size, education, age breakdown, gender proportions, income levels, job categories, religion, race, nationality, and population density. Population density refers to the number of people per square mile residing in a given area. It is an important element for the success of businesses that rely on high traffic volume. For example, the customers of beauty spas will likely live or work within an 8- to 10-mile radius of the spa. If a sufficient number of residents within the target market are not within this range, then it may not matter how good the spa services are. An example of a city with a growing population density is Atlanta, Georgia. Atlanta has experienced a rapid growth rate in the population of high income, young professionals. With an average age of inhabitants at 29 years, Atlanta has seen an explosion of fashion businesses aimed at young people with rising incomes and appetites for fashion apparel, services, and home furnishings.

Another factor the entrepreneur will want to assess about a city is competition. One variable to consider is the number, quality, and locations of competing firms. The entrepreneur will want to examine competing companies in terms of the differences and similarities among their offerings and those of the entrepreneur's business, as well as quality and pricing variances. Additionally, the entrepreneur will want to examine the success and failure rates of competitors within the city. The entrepreneur may also find that the chamber of commerce, or similar city agencies, will share information on firms that will soon be opening in the city. An entrepreneur who had intended to open a home accessories business in the downtown shopping district of Boulder, Colorado, provides an illustration. She has done all her homework, thoroughly studying the competition and carefully choosing a site for her future store. By chance, she mentioned her business concept to the director of small business development at the chamber of commerce and was stunned to learn that two similar businesses were opening in her targeted area within the

Figure 5.1 Sample Demographic Report

···

U.S. Census Bureau
State and County *QuickFacts*

Fulton County, Georgia

People QuickFacts	Fulton County	Georgia
Population, 2000	816,006	8,186,453
Population, percent change, 1990 to 2000	25.8%	26.4%
Persons under 5 years old, percent, 2000	7.0%	7.3%
Persons under 18 years old, percent, 2000	24.4%	26.5%
Persons 65 years old and over, percent, 2000	8.5%	9.6%
White persons, percent, 2000 (a)	48.1%	65.1%
Black or African American persons, percent, 2000 (a)	44.6%	28.7%
American Indian and Alaska Native persons, percent, 2000 (a)	0.2%	0.3%
Asian persons, percent, 2000 (a)	3.0%	2.1%
Native Hawaiian and Other Pacific Islander, percent, 2000 (a)	Z	0.1%
Persons reporting some other race, percent, 2000 (a)	2.6%	2.4%
Persons reporting two or more races, percent, 2000	1.5%	1.4%
Female persons, percent, 2000	50.8%	50.8%
Persons of Hispanic or Latino origin, percent, 2000 (b)	5.9%	5.3%
White persons, not of Hispanic/Latino origin, percent, 2000	45.3%	62.6%
High school graduates, persons 25 years and over, 1990	323,055	2,853,605
College graduates, persons 25 years and over, 1990	131,001	777,158
Housing units, 2000	348,632	3,281,737
Homeownership rate, 2000	52.0%	67.5%
Households, 2000	321,242	3,006,369
Persons per household, 2000	2.44	2.65
Households with persons under 18, percent, 2000	32.5%	39.1%
Median household money income, 1997 model-based estimate	$39,047	$36,372
Persons below poverty, percent, 1997 model-based estimate	18.3%	14.7%
Children below poverty, percent, 1997 model-based estimate	29.8%	22.8%

Business QuickFacts	Fulton County	Georgia
Private nonfarm establishments, 1999	30,590	197,759
Private nonfarm employment, 1999	726,101	3,363,797
Private nonfarm employment, percent change 1990–1999	35.6%	34.6%
Nonemployer establishments, 1998	52,085	435,338
Manufacturers shipments, 1997 ($1000)	14,240,886	124,526,834
Retail sales, 1997 ($1000)	9,248,184	72,212,484
Retail sales per capita, 1997	$12,779	$9,646
Minority-owned firms, percent of total, 1997	20.7%	15.6%
Women-owned firms, percent of total, 1997	27.3%	25.6%
Housing units authorized by building permits, 2000	9,621	91,820
Federal funds and grants, 2000 ($1000)	7,409,352	42,459,795
Local government employment–full-time equivalent, 1997	37,077	324,480

Geography QuickFacts	Fulton County	Georgia
Land area, 2000 (square miles)	529	57,906
Persons per square mile, 2000	1,542.5	141.4
Metropolitan Area	Atlanta, GA MSA	

Source U.S. Census Bureau: State and County QuickFacts. Data derived from Population Estimates, 2000 Census of Population and Housing, 1990 Census of Population and Housing, Small Area Income and Poverty Estimates, County Business Patterns, 1997 Economic Census, Minority- and Women-Owned Business, Building Permits, Consolidated Federal Funds Report, 1997 Census of Governments year. With this critical information, the entrepreneur reevaluated her plans and opened a different type of store—one that became quite successful.

Studying the size of the market for the business's products and/or services will help the entrepreneur determine whether or not he or she can capture a market share large enough to earn a profit. Again, U.S. Census Bureau reports (www.census.gov) can provide valuable demographic data (Figure 5.1). Once the entrepreneur has completed an examination of the city, he or she should know more about the city and its neighborhoods than do its residents. The next stage is to determine the type of area within the community in which the business will be placed.

The Site

There are five basic areas where businesses can be located: a central business district, neighborhoods, shopping centers and malls, outlying areas, and at home. The central business district is the often the historical center of a city or town, the area where downtown businesses were established early in the development of the city. Neighborhood locations are those in which residential areas are heavily concentrated. The city of Olathe, Kansas, provides a good illustration of a neighborhood location. As many young families moved into this area, children's wear boutiques, dry cleaners, and fitness centers have found success through a very localized and congruent target market.

Shopping centers and malls provide the customers with one-stop shopping. They are classified as follows: neighborhood shopping centers, community shopping centers, regional shopping malls, and power centers. A power center combines the drawing potential of a large regional mall with the convenience of a neighborhood shopping center. Anchored by large specialty or department stores, these centers frequently target affluent baby boomers who desire broad selection choices and convenience. Although they still account for the majority of retail sales in apparel and soft goods, malls have declined in popularity over the past decade. Sameness and staleness are two of the adjectives used by shoppers to describe the reasons for this downslide. As a result, mall and shopping center developers are trying new formulas. Many are adding entertainment to retailing. "Entertailing," as it is called, combines an interesting environment with appealing activities and desirable merchandise. All this is developed with a specific target market in mind. It is lifestyle merchandising, a significant trend in fashion marketing and retailing.

LOCATION FACTORS

Analyzing the potential location of the business, whether from a regional, state, city, or site perspective, requires an examination of many factors. Before examining actual location factors, the entrepreneur must prioritize the qualities that are most necessary to the success of the business. For example, the entrepreneur may be looking for a facility in which to locate offices and to warehouse merchandise. He or she may intend to sell the product lines through catalogs or on-line. In such cases, the entrepreneur may find the factors of visibility, competition, neighbor mix, and image to be less important than if the entrepreneur were choosing a storefront location where 100 percent of the business's sales would take place.

Once the entrepreneurs have prioritized the location characteristics for their businesses, where do they go for general location information? There are a number of good sources available in print and on-line, such as census tracts which can usually be found in public and university libraries. Census data range from the general to the specific. Zip code catalogs also provide general data about populations in geographic areas. Additionally, city government and tourist offices, as well as chamber of commerce offices, often provide demographic data on neighborhood clusters. Finally, media sources may also collect and distribute demographic data that pertain to their promotional regions. Prospective entrepreneurs are their potential customers; therefore, they are likely to share this information.

National Retail Traffic Index

There are a number of retail business information sources that provide location data in terms of customer traffic. The **National Retail Traffic Index** (NRTI) provides information about shopper traffic and conversion trends (i.e., sales volume) for retail executives, mall developers, industry analysts, real estate consultants, and advertisers. More specifically, the NRTI evaluates department store traffic from two perspectives—the mall in which the department store is located and the department store itself. As built-in traffic can reduce the need for advertising expenditures and increase the potential for sales, this information can be very helpful to the entrepreneur when considering a mall location. Think about the number of large, successful retail apparel chain stores that are located in malls and that do little or no advertising. Instead, they contribute to institutional advertising of the mall and/or they rely on national advertising. It is important for the entrepreneur to ask about the level of customer traffic in a given area, past and present.

Location Checklist

Following are a number of questions the entrepreneur should ask and prioritize in order to decide on the location of the business. If the entrepreneur plans to have the company's headquarters in a location separate from other parts of the business, then the questions should be answered and weighed for each site.

- *Target market.* Is this location easily accessible to the prospective company's specified target market? Does this location meet the needs and desires of the target market?
- *Quality of life.* Does the area fit the business's needs and the personal preferences of the entrepreneur?
- *Image.* Is the image of this location appropriate for the prospective business and its target market?
- *Compatibility with the community.* Does the business's image fit with the character of the place and the needs and wants of the residents?
- *Neighbor mix.* Is the assortment of neighboring businesses appropriate for the company and its target market?
- *Proximity to suppliers.* Are suppliers accessible and are shipping alternatives readily available?
- *Transportation networks.* Are transportation alternatives available and cost-effective for the company's customers and suppliers?
- *Competition.* Where are direct and indirect competitors located in relation to the location?
- *Security/safety.* Is the location secure for employees, customers, inventory, and facilities?

- *Labor pool.* Is there an adequate number of qualified people available for employment near the business area? What are wage rates in the area? Is there a strong union presence?
- *Restrictions.* Are there any city or county laws governing business locations that will affect the choice of location?
- *Business climate.* What is the overall attitude of customers, residents, and government officials toward this type of business? Are there any "blue laws" that prohibit business on Sundays? Are small business support programs, financial assistance, or incentives offered to entrepreneurs?
- *Services.* Are the services required for the company accessible and affordable in this location? For example, if alterations are needed by the company's customers, are alteration sewers available and affordable?
- *Ownership.* Is it more cost-effective to purchase or to lease in this location? Is ownership an option?
- *Past tenants.* Who were past tenants in this location? What types of businesses were they? Why did they leave? Where did they go?
- *Space.* Is the space adequate in this location? Is there room for growth?
- *Physical visibility.* Is the location visible to the target market? Is visibility necessary to the success of the business?
- *Life cycle stage of the area.* What is the maturation of the area—emerging, growing, peaking, or declining?
- *Expenses.* Will costs for this location fit within the company's budget?

When all the location factors are analyzed, the factor that is often most critical is cost. Often, locations vary enormously in terms of price. How does the entrepreneur determine which locations are true options? An estimate of monthly income and expenses is necessary in order to determine a range of realistic location alternatives.

FINANCES AND LOCATION

It is possible to find the perfect location when money is no object. In the real world, however, budget limitations often create choice limitations. What if, after months of looking, the entrepreneur finds a hundred places that would be perfect for the business? What if all 100 locations must be ruled out when costs are considered? A better approach is to begin by estimating location costs and then limiting the number of locations the entrepreneur investigates to those that fit within the budget.

Estimating Location Costs

In the Merchandising and Operating Results (MOR) report, the National Retail Federation (NRF) has compiled annual data provided anonymously by retailers from across the country. The data are categorized by merchandise classification (e.g., men's sportswear or ladies' dresses) and store type (e.g., specialty store or department store). The results are then sorted to show levels of sales performance in terms of high, medium, and low annual volume. Markdowns, inventory turnover, and sales per square foot are also indicated. The simplest way to determine a rough estimate of monthly sales for the business is to multiply average sales per square foot for the business type by the

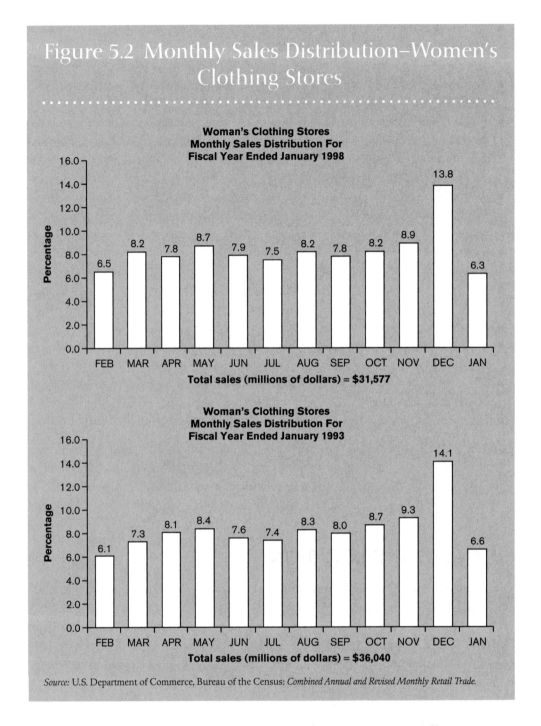

Figure 5.2 Monthly Sales Distribution–Women's Clothing Stores

Woman's Clothing Stores
Monthly Sales Distribution For
Fiscal Year Ended January 1998

FEB 6.5 | MAR 8.2 | APR 7.8 | MAY 8.7 | JUN 7.9 | JUL 7.5 | AUG 8.2 | SEP 7.8 | OCT 8.2 | NOV 8.9 | DEC 13.8 | JAN 6.3

Total sales (millions of dollars) = $31,577

Woman's Clothing Stores
Monthly Sales Distribution For
Fiscal Year Ended January 1993

FEB 6.1 | MAR 7.3 | APR 8.1 | MAY 8.4 | JUN 7.6 | JUL 7.4 | AUG 8.3 | SEP 8.0 | OCT 8.7 | NOV 9.3 | DEC 14.1 | JAN 6.6

Total sales (millions of dollars) = $36,040

Source: U.S. Department of Commerce, Bureau of the Census: *Combined Annual and Revised Monthly Retail Trade.*

average number of square feet in selling space per store type. From this figure, the cost of goods can be estimated and then subtracted. The result is a rough estimate of monthly capital available for all expenses, except cost of goods. An example of this process follows:

- The MOR report indicates that annual sales for a specialty store featuring ladies' sportwear are, on a national average, $160 per square foot. (Assume that the location being considered has 2,000 square feet of selling space.)
- $160 per square foot × 2,000 square feet = $320,000, which is the sales estimate for the year.

- Using 50 percent retail markup as the industry average for apparel, the cost of goods is estimated at $160,000 (half of the $320,000 in annual sales volume).
- This leaves a balance of $160,000 for the estimated annual expenses, excluding inventory purchases. When the $160,000 is divided by 12 to find a monthly amount for expenses, the result is $13,333 per month. Figure 5.2 (page 101) illustrates the distribution of monthly sales for a women's apparel store.

In the preceding scenario we can see that rent above or even close to $13,000 per month will not fit within the potential business's budget. Payments for utilities, taxes, payroll, insurance, and remaining budget items must be added to the list of monthly expenses. The entrepreneur must estimate fixed and variable monthly costs and deduct these from the monthly amount for expenses before establishing a monthly location cost. For example, let us assume that the estimate for monthly expenses (not including cost of inventory and location) is $5,000 for the business. If the entrepreneur agrees to a lease of $8,000 per month and if the business performed in alignment with similar stores, the business would lose money every month.

Another method of estimating income and expenses for a location budget is through the Index of Retail Saturation (IRS). For retailers, the number of customers in the trading area and the amount of competition are essential factors for predicting success. The Index of Retail Saturation is a measure that calculates the number of customers in a specified area, customers' purchasing power, and the level of competition. It combines the average retail expenditures with the average dollar amount that each person spends for a certain type of merchandise in a given trading area. These data can be found through the U. S. Census Bureau (www.census.gov) in two reports, *County Business Patterns Economic Profile* and *Economic Census*. Additionally, city governments and chambers of commerce offices often provide this type of information. Once the number of customers in the trading area, dollar retail expenditures per person in the product category, and the amount of square footage owned by competitors are determined, the IRS can be determined. It is calculated as follows:

IRS = Number of customers in the trading area × Retail expenditures (per person)
= Retail facilities (total square feet of selling space allocated to the product category in the trading area)

For example, suppose an entrepreneur is looking at two sites for an active footwear store. Through the MOR reports, the entrepreneur learns that the national average sales for a store selling shoes is $175 per square foot. Location 1 is in a geographic area that has 20,000 potential customers, each of whom spends an average of $62 on sports shoes annually. The only competitor in the trading area has an estimated 6,000 square feet of selling space. Location 2 has 25,000 potential customers who spend an average of $65 on sports shoes each year. Near this location, two competitors occupy a combined space of about 8,400 square feet. The IRS values for these two sites are computed as follows:

$$\text{IRS of Location 1} \quad \frac{20,000 \times \$62}{6,000} = \$206.67 \text{ per square foot}$$

$$\text{IRS of Location 2} \quad \frac{25,000 \times \$65}{8,400} = \$193.45 \text{ per square foot}$$

At first glance, Location 2 appears to be the more productive, however, when the IRS is calculated, Location 1 proves to be better. Both IRS figures surpass the industry average of $175 per square foot.

It is imperative for the entrepreneur to remember that this estimate is just that—an estimate. It is a starting place; it is not the actual or final calculation that the entrepreneur will make in the financial section of the business plan. There are many factors that influence sales and expenses. A number of monthly expenses unrelated to location have not been taken into consideration at this point. Monthly costs associated with start-up expenses, loan repayment (principal and interest), payroll, sales taxes, shipping, advertising, markdowns, and much more, have not been included in this estimate. This is simply a logical way for the entrepreneur to limit the number of location alternatives. The completed financial plan will be the determining factor as to whether or not the costs associated with each location will actually work for the company.

Monthly Expenses Related to Location

What are the monthly expenses that the entrepreneur must consider with respect to location? They vary with each location, whether a new building, a purchase, or a lease agreement, and with each contract. Following is a list of expenses that often relate to the location of a business:

- Utilities (e.g., electricity, gas, and water).
- Maintenance.
- Commons fees (e.g., charges for maintenance of areas shared by tenants, such as courtyards, plants, fountains, etc.).
- Facilities improvements.
- Insurance.
- Property taxes.
- Advertising and other promotion costs (e.g., charges for promotional activities sponsored by the shopping center).

When comparing locations that fit within your rough estimate for monthly expenses, compiling a chart of monthly costs for each and every alternative is an effective way of comparing locations. This allows the entrepreneur to make adjustments, if needed, when the financial section of the business plan is completed. For example, the least expensive alternative may end up being the actual location choice when the financials are completed. On the other hand, the entrepreneur may find that a more expensive location, with its added benefits, may fit easily into the final financial plan.

BUILD, BUY, OR LEASE?

Once the entrepreneur has decided on the general geographic location and has reviewed a number of specific locations that fit within the company's budget, then the location decision shifts to that of a specific facility. Which factors should the entrepreneur consider when determining whether to build, buy, or lease a site for the business?

Building a Facility

A critical decision for the entrepreneur is whether or not to build a facility. The decision to build is largely influenced by the entrepreneur's money situation. If the entrepreneur has unlimited funds, he or she could design and build a perfect facility. Few people have this luxury; however, constructing a new facility can project a positive image to prospective customers. A new building can incorporate the most needed and efficient features, which can significantly lower operating costs and increase productivity.

In some areas, there are only a few or no existing buildings to buy or lease that correspond to the entrepreneur's needs. In these situations, the entrepreneur must consider the cost of constructing a building as part of the start-up capital. Constructing a building creates a high initial fixed cost that the entrepreneur must weigh against the facility's ability to generate revenue. It plays a critical role in calculating the break-even point of the business. Time is also a factor to consider when assessing the build, buy, or lease alternatives. Building a facility will require more lead time than the other options. Finally, building a structure can be viewed as an investment. If the building has the potential of becoming a profitable investment because of its location, then the entrepreneur, as well as potential funders, may determine that constructing a facility is the best way to go.

Buying a Facility

In some cases, there may be an appropriate building in the area where the entrepreneur wants to locate. If the building will require remodeling, buying it may be the best option. Although buying a building requires considerable financial resources, the entrepreneur will know exactly what the monthly payments will be. As with the alternative of building a facility, the entrepreneur may have significant reasons to believe that the property will actually appreciate in value. In such cases, choosing to purchase may be a wise decision. Additionally, the entrepreneur can depreciate the building each year. Both depreciation and the interest on the loan for the facility are tax-deductible business expenses.

On the downside, building or buying a facility may limit the entrepreneur's mobility. Some entrepreneurs prefer to stay out of the real estate business and focus on what they know best, running their businesses. All real estate does not appreciate in value. Surrounding properties can become run-down or unsafe and consequently lower property values in the area despite the owner's efforts to keep the building in prime condition. Many downtown locations in large cities have experienced this problem. Additionally, the entrepreneur may decide that flexibility and mobility are necessary to maximize the business. If this is the case, then leasing a facility offers the most flexibility, the greatest mobility, and the lowest initial cash outlay.

Leasing a Facility

The major advantage to leasing a facility is that leasing requires less money. This frees up funds for purchasing inventory, promoting the business, and supporting the business's operations. Monthly rental fees may be tax deductible. What are the disadvantages of leasing a structure? The property owner may decide not to renew the lease or to increase the rent drastically at the time of lease renewal. As a result, a successful business may be forced to move to a new location, which can be costly. Relocation can also result in a loss of customers.

In cases where the building owner wants a large increase in rent when the lease is up for renewal, the landlord has the upper hand. He or she is well aware of the tangible and intangible costs associated with moving. Another disadvantage to leasing can be the limitations to remodeling the building. For example, the building owner may believe that modifications of the facility will adversely affect the future value of the property. In this case, the landlord may likely refuse to allow remodeling or will require a long-term lease at a higher monthly rent. Additionally, permanent modifications of the structures, such as wallpaper, track lighting, and electrical improvements, usually become the property of the building owner.

The length and terms of a lease can benefit or hinder a business. Obviously, a long-term, low-rent lease for an excellent facility in a desirable location can be viewed as a true business asset. In contrast, a short-term lease may spell trouble for a company. In addition to length of lease, there are a number of issues that need to be discussed and specified in the rental contract. Following is a list of questions that should be discussed and clarified with the facility landlord. The result of the discussion should then be specified in the lease:

- What will be the terms and the length of the lease?
- Will the lease be a straight rental or rent plus a percent of gross or net profits?
- Will a sublease be permitted?
- Will there be a "due on sale" clause in the lease stipulating that the remaining lease payments are due if the facility is sold?
- Who will pay for exterior and interior improvements?
- What restrictions will the lease contain? (e.g., hours of operation or joint promotional activities).
- Will there be any energy-efficient requirements?
- Will electronic and computer needs be accommodated? If not, who will pay for these?
- Can the facility be expanded, if needed?
- What additions, such as walls or signage, can be made? Who will pay for these?
- How much will the deposit be for the lease, if required?
- What will be the monthly utility costs? Will these be included in the monthly rental fee?
- Will there be additional fees for janitorial, trash removal, or other facility maintenance needs?

Let us assume that the entrepreneur has investigated these questions and determined that leasing a specific facility is the best option. What does the entrepreneur need to know about negotiating and committing to a lease? In some instances, the building owner may require a percent of the tenant's gross sales, in addition to the monthly rent. If this is the situation, then the entrepreneur may elect to request a long-term lease with a lid or cap that limits or prohibits monthly rental increases. Following are a number of suggestions that the entrepreneur may want to consider before signing a lease:

- Read the lease agreement thoroughly; then ask an experienced and reputable attorney to review it before signing it.
- Incorporate, or form a limited liability corporation, before signing a lease.
- Get all promises in writing.
- Be certain that insurance will cover any damage to the property.
- Verify the lease's provisions on such issues as parking spaces, improvements, repairs, maintenance, operating hours, air-conditioning and heating, and cleaning and other services ranging from grounds keeping to promotional activities.
- Be sure that subleasing is permitted.
- If the facility is in a shopping center or mall, include a clause that guarantees that the building owner will not lease to a competing business.

Figure 5.3 Factors to Consider for Building, Buying, or Leasing a Site

4 = most preferable; 1 = least preferable

	Build				Buy				Lease			
	4	3	2	1	4	3	2	1	4	3	2	1
Building exterior												
Building interior (office and work areas, selling space, storage, traffic flow, and parking)												
Zoning												
Maintenance needs												
Insurance requirements												
Security												
Identification (signage)												
Parking												
Vehicle traffic and speed limit												
Nearby businesses												
Proximity to customers and suppliers												
Area demographics												
Population of trading area												
Economic conditions												
Property potential												

- Also for shopping centers or malls, request an occupancy clause, stating that rent will be reduced or eliminated until the center reaches a specific level of occupancy.

Funders evaluating the entrepreneur's business plan will carefully examine plans for the business's facility. They will assess initial costs relating to the structure, the value of the property, any equity that may be associated with the facility, and the potential contribution of the building to the success of the business. Figure 5.3 provides a list of factors and a rating system from excellent to poor for each of the three location options.

LOCATION AND THE BUSINESS PLAN

In the business plan, the entrepreneur will list the location of the company's headquarters, the main place of business (if different), and any branch locations (if applicable). The entrepreneur will indicate whether the facility will be constructed by the entrepreneur, purchased as an existing building, or leased. Additionally, the square footage and how this sqaure footage will be allocated for office space, warehouse, and retail will be described. It will be important to discuss access to parking and transportation. If visibility is a key factor to the business's success, the entrepreneur will want to discuss this in the location section of the business plan. A description of the geographical area the company will serve should also be included. The following statements provide an example of the location section of a formal business plan:

> The corporation offices of Annie's Vintage Apparel, Inc., will be located in a 3,000-square-foot brick building at 2112 East Main Street, Columbus, Ohio. The building will be leased

from Commercial Properties, Inc. In addition to the corporate offices, this facility will also contain receiving, warehouse, and distribution space. Approximately 1,000 square feet will be allocated to offices, and 2,000 square feet to inventory. Annie's Antique Accessories will be located in a 1,000-square-foot storefront at 3145 Broadway in Columbus, Ohio, leased through Commercial Properties, Inc. Annie's Attic, an apparel retail outlet, will be located in a renovated train station at 2268 South Crossroads in Columbus, Ohio. This property will be leased through the city of Columbus. The train station, which is located in the center of the downtown area, accommodates 1,500 square feet of retail floor space and 500 square feet of office space. The two retail outlets will serve a high-income area in Ohio, represented by a 60-mile radius of Columbus.

A copy of the actual unsigned lease and a letter of commitment from the building owner should be attached to the business plan. Further details about location will be provided in the business plan in the form of a blueprint and layout that denote specifics about the exterior and interior of the facility

DESIGNING EFFECTIVE SELLING SPACE

Retail facilities must make maximum use of the space available with respect to efficiency and appearance. Both the exterior and the interior of the building should be carefully planned by the entrepreneur.

The Exterior

Customers develop opinions about a store before they enter it. They form opinions about the image, price range, quality, and exclusivity of the merchandise that are inside the store from outside. The following four factors influence the opinions that customers form before they enter the retail operation: exterior design, signs (e.g., logo and name), approach, and display windows. The exterior design of the building influences the consumer's initial opinion.

Since the expectation level of the customer is established outside the store, if the potential customer does not like the look of a retail store from the outside, he or she may never go inside to get to know the operation better. The exterior should reflect the personality of the business—similar to the way the choice of clothing expresses the personality of its wearer.

The Design of the Exterior   The architecture of shopping malls has neutralized the impact of individual store architecture. Even when successful fashion stores are clustered in spaces as beautiful as London's Burlington Arcade or as unique as Les Halles in Paris, few shoppers remember the individual store's façade. Downtown shops, stores in strip centers, and free-standing stores have the opportunity to use exterior design as a tool to create image and visual uniqueness. As customers approach these types of stores, effective architecture can generate a powerful first impression. The early entrepreneurs who pioneered the growth of fashion retail businesses knew this. The first department stores in New York and Chicago were, in essence, theatrical emporiums. It was the desire of these retailing leaders to create a structure that would fulfill the fantasies of their clients. They made the building part of their total image. Today, storefronts can represent attitude, price perception, value, and target market through a combination of architecture,

location, and signing. J. C. Penney, Urban Outfitters, Harrods, and Banana Republic are a few examples of retailers that effectively use these tools to project image.

Logos and Signs   Today, in place of eye-catching façades, the exterior image of stores in shopping centers is communicated primarily by the company name and the design of the logo. The sign, and occasionally the façade, has replaced the building as an exterior signature. The choices of signs and designs include script, block letters, backlit, neon, pictorial, metal, wood, and plastic. The configuration of fonts, sizes, and materials for signs is unlimited. There are some interesting messages that may be communicated to customers through signage. Some designer boutiques, for example, have no significant signs, except for plaques at the entry. These prestige retailers are allowing the building itself to communicate the store's image. Additionally, they are implementing the subliminal understanding that the smaller the sign, the more exclusive and higher priced the merchandise. Most department stores in downtown locations have their names on marquees or in large illuminated letters on the façade. Free-standing stores more often use logo or graphic and name combinations. Each variation creates a different perception of image and, subsequently, price.

Approach   As customers approach the store, even before they see the merchandise in the window, they become aware of automobiles in the parking areas, the grounds and common areas, and people moving to and from the entry. The customer quickly develops a perception of the location. The entrepreneur needs to anticipate these perceptions when selecting a location. For example, feelings of prestige may turn to concerns about safety when panhandlers are begging in an exclusive strip center. The clothing and image of shoppers in the area also elicit an image. Observing other shoppers does influence customers in categories such as exclusivity, price expectation, and fashion availability.

Windows   The last visual stimulus communicated to the customer before entry to the store is the window. It is here that the last of the prejudged expectations is made. Because the windows are what shoppers see right before they enter the store, the appearance of the windows carries the most weight in the shoppers' mind. Windows must have an overall consistency with the merchandise within the store. The size and number of windows should relate to the type of merchandise being sold. Bloomingdale's projects a fashion-forward and creative image through large display windows that surround the building. Compare this vision with the windows of Tiffany's. Tiffany's exterior features small windows at eye level, tertiary windows designed to present vignettes using beautiful jewelry. On a winter afternoon, Bloomingdales's windows may feature eye-catching coats by "hot" designers shown on gorgeous mannequins who resemble Kate Moss and Shalom. On that same day, Tiffany's windows may display tiny snowmen with diamond earrings as eyes and miniature pine trees wrapped with glittering bracelets and topped with star-shaped and diamond-encrusted pins. In both cases, the windows are in proportion to the featured products; they frame the merchandise and give it importance. Additionally, in both cases, the image of the retailer is enhanced and communicated by the exterior of the store.

The Interior

The goal shared by fashion entrepreneurs planning a retail space is a simple one—to create an environment that will entice the customer to buy. The size and layout of the store, the colors of the décor, the displays, the fixtures and mannequins, the lighting, the fitting rooms, and even the placement and look of the cash desk come together to create the visual environment that can make or break a retail business. When selecting a location, the entrepreneur will want to envision and plan how the interior space will be allocated and decorated.

Size of the Sales Area   The amount of space within a sales area can communicate an image. When most customers see an open, spacious department, they automatically think of higher prices and exclusivity, as well as excellent customer service. Bergdorf Goodman is an excellent example of this concept. It has less merchandise per square foot than any large specialty store in Manhattan; however, it reports one of the highest sales volume levels per square foot in the country. In contrast, some retailers have been able to use small spaces to their advantage, often depending upon the merchandise assortment. These retailers create the feeling of a boutique by using small, intimate spaces that showcase unique goods and allow for a high level of service. Sock Shop of London is a perfect example of a boutique concept. The inventory is moderately priced and includes fashion and basic socks and hosiery for men, women, and children. The sales associates are approachable, friendly, and informed. The small stores are well-merchandised with wall fixtures and carefully placed floor racks to create pathways or aisles. Aisle width is a feature of retail floor space. It is important to recognize that customers often equate wider aisles with higher prices. A planned balance of merchandise, display, and aisle spaces is necessary to project a desired image and to maximize sales.

Layout   Layout is the arrangement of the physical facilities in a business. An ideal layout contributes to efficient operations, increased productivity, and higher sales. Retail layout refers specifically to the arrangement and method of display of merchandise in a store. A retailer's success depends, in part, on a well-designed floor plan. The retail layout in an apparel and accessories business should put customers into the store and make it easy for them to locate merchandise; compare price, quality, and features; try on the merchandise; and, ultimately, make a purchase. Additionally, the floor plan should take customers past displays of the items they may buy on impulse. An effective layout can generate sales through suggestive selling initiated by planned visual merchandising efforts. For instance, when a handbag department is located next to the footwear department, multiple sales may result as the customer is tempted to purchase a bag to match a new pair of shoes.

Successful retailers recognize that some locations within a store are superior to others. Customers' traffic patterns give clues to the best locations for items with the highest profit potential. The location with the highest level of customer traffic is referred to as prime selling space. For example, merchandise purchased on impulse and convenience goods should be placed near the front of the store, preferably adjacent to the cash desk. Customer jewelry, care products for shoes and apparel, as well as inexpensive gift items are ideal add-on items to place in the prime selling space near the cash register. New fashion merchandise is most effectively positioned at the entrance of the store.

Some retailers generate significant increases in sales by intentionally directing customer traffic patterns. These retailers use the placement of a department or the design of aisles within the store to increase the customer's exposure to the merchandise assortment. The retailer may create a circular traffic pattern that requires the customer to walk around the store from entrance to exit. Another traffic pattern designed to require the customer to circulate throughout the store is formatted like a bicycle wheel with aisles, like spokes, attached to the circle or outer rim. In either case, the customer will pass through a number of departments before leaving the store.

Another technique used by retailers to increase sales is to locate a high-volume department in the rear of the store. Generally speaking, space values in a retail store depend on the space's relative position to the store entrance. Space value is the value of each square foot of space in the store with respect to generating sales revenue. Typically, the farther away an area is from the entrance, the lower its value. Furthermore, space values typically decrease as distance from the main entry-level floor increases. Selling areas on the main level contribute a greater portion to sales than do those on the other floors because they offer greater exposure to customers than either basement or higher-level locations. Some retailers, however, work to offset lower space values through the placement of successful departments. For example, if a retail operation specializing in apparel and accessories is known for its shoe selection, the shoe department may be situated in the back of the store on a platform level. This way, customers can see the shoe department upon entering the store, yet they must walk through the other departments to get to it. If customers come into the store for specific products and have a tendency to walk directly to those products, it may benefit the retailer to place complementary products in their path. In essence, customers are tempted to make more purchases by seeing or coming in contact with more merchandise.

Still other retailers have found success by adding entertainment facilities to their stores. Sephora, a French retailer that sells beauty and fragrance products, has successfully attracted customers by integrating computer terminals into its store design. The company installed computer facilities with Internet and e-mail services as a test market in the back of its Champs d'Elysée location in Paris. The idea was to present an open invitation to customers to "come in and hang out." Additionally, Sephora constructed a stage area in the front of the store where bands and singers regularly perform. It is a drawing card that pulls people in off the busy street. Similarly, the Donna Karan flagship store on Madison Avenue in Manhattan features a juice bar as well as a music and magazine department on its second floor. This, too, pulls customers into and through the store, encouraging them to lounge awhile. More and more, retailers are including cafes, coffee shops, music areas, arcades, computer facilities, and other nonapparel entities as part of the store layout. The entertailing trend in retailing is one that has resulted from a keen understanding of the target customer's lifestyle and interests.

Effective layout in a retail store emerges from in-depth knowledge of the target customers' buying habits by the entrepreneur. Observing customers' behavior can help the entrepreneur identify the "hot spots" where merchandise sells quickly and the "cold spots" where it may sit untouched. A plotted pattern that is created from observing the movements of random samples of shoppers in the store is called the tracking plan. The flow of customer traffic, as well as the places where customers tended to touch merchandise, pick it up, and buy it, are indicated on a floor plan of the store. The tracking plan is used as a reference when planning the design of new spaces, and when adjusting stock content by area. It is an excellent and inexpensive method that can be used to maximize the sales potential of floor space. What, however, does the entrepreneur of a new business do about layout for the opening of the business when observation time is nonexistent?

Retailers have the following three basic layout patterns from which to choose: the grid, the free-form layout, and the boutique. Figure 5.4 illustrates these layout patterns. In the grid layout, displays are arranged in a rectangular fashion so that aisles are parallel to one another. It is a formal layout that controls traffic in the store as it uses the available space efficiently, creates a neatly organized environment, and facilitates shopping by standardiz-

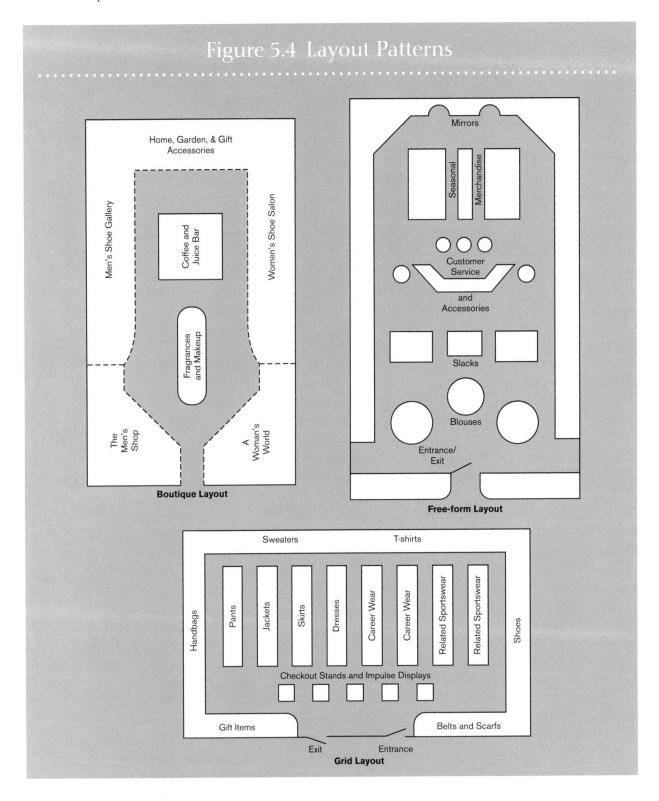

Figure 5.4 Layout Patterns

Boutique Layout

Home, Garden, & Gift Accessories

Men's Shoe Gallery

Coffee and Juice Bar

Fragrances and Makeup

Women's Shoe Salon

The Men's Shop

A Woman's World

Free-form Layout

Mirrors

Seasonal

Merchandise

Customer Service

and Accessories

Slacks

Blouses

Entrance/ Exit

Grid Layout

Sweaters

T-shirts

Handbags

Pants

Jackets

Skirts

Dresses

Career Wear

Career Wear

Related Sportswear

Related Sportswear

Shoes

Checkout Stands and Impulse Displays

Gift Items

Belts and Scarfs

Exit

Entrance

ing the location of items. Many discount stores in apparel and home furnishings use the grid layout because it is well suited to self-service operations.

In contrast, the free-form layout is informal as it utilizes displays of varying shapes and sizes. Its primary advantage is the image it creates. This image is one of a relaxed and friendly shopping atmosphere, which encourages customers to take their time, thereby spending more time in the store with the potential for making more purchases. Additionally, the free-form layout has been shown to increase the number of impulse purchases customers make. Related merchandise can easily be placed in a common area to encourage multiple sales. For example, a circular rack of girl's dresses and a shelf unit featuring Easter hats may be placed adjacent to the children's shoe department. The major disadvantage of the free-form layout is that it can create security problems if not properly planned and staffed. It may be difficult for a small staff of sales personnel to observe customers and watch for theft in a free-form layout due to visual obstacles. Another disadvantage is that is can appear to be disorganized and may be challenging to the consumer who wants to be directed to a specific merchandise department.

The boutique layout divides the store into a series of individual shopping areas, each with its own theme. It is much like building a series of specialty shops in a single store. The boutique layout is informal and can create a unique shopping environment for the customer. Additionally, it allows the retailer the freedom to create new departments based on seasonal merchandise trends. Henri Bendel and Bloomingdale's are two examples of retailers that use the boutique layout. The look and the configuration of these retail stores may dramatically change to feature the key looks and/or new and prevalent designers of the season. Specialty stores often use the boutique layout to project a distinctive image, one that tells the customer something new is always happening in the store.

Interior Display Elements Customers' eyes focus on displays, as they tell the customer the type of merchandise the business sells. Merchandise displays are often referred to as "silent sales associates," because they market the goods and influence sales. There are a number of guidelines upon which visual merchandisers base their decisions for interior displays. First, retailers can make it is easier for the customer to focus by creating a display, rather than by presenting simply a rack or shelf of merchandise. Open fixtures of merchandise can surround the focal display, creating an attractive and merchandise-specific selling area. Second, retailers can boost sales by displaying together items that complement each other. For example, men's ties may be displayed near dress shirts

Interesting Facts for Planning Interior Displays

- The average man is 68.6 inches tall, and the average woman is 63.6 inches tall.
- The average person's normal reach is 16 inches, and the extended reach is 24 inches.
- The average man's standing eye level is 62 inches from the floor, and the average woman's standing eye level is 57 inches from the floor.
- The average customer will turn to the right upon entering the store and will move around it counterclockwise.
- Using the traditional grid layout, only about one-fourth of a retailer's customers will go more than halfway into the store.
- The average consumer spends 8 seconds in front of a store window.

to encourage multiple sales. Third, retailers can recognize that spacious displays provide shoppers with an increased view of the merchandise, generate an expensive image, and reduce the likelihood of shoplifting. Finally, retailers must remember to separate the selling and nonselling spaces of a store. Prime selling space should not be wasted on nonselling functions, such as storage, office, or receiving operations.

Lighting   Effective lighting has two main purposes. First, it enhances the merchandise selection. Second, it allows employees to work at maximum efficiency. A jewelry store retailer, for example, has lighting needs specific to its repair department, as well as lighting needs associated with its display cases. Proper lighting is measured by what is ideal for the job to be done. New lighting systems offer greater flexibility, increased efficiency, and lower energy consumption than do older systems. Lighting is often an inexpensive investment, considering its impact on the overall appearance and operation of the business. As layout and the other interior characteristics generate an image for business, lighting, too, contributes to store image. A dimly lit business conveys an image of untrustworthiness. The effective combination of natural and artificial light can give a business an open and cheerful appearance. Lighting can have a critical influence on the attitude of the customer in a fitting room. Often, stores use a single overhead fluorescent light in the fitting room. Such lighting is unflattering to the consumer. Better choices include diffused and back lighting that create a halo effect as in a portrait photo session.

Fitting Rooms   For an apparel store, the fitting rooms play a significant role in the sale of merchandise. Fitting rooms are usually regarded as nonselling space and, subsequently, are often pushed to small, dark corners in the back of the store. Fitting rooms, however, are often the place where the customers actually make their buying decisions. The effective fitting room is spacious, well lit, clean, convenient, and pilfer-proof. There should be adequate places for hanging the merchandise. Mirrors should provide an accurate image and be accessible to the customer. Three-way mirrors that provide a back and front view may be intentionally positioned outside, but adjacent to, the fitting rooms. This placement encourages the customer to come out of the dressing room, wearing the garment in which he or she is interested. Once the customer exits the fitting room to take a look in the mirror, the salesperson has the opportunity to assist him or her with suggestions for alterations, accessories, or alternative merchandise. While the space should be comfortable, the retailer must minimize the opportunity for shoplifting in the fitting room. Furnishings, such as covered tables, cabinets, and skirted chairs, can become hiding places for the hangers of stolen merchandise. The location of a fitting room is also important. It should be situated away from exits and near the sales personnel to ensure privacy and service for the customer, without compromising store security.

Checkout Area   The checkout area, or cash-wrap desk, should be strategically located so that it is visible to the customer from all vantage points. Additionally, the checkout area can serve as a security point when it is placed near the entrance or exit. The area should be clearly signed, organized, and well lit. It should be outfitted with all the equipment and materials needed to smoothly process the sale. For example, the computer terminal, cash drawer, and telephone should be installed at the checkout area, in addition to materials such as tissue paper, bags, and credit card supplies.

CONCLUSION

The entrepreneur will have a number of decisions to make when deciding on a location for the business. Each decision affects the others. The entrepreneur may find an ideal regional location, and then later identify several states appropriate for the business. Once a city has been selected, the entrepreneur may learn that there are few appropriate building choices in the area. At this point, the option to build, buy, or lease becomes a key decision. Once a site is selected, the entrepreneur will determine an exterior and an interior layout. Among the components of the interior layout are the size of the sales area, display elements, and lighting. Finding the right location requires research, patience, and a multitude of decisions. It is one of the most significant factors related to the success of a new business.

WRITING THE PLAN

Develop the Location Section on the business plan by using the following topics from Chapter 14 as a guide:

SECTION	TOPIC
Location	Region, state, city
	Demographics and psychographics
	Competition
	Site
	Location factors
	Physical visibility
	Finances and location
	Facilities and layout

There is no separate section on the Business Mentor™ CD-ROM for Location. While not significant for every business in every industry, location is frequently a critical factor in the success of a fashion business. This information should be entered in the Product Section of the Business Plan on the CD-ROM, or appended to the CD-ROM template as a separate section.

KEY TERMS

boutique layout
business location
central business district
customer traffic patterns
entertailing
free-form layout
grid layout
Index of Retail Saturation

layout
National Retail Traffic Index (NRTI)
population density
power center
prime selling space
retail layout
space value
tracking plan

QUESTIONS

1. Select a major fashion retailer and list its target customer in terms of age, education, family size, income, and nationality. For some retailers, this information may be found on the company's Web site as part of the mission statement or company description.

2. If you were hired to design a building for an upscale designer boutique, how would you plan the exterior look? Defend your plan by explaining why you selected specific types of architecture, exterior design, signing, and windows.

3. Where can you locate regional data that will identify the top states in which to locate a fashion retail business? Include Internet and print resources in your response.

4. Are there any types of fashion businesses for which population density is not a critical factor? If so, what are these?

5. In which of the following business locations do you project growth over the next decade: the central business district, neighborhoods, shopping centers and malls, outlying areas, or homes? A decline in growth? Why?

6. Which components of Figure 5.1 are most important to you? Why?

7. An entrepreneur projects annual retail sales for her accessory boutique of $140 per square foot. The average initial markup on goods, at retail, is 50 percent. She wants to lease a 1200-square-foot store for $1200 per month. Should she pursue negotiating this lease or look elsewhere?

8. For a specific merchandise classification and a specific location, determine the index of retail saturation by reviewing U.S. Census Bureau data available in most libraries and on-line at www.census.gov.

9. What advantages exist in being able to sublet a facility?

10. Describe the types of information that would be found in a report of the National Retail Traffic Index.

11. List the advantages and disadvantages of each of the following alternatives for locating a business: building, buying an existing facility, or leasing.

SUGGESTED READINGS

Susan Abramson and Marci Stuchin, *Shops and Boutiques 2000: Designer Stores and Brand Imagery* (Godalming, England: PBC International Publishers, 2000)

Rasshied Din, *New Retail* (London, England: Conran Octopus, 2000)

William Green, *The Retail Store: Design and Construction* (New York, New York: Excel Inc, 2000)

The Institute of Store Planners and Visual Merchandising and Store Design, *Store and Retail Spaces 2* (London, England: Watson-Guptill Publishers, 2001)

CASE STUDY

When it comes to visual merchandising, fashion retailers are among the first to try a new look. "Fashion retailing has come a long way in the past 20 years and a lot of this is due to in-store design," says Hugh Phillips, senior lecturer in retailing at DeMontfort University. "The fashion retailers are way ahead. In fact, they are almost unique in supplying an in-store environment to suit their customer's needs." Ask fashion retailers about their visual merchandising and store planning strategies, and they immediately start talking about such issues as flooring—if it is soft, it slows customers down and encourages them to browse—or lighting, which can magically turn dead space into a bright spot in terms of sales volume. Design is no longer solely the concern of the fashion designer. In the highly competitive world of fashion retailing, retail design communicates brand identity, and brand identity stimulates revenues.

Those involved in the design of fashion stores stress that the key to making the purchase environment appealing to the consumer is to develop an integrated strategy that reflects the advertising that has brought customers to the store. Ultimately, this is a two-step process. First, a clear brand identity must be established. It is much like creating a personality for the retail operation. Next, this image, or personality, must be reflected in every aspect of the design from the window displays to signage. A typical shopper will wander in and out of shops, making comparatively a quick judgement about the retail brand. An assessment of both the product and its price is often made on the basis of the environment. While each customer will be attracted to a store he or she perceives as affordable, he or she will also impose a limit on the amount of time given to evaluate the product. In the competitive world of fashion retailing, this means ensuring that the in-store environment reflects that brand as clearly, and immediately, as possible. "The price of the product is not just what is on the ticket, but the effort and frustration of finding the right product. The fashion retailers are good at cutting down on the effort and frustration and then using the design to draw the customers to pursue further—thus increasing their time in-store," says Phillips.

French Connection is an example of a retailer that has successfully managed to make its brand stand out from the rest of the crowd through establishing a distinct position. Its personality is irreverent and bold, a certified rebel of retailing. French Connection employs a design consulting firm, Section d, to create its windows displays. The firm recently developed an installation for its windows entitled "Do you know enough to survive?" It featured a one-night stand kit, complete with birth control, underwear, soap, and spray cologne. The display not only stopped traffic, but the kit proved so popular that the retailer has started to sell it in-store.

A high level of competition and a high price for promotional efforts have led fashion stores to differentiate themselves by incorporating a lifestyle element into their designs. The store itself has become a three-dimensional advertising vehicle. Madison Avenue in Manhattan is home to several key players in lifestyle merchandising. Donna Karan's flagship store features a full glass facade that houses fresh flowers, a juice bar, vintage apparel, and, of course, Karan's lines of men's wear, women's wear, shoes, and accessories. It reflects the New York skyline, as well as the personality of the New York customer. Passersby can see the merchandise and activity within the store before they walk through the door. Across the street, Calvin Klein's store is a monument to understated elegance. Its clean lines and impeccable quality are in evidence through marble, priceless woods, and polished concrete. Furnishings are minimal and elegant. Up the street, Ralph Lauren's retail operation is situated in a magnificent mansion that is furnished like an English hunting lodge, an African plantation home, or a French Riviera summer maison—depending on the look of Lauren's latest apparel lines.

What is the catch in store design? In contrast to earlier decades, retailers of today have discovered that it is more difficult to guarantee that a substantial investment in a complete store redesign will pay off. Additionally, for retail operations that are not selling their own private brands of merchandise, there needs to be a balance between the identity of the retail store and those of the individual brands carried by the merchant. How does the fashion retailer introduce a common thread of unity between different brands on the floor, while expressing a store identity that remains after these brands have come and gone? Creating a shopping experience and communicating an identity through store design is the goal. There are a number of ways to get there. In the end, it comes down to the personality of the customer purchasing the products and putting these products together in an interesting environment in which knowledge of the target market is everything. H. Marsh, "Pop Stars of the Retail World: Fashion Retailers Lead in Point-of-Purchase Marketing," www.findarticles.com, January 7, 1998.

CASE STUDY QUESTIONS

1. Which characteristics of store design would you look for in a location that may allow you to develop a store brand identity with limited funds?
2. How have small retail operations successfully managed to create a clear image while carrying a variety of branded lines? Provide examples and descriptions of such retailers.
3. How does a retailer develop a lifestyle experience in the shopping environment? What factors combine to create this ambiance? Think about the five human senses of sight, smell, taste, touch, and hearing.

ENTERING THE WORLD OF THE ENTREPRENEUR

1. The location hunt is one of the toughest searches the entrepreneur will undertake. It significantly affects the potential for success of the business, and it is greatly influenced by the availability of funds for the start-up of the business. While you are in-

vestigating location options, you will have the opportunity to collect a great amount of data about the geographic location in terms of population demographics and customer psychographics. You will want to maintain a file of all of this information, as you can use it to construct parts of the business plan. Statistics on population growth, income, family sizes, and employment rates, for example, can be incorporated into the consumer section of the business plan.

2. Visit a number of existing store locations to gain a feel for size as it pertains to square footage. Most store owners and managers will share information about this with you. You may want to ask about the amount of square footage allocated to selling space, dressing rooms, receiving/warehousing, and offices.

3. If you are considering a mall location, contact mall management for pricing information. Ask about lease terms, leasehold improvements, promotional fee requirements, and commons fees that may be charged for maintenance of the general mall space. In some malls, the entrepreneur will be able to lease temporary space as a short-term arrangement, either in vacant store space or as a kiosk. This allows the entrepreneur to conduct a trial run in the mall, while providing mall management with filled space.

4. Contact commercial real estate agents for information about pricing and availability in shopping areas. You may want to ask about zoning restrictions if you are considering a nontraditional store location, such as a residential home. The agent may also be able to talk with you about average costs of utilities and terms of leases.

5. Talk with the local regional director of the chamber of commerce in the area you are considering. The chambers of commerce in most cities have Web sites that provide demographic data about the city. Often, the chamber of commerce has a department assigned to supporting small business growth. This office specializes in recruiting new businesses and working with prospective entrepreneurs interested in the geographic area. Some cities have a Regional Economic Development, Inc. (REDI) office that will provide demographic statistics on a specific area. Again, through these interviews with people at such places, you may have the opportunity to collect information about the potential consumer in this area that can be incorporated into the business plan.

6. One of the key steps to preparing for the location decision is estimating sales volume for the business, using variations in location size and cost. Using the resources detailed in the chapter, such as MOR by the National Retail Federation and RMA, determine average sales per square foot for your business type. By using this figure, you can estimate the amount of sales volume you will need to support the cost of each location alternative. As you develop your financial statements, you may find that you will be able to afford one of the more expensive locations. On the other hand, you may learn that you will need to trade down in terms of location preference or that you will need to reduce the size of the space you intended to lease. As long as you have the information organized and accessible, you will be able to make a location adjustment to the business plan more easily.

7. After you have previewed a number of location options, it is time to construct a comparison chart of all the factors that will influence your location choice. Some of the categories to compare are the specific address of the location, the amount of square footage available, the potential for allocation of the space to fit the business's needs (e.g., selling, receiving, and office space), the cost per square foot, the total cost of square footage, the amount of deposit required, the terms of the lease (e.g., length

of the lease, renewal terms, etc.), building improvement cost estimates to include technological needs, insurance estimates, utility costs, neighboring businesses, parking facilities, merchandise receiving access, required hours of operation, and others. Review the chapter to find additional categories that pertain to your particular type of business for this comparison. It is a lengthy and detailed process, but it is one that will significantly affect the profit potential of your business.

. . . .

ENTERPRISING ENTREPRENEUR

. . . .

MacKenzie-Childs Ltd. is an entrepreneurial company for the young at heart. In 1983, artists Victoria and Richard MacKenzie-Childs founded the innovative company inspired by "commitment to the qualities of home and the gumption of their little girl, Heather" (www.mackenzie-child.com). Today, with a staff of over 200 artisans and employees, the company creates whimsical pottery, floor cloths, furniture, paper products, tassels and trims, linens, cushions, glassware, enamelware, and even elegant trailer interiors. To fit with such a diverse and unique product line, the locations for the headquarters and U.S. retail operation of MacKenzie-Childs Ltd. were significant choices that needed to reflect the playful spirit of the company. MacKenzie-Childs Ltd. opened its American flagship store at the key location of 84 Madison Avenue in New York City. Every surface, from floor to ceiling, is covered with MacKenzie-Childs' colorful tiles, mosaics assembled from uncooked pasta, tapestry print wallpapers, and floral hooked rugs. The stairs resemble those in a tree house. A gigantic dollhouse of miniatures replicates the MacKenzie-Childs's family home, as does the actual merchandise in the store. The corporate headquarters is situated on a nineteenth-century estate. Here, in a hand hewn chestnut barn, one-of-a-kind pieces are sold to the public. The image of the company and these environments are a perfect match, much like Victoria and Richard MacKenzie-Childs.

Chapter 6

BECOMING AN E-TREPRENEUR

by Jana Hawley, Ph.D.,

Department of Textile and Apparel Management,

University of Missouri, Columbia, Missouri

INTRODUCTION

As long ago as 1967, Doody and Davidson envisioned consumers shopping electronically. Their vision incorporated a comprehensive, flexible shopping and distribution system for such products as groceries, drugs, and other common household items. Computer-type consoles would be linked electronically to a central distribution facility that, in turn, would automatically fill orders, process electronic funds transfers, and deliver goods the next day.[1] This 35-year-old foresight proved to be astonishingly exact with regard to today's e-commerce business models.

Electronic commerce was launched commercially in 1991 and has since grown to be a major force. By the end of 2000, the Online Computer Library Center (OCLC) office of research determined that 7 million unique sites exist on the Web, up 50 percent over the previous year's total of 4.7 million.[2] Some people have referred to this as a revolution affecting government, businesses, and consumers. Others argue that it is not a revolution, but simply a profound evolution of business with many foreseeable changes to come. Either way, the rapid acceptance of the Internet, advances in technology, escalating global competition, and rising consumer expectations will require company owners to substantially rethink how they must conduct business. As Sheth and Sisodia claim, "No longer will goods and services be offered primarily at the convenience of the seller. . . [rather] 'anytime, anywhere' purchasing as well as consumption will become commonplace."[3] Richards (2000) pointed out that "Successful retailers will not waste their energy trying to avoid the Internet—that's a battle they can't win. Rather, they will devote their energies to defining how it can make them more successful."[4]

HISTORY AND FUTURE PROJECTIONS

Not since the Industrial Revolution brought to the business world new inventions that improved effectiveness, production levels, and quality has there been such a remarkable change in the way business is conducted. The inventions made during the Industrial

Revolution introduced major advances in both lifestyle and business practices. But with the invention of computers, a new era was born that allowed business people around the globe to communicate electronically. We are now in the information age, and its impact is happening at tremendous speed with tremendous force.

Currently, the central component of the information age is the Internet. No other disruptive technology has been adopted as quickly—not telephones, not fax machines, not the cell phone. Whereas it took radio 38 years to get 50 million listeners and the cell phone 20 years, it has taken the Internet less than 5 years. The result has been a dramatic technological shift that has affected the world.

Early channels of electronically connected communication began in 1969 and were coined ARPANet (for Advanced Research Projects Agency Network). The primary purpose of ARPANet was to link computer systems for the U.S. Department of Defense, scientists, and academics in a global, electronic, and collaborative environment. ARPANet was conceived to allow multiple users to send and receive information at the same time over the same communication paths (phone lines). Eventually, the government decided to allow commercial access to these networks, and the Internet was born. Once businesses were allowed access to the Internet, capital investments enhanced by hardware and software applications ultimately improved the effectiveness of the Internet.

Even though the Internet is now over 30 years old, the World Wide Web (WWW) is a relatively new phenomenon. Early in the 1990s, Tim Berner-Lee of the European Laboratory of Particle Physics developed the foundation for the World Wide Web using several communication protocols. The WWW allows computer users to locate and view multimedia-based documents including graphs, text, audio, animation, and videos. Now the Internet and the World Wide Web are considered a mass medium for public use, allowing for information searches and business transactions including shopping. The impact of the Internet as an agent of social change can be seen in all aspects of our lives: buying medicine, taking care of finances, playing games, conducting family genealogy searches, searching for friends, getting directions, and ordering dinner, to name a few.

As Peterson, Balasubramanian, and Bronnenberg contend, "It is not possible to predict precisely the specific impacts of the Internet, especially given the velocity with which Internet-related changes are occurring and the increasingly assertive and unpredictable behavior of consumers."[5] Undoubtedly, even if the projections highlighted in the following box seem somewhat exaggerated and based on assumptions rather than reality, it is evident that all predictors agree: e-commerce will have a giant impact on global business. Even though Wall Street shows evidence of dot com struggles and failures, electronic commerce is here to stay and provides opportunity for entrepreneurs to reap some benefits. Though the numbers seem staggering, it must also be remembered that the total economy is huge. Even though e-commerce will play an important role, it will not take over the economy. Szydlik and Wood predict that in the near future, "E-commerce as a separate and distinct way of doing business will fade away. In its place would be business, just business, some of which would be conducted on-line."[6] This suggests that having an on-line presence will be the norm and perhaps a necessary way to conduct business in the not too distant future.

Today's Internet users, including customers, retailers, manufacturers, and suppliers are computer-savvy with increasing expectations for e-commerce. As the comfort level continues to increase, businesses will need to regularly update their Web presence to meet

E-Commerce Projections

Projections for e-commerce are mind-boggling. Consider the following

- In June 1999, International Data Corporation (IDC) predicted that Internet commerce in the United States would reach $56 billion, and $1 trillion world-wide in 2001. IDC now maintains that by 2003 trade volume on the Internet will reach $2.8 trillion.
- Forrester Research predicted in December 1999 that on-line commerce in the United States would reach $1.3 trillion by 2003, or more than 9 percent of total business sales. It also predicts that use and dependence on the Internet will accelerate.
- The Gartner Group estimated in January 2000 that by 2004, 7 percent of the globe's business-to-business commerce will take place on-line. That equals $7.3 trillion.
- Boston Consulting Group predicted that by the year 2003, one-fourth of all business-to-business purchasing in the United States will be done on-line, a staggering $2.8 trillion with an ongoing growth of 33 percent per year. Furthermore, 65 percent of all business-to-business e-commerce will come from six industrial sectors: retail, motor vehicles, shipping, industrial equipment, high technology, and government.
- Jupiter Communications, in 1999, projected that consumer-related commerce is doubling every year and should amount to about $41 billion in 2003.

S. Syzdlik, and L. Wood, *E-trepreneur!* (New York, New York: John Wiley & Sons, 2000)

customer demands. Following is a list of some of the expectations that today's e-consumers have:

- Saving time in a time-constrained world.
- Increasing the number of choices of products and services.
- Increasing information to assist in decision making.
- Price-competitiveness.
- Accessibility anytime, anywhere.
- Convenience.

WEB DEMOGRAPHICS

At first, many consumers were reluctant to give credit card information over the Web. The banking industry began to require secure encryption technology (SET) to protect their Net-using customers. Once consumers reached a comfort level with credit card security, exponential growth of shopping on-line began occurring. Consider this scenario. Scott loved his trip last year to Italy. One of the things he came to fully appreciate was the suit that he had custom-tailored at one of the family-owned tailor shops that specialized in suits made from Italian wool. When he returned to the United States, he decided to get a second suit. Because the boutique had a Web site and Scott's measurements on file, Scott was able to contact the company through the Internet, view graphics of fabric swatches, and order his second custom-tailored suit. Scott had never purchased anything on-line before. However, because he recognized and appreciated the fine craftsmanship of both the custom tailoring and the fine Italian wool, he trusted that he would be satisfied with his on-line purchase. After reading the pop-up boxes that ensured credit card security, Scott ordered his second suit. Within a month, Scott received his purchase. Even though the cost of shipping seemed high, Scott was able to add a second beautifully tailored suit to his wardrobe. Not only had Scott now made his first Internet purchase, it was a global experience at that!

Who else is shopping on-line? Originally it was the well-educated, white male with a high income and often with a career in the technology industry. But as consumer acceptance grows, payment security increases, and technology gets faster and cheaper, the profile is beginning to mirror the demographics of the population as a whole. Today grandmothers, children, professionals, teenagers, and all college students are on-line. The profile cuts across urban, suburban, and rural tracts, all races, both genders, a wide swath of income groups, and all education levels.

There are two basic types of Internet users: those who browse and those who buy. Internet browsers use the Internet to check stock prices, read the news, research information, send cash reserve, e-mail, and conduct other types of activities that do not involve buying anything. Internet buyers, on the other hand, may conduct browsing activities, but ultimately they purchase goods. Currently there are many more Internet browsers than Internet buyers. But as time passes, e-commerce sites will continue to improve by adding value to the e-commerce buying experience. Ultimately, the Internet browser will evolve into an Internet buyer. As Tomsen states, "The leap to net buyer occurs when the content, service, or product strikes the right note of relevance for the net user."[7] This note of relevance can be in the form of cost savings, product uniqueness, or customer service. Figure 6.1 illustrates that process.

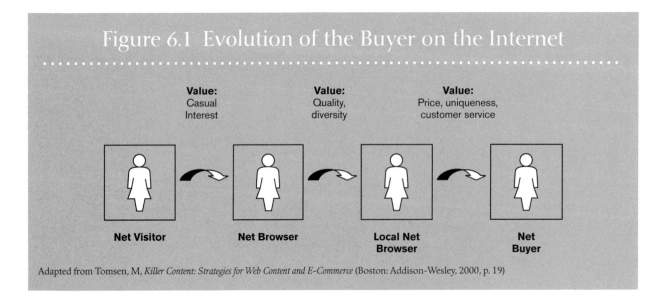

Figure 6.1 Evolution of the Buyer on the Internet

Value:
Casual
Interest

Value:
Quality,
diversity

Value:
Price, uniqueness,
customer service

Net Visitor   **Net Browser**   **Local Net Browser**   **Net Buyer**

Adapted from Tomsen, M, *Killer Content: Strategies for Web Content and E-Commerce* (Boston: Addison-Wesley, 2000, p. 19)

BENEFITS AND LIMITATIONS OF GOING ON-LINE

Many benefits exist for going on-line. Depending on what the consumer is looking for, the Internet may serve as a powerful tool for shopping. For example, the search engines on the Internet can be useful for finding unique items such as antiques, handmade crafts, mint-condition collectibles, or a particular book. Similarly, many consumers browse the Internet for product information including specifications, features, and prices. Once that information is gathered and studied, the information-empowered consumer heads to the retailer to make the purchase. This allows local retailers to benefit from the information on the Internet. Arguably, this becomes yet another reason for traditional retailers to establish a Web presence. Even if the customers never make a purchase on-line, they have gained product knowledge and will become destination shoppers who head to the mall or to the downtown store to buy products they found on the Internet.

Benefits of electronic commerce exist for businesses, suppliers, consumers, and society as a whole. (See Table 6.1.) Although many benefits do result from e-commerce, there are also limitations. Turban, Lee, King, and Chung have identified several limitations that e-trepreners must be made aware of.[8] (See Table 6.2.) As you can see, although the limitations may seem formidable, the benefits outweigh the limitations. That, coupled with the projected growth of Internet usage and e-commerce outlined earlier in this chapter, makes it apparent that today's business owners should consider a Web presence (becoming a click-and-mortar business) as a supplement to their traditional business. If a brick-and-mortar presence is not already established, perhaps the entrepreneur should consider establishing a Web-only business. Regardless, a strategic plan is necessary to go forward with business on the Web.

BUILDING A BUSINESS PLAN FOR E-COMMERCE

Entrepreneurship reigns on the Internet. Successful on-line retailers have exercised their entrepreneurial spirit to launch interesting new ways for consumers to shop on-line. But, like traditional retail stores, a plan must be in place that can guide the retailers through the process. Many how-to books exist to help e-trepreneurs learn about doing business on-line. It is advisable to study the various techniques, tips, and tricks available through these sources.

For those fashion business owners who already have a retail store, adding an on-line presence may be a logical next step. But it takes a lot of planning before a successful Web presence can be launched. Plans must also be in place for those interested in forgoing the bricks-and-mortar operation and establishing a click-only store. Setting up and running an e-commerce site takes technical, marketing, and advertising experience. Those e-trepreneurs who can offer their customer 24/7 accessibility that is user friendly, reliable, and functional will have a good chance for success. (See Figure 6.2.)

E-commerce includes the "transaction, pre-transaction, and post-transaction set of activities that are performed by buyers and sellers through the Internet (or an intranet), where there is a clear intent to buy or sell."[9] The ways in which e-commerce is incorporated into businesses include business-to-business (B2B), business-to-consumer (B2C), consumer-to-consumer (C2C), consumer-to-business (C2B), and government to business or public sector.

Table 6.1. Benefits of the Internet

Benefits of Business

Is flexible

Improves supply–chain management

Size and location of company is irrelevant

Reduces inventories

Increases availability of sourced products

Improves image

Reduces transportation costs

Provides a competitive edge

Makes it possible to react quickly to sales trends

Streamlines business processes

Contributes to shareholder value

Builds brand identity

Enables people to work from home

Provides people in remote areas access to shopping

Expands the marketplace

Reduces transportation costs

Suppliers

Become highly specialized

Reduce overhead and inventories

Reduce time between payments going out and payments coming in

Lower telecommunication costs

Create new business partners and strategic alliances

Benefits for Consumers

Provides 365/24/7 access

Expands choices

Shortens shopping time

Increases customer service

Allows for customization

Facilitates discounts/competition

Provides in–depth information

Lowers prices

Benefits for Society as a Whole

Eliminates paper

Provides people in remote areas with access to shopping

Enables people to work at home

Lowers pollution

Facilitates delivery of public services

Adapted from E. Turban et al., *Electronic Commerce: A Managerial Perspective* (Upper Saddle River, New Jersey: Prentice-Hall, 2000, p. 16–17)

Table 6.2. Limitations of Electronic Commerce

Technical Limitations

Lack of system security and reliability

Insufficient bandwidth

Evolution of software

Integration of new technologies with existing technology structures

Nontechnical Limitations

Cost and justification

Security and privacy

Lack of trust and user resistance

Unresolved legal issues

Lack of stability of e-commerce as a discipline

Lack of quality support services

Not yet enough sellers and buyers to create profit (has not reached critical mass)

Breakdown of human relationships

Accessibility

Adapted from E. Turban et al., *Electronic Commerce: A Managerial Perspective* (Upper Saddle River, New Jersey: Prentice-Hall, 2000, p. 16–17)

First, a distinction must be made between e-commerce and e-business. E-commerce includes the exchanges that occur among businesses, vendors, and customers. For example, textile companies interact with apparel manufacturers, fashion buyers interact with vendors, and customers interact with retailers. Once these relationships are established and transactions occur over the Internet, e-commerce becomes a reality.

E-business, on the other hand, involves all the transactions for e-commerce, plus in-house business elements, such as inventory control, product development, and operation management. Electronic links for in-house communication are usually made through intranet or extranet relationships or what are sometimes called interorganizational systems (IOS). Implementing an IOS facilitates inter and intraorganizational flow of information, communication, and collaboration.[10] As an example, when a fashion retailer sets up an IOS, he or she is able to facilitate in-house operations such as payroll, inventory control, and customer databases as well as external operations such as vendor information, purchase fulfillment status, and electronic transfer of funds.

As electronic data interchange options became available, some retailers opted to reduce back-stock inventory and have automatic replenishment for restocking. For example, Wal-Mart's just-in-time inventory system was a major innovation that helped make that company the price leader in the United States retail market.[11] The World Wide Web and the Internet then made it possible to extend those electronic links to customers as well. When electronic links to suppliers were coupled with electronic access by customers, the virtual retailer was born. This allowed business owners to sell everything while stocking nothing.

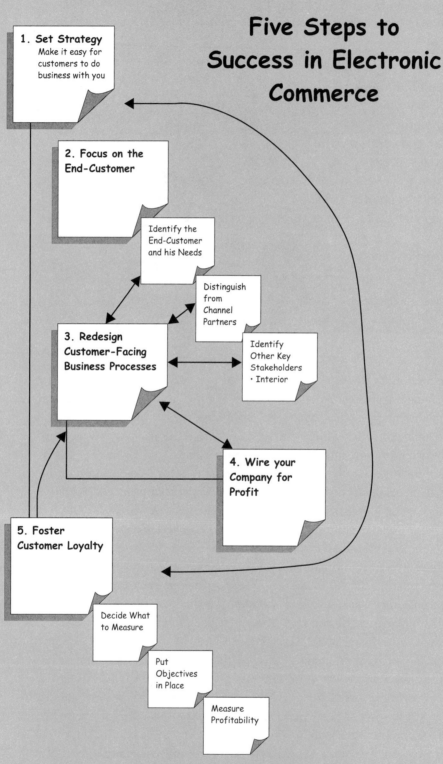

Figure 6.2 Five Steps to Success in Electronic Commerce

Seybold, P.B. *Customers.com: How to Create a Profitable Business Strategy for the Internet and Beyond* (New York, New York: Times Business, 2000, p. 7)

This elimination of inventory and of intermediaries through the use of digital networks is called disintermediation. When the intermediaries such as wholesalers, distributors, and retailers are eliminated from the supply chain, disintermediation occurs. But true virtual retailing is not disintermediation. It is reintermediation. Reintermediation occurs when new intermediaries use electronic networks to add value to the intermediation process and replace traditional intermediaries. Perhaps Amazon.com represents virtual retailing at its best. Amazon.com is dependent on the publisher-to-wholesaler supply chain which eliminates the need for Amazon to stock inventory. This is how Amazon is able to add value with lower costs while at the same time improving upon traditional retail bookstore services.

E-MODELS

Many models for conducting business on-line exist. Entrepreneurs interested in e-commerce should be aware of the options and even consider developing hybrids unique to their business. For example, a hybrid e-model could be an affiliate model coupled with an e-catalog model. When the Internet first began, the most common business model focused on importing existing business practices into the digital environment. Now new business models specifically designed for e-commerce are emerging.

Traditional retail establishments (brick-and-mortar) are defined by their storefronts and the inventory. This often translates to brand and store identity. The typical retailer opened shop either in the mall or on Main Street, stocked the racks with inventory, and sold to customers who came through the door. Although this is a proven business model, some people who have dreams of becoming fashion entrepreneurs find the traditional brick-and-mortar model cost prohibitive. In that case, it may be possible for fashion entrepreneurs to establish an on-line presence for significantly less capital outlay. The following e-models, then, may be of particular importance to the fashion e-trepreneur.

Storefront Model

A storefront model is a basic model for retailing on-line and is conceived very much like a brick-and-mortar store. These Web stores are independent on-line stores that are generally large-scale retail establishments. These sites use shopping cart technology and accept credit cards charges via a secure server. Shopping cart technology is software that allows the consumer the opportunity to pick and choose items to accumulate in their shopping basket before they proceed to payment. In addition to transaction processing and on-line payment, the storefront model also stores customer information and manages inventory data in a secure environment.

To start a storefront model Web presence, e-trepreneurs must organize an on-line catalog of merchandise, take orders through their Web sites, securely accept payments, and deliver the goods to the customer in a timely manner. In addition, they must market their Web site (discussed later in this chapter) in order to gather additional customers. These operations require a lot of independence because the site that is built "stands alone" from other businesses.

Many Web sites that have implemented the storefront model use shopping cart technology. This technology operates much like getting a shopping cart at the local supermarket. As shoppers peruse the Web site, they select items and place them into the virtual shopping cart. As the shopping excursion comes to an end, the customer proceeds to the virtual checkout counter to pay for the items. The latest shopping cart technology allows customers the option of removing items if they decide not to purchase them, just as if they were hanging clothes back on the rack at the store. On-line shopping carts also total the purchase and add shipping and handling costs. Some companies that use shopping cart technology include Amazon.com, Sephora.com, and JCPenney.com.

E-Catalog Model

Brick-and-mortar operations often enhance their businesses with catalogs that feature select merchandise. The problem with paper-based catalogs is that they require that large inventory be kept to meet orders. Interestingly, some of today's top e-retailing sites include companies that started as print catalog companies. Powers such as L. L. Bean, Lands' End, and Eddie Bauer are generating consistently high levels of traffic on the Web. Part of the Web success of catalog companies can be attributed to a customer base that is already accustomed to buying without touching. Brand recognition and trust play an important role, as does a distribution system in place for mail delivery of goods. For small business owners who are already in the catalog business or wish to start one, there is Catalogcity.com. This is a site containing more than 17,000 catalogs that can be requested; more than 2,400 of these catalogs have an arrangement with Catalog City to put a digital version on-line. Shoppers can use the Catalogcity.com shopping cart to buy from any of the 2,400 on-line catalogs. This provides a significant opportunity for e-trepreneurs. (See Figure 6.3.)

Portal Model

When most people hear the word "portal," they think of search engines. In reality, a portal aggregates information on a broad range of topics. In the e-commerce arena, the portal model links on-line merchants, on-line shopping malls, and auction sites to provide several advantages to both the shopper and the e-trepreneur. These portals assist users in collecting information and browsing independent storefronts. An example of a Web portal model is uniquelyme.com, which is featured in the case study at the end of this chapter.

Distributed Storefront Model

Distributed storefronts are based on the principle of connectiveness, where a Web site serves as an umbrella site for a wide range of products and companies that have similar attributes. In a bricks-and-mortar shopping mall, various storefronts feature different kinds of merchandise, and customers move from one store to another to get the things they want. Perhaps a prime example of this are the stores owned by the Limited Corporation, including Limited Express, The Limited, Lerner New York, New York and Company, Henri Bendel, Victoria's Secret, Structure, Bath and Body Works, and the White Barn Candle Company. For instance, fashion-savvy women can go to Limited Express to buy the latest fashions, Victoria's Secret to buy beautiful lingerie, Bath and Body Shop to get their favorite fragrances and skincare products, Structure to buy their favorite guy a new shirt, and White Barn Candle Company for candles to set a romantic mood. Could the same brick-and-mortar store provide all these products? Probably not, because in the physical world the logistics of dealing with multiple suppliers, competition for expensive floor space, and limited sales staff expertise create problems.

Figure 6.3 Home Page of www.catalogcity.com

Source: CatalogCity.com

In a distributed storefront, however, that same customer is linked directly from the fashion apparel site to the lingerie site to the candle shop site. Extend this model to the other stores—for example, imagine a kitchen wares Web site that sells cookbooks, pots and pans, travel books to the French wine country, cooking lessons, reservations at gourmet restaurants, and tickets to wine-tasting events and you begin to see the connectiveness in the shopping experience. On the Internet, these links can be electronic. If the on-line kitchen wares shop can provide a link to a bookstore's Web site, then the bookstore is no longer selling books from just one site. By making strategic links to several hundred (or thousand) Web sites, a distributed storefront model is created.

Affiliate Model

Companies need people to visit their sites. A good way to get people to the sites is through the affiliate model. Affiliate programs are among the fastest growing and most profitable revenue-sharing opportunities available. As e-commerce grows, so will affiliate program opportunities. The main participants in a revenue-sharing program are merchants and affiliates. A merchant is an on-line retailer who has products or services for sale. An affiliate is a Web site owner who places merchant promotions on his or her site and makes a commission when a sale is generated from that Web site. Benefits of affiliate programs include:

- New channels for making money.
- Sales generated through the many affiliations that are bringing customers to the merchants' sites—a win-win situation.
- Ease of maintaining and marketing the site.
- Complementary product/service offerings that increase value.

In an affiliate model, the Web site (the affiliate) agrees to promote goods being sold by an on-line merchant. The representation of these goods on the affiliate's Web site has a hypertext link to the merchant. A hyperlink will connect the shopper to a new page or sight on the Internet. If a visitor to the site clicks through (continues toward the purchase process) to the merchant and buys the product, the affiliate receives a commission and generates revenues from the other services offered on its Web site. On-line merchants benefit because buyers who are nearly committed to making a purchase are directed to their site, and the commission cost of affiliate-generated sales is typically less than sales generated from banner advertising. Banner ads often appear at the top or side of another Web page. (See Figure 6.4.) Shoppers benefit, too. When shoppers find a product that they are interested in, search time is minimized. The affiliate model becomes a plus-plus-plus arrangement made possible by the hyperlink connectivity of the World Wide Web.

Several companies serve as clearinghouses for affiliates. Some highly service-oriented sites include www.associate-it.com and www.refer-it.com. On these sites a fashion etrepreneur can identify fashion apparel and accessories companies that are willing to be merchants for the Web site. Not only do these sites list willing merchants, but they also provide business strategies, articles, and research for businesses that want to start an affiliate program Web site.

Amazon.com Associates Program is the foremost leader in the affiliate model. This program allows anyone with a Web site to open a bookstore and sell Amazon.com books, CD-ROMs, and videos to the world. Once a customer has clicked through, Amazon.com takes care of accepting the order, collecting the money, and shipping the product. All the affiliate (or associate) has to do is wait for the 5 to 15 percent commission check to arrive. Other merchants with affiliate programs include avon.com, gap.com, totalwoman.com, and focusonstyle.com.

Auction Model

The on-line auction model is a proven success. Part of the success of on-line auctions comes from the excitement of bidding with the opportunity of getting what is perceived to be a real bargain. A popular example of an auction site, eBay, ranks among the top of

Figure 6.4 An Example of Banner Advertising

Source: Style.com

all B2C e-commerce sites. Founder Pierre Omidyar recognized that both buyers and sellers needed a platform where they could come together for transactions. Featuring unique items in more than 1,600 categories, eBay makes money by earning commission on each sale.

For the fashion e-trepreneur, the auction model can be used to sell end-of-season fashion goods. This way, the shop-tired goods can be moved off the floor, thereby saving floor space for new merchandise that can provide the opportunity for greater profit margins. Additionally, the auction site for end-of-season goods may be able to get a higher price than if the goods had remained on the sales floor competing with new-season merchandise. Some examples of auction model Web sites include eBay.com, Ubid.com, and Liquidprice.com.

On-line Shopping Malls Model

The on-line shopping mall model allows customers to "go shopping" much as they would if they had driven to their local mall. In the mall model, customers can shop at a variety of vendors for health and beauty suppliers, clothing, books, music, and a variety of other products. At the end of the shopping spree, the customer can use the mall's shopping cart technology and pay for the items in a single transaction. Often these on-line shopping malls offer the same stores that one would find at the local mall. (See Figure 6.5)

Participating in a mall can be a great way to promote and sell products to both businesses and consumers. This model can prove viable for the small business owner because the mall owner is responsible for creating and managing the mall site. Therefore, the construction

Figure 6.5 An Example of an On-line Shopping Mall

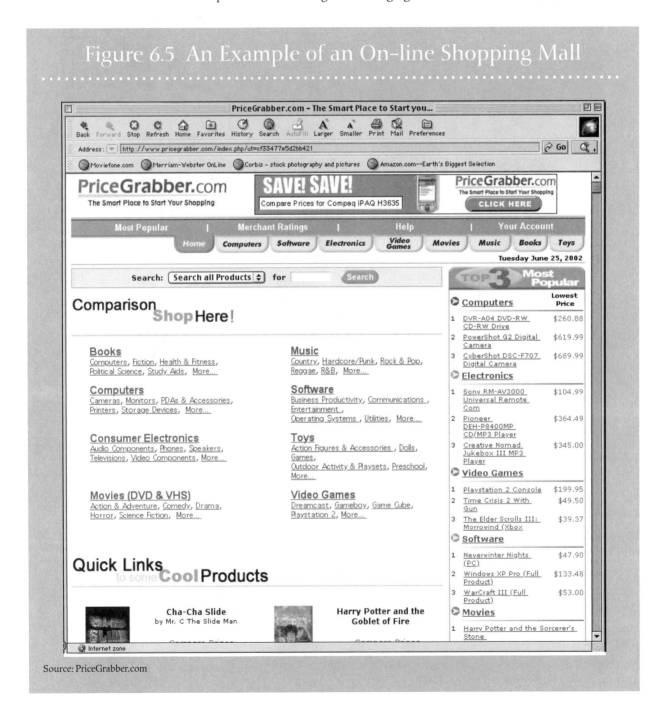

Source: PriceGrabber.com

costs of the mall and merchant solicitation costs are incurred by the mall owner. In addition, the mall owner is responsible for the promotion that will bring shoppers to the site. Finally, because the mall can attract a large number of visitors, critical mass can be achieved with positive results in Web site profits. These advantages reduce the start-up costs for small business owners and provide them with an opportunity to focus on their own merchandise offerings and customer relationships rather than needing to focus on Internet technology.

However, there are some disadvantages in choosing the on-line shopping mall model. There are often restrictions on how merchandise and services are presented. This limits flexibility, which is a tough constraint for the entrepreneur who often places high value on flexibility. In addition, while the mall might bring a lot of visitors to the business owner's Web site, the visitors might not translate to sales. And finally, surfers, prospects, and customers are forced to start shopping from the mall's home page, thus reducing direct access to the entrepreneur's Web site. Examples of on-line mall sites include utopion.com, excitestores.com, and pricegrabber.com.

Content-Attraction Model

Sites that offer customer service through informative content have a better chance of keeping shoppers at the site (sometimes called stickiness) or returning for more information at a later time. As more and more sites launch on the Internet, they start to look similar. Content can be a method for connecting to customers, offering them relevance and information.[12] One way of adding significant value to an on-line store is to add relevant content that piques the interest of on-line shoppers. For specialty stores, this can help to distinguish them from the competition. The shopper is able not only to shop for merchandise at that site, but also to read stories, get product reviews, find links to similar pages, and so on. An example of an on-line content store that has successfully implemented this model is www.rei.com. REI is a specialty store that sells quality outdoor gear. REI has been in business for six decades and uses traditional brick-and-mortar stores, both print and e-catalogs, and direct marketing through the Internet. The site sells outdoor apparel and sporting goods equipment, but REI offers an internal link called "Learn and Share" that offers sporting information including instructions, clinics in the geographic area, shopping assistance, contact information for equipment repair shops, and the like. This model offers added value to outdoor enthusiasts and is developing a loyal customer base. Although it can be argued that the content model adds value and can serve as a competitive advantage, this model also requires time, quality content writers, and excellent Web design. Thus it is important to plan well in order to launch such a site without costly mistakes. (See Figure 6.6)

Lowest Price Model

Today's customers have become accustomed to buying apparel at below retail prices. This is due in part to the strategies adopted by large fashion retailers who slash prices in order to compete. It is not surprising, then, to find consumers who are shopping on-line for the lowest price. What makes this model enticing for fashion entrepreneurs who are considering distribution through the Internet is that the use of the Internet can eliminate some of the traditional costs incurred by brick-and-mortar retailers. For example, an on-line retailer can eliminate mannequins, gift wrapping services, store atmosphere, labor costs for steaming clothes, and so on. Those savings can be passed on to the on-line customer. Using the absolute lowest-price model may not be the wisest strategy, however, because

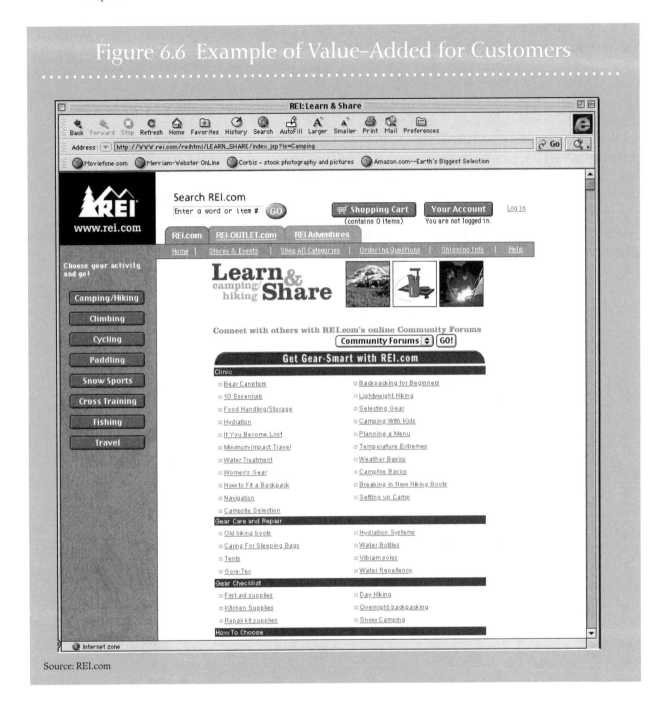

Figure 6.6 Example of Value-Added for Customers

Source: REI.com

customers who are attracted to a site based on price alone will continue to search for any site with the best prices, while possibly disregarding any other services or information offered on the site. Profits will be low, making it difficult to be successful with this setup.

Click-and-Mortar Model

"Click and mortar" is becoming a recognized term used to describe stores that have a traditional brick-and-mortar presence and an on-line presence as well. Typically, the entrepreneur recognizes the advantage of offering at least some services or products on-line as a supplement to the traditional storefront; this strategy complements the traditional store and suggests that on-line and traditional stores "are truly symbiotic."[13]

In this model the sum of the parts is greater than the whole. Some larger retailers have promoted this model by encouraging customers to buy on the Web and make necessary returns locally. This enhances customer relationships by saving customers the hassle of repacking the item and making a trip to the shipping company. Furthermore, if a customer wants to return the item to the store, there is the additional benefit of being able to increase sales by offering add-on items. For example, if a customer ordered a silk blouse on the Web and decides to return it because of poor fit, an astute salesperson could save the sale by helping the customer find a similar item that fits and by adding accessories or other apparel items to increase the sale.

Members-Only Model

When traditional brick-and-mortar companies like Sam's Club offer low prices, bulk packaging, and other services to members only, they are able to glean substantial income just from membership dues. Members-only models require customers to pay dues before they can gain access to the site. Once members, a user-ID and password allow customers to log in and take advantages of the Web site offerings. Consider a members-only store that has 100,000 people paying an annual membership fee of $25. This translates to an annual income of $2.5 million in membership fees alone. This helps to offset the low prices offered on products. Typically, the traditional small fashion retailer would not consider membership-only models, but on the Internet, the model becomes more attractive, particularly for stores that offer unique merchandise such as luxury items or those that offer impeccable customer service.

The goal of this model is to build a loyal customer base that recognizes the advantages of being a member and that continues to return to the Web site rather than going to the competition. It would be possible for an on-line store to offer two different prices: one for members and one for non-members. The member price must be significant enough to entice the buyer to become a member. Member prices must also be significantly different from the prices of competitors. Finding that magic price differential will take time, number crunching, and trial and error. Remember, adding value for members through content, product selection, or other advantages may be a solution to entice buyers to pay for membership. Examples of members-only models include http://www.virtual-encore.com and http://www.freebieclub.com.

These and many other e-models exist for e-commerce. In each case there are examples of successful on-line businesses. Yet, no single model is best. As time passes, hybrids will materialize, technology will evolve, and new models will continue to emerge. Deciding which model to implement will depend on how the e-trepreneur wants to get products into the hands of the customer and meet customer expectations.

CUSTOMER RELATIONSHIP MANAGEMENT

In the new economy (global, digital, and mobile), customers are in charge. For Internet e-trepreneurs to succeed, customers must be central to the plan. Then the plan must be skillfully executed to make sure that the customers have a positive on-line buying experience. When customers get frustrated with a site, they leave before they make that all-important final purchasing click. On the other hand, when the customer has a positive buying experience, the likelihood of repeat purchases increases.

As Seybold claims in her best-selling book, *Customers.com*, "There's a profound revolution afoot of electronic business technologies. Every organization, no matter how big, now has the wherewithal to interact directly with its end customers. Every company, no matter how decentralized, now has the ability to consolidate customer information and to gain a much better picture of who its customers are, what products and services they buy, and how they like to be served." [14]

In traditional business models, customers get information through print, audio, and visual means, all being one-way communication. With e-commerce, on the other hand, communication can be a dialogue, where the customer has an opportunity for significant input.[15] The very nature of the technology allows business owners to electronically implement customer-focused solutions.

Several important issues need to be highlighted here. Customers can interact with the Web site through e-mail, chat, bulletin boards, and selection and control of content choices. If Shelly, a time-constrained customer, wanted to learn more about this season's fashion trends to prepare herself for her fall fashion trip to the mall, she could log on to *Vogue* on-line, called style.com, and she could interact with the images from designer collections, stories about what the stars are wearing, trend reports from fashion gatekeepers, and advertisers. If she still has questions, she can contact style.com through e-mail or offer feedback. Now the fashion-savvy yet time-poor shopper can be armed with the latest trend information before she heads to the mall. The magnitude and scope of this interaction will have a revolutionary impact on how marketing strategies are planned.

It cannot be emphasized enough that the on-line business owner must provide a user-friendly experience for the customer. Sites must be carefully constructed to help the customer search easily, evaluate alernatives, make informed purchase decisions, and have postpurchase satisfaction so that they return for future purchases. As Brady et al., advise, business owners must encourage customers' involvement on their sites.[16] Customers must realize value in order to become loyal to the Web site. This can be implemented through creating an inviting,

Strategies for Customer Involvement

- Create an inviting, intuitive interface for content.
- Link the Web site to a logical site that will serve as a gateway to the site.
- Leverage brand equity.
- Integrate the Web address with traditional marketing communication media (e.g., letterhead, calling cards, print advertising).
- Update and refresh content regularly
- Sponsor and moderate interesting and stimulating chats with expert guests and/or interesting topics that match the target customer profile.
- Create direct links from the home page to bulletin boards where customers can voice their opinions.
- Align with other content providers or strategic partners by using hypertext links to one another's sites.
- Offer sophisticated search mechanisms that help customers pinpoint specific information.

Adapted from R. Brady et al., *Cybermarketing: Your Interactive Marketing Consultants* (Lincolnwood, Illinois: NTC Business Books, 1997, p. 39–40) intuitive Web site where customers want to stay, learn, have fun—and shop. The following list offers several suggestions for enhancing customer on-line involvement:

Perhaps the most important goal of an on-line business is to hone customer relationships. An Internet site can increase customer loyalty. However, to establish that loyalty, e-trepreneurs must make it easy for customers to visit their Web sites. It is important to understand who the target customer is. What is his or her profile? In other words, don't waste the customers' time, remember who they are, make it easy for them to use the site, delight them with services, and offer customized products and services to meet their needs and wants. The following list suggests ways to focus on the customer:

Focus on the Customer

- Target the right customers.
- Streamline the customer's on-line buying experience.
- Develop a relationship with the customer.
- Establish a total experience for the customer.
- Make shopping easy for the customer.
- Let customers help themselves.
- Deliver personalized service.
- Foster community.

S. Syzdlik and L. Wood, *E-trepreneur!* (New York, New York: John Wiley & Sons p. 248–9)

SECURITY AND PRIVACY

At first glance, security and privacy may not be customer relationship issues, but they are paramount. Although the Internet has become an increasingly secure place to shop, some customers will still have reservations about using their credit cards or providing personal information. To offer assurance to Web shoppers, two things must happen: (1) the Web retailer must implement all the appropriate mechanisms to ensure privacy, and (2) a privacy statement must be posted, which lets the customers know that appropriate security measures have been implemented. At some sites, it is difficult to find that security statement, which make customers uncertain.

To implement security on a Web site, a retailer must install and configure security systems such as firewalls, which are software applications that act as filters between a company's network and the Internet, and up-to-date security software. It is important to back up systems on a regular basis. Even if the Web site was built by the retailer, privacy and security issues are areas for which e-trepreneurs should seek expert assistance. Also, an expert should be hired to periodically run a security check to make sure there are no leaks.

Success of electronic commerce depends heavily on security and privacy. E-commerce necessitates new payment systems between remote buyers and sellers. Many retailers use Secure Socket Layers (SSL), which encrypts online communications to make Web transactions more secure, to provide security, and privacy. But a more secure protocol is Secure Electronic Transaction protocol (SET), which was jointly developed by Visa and MasterCard for Internet transactions and was designed to secure credit card transactions, for both consumers and merchants. Whereas SSL is built into the browser, SET requires that users be conformed to SET protocol with additional software technology. Consult an e-commerce professional to ensure proper security for a Web site.

Regardless of the type of business, credit card fraud is possible. The two main concerns are theft of information during transmission and credit card user authentication. Secure Electronic Transaction protocol offers the most secure protection when information is transferred digitally. But for credit card authentication, even a password cannot completely eliminate risk. It is predicted that consumers will eventually have an authenticating certificate stored in a smart card so that counterfeiters cannot abuse card information.

There are other ways that e-trepreneurs can complete transactions on their Web sites. These include electronic check systems, store-value or e-cards (e-cards work like a pre-paid phone card), electronic funds transfers, and electronic money, to name a few. E-trepreneurs should research which system will best serve their needs and then consult an expert. (For a complete discussion of the topic, see Chapter 8 of E. Turban et al., *Electronic Commerce: A Managerial Perspective,* England Cliffs, NJ, 2000.)[17]

PROMOTION AND MARKETING

When a site is developed and it is time to launch, promotion and marketing must be implemented in order to attract customers. Objectives for promotion and marketing of the site are the same as those for any other business model, namely, to attract customers and persuade them to buy. This can be accomplished in a variety of ways:

1. Build brand recognition.
2. Establish a domain name that represents the company.
3. Register with search engines from inside the Internet. Many prospective customers surf the Web using search engines to find what they are looking for.
4. Build strategic alliances with other businesses to establish links with each other's sites.
5. Use the Web address (URL) on all printed materials including catalogs, print advertisements, calling cards, brochures, etc. It is important to treat the Internet address with the same importance as the telephone number.
6. Use publicity and promotional efforts to reach target customers. Offer something of value to users who want to visit the Web site. Do not, resort to spamming (the use of mass e-mailing to people who have not expressed interest in receiving e-mails) as a way to promote the site.

Brand Recognition

Perhaps the first thing that needs to be addressed is the company domain name and its link to brand and brand equity. Customers need to be able to make a logical link between the business and the Web site. Branding is defined as "a name, logo or symbol that helps one identify a company's products or services."[18] It is important to have uniformity across all channels of distribution. In other words if the business offers print catalogs and an on-line version, there should be a sense of uniformity across both media. For many retailers, the Internet serves as a tool for further branding the company and its products.

The Domain Name

What's in a name? Perhaps everything. It is well established that humans prefer names over numbers when it comes to remembering. Thus, Internet systems established the domain naming convention called the Domain Naming System or DNS. This system administers names by giving different groups responsibility for subsets of the names. It is based on hierarchal levels where each level is called a domain. For instance, in the URL (uniform resource location) http://www.eddiebauer.com/ebh/custserv/eb_storelocator.asp, Eddie Bauer is the name of the host. But the hierarchical address also tells us that the customer service department is telling us where other stores are located. Finally, the .com portion of the address is considered the top-level domain and tells us that it is a commercial site. Originally there were six top-level domains. They were .gov for government sites, .org for nonprofit organizations, .edu for academe, .mil for the military, and .net for networking organizations like Internet service providers. In 1997, seven new domain names extensions were implemented. They include:

- arts—entities emphasizing cultural and entertainment activities.
- firm—businesses or firms.
- info—entities providing information services.
- nom—individual or personal designation.
- rec—entities emphasizing recreational or entertainment activities.
- store—businesses offering goods for purchase.
- web—entities emphasizing activities related to the World Wide Web.

As the need arises, new domain extensions will be added.

Domain names are registered with a pool of recognized companies that shares a database of registrants. The fees for establishing a domain name are market-based with each registering company being permitted to set its own fees in a competitive environment. When the Internet became truly international, domains corresponded to two-character ISO country codes (e.g., .ca for Canada, .us for United States, .it for Italy, and so on). When entities established a Web presence, they selected a domain name, which was issued on a first-come first served basis. This system worked fairly well until the .com domain became so valuable. As more and more companies try to establish their Web presence, they find that their desired domain names are already taken. For example, what if Wendy's Whirligigs established wendys.com as its domain name before Wendy's fast-food chain? So far, the courts have ruled that trademark names do not necessarily take precedence in the on-line world. As Conner-Sax and Krol point out, trademarks and names are established by industry and geography and not distiguished in the same way on the Internet.[19] Because so many companies are now establishing a Web presence, challenges over domain names are on the rise. Some companies are now using the extensions .net or .org, but this is not legitimate alternative because those top levels are intended for other purposes.

While the Domain Naming System may appear complicated, it is, in fact, one of the things that makes the Internet a comfortable environment. It is through domain names that the gigantic World Wide Web is segmented into manageable, perhaps even rational, sectors, making it easier for Internet users to remember important sites. Consumers gain confidence when they recognize that the Internet address is related to the item for which they are searching.

Search Engines

Once the domain name is established, a Web site should be submitted to a search engine. Search engines serve as the preferred and most often used method by internet users to find information. A search engine is software that searches the entire Internet for key words. What happens, however, is that when key words are submitted, thousands of hits can result. Internet users may visit the first ten or so sites, but may not go to the next hundred or thousand hits that the search engine finds.

In order to best position an on-line company to rise to the top when a customer does a search it is important to understand how search engines work. The term "search engine" is often used generically to describe both crawler-based search engines and human-powered directories. These two types of search engines gather their listings in radically different ways.

Crawler-based Search Engines

Crawler-based search engines, such as HotBot, create their listing automatically. They use crawlers or spiders to peruse all Web pages including page titles, contents, graphics, audio clips, animation, and other elements. After the pages have been crawled, people search through what they have found. With this technology, if a Web page is updated or changed in any way, the crawler or spider eventually finds these changes, which effects how the Web pages are listed on search results.

There are three major elements to crawler-based search engines. First, an electronic spider or crawler visits a Web page, reads it, and then follows links to other pages within the site. So if someone says that a site has been spidered or crawled, this is what they are talking about. The spider returns to the site on a regular basis, usually every month or two, to look for changes. The second part of the search engine then indexes everything that the spider has found. The index is like a giant catalog that contains every Web page that the spider found on that topic. Every time the spider revisits a site, it recognizes any changes that have been updated on the Web site. But it sometimes takes a while for the indexing to catch up with the spider, so edits and changes may not appear for a while (sometimes a month or two). Until Web sites are indexed, they will not be found on a search.

The third step of the search engine is software that sifts through the giant catalog of recorded and indexed Web pages to find matches to a search and ranks them in order of what it believes to be most relevant. Examples of crawler-based search engines include www.google.com and www.altavista.com.

Human-powered Directories

A human-powered directory, such as Yahoo, depends on humans for its search results. The Web site owner submits a short description to the directory, which summarizes the Web site. Additionally, companies hire editors who write descriptions of Web sites they review. When key words are put into a search, the search looks for matches only in the descriptions submitted, rather than in the entire Web site as in the crawler method. Changes to the Web sites have no effect on the search results. So when a Web site is improved to make it more interesting, attractive, or useful, it will not affect search listing unless the directory is changed as well. The only exception is that a good site, with good content, might be more likely to get reviewed by editors than would a poor site.

Hybrid Search Engines

In the early days of the Web, site owners had the choice of either crawler-based or human-based search engines. Today, it is more common for both types of results to be presented. Companies will usually favor one over the other. For example, Yahoo favors human directories but also provides crawler-based results through its partner company, Google. If one tested these two sites, one would probably learn that the crawler-based engines have the basic parts as described above, but there are differences in how these parts are tuned. That is why the same search using different search engines produces different results. Some of the significant differences between the major crawler-based search engines are summarized at http://searchenginewatch.com/webmasters/features.

Understanding the differences in search engines and how they work will help the e-trepreneur. Savvy e-trepreneurs will pay attention to the content of their Web pages and the description of their Web sites that is submitted to the human-generated directory so that a search can assist customers in finding what is located on the Web site and ultimately contribute to a more profitable Web site. E-trepreneurs can have their Web sites automatically submitted to a search engine. This method takes little time, money, or expertise but there is no assurance that the site will appear at the top, middle, or end of the hits. To ensure better results, e-trepreneurs should write careful descriptions of their Web pages, research the various search engines to see how they function, and perhaps even pay some search engines to maximize their ranking.

Hyperlinks

Another way to get customers to come to the site is to build strategic partnerships that allow hyperlinks with and from another site. Hyperlinks link the net user to other Web pages, Web sites, or areas within the current site. Often this method uses topic-specific link pages and directories. While it might be inconceivable that competitors would form an alliance, it is not impossible. Many Internet companies have come to realize that these partnerships may prove to be more valuable than their sitting back and waiting for customers to surf the Web in hopes that they will end up at their site.

Print Web Address on All Communication Materials

Everything that comes from a company should have the Web site address printed on it. This includes e-mail messages, printed brochures and catalogs, calling cards, paid advertising, letterheads, and so on. This is a low-cost method of advertising the Web site, because all these materials are part of the day-to-day operations costs anyway. When customers see any marketing materials from the company, they can also see the Web address.

Publicity and Promotional Efforts

Promotions can be implemented to attract customers to a Web site, to increase brand loyalty through schemes or reward (frequent-user) programs, and ultimately influence purchases. One site, www.promotionalworld.com/tutorial/ooo.html, offers a tutorial on how to promote a Web site.

Use of Cookies Cookies allow e-commerce sites to collect and record visitor information and identify customers that best fit the target customer profile. This is achieved by automatically assigning an ID number to each customer. Then when the customer

browses for information, the browsing behavior is automatically recorded by the Web site software. This information can be used to enhance customer profiles, shoppers' preferences, and the like. Additionally, this information could allow the Web site owner to follow up with promotions directed to that shopper. Many consumers are not aware that cookies are being stored in their computers as they browse various sites. Therefore, privacy issues are at stake. Many e-trepreneurs have opted for self-registration rather than the use of cookies, because it reduces the privacy concerns over using cookies.

E-Mail Marketing   E-mail campaigns, in combination with other marketing strategies, can be used to improve customer service, target specific customers, translate various languages for the global consumer, and in combination with other marketing strategies. Campaigns that are implemented over e-mail systems can be an inexpensive and effective way of getting the word out about the Web site. However, one should avoid unsolicited mail to people who have not given permission or shown interest in the product of services offered. As noted earlier, this is spamming and is negatively perceived by most Internet users. Participating in spamming campaigns can result in a poor reputation. To avoid being accused of spamming, companies have implemented an opt-in strategy whereby messages are sent to people who have granted their permission to be sent messages.

Concerns on the Internet

When going on-line, people have many concerns. In order to provide a solution, e-trepreneurs must take these concerns into account:

- *Channel confict.* Disintermediation may happen.
- *Competition.* The competition is growing from local competition to worldwide competition.
- *Copyright.* Once information has been published on the Internet, it becomes easy to copy
- *Customer acceptance.* Many companies are afraid that their customers won't accept the new channel.
- *Legal issues.* There is no legal framework for the Internet that is binding on a worldwide basis.
- *Loyalty.* The Internet is less personal, so people are not bound to a certain vendor.
- *Pricing.* The new economy makes it easier to compare prices. Prices will drop, so quality and add-on services become more important.
- *Security.* Most companies are very concerned about security on the Internet.
- *Service.* A customer can compare the offerings of a certain company with those of another much more easily.
- *Viability.* Many companies are unsure about the viability of their digital business case.

Adapted from D. Amo, *The E-Business Revolution: Living and Working in an Interconnected World* (Upper Saddler River, New Jersey: Prentice-Hall, 2000, p. 23)

E-COMMERCE CHALLENGES AND CONCERNS

When the small fashion retailing entrpreneur thinks about establishing an on-line presence, many concerns must be considered. Traditional brick-and-mortar companies usually have their business strategies in place, understand their competition, and have established their vendor and customer relationships. To invest in new technologies, processes, and ideas can seem overwhelming to small business owners who already have little time (and perhaps money). But as noted above, a presence on the Internet may be a neccessary strategy to complement their existing business. Amor highlights the concerns that businesses have about establishing (or not establishing) an on-line presence, as shown in the preceding box.[20]

CONCLUSION

The Internet will continue to evolve. It has grown from a scientific network into an enabling platform for a new generation of business strategies. It has moved from an information exchange system to an interactive and viable form of commerce. In essence, it requires a paradigm shift in the ways in which entrepreneurs stategize, plan, develop, and implement their operations.

It is also affecting society in both positive and negative ways. Still in a transition phase, it is uncertain just how the Internet will affect social structures, but it is certain to do so. Internet technologies offer opportunities for the whole world. It will affect the ways in which people do their jobs, eliminating some jobs while creating many new ones. It will change the way people communicate with one another—some argue to the detriment of relationships. Others argue that the freedom of time and space will enhance relationships.

Regardless, the Internet and its evolving technologies are here to stay in some form or another. They are part of the real world and real business. A time will come shortly when it is realized that "the most important part of e-business is not the 'e', but the actual business" and the boundaries between the two will blur because they have been fully integrated with each other. As Pete Cooper said, "The hype surrounding e-commerce may have peaked and now fallen flat on its face, but e-commerce success stories are being created every day."[21]

WRITING THE PLAN

Developing a business plan for an e-tailing business, or a retail business with a Web presence, encompasses all aspects of the plan. Use the topics covered in Chapter 14 to address e-tailing issues. The topics should be approached from an e-trepreneur perspective.

KEY TERMS

affiliate

ARPANet

banner advertising

click through

connectiveness

cookies

crawler

disintermediation

domain

domain name

Domain Naming System (DNS)

extranet

hypertext link

Interorganizational Sytem (IOS)

intranet

merchant

privacy statement

reintermediation

Secure Electronic Transaction (SET)
   protocol

Secure Socket Layers (SSL)

shopping cart technology

spamming

spider

stickiness

uniform resource locator (URL)

QUESTIONS

1. Define ARPANet and its role in electronic commerce.
2. Explain the difference between the Internet and the World Wide Web.
3. What is the difference between e-commerce and e-business?
4. What is crawler technology?
5. Why is it important for a merchant to understand how search engines work?
6. List four communication media that e-trepreneurs can use to promote their e-commerce sites.
7. In a merchant/affiliate partnership, who is the merchant? Explain.
8. Why is it important for an electronic commerce company to arrange for SET technology?
9. List five different ways to ensure customer service.
10. What is spamming and how is it perceived by most e-commerce professionals?

REFERENCES

1. A. F. Doody and W. R. Davidson, "New Revolution in Retailing," *Harvard Business Review 45,* May-June, 1967, p. 4–16, 20, 188

2. http://www.oclc.org/press/20001016a.htm, August 14, 2001

3. J. N. Sheth and R. S. Sisodia, "Consumer Behavior in the Future." In Robert A. Peterson (Ed.), *Electronic Marketing and the Consumer* (Thousand Oaks, California: Sage, p. 17)

4. K. Richards, "The Art of Web: Rules of 'E-tail' Engagement," *Perspectives on Retailing*, Summer, 2000, p. 2

5. R. A. Peterson, S. Balasubramanian, and B. J. Bronnenberg, "Exploring the Implications of the Internet for Consumer Marketing," *Journal of the Academy of Marketing Science, 25*(4), 1997, p. 330

6. S. Szydlik and L. Wood, *E-trepreneur!* (New York, New York: John Wiley & Sons, 2000, p. 246)

7. M. Tomsen, *Killer Content: Strategies for Web Content and E-Commerce* (Boston, Massachusetts: Addison-Wesley, 2000, p. 19)

8. E. Turban, J. Lee, D. King, and H. M. Chung, *Electronic Commerce: A Managerial Perspective* (Upper Saddle River, New Jersey: Prentice-Hall, 2000)

9. C. Fellenstein and R. Wood, *E-commerce, Global E-business and E-societies* (Upper Saddle River, New Jersey: Prentice-Hall, 2000, p. 1)

10. Turban et al., *Electronic Commerce: A Managerial Perspective,* p. 280

11. E. Clemons and M. Row, "Sustaining IT Advantage: The Role of Strutural Differences," *MIS Quarterly,* September 1991, 15(3), pp. 275-292

12. M. Tomsen, *Killer Content: Strategies for Web Content and E-Commerce,* p. 39

13. B. Sawyer, D. Greely, and J. Cataudella, *Creating Stores on the Web,* 2nd ed. (Berkeley, California: Peachpit Press, 2000, p. 97)

14. P. B. Seybold, *Customers.com: How to Create a Profitable Business Strategy for the Internet and Beyond* (New York, New York: Times Books, 1998, p. 20)

15. R. Brady, E. Forrest, and R. Mizerski, *Cybermarketing: Your Interactive Marketing Consultant* (Lincolnwood, Illinois: NTC Business Books, 1997, p. 39)

16. Ibid.

17. E. Turban et al., *Electronic Commerce: A Managerial Perspective*

18. H. M. Deitel, P. J. Deitel, and K. Steinbuhler, *E-Business and E-Commerce for Managers* (Upper Saddle River, New Jersey: Prentice-Hall, 2000, p. 220)

19. C. Conner-Sax and E. Krol, *The Whole Internet: The Next Generation* (Sebastopol, California: O'Reilly, 1999, p. 49)

20. D. Amor, *E-Business (R)Evolution* (Upper Saddle River, New Jersey: Prentice-Hall, 2000, p. 23)

SUGGESTED READINGS

J. Cannon, *Make Your Website Work for You* (New York, New York, McGraw-Hill, 2000)

J. C. Levinson and C. Rubin, *Guerilla Marketing Online: The Entrepreneur's Guide to Earning Profits on the Internet*, 2nd ed. (Boston, Massachusetts, Houghton Mifflin Company, 1997)

P. Edwards, Linda Rorhbaugh, and S. Edwards, *Making Money in Cyberspace* (New York, New York: Penguin USA, 1998)

D. Greeley and J. Cautadella, *Creating Stores on the Web* (Berkeley, California: Peachpit Press, 1999)

B. Tiernan, *E-tailing* (Chicago, Illinois: Dearborn, 2000)

CASE STUDY

Uniquelyme.com was launched on August 1, 2000, when president and CEO Susan Barone, partnered with her sister Cheryl Anderson, executive vice president, decided to live out their life-long dream of owning a business together. Susan started in 1985 in the heart of the fashion industry, New York City. She worked as a sales manager for top fashion companies and, as a result, built a strong network with fashion leaders and experts. Cheryl Anderson's forte has been in business management of health-care facilities. She was always in management positions, an "operations person," and had to oversee more than 250 employees at a time. She has a masters degree in business and is a "planner." After lots of contemplation, planning, and soul-searching, the sisters decided to do something about their dream: start their own on-line business, marketing to the plus-sized woman. They had several goals:

1. To be able to work from home so that they could be with their young children. Barone also recognized that many women longed for that same opportunity, so she wanted to extend that opportunity to other women whom she now hires as free-lance writers and technologists. Barone refers to these talented women as her "creative contributors" and their personal stories can be found on the Web site.

2. To meet the demands of an important market segment, the plus-sized woman. Barone's connections from her years in the fashion industry in New York allowed her to present her plan to companies that manufacture plus sizes.

3. To establish a Web site that would be the most profitable and recognizable site for plus-sized clothing.

Uniquelyme.com started as a Web portal model Web site that connected plus-sized women to some of the best companies in the world that manufacture and market plus-sized clothing. The site goes beyond most Web portal models in that it is linked directly to the products rather than simply having a banner ad mentioning the site. With each purchase, Uniquelyme.com gets a commission, which has been tracked through Affiliates Solution Providers which handles the link tracking and the distribution of commission checks.

Barone has also worked in developing stategic partnerships with Emme, Catherine Schuler, *Working Woman* magazine, and *Mode* magazine to raise positive consciousness for the larger woman. She also uses uniquelyme.com to educate manufacturers on how to generate more exposure with the market.

Recently, Uniquelyme.com added an additional domain site—www.AlwaysForMe.com implements the e-commerce model where proven styles are inventoried in a warehouse and shipped directly from the warehouse to the customer. This has allowed Uniquelyme.com the ability to glean higher profits while at the same time responding more quickly to customer requests. The AlwaysForMe.com site has been instrumental in generating the revenues to keep Uniquelyme.com alive. In addition, the AlwaysForMe.com site is for "A Woman of Any Size" and carries sizes 4-26. This site will be used to launch new designers and develop private label merchandise with the UniquelyMe label. It is directly linked from the Uniquelyme.com site, so the traffic benefits the sales there.

Uniquelyme.com realized a surge in its business when *Working Woman* magazine recognized the site at its national conference in May 2001. Other awards Uniquelyme.com has received include third place in the lifestyle and travel category at the WALI Awards. This is an award given by the Long Island Web Developers Guild for the best Web sites on Long Island. In additon, the site was featured in *Mode* magazine's June 2001 issue and has been written about in the *L.A. Times* and the *Long Island Business News*. Combined, these awards and recognitions, plus Barone's and Anderson's tireless energy and vision, have allowed Uniquelyme to continue to grow into a viable powerhouse of merchandise, lifestyle, shopping, personal, and spiritual connections for the larger woman.

CASE STUDY QUESTIONS

1. Discuss ways in which Uniquelyme.com could receive additional publicity to promote its site and ultimately realize increased sales.
2. Visit www.uniquelyme.com and determine the e-model used to enhance lifestyle and other needs of the plus-sized woman.

ENTERING THE WORLD OF THE ENTREPRENEUR

1. Search the Internet for five different fashion-oriented sites and determine the various payment options that each company offers. Also note whether the site offers secure encryption technology.
2. What considerations are given to determining which e-commerce model would best serve the needs of the small fashion e-trepreneur?
3. Visit www.eluxury.com. Does this site achieve the image it wants through its offerings? What customer services are offered?
4. Visit www.google.com (a crawler technology) and www.yahoo.com (a human-powered directory) to do a search for designer handbags. How do the results differ between these two search engines?
5. Set up a spreadsheet containing a column for each of the following business models:
   a. Storefront model
   b. Auction model
   c. Distributed storefront model
   d. Affiliate model

In each column, list three e-businesses for each model. Visit the sites for each of the businesses and answer the following quesions:

   a. Do any of the companies implement more than one of the models?
   b. Are the companies Internet-only companies, or do they have catalog or brick-and-mortar operations as well?
   c. Do any of the sites have more than one revenue-generating stream? If so, what are they?
6. Find a traditional company located in your hometown area that also has a Web site. Talk to the entrepreneur and find out how the site is promoted.

7. Visit www.barbie.com and experiment with the Barbie™ customization services that are offered. How could this technology translate to customization for humans on a fashion-oriented Web site?
8. Visit www.globalset.com and take the animated tutorial for demonstating the use of an electronic wallet in an secure electronic transaction.
9. Visit www.keytronic.com and www.josoftware.com to learn about the latest technologies in fingerprint verification for security.
10. To keep up on the latest laws relating to the digital world, log on to www.findlaw.com or www.fcc.gov to find the latest court decisions or government regulations on the subject.

. . . .
ENTERPRISING ENTREPRENEUR
. . . .

"We guarantee every item purchased from us. No more, no less. Your satisfaction is the sole purpose of our transaction." Clinton C. Filson, 1897

When people were rushing to the Klondike during the gold rush in 1897, someone had to specialize in clothing and accessories to outfit these rugged adventurers. C. C. Filson, an enterprising man himself, opened C. C. Filson's Pioneer Alaska Clothing and Blanket Manufacturers, specializing in goods to outfit the new arrivals.

Distressing stories of the Yukon were widely reported. In 1897, the diary of Hume Nisbet reported, "Try to recall your sensations on the coldest night you have ever known; try to intensify the most bitter ice blast that has ever pierced your marrow by the thousand fold; even then you will not be able to realize spring in the Chilkoot Canyon, far less midwinter on the Klondike."

Recognizing the need for these gold rushers to keep warm, Filson started his own factory and designed clothes and blankets to fill this niche. To make sure that the goods were designed to fill their needs, Filson kept in close contact with his customers, improving his goods to meet their specific requirements. The gold rushers depended on Filson. In that era, clothing was a matter of survival.

The gold rush ended, but the need and desire for rugged outdoor clothing did not. For well over 100 years the Filson Company, a family-owned business, has been supplying rugged outdoor clothing to people with discriminating tastes. Its motto, "Might as well have the best," is an indicator of the company's focus on quality. Some have argued that their longevity stems from their top-quality fabrications such as the 100% virgin wool, extra-thick, extra-sturdy, extra warm Tin Cloth. Customers have begged them to "not change anything" which is evident from their hunting vest, which has been made from the same design, fabric, and quality construction methods since 1911. As founder C. C. Filson said in 1914, "our materials are the very best obtainable, for we know that the best is none too good and that quality is of vital importance."

Filson developed his business into a world-class operation based on honesty, quality, and durability. Today, the Filson reputation as the premier outfitters for outdoorpeople is unsurpassed. Still based on the time-tested philosophy of C. C. Filson himself, today's Filson Company strives to meet its customers needs. Filson is also known for applying its motto, "might as well have the best" to the customer service arena too.

While these are certainly strong indicators of the cliche "if it's not broken, don't fix it," a problem arose for the Filson Company. Its satisfied customers were now located all over the world. To meet this worldwide demand, the Filson Company launched www.Filson.com in 2000. A visit to the Web site will quickly reveal that time-honored customer service and product quality remain top priorities to this 100-year-old enterprising family business. A shopper at its site can be assured of in-stock items that are manufactured in Seattle where the home office and flagship store are located. This "made in the USA" approach allows Filson to quickly respond to product shortages, but it also allows the company to make custom sizing for tall customers and free hemming of pants. As a special service to its especially rugged outdoorpeople, leather binding can be added at the bottom of pants for a small fee. The site also offers a place for customers to share their stories, order a catalog, and order gift certificates. When it comes to offering outdoorpeople the best there is, Filson does it in a time-honored way—but now, with the help of the Internet, this 100-year-old company is just getting started.

Chapter 7

STRATEGY FOR PENETRATING THE MARKET

INTRODUCTION

Chapters 3 through 5 of this text focus on how the entrepreneur can obtain information to objectively analyze the industry and zero in on a potential target market. The industry analysis and market feasibility study emphasize obtaining information through research for the purpose of developing a comprehensive marketing strategy. By exploring the fashion industry's current trends, norms, and standards through market research, the entrepreneur will have the information needed to determine the avenues of advertising and promotion that help create a successful business. In this chapter, the entrepreneur will examine ways of penetrating the market. Entrepreneurs will look at methods of differentiating their business from those of competitors through price, product, placement, and promotion to the right people—the target market.

THE ROLE OF THE MARKETING STRATEGY

Determining a successful marketing strategy is key to leading the business to success. To be successful in business, the entrepreneur must formulate and implement a plan to reach customers and to motivate those customers to buy. The marketing plan helps to define and quantify user benefits; establishes the market size as well as potential customer interest; and assesses the competition. Entrepreneurs must tackle these issues convincingly because investors want to put their money into market-driven companies rather than technology-driven companies.[1] The marketing plan serves a number of purposes. First, it will help the entrepreneur determine how potential customers will become aware of the product or service. Second, it will help define the message the entrepreneur wishes to convey about the product, service, or company. Third, it will help identify the methods that will be used to deliver and reinforce that message, and how sales will be achieved. Finally, the marketing plan will address how the company will position itself relative to its competition.

MARKET VARIABLES: THE Ps OF MARKETING

The elements needed to determine the marketing strategy include the four Ps of marketing: product, place, price, and promotion. A fifth P of marketing can be added—the people or consumers who will be targeted as potential customers or product users. These market variables, or decision areas, when combined, must reinforce the image of the company's product to the potential customer. All five elements should complement one another in order to achieve the marketing objective.

Before examining the five Ps of marketing, let us first view a case in which the lack of thorough research into the necessary marketing mix led one company to bankruptcy. The company's owner, Marshall Smith, was on target in his identification of a consumer trend—educational merchandise; however, the placement, products, and price did not combine for success.

"A general store for the curious mind." That's what Marshall Smith called the first Learningsmith store, which he opened in a shopping mall in a Boston suburb. The store was founded in 1991. The 4,500 square-foot store was organized thematically. A section devoted to aviation, for instance, stocked airplane models for children alongside books for adults. "If you wanted to learn French, there'd be dictionaries, phrase books, videos, CD-ROMs, children's games, Dr. Seuss in French, flash cards. We were selling knowledge rather than products as such," recalls Smith. The goal: promoting lifelong learning. Smith, who'd previously founded the Booksmith and Videosmith chains, oversaw the growth of Learningsmith to a dozen stores and, in 1994, sold a majority stake in it to the Boston venture-capital firm Halpern, Denny & Co.

The company continued to expand, peaking at 87 stores (all but one in shopping malls) in 40 states. According to industry sources, the chain's greatest strength—as a browser's delight—ultimately did it in. "They tried to do too many things at once. They had toys, books, little novelties, but they didn't really have enough of any one thing to make it a destination store," says Cliff Annicelli, managing editor of *Playthings* magazine, based in New York City. Rather than making a beeline to Learningsmith for a specific purchase, many mall goers wandered into its stores "to take a break from real shopping," Annicelli suggests.

The extensiveness of the stores' inventory had serious shortcomings. "They tried to cherry-pick and offer the best of the best," says John Lee, president and founder of developmental toy maker Learning Curve International, "but with a brand like our Thomas the Tank Engine wooden railway system, if you're a loyal customer and want to go back and pick up the secondary pieces to build your system, they wouldn't have them."

Four presidents in four years followed Smith and tried tinkering with the product mix. Competitors were offering broader and deeper toy selection, generally lower prices, and more convenient locations to serve their core customers. The competitors had another critical edge: less expensive leases. Rent at Learningsmith's mall locations came to 20 percent of sales, about twice the industry average, according to a source close to the company's finances.

On December 10, 1999, Learningsmith filed voluntary bankruptcy. Cause: unfocused product mix.[2]

Product

A product is anything offered to a market for attention, acquisition, use, or consumption. It can be defined as any item or service that satisfies the need of a consumer. Whether the fashion retail business is providing a tangible product or an intangible service, such as convenience or comfort, consumers buy based on the ability of that product or service to satisfy a need or provide a benefit. The product and product life cycle are examined in Chapter 2. In this chapter, the product is discussed as an integral component of the total marketing strategy. Successful fashion companies often use the product to build a marketing strategy and to penetrate the market. To stay competitive in the marketplace, entrepreneurs must be open to innovation and change in their current product lines. They must also be willing to explore bringing in new products. In Chapter 2, we discussed an article published in *Bobbin* by Jules Abend ("Jockey Colors Its World," February, 1999). Jockey's team analyzed the essence of the Jockey brand to modern-day consumers. Jockey's new fashion products and marketing approaches are aimed at attracting a younger audience while retaining the loyal and traditional customers. The company is looking for ways to increase sales through aggressive and effective marketing strategies driven by products. The company will do battle in a very competitive arena by selling, for the first time, a line of fully constructed bras.[3]

The product life cycle must be understood in order for the entrepreneur to determine if and when to introduce new products into the existing product line and to revise existing ones. The product life cycle for fashion goods can be short. The product life cycle of a fad item may last as little as 4 to 6 weeks. Fashion trends can last for a season or a decade. The trick for the entrepreneur is to anticipate when to get into a fashion and when to get out. The time to introduce a new product is during the early life cycle of the current product when sales are strong and profit margins are higher. To successfully launch a new product, the entrepreneur must be committed to the new product and be willing to adjust to changes in the environment. Adequate planning and knowledge of the market are important. The entrepreneur must be able to differentiate the new product from existing products, usually through promotional efforts.

Place

This is a culture of immediate gratification. Consumers want what they want when they want it. They are looking for products and services that are convenient to purchase when they are wanted or needed. In selecting the *channel of distribution*, the avenue selected for moving goods from producer to consumer, careful consideration should be given to using distributors that can provide good service at a reasonable price. The primary channel of distribution for the fashion retail industry moves from manufacturer to retailer to consumer. Some manufacturers, however, sell directly to the consumer through catalogs, Web sites, or factory outlets. An alternative, and less often used, channel of distribution in the fashion industry is the wholesaler. In this case, the manufacturer sells merchandise to a wholesale company, one that sells the goods to the retailer for subsequent resale to the consumer. Gerson, Inc., a jewelry company based in Olathe, Kansas, is an example of a successful wholesale operation. Figure 7.1 illustrates the position of the wholesale operation in the common channels of distribution.

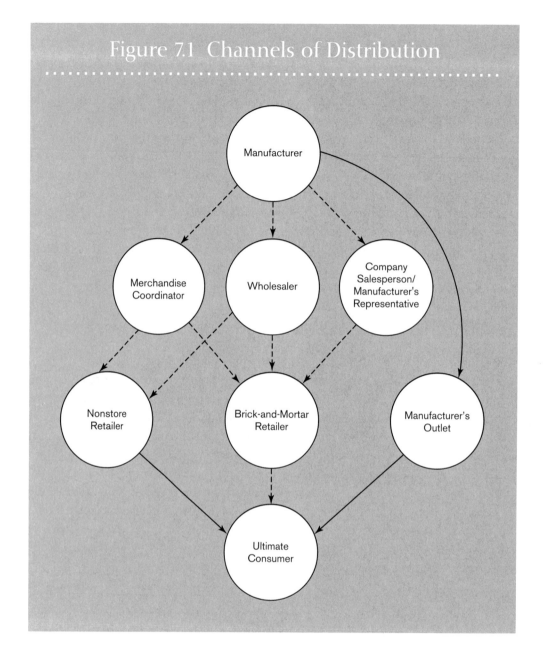

Figure 7.1 Channels of Distribution

Price

Pricing is a key factor for consumers when deciding whether or not to buy. To establish price, the entrepreneur should take into consideration the company's cost variables, markups, desired image, and the prices consumers will be willing to pay. Prestige specialty stores, such as Neiman Marcus and Saks Fifth Avenue, as well as designer boutiques, such as Chanel and Versace, can use their image and exclusivity to demand higher prices. A Gucci key chain may actually cost as much to manufacture as one available at Kmart, but the Gucci customer is willing to pay much more for the status name.

It is important to note that large retail companies can offer products at a lower price because of a larger sales volume and the resulting product discounts. For many smaller businesses, price may not be an effective basis for competing. Other considerations such as sponsoring special promotions, focusing on the quality of the product, or providing exceptional customer service may prove to be a more cost-effective way to compete. (Customer service is discussed later in this chapter.)

Setting the Price Pricing strategy is a difficult one for entrepreneurs, but it is crucial to the success of the business. The price of the product or service must take into account costs, customers, competition, and the market. Setting prices too high may result in a high profit margin, but may also result in low sales volume (which would lead to high markdowns), the inability to establish a customer base, and ultimately, the company's inability to survive. Setting prices too low may limit profits and lead the consumer to believe the product lacks quality. Price represents the value of the product for both seller and buyer. It plays a role in establishing an image of the product in terms of value, and it determines profit margin. The image projected by a store selling designer apparel will be completely different from the image projected by a discount store. To consumers, price may distinguish the type of stores in which they are shopping. Price sends a message to the consumer about the quality and value of the product.

Too often entrepreneurs will price their products on a guess or on what the competition is doing. An awareness of the price established by the competition is important, but other factors must be taken into consideration, such as the following:

- Product or service costs
- Market factors: supply and demand
- Sales volume
- Economic conditions
- Business location
- Seasonal fluctuations
- Psychological factors
- The company's competitive advantage
- Credit terms and purchase discounts
- Customer's price sensitivity
- Desired image[4]

In addition to cost considerations, the selling price should be consistent with the consumer's perception of the product, the marketing goals, and the image the business wants to project. The British retailer, Holland & Holland, on Rodeo Drive in Beverly Hill, sells a thorn-proof tweed jacket for $750, as well as a hand-engraved hunting rifle for $60,000. The location of the business and the perceived value based on the brand name create a market for a $750 jacket and a $60,000 rifle.

"Without an understanding of how customers perceive the value of your product or service, it's almost impossible to set a price they'll be willing—and able—to pay," says one business writer.[5] Ralph Lauren is a high-end fashion retailer whose products define quality. "Ralph Lauren's line of interior latex paints, whose price can exceed $30 a gallon, has tested the limits that consumers are willing to pay for coatings, even when marketed as home design products. Ralph Lauren may mean different things to different people, but it's a positive story, and a brand name that is exciting."[6] The higher price is an indicator to consumers that Ralph Lauren and Holland & Holland want to create an image of quality and that the product can stand the test of time. Would consumers question the quality of Ralph Lauren paint if it sold for $10 a gallon?

While conducting market research, Ralph Lauren's home improvement division made a determination about the target market—specifically the demographics and psychographics of that target market. Research was conducted to determine income levels, age, gender, where consumers buy, why they buy, and when they buy. This information played a significant role in setting the price of the paint line. Entrepreneurs must be aware of the consumer's perception of value. Most products carry an acceptable price range as opposed to one ideal price. Fashion retailers must determine the maximum price a consumer is willing to pay (price ceiling) and the minimum price that can be charged based on costs (price floor). As stated previously, fashion entrepreneurs must be aware of the pricing structure set by the competition, but this should not be the sole influence on pricing. Selecting a price based only on the prices charged by competition carrying similar or identical products assumes that the cost structures are the same. The entrepreneur must be aware of the costs involved in obtaining and carrying products. (See Chapter 12, Developing Operating and Control Systems, for more on this.) Good financial records will help ensure that the entrepreneur has a handle on costs and, therefore, can price merchandise to make profit.

In summary, the entrepreneur must set prices high enough to cover costs and earn a profit and low enough to establish and maintain a customer base and generate adequate sales volume. (Pricing is discussed from a merchandising perspective in Chapter 9.) The entrepreneur must be aware of changes in external factors, such as competition and changes in market conditions. An example of changes in external factors can be found in examining companies that produce products made from petroleum, such as hosiery manufacturers. When the price of petroleum rose, Hanes, Inc., found it necessary to increase the cost of its products. As a result, retailers carrying Hanes hosiery were forced to increase the retail prices. Finding alternative product lines resulted when retailers were faced with complaints from their customers.

In *Writing a Convincing Business Plan*, DeThomas and Fredenberger, provide four guidelines that can be used in determining price:

1. *Know the full costs.* Research indicated that new entrepreneurs rarely understand the full cost of operating their businesses. The most effective method for understanding cost is to perform a break-even analysis (break-even analysis is defined in Chapter 11) for the business as a whole and for individual products/services or product lines.

   A company's break-even point is the level of operations at which revenue from sales and total costs (expenses) are equal. There is neither a profit nor a loss. By performing this calculation, the entrepreneur can identify the minimum level of sales or activity required of the business to keep the business in operation. Break-even can be calculated in terms of either units or sales revenue. It can be calculated for a single product, a product line, or for the overall operations of the business. (Break-even analysis is discussed in further detail in Chapter 11.)

2. *Price, image, and goals are interrelated.* Pricing policy cannot be established in a vacuum. The selling price of the product/service should be consistent with the entrepreneur's marketing goals, the image he or she is attempting to project, and the perceptions and expectations of the target market.

3. *Price, product differentiation, and market power are inseparable.* The ability to set price independent of competition depends on the degree of differentiation the product or

service commands and the market power of the firm. The more difficult it is to differentiate the product or service from that of the competition, the more likely it is that the firm will have to accept the going market price. The same is true of market power. Larger firms and industry leaders have more flexibility in setting selling price than do smaller firms and industry followers.

4. *Price and nonprice perceptions are significant.* While selling price is an important influence on consumer purchases, it is not the main reason consumers buy. More important are the ways price and nonprice considerations are perceived by consumers. In the fashion industry, consumers will take into account price, quality, exclusivity, and service. These areas are closely interrelated in the minds of consumers when they determine which fashion merchandise they will buy.[7]

Establishing Pricing Policies   Various strategies may be used in establishing price. As today's consumers become more price conscious, fashion retail entrepreneurs have been forced to take a hard look at their pricing strategies. They have begun to focus on the value of their products and/or services. Advertising and promotion strategies have been changed to relate the value of the product or service to the consumer. Common among retailers are strategies such as markup, odd pricing, competitive pricing, price skimming, price lining, and below-market pricing.

■ MARKUP   Markup is the amount added to the cost of the product to establish the selling price. The amount of the markup may be determined by the type of merchandise sold, services provided by the retailer such as free alterations, how often the product sells, and the amount of profit the entrepreneur wants to make. The markup can be expressed in terms of dollars and cents, or as a percentage of cost or selling price. It is most commonly expressed as a percent of the retail price.

Dollar markup = Retail price − Cost of the merchandise

$$\text{Percentage (of retail price) markup} = \frac{\text{Dollar markup}}{\text{Retail price}}$$

$$\text{Percentage (of cost) markup} = \frac{\text{Dollar markup}}{\text{Cost of unit}}$$

For example, assume that the retailer is pricing a new sweater that costs $50. The selling price (retail price) is set at $100. The markup, then, is:

Dollar markup $100 − $50 = $50

$$\text{Percentage (of retail price) markup} \quad \frac{\$50}{\$100} = 0.50 = 50\%$$

There are a number of costs associated with moving product from manufacturer to consumer in addition to the wholesale cost of goods. Operating costs, which can be defined as the day to day expenses incurred in running a business such as rent, utilities, and telephone, and incidental costs, which can be defined as those costs which may occur sporadically such as shipping charges and ticketing expenses, need to be taken into account when establishing a pricing strategy. Having a handle on costs will enable the entrepreneur to establish the initial markup. The initial markup (the first markup added to the cost of merchandise to determine an original retail price) takes the following costs into consideration: the wholesale price of the merchandise; any reductions, such as customer discounts, employee discount, markdowns, and special sales; and the amount of reasonable profit the business wants to make. Initial markup is calculated as follows:

$$\text{Initial markup} = \frac{\text{Operating expenses + reductions + profits}}{\text{Net sales + reductions}}$$

For example, Great Line Retail, Inc., has decided to open an apparel shop in Achieve, U.S.A. It has forecasted sales of $425,000, expenses of $195,000, and $30,000 in reductions. Profits are expected to be $36,000. Using the above formula, the markup percentage is calculated as follows:

$$\frac{\$195,000 + \$30,000 + \$36,000}{\$425,000 + \$30,000} = \frac{\$261,000}{\$455,000} = 57.36\%$$

To cover costs and generate a profit, the initial markup on all merchandise would have to average 57.36 percent.

A fashion retail store carrying related products may sometimes use a technique of applying a standard markup on all its merchandise. Fashion retailers offering an array of merchandise often find it more effective to use a flexible markup policy. Using a flexible markup policy allows the entrepreneur to apply different levels of markup to varying merchandise classifications. For example, retailers carrying apparel lines frequently carry accessory lines to accompany the clothing. The initial markup on a line of belts may be different from that on a line of dresses.

■ ODD PRICING   Odd pricing is the technique of setting prices that end in odd numbers such as $399.95, as opposed to $400. It has been traditionally believed that this form of pricing leads consumers to assume that the price is a bargain. The psychology of this technique is not as effective as it was in the past. Consumers have become aware of this strategy and the psychology behind it.

■ COMPETITIVE PRICING   Competitive pricing is a strategy in which a retailer bases its prices on those of the competitors. It is important in this type of pricing to base figures on stores comparable in size and merchandise. Larger stores often buy in large volumes, enabling them to have a lower cost per unit price. Retail prices may be set either above or below the competition. To price below the competition often requires the business to increase its sales volume and reduce costs. As a result, inventory needs to turn over at a faster rate. Subsequently, it is important to closely monitor the inventory. The entrepreneur will want to be aware that pricing below the competition can bring about price wars. Competitors can cut prices too, leaving both businesses to find alternative ways to generate profits.

Pricing above the competition is possible when considerations other than price are important to the buyer. Retailers carrying exclusive merchandise or brand names that are not available in other nearby stores may be able to price above the competition. Escada, Burberry, and Armani are examples of retailers that are able to price above competition because of the exclusivity and prestige of their merchandise assortments. Boutiques offering exceptional customer service can sometimes price higher than other stores.

■ PRICE SKIMMING   Price skimming refers to pricing merchandise at the top of the relevant price range. It may be viewed as the technique that can be offered by retailers selling a product that is new to the market, or to an elite group of buyers not sensitive to price.

The product is marketed to be perceived as top quality and must project a prestigious image. The higher price enables high promotional costs to be recovered quickly. Price skimming does have its drawbacks. The competition may be quick to take advantage of the higher prices.

■ PRICE LINING   Price lining refers to a marketing strategy based on maintaining a consistent pricing philosophy for all products. The merchandise within each category will be similar in quality, cost, appearance, and other attributes. For example, a fashion retailer may buy various name brand sweaters and price all of them at $39.99 each, regardless of the wholesale cost. The retailer is using one price to effectively promote the product or products. One price allows the retailer to promote the merchandise with impact, simplifying the message with a single retail price.

■ BELOW-MARKET PRICING   To stay competitive when prices are below market, the entrepreneur has to move a larger amount of inventory than when prices are the same as the market. Sufficient sales volume is needed to offset lower profit margins. It may also mean eliminating services such as sales assistance and credit services. Retailers offering below-market prices should be aware that they are creating a discount image.

Promotion

Promotion involves the activities used to inform the potential consumer about the product. Advertising requires capital. Because start-up and early stage companies are usually working on a tight budget, entrepreneurs must be creative in the avenues they use to get the message out. Retailers use promotional efforts such as window displays, product labeling and packaging, and store signage as ways of promoting the product.

What's the message? Developing an Advertising Strategy   Victoria's Secret is not simply selling underwear. The company has created a brand with sex appeal. "He's done an extraordinary job branding Victoria's Secret," says retail consultant Wendy Liebmann of WSL Strategic Retail, N.Y. about Ed Razek, president and CMO for The Limited and Intimate Brands, Columbus, Ohio. "He's taken it from what was viewed as a sexy catalog business not far removed from Frederick's of Hollywood, and made it into a sexy lifestyle brand for men and women. They've turned what once was a fairly sleepy category into a fashion business."[8]

Advertising is paid, nonpersonal communication delivered through mass media. Businesses send messages in their promotional strategies and advertising campaigns. In addition to reaching and motivating targeted consumers, the advertising message will position the company relative to the competition. In other words, the company will emphasize particular attributes and/or focus on targeting how the consumer feels about herself or himself. Victoria's Secret sells self-image. Print and television advertisements using supermodels dressed in sexy lingerie imply that buying Victoria's Secret lingerie will make the consumer feel sexy and look attractive.

Avenues of Promotion—Selecting the Media   The entrepreneur must decide on the message to be conveyed and to whom that message will be sent. The first question the entrepreneur should ask when developing an advertisement is, "What do I (as a business) want or need to communicate?" The entrepreneur should also want to ask, "What is the objective of the advertising? What is it intended to accomplish and when?" The

answers to these questions will help ensure that the advertising objectives will be clear, specific, and targeted.

The primary goal of any advertising campaign is to increase sales. To determine the effectiveness of the campaign, the entrepreneur needs to decide not only what should be accomplished through advertising, but also should establish ways in which to measure the results. Retailers can measure the effectiveness of an advertising campaign by tracking increases in store traffic and/or sales volume, by experiencing an increase in orders placed through the Web site, or by tracking sales of the specific product promoted through the advertising campaign. The entrepreneur will need to determine the goal of the advertisement. Is the objective to get the consumer to make a buying decision in the near future? Is the goal to introduce a new product or service? The goal of the advertising campaign will influence the medium used to convey the message.

Media Options   To determine which medium to use to reach the consumer, the entrepreneur must know the target market he or she is trying to reach. This requires an understanding of the characteristics of the target market, including buying behavior, benefits the target market will receive from purchasing the goods or services, where to reach the target market, and knowing the advertising approach used by the competition.

Selecting the right medium to make advertising work consistently is no easy task. There is no magic formula that will guarantee success. It is important, therefore, to know and understand some of the advantages and disadvantages of the various forms of media. Not every medium works for every business. Not every medium will work for every advertisement that the entrepreneur wishes to place. The goal is to select the medium that has the highest likelihood of producing the best results for the business. Through advertisements, entrepreneurs must reach as many potential customers as possible on a consistent basis. The entrepreneur must also send the right message. Advertisements and the medium chosen to relay the message reflect the personality and image of the company.

Understanding the target market will help determine the unique selling proposition (USP), a key benefit of the product or service to the consumer, that sets it apart from its competition. In an article published by *Inc. Magazine*, Arthur Lubow describes Barry and Eliot Tatelman, owners of Jordan's Furniture in Boston, Massachusetts:

> [they're] selling an image of their stores and themselves as honest, reliable, and amusing. In a price-sensitive furniture industry, Jordans's Furniture maintains a single-price policy and never holds sales. Instead of running the standard newspaper ads for a "year-end-clearance!" with "an additional 10% off our lowest tagged price," Jordan's relies solely on tongue-in-cheek radio and TV commercials, which never mention an item's cost. Inventory items are never named in the Jordan's Furniture advertising. The Tatelmans have taken a unique approach to advertising and penetrating the furniture market. The Tatelmans say they spend only 1 percent to 2 percent of their gross revenues on advertising (far below the industry norm of 6 percent). In spite of this low advertising budget, Jordan's four stores grossed close to $250 million in 1999 with sales of almost $1,000 per square foot. The average furniture store sells between $150 and $200 per square foot. Jordan's Furniture continually saturates the airwaves, buying on average 150 television and 500 radio spots a week. Although a small amount is spent on advertising, the Tatelmans are well known in their market. Consumers like them and find their prices fair. They state that their consumers believe in the company and believe that it is one reason for their success.

The brothers' great conceptual breakthrough revolved around waterbeds. "The only people selling waterbeds were waterbed stores," Eliot recalls. "And we said, we'll take the bed and match it with the rest of the bedroom set. . . . we had something unique and people wanted it." Jordan's furniture was selling 25 beds a day, for about $600 per bed. In the ads, the Tatelmans emphasized the benefits of sleeping on one, not harping on what one would cost at Jordan's. "Everyone else was talking about price," Eliot says. "We came up with this 'underpricing'—one price. We've been doing it for 25 years. One price, no sales. We realized we were spending more time changing tags and more money paying for tags. And it wasn't legit. Your staff couldn't feel good about it, not if they were honest. How could it be $899 this week and $799 the next week? It didn't make sense."

The Tatelmans have turned furniture shopping into a source of entertainment. Lubow states that "when they walked me through their newest store, in Natick, customers were being waylaid at the entrance not, as you might expect, by a fast-talking salesman itching to close a deal but by a friendly young woman handing out strands of beads. The necklaces were Mardi Gras attire, in keeping with the décor of the central hall of the 130,000 square-foot store, which is a theme-park version of Bourbon Street.

The Tatelmans believe that if they can generate traffic in their stores, the sales will follow. "We realized that the only reason people go into a furniture store is if they need furniture," says Eliot Tatelman. "And yet we are in a fashion business that's constantly changing. If you don't show people the new styles, you won't get them motivated. We need another reason to get them into the store. And that is fun."[9]

■ TELEVISION   According to the Television Bureau of Advertising, Inc. 1999, cover, "TV remains the primary link to the American consumer. More than 52 percent of consumers say they are most likely to learn about products or brands they would like to buy from television commercials."[10] Television combines the use of sight, color, sound, and motion to attract attention. Small businesses often do not have enough promotional dollars to make advertising on national TV cost-effective. A 30-second commercial on national television can cost over $500,000. A 30-second advertisement during the Superbowl can cost over $2 million. However, advertising on local cable channels may be an effective means of reaching a customer base. Cable advertising time may be only 10 to 20 percent of the cost of regular broadcast time.

Following is a list of the potential benefits of television advertising:

- *Television has a sensual impact.* The visual nature of television is beneficial to fashion retailers. Television allows consumers to view or experience the business before setting foot through the door. Consumers can see the environment, as well as the product offered.
- *Broad and specific coverage.* Television can reach large groups of consumers in a short time period. It appeals to a mass audience. Almost 97 percent of homes in a given area have a television and keep it on a large portion of the day. In addition to broad coverage, cable television offers channels that broadcast specific topics to a select audience. With this option, businesses are able to reach a targeted group. For example, fashion retailers offering clothing and accessories that appeal to the teenage customer may choose to advertise on MTV.
- *Television is intrusive.* The viewer does not have to be actively involved to receive the message.
- *Targeted selection.* Television allows for targeted selection based on geography, time of day, programming, and networks.

- *Prestige.* Television is often considered the big league of advertising. It is assumed that a company is doing well if it has the ability to place an advertisement on television. It is important to note that the quality of the commercial plays a large role in how the audience perceives the company. (See Figure 7.2.)

Television advertising has disadvantages that should be assessed by the entrepreneur. A list of these follows:

- *Cost.* The cost of television advertising is primarily based on the number of viewers who watch the program and the time of day the program airs. One 30-second television commercial aired during prime time can cost 10 to 30 times more than one radio spot during drive time. Production fees are then added to the cost of airtime. Professional design firms offer assistance in creating commercials for television, but the expense can be prohibitive to an early-stage company.
- *Clutter.* The number of television advertisements increases daily. The position sequence in the lineup may affect the viewer's attention.
- *Zapping.* Viewers often channel surf during commercial breaks. This can affect the probability of a commercial being seen and remembered. In addition to zapping, viewers take breaks from television during commercials.

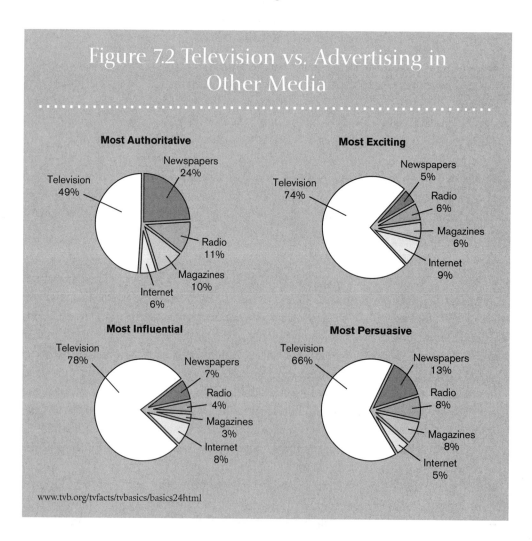

Figure 7.2 Television vs. Advertising in Other Media

www.tvb.org/tvfacts/tvbasics/basics24html

■ RADIO   Radio can be an inexpensive option to reach the target market. To the fashion retailer, radio works for institutional advertising, but it lacks the ability to show specific goods. The Radio Advertising Bureau reports that the average weekday time adults spend listening is 3 hours and 17 minutes; the average weekend amount of time is 5 hours and 30 minutes.[11] A list of benefits related to radio follows:

■ *Mobility.* Advertisements can be heard at work, at home, in cars, in stores, and in a multitude of other places.

■ *Flexibility.* Advertisements can be changed easily and updated often. Because they deal in seasonal merchandise, fashion retailers must be able to change a commercial quickly to promote apparel appropriate for current weather conditions. Furthermore, advertisements can be revised to promote sales.

■ *Target demographically.* Because radio formats are designed to appeal to a specific demographic group, entrepreneurs are able to advertise on a radio station that matches the targeted customer.

■ *Audio advantage.* Regardless of how something is said—whether serious, friendly, or humorous—radio sends a message. Fashion retailers can use tone of voice to persuade consumers to buy. Unlike television with its images, radio allows the listener to create an image that is personal and unique. The mind's image for one person will most likely be different from that of the next. It is important, therefore, to ensure that image and message align with the marketing plan.

■ *Cost-efficiency.* Radio advertisements can be more cost-efficient then promotional television. The cost of frequency, the number of times that a commercial will be run, is less expensive for radio than television. The more times a commercial is aired, the greater the chance of reaching the market.

Disadvantages do exist for radio advertising. Some of them include:

■ *No visuals.* This can be challenging to fashion retailers. Products can be difficult to describe. The listener would need to be familiar with the product in order for the advertisement to be effective, unless the entrepreneur is using radio to promote the business as an institution.

■ *No hard copy.* Radio commercials cannot be carried around for reference at a later date. Consumers may have difficulty remembering phone numbers and details regarding location. Since radio spots are often sold in 60-second, 30-second, and 20-second spots, it is difficult to incorporate many details.

■ NEWSPAPERS   Almost every home in the United States has a newspaper present. People often purchase newspapers solely to read the advertisements. Given the different sections in a newspaper such as news, sports, and lifestyle, advertisements can be placed in the section most likely to reach target customers. The advantages of newspaper advertisements are indicated below:

■ *Flexibility.* Like radio ads, newspaper advertisements can be changed on short notice. Often, newspapers do not require more than 24-hour notice to place or change an advertisement. Entrepreneurs have the ability to choose the days they want the advertisements to run, how often, and where in the paper they will be placed.

- *Geographic coverage.* Newspapers typically focus on a specific geographic area. For businesses targeting consumers in a certain geographic area, newspapers offer a key advantage in that the audience is regionally or locally concentrated.
- *Cost.* Newspaper advertisements are relatively low in cost. A large amount of information can be conveyed to consumers for less money than in TV or radio ads.

It is important to recognize the disadvantages of newspaper advertisements. A list follows:

- *Price-sensitive shoppers are an audience.* People who purchase newspapers to look over the ads tend to make buying decisions based on price, thus making it difficult to sell higher-priced items at full retail price.
- *Reproduction of photos.* Newspapers are printed on inexpensive paper, so good quality reproduction of color and images is difficult to achieve.
- *Appeal to immediate needs.* Consumers have a tendency to screen information. As a result, a newspaper advertisement may not drive consumers to make a purchase unless they are already looking for the product or service. Therefore, the cost of running the advertisement could be wasted.
- *Decline and shift in readership.* Between 1986 and 1996 newspapers lost nearly 5.5 million readers. Research also indicates that the newspaper is a good medium to reach adults over 40 years old. What is the significant shift in newspaper reader demographics? The decline is based primarily on the younger population turning to electronic media as the primary source of information. The people who spend the most amount of time reading the newspaper are those people who grew up with the newspaper as their primary source of information.[12] Increases in cost and reduced readership can make newspaper advertising less cost-effective for many businesses.
- *One of many ads.* Newspapers are filled with ads. Without the use of color or an exaggerated size, one ad can become lost in the crowd. Statistics show that the use of color advertisements can increase readership by as much as 80 percent over black-and-white ads.[13]

■ INTERNET ADVERTISING   The growth of the World Wide Web with its ability to reach the global market has made Internet advertising an appealing option for businesses. Demographics of Internet users are broad, attracting young, old, educated or not, and wealthy or not. The ability of the Internet to incorporate sound, color, visual appeal, and video offers Internet advertisers the same advantages as television, but at a lower cost.

Advertisements on the Web take different forms, such as the following:

1. *Full-page advertisements.* These are downloaded to the screen before users can access certain Web sites.
2. *Banner advertisements.* A banner is a component of the Web page that is usually an inch or less tall (rectangular in shape) and spans the width of the Web page. The banner contains a link to the advertiser's Web site.
3. *Push technology advertisements.* This technology sends information to users before they actually request it. Push technology ads appear on the screen of the user when information is downloaded from another site.
4. *Cookies.* A cookie is a file written to the hard disk when certain Web pages are accessed. Cookies are used to track locations that users visit while at the site so that pop-up advertisements can be used that would be of interest to the user.

The advantages of Internet advertising are many, and the number of users is growing. Following is a list of advantages to advertising on the Internet:

- *Global potential.* The Internet allows the business owner to market outside the business's immediate area. The business and its products can be marketed internationally.
- *Extensive ads.* Ads on the Internet may incorporate such features as sound, color, video, visuals, and maps. The amount and type of information that can be included in an Internet advertisement is endless.
- *Interactivity.* Web sites allow users to give feedback, place orders, or ask questions. Consumers can purchase goods immediately, provided the site is set up to take orders. Businesses can track consumer information to help them in future marketing endeavors.

Disadvantages do exist for Internet advertising. The negative aspects of advertising on the Internet include:

- *Labor.* To entice customers to continue to visit a Web site, the site must contain new information. Therefore, the entrepreneur must continually update the content of the site to encourage repeat visits.
- *Image.* The visual appeal and ease of use of an Internet site will affect the consumer's perception of the business. If it looks good and is simple to access, this perception will be positive. If not, the consumer may move on to another site.
- *Traffic.* Traffic in this context refers to the number of consumers visiting the Web site. With the vast number of sites available for any given merchandise classification or service, it is challenging to position the site to receive a significant number of visitors. For example, if a consumer enters the key words "fashion retail store," he or she will receive a listing of over 117,000 Web sites.

- MAGAZINES   Magazine advertising includes the following benefits:

- *Layout flexibility.* Advertisers have many options with the layout of magazine ads. Flexibility in magazine ads allows for creativity, which will grab the readers' attention. Color, fragrance samples, foldout photos, and moving pieces are some of the tactics used to get the attention of the reader.
- *Long life span.* People have a tendency to keep magazines and reread them from time to time. The advertisement, therefore, has the potential of being viewed several times. Additionally, magazines are often passed from one person to another, thereby increasing the number of readers.
- *Narrow audience focus.* Magazines exist that target the specific fashion customers. *Glamour, Elle, Mode,* and *In-Style* are a few of these. Selecting a magazine with reader demographics that match the demographics of the retailer's target market is a key to effective magazine advertising.
- *High-quality ads.* The use of slick or high-grade paper allows for high-quality images when photographs are reproduced.

Disadvantages of advertising in magazines are as follows:

- *Costs.* The same equipment and technology used to create high-quality advertisements also increases costs. In addition, as with newspapers, the higher the circulation, the higher the advertising rate. Advertisers may want to consider exploring advertisement options and prices in local magazines and publications. Costs are often much lower in local publications than in national magazines.

■ *Tight deadlines*. Magazines work on tight deadlines. The publisher may need to receive the final advertisement several weeks in advance of the issue's publication.

■ DIRECT MAIL   Direct mail reaches consumers through such materials as brochures, catalogs, postcards, letters, coupons, statement enclosures, and computer disks. Clothing rates as one of the most popular items purchased through mail order.[14] The U.S. Small Business Administration offers some rules to remember when planning a direct-mail strategy:

Direct Mail-Rules to Remember

■ *Define your audience.* Figure out whom you want to reach before you develop your direct-mail program. This allows you to specifically target your message to fit common needs. It is the best advertising medium for tailoring your appeal.

■ *Locate the right mailing list.* You can either build a "house list" by doing the research yourself and compiling the information on a computer; or you can purchase an outside list from a listhouse or mailing organization. The list is prepared and ready to go immediately. There are many ways to purchase lists. You can buy them demographically (by age, profession, habits, or business), or geographically (by location, state, and zip code). You can also buy a list with both qualities. More than likely, there is a mailing list company in your area that would be happy to consult with you on your needs. If not, there are a number of national mailing lists available. On the average, you should pay between 4 to 5 cents a name.

■ *Prepare materials for mailing.* For assembly, addressing, and mailing your project, you also have the choice of doing it yourself or locating a mailing service company to do it for you. As the numbers of your direct mail pieces increase, the more practical it is for you to enlist such an organization for assistance. Such organizations are very good at getting you the lowest postal rates.

■ *Encourage returns.* Consider using a self-addressed reply card or envelope to strengthen returns. Use a business reply postage number on the envelope, and you'll pay only for cards that are returned to you.

There can be advantages to utilizing direct mail. They include:

■ *A defined audience.* Direct mail allows the advertiser to target a specific audience. As noted above, mailing lists may be obtained from other businesses, or they may be developed by the business owner. For example, to announce the opening of Blue Gallery, located in Kansas City, Missouri, owners Kelly and David Kuhn sent postcards to over 7,000 art collectors and art enthusiasts throughout the country. They developed the list by contacting other local galleries and associations. The mailing brought over 1,000 visitors to the grand opening.

- *Known responses.* By comparing the number of responses to the number of pieces mailed, the effectiveness of the direct-mail advertisement can be measured. The inclusion of coded coupons or response cards help track exactly who responds and from where. Business owners can expect quick results from a successful direct-mail piece. Most sales take place within 3 to 4 days of receipt of the advertisement.
- *Attention of the reader.* The direct mailer is not competing with other advertisements. The recipient's attention will be focused on the one advertisement.

Direct mail is not entirely advantageous. The disadvantages of direct mail are as follows:

- *High cost.* A well-thought-out mailing list is necessary for direct mail to be cost-effective. The costs of production and handling, postage, design, and printing must be calculated at the earliest stages to determine whether costs will be proportionate to the size of the audience that will be reached.
- *Perception of junk mail.* Because of the vast amount of direct mail consumers receive, it is important to develop the right mailing list. Sending the wrong mail to the wrong customer will be costly and ineffective. Even if the piece is well designed and sent to the right consumer, it may end up in the trash as the consumer may perceive all direct mail as junk mail.[15] (See Figure 7.3.)

The Advertising Budget.   Advertising takes money; start-up businesses usually have limited advertising budgets. Careful consideration should be given to how much to

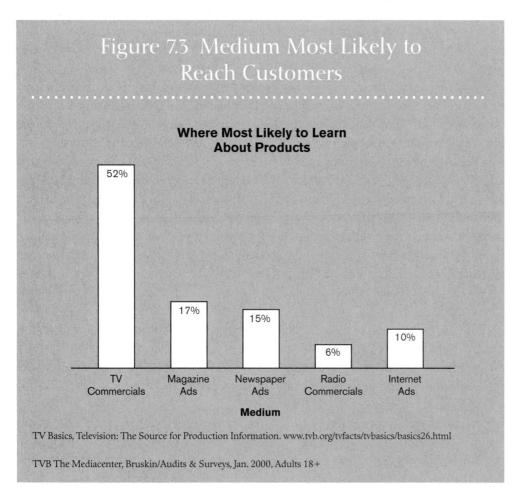

Figure 7.3 Medium Most Likely to Reach Customers

Where Most Likely to Learn About Products

TV Basics, Television: The Source for Production Information. www.tvb.org/tvfacts/tvbasics/basics26.html

TVB The Mediacenter, Bruskin/Audits & Surveys, Jan. 2000, Adults 18+

include in the advertising budget. Knowing how much money to allocate for advertising is not an easy task. Consumers have to know that the business exists before they can buy anything. To build sales, the business must be advertised. The entrepreneur should determine the type and amount of advertising necessary to get the message out. Various methods exist for determining the advertising budget. Not all methods work for all businesses. Two methods are primarily used to establish advertising budgets for fashion retail businesses. They include the percentage of sales (or profits) method and the objective and task method.

■ PERCENTAGE OF SALES OR PROFITS METHOD   In the percentage of sales method, costs are budgeted as a percentage of sales. Most business owners use this method to establish the advertising budget. This approach works as long as it meets the needs of the company. The exact percentage can be affected by competitive factors and the marketing strategy. Using the percentage of sales method avoids problems that can result from using profits as the base because sales tend to fluctuate less than profits.

Sales can be based on past sales, estimated future sales, or both. Determining the typical ratio of advertising expense to sales for a particular industry can be found through Census Bureau and Internal Revenue Service reports, Dun & Bradstreet, and the Robert Morris Associates Annual Statement Studies. Industry standards may also be found through the Accounting Corporation of America (www.bizmove.com/marketing/m2j1.htm). A figure explaining how to read the Annual Statement Studies is introduced in Chapter 11. Industry averages are just that—averages. Because each business and market is different, it may be necessary at times to increase advertising to bring more customers in the door. Also, a fashion retail business may carry seasonal merchandise. If the business primarily offers swimsuits, a larger amount of advertising money may be allocated just before the swimwear season hits.

■ OBJECTIVE AND TASK METHOD   The objective and task method links advertising expenditures to specific objectives. This method is more difficult to use, but is the most accurate. To establish the budget using this method, a coordinated marketing strategy with specific objectives based on a thorough survey of the markets and their potential must be established. Advertising expenditures are linked to specific objectives. Costs are calculated after the task method establishes what must be done in order to meet objectives. For example, the entrepreneur of a children's wear store wants to attract mothers of small children to the new brick-and-mortar store. The entrepreneur must determine which media channels will best reach this target market. The entrepreneur will want to estimate how much it will cost to run the number and types of advertisement for each media choice to generate the opening month's sales. Next, the media alternatives are compared in terms of cost and reach for the target market. The costs are totaled and calculated into the projected budget.

Once the budget has been established, the entrepreneur must be flexible to adjust to changes in the marketplace. A planning calendar will help ensure that deadlines are met and will help keep the advertising budget on track. The shorter the budget period, the more flexibility the entrepreneur will have to change tactics.

PEOPLE: EXCEPTIONAL CUSTOMER SERVICE

Promotion alone will not generate all a company's sales. Customer service is an important element for most successful retail operations. Poor customer service can put a fashion retail store out of business quickly. "In this age of information, where we communicate by fax, modem and e-mail, face-to-face interaction is all but obsolete. It is vital that we do not lose touch with our most valuable assets: our customers."[17] Studies show that "fewer than 10 percent of dissatisfied customers repurchase a product." More importantly, these individuals relate their dissatisfaction to others at a rate five times that of a satisfied customer.[18] Good customer service makes a difference in customer retention. Statistics indicate that by retaining 5 percent more customers, profits can be increased by 25 to 125 percent. Additionally, research indicates that it costs up to five times as much to acquire a new customer as it does to retain an existing one.

One of the ways small businesses can differentiate themselves from and compete with larger companies is by providing exceptional customer service. Effective customer service helps smaller businesses attract and maintain a loyal customer base. In "Customer Relationships" (www.sales.about.com), Gemmy Allen discusses the significance to business owners of recognizing that relationship selling, working closely with customers to build lasting relationships, is important in retaining lifelong customers. The lack of good customer service often leads to failure.[19]

How to Determine the Lifetime Value of a Customer

1. Compute your average price per sale (total sales revenue minus sales expenses, such as advertising and product or service fulfillment, divided by number of sales).
2. Determine how many times the average customer will purchase from you over a one-year period.
3. Calculate the amount you make from that customer in one year.
4. Multiply that one-year amount times the number of years that the customer is likely to continue to purchase.

Example: Lifetime Value of a Customer for the Fashion Retailer

Average spending (from sales data) = $65.00

Average number of orders (from survey research or database system) = 2 times per month

Average monthly revenue = $130 ($65 × 2)

Average yearly revenue = $1,560 ($65 × 2 × 12)

Residency (from Bureau of Census on residency) = 3 to 5 years

The lifetime value of the customer (5 years) = $7,800

Adapted from Gemmy Allen. "Customer Relationships," www.about.com
http://sales.about.com/careers/sales/library/weekly/aa112000a.htm

Nordstrom is committed to exceptional customer service. It enhanced its Web site to include a live chat room, which allows customers to chat on-line in real time with personal shoppers. The representatives are available 24 hours per day, 7 days per week during the holiday season in order to deliver an always-open on-line store. Representatives are available to help with on-line browsing. In addition, Nordstrom.com has implemented a hassle-free return policy: a Tyvek postage-paid envelope included with each order to allow customers to return merchandise to any Nordstrom store. It has improved on-line merchandising and fulfillment initiatives designed to answer the needs of the customer. The goal was to create hassle-free shopping during the holiday season.[20]

Successful retailers recognize the importance of providing customer service beyond customer expectations. As today's culture becomes less personal, a focus on individualized attention by the business can set it apart from the competition. Personalized attention includes calling the customer by name or providing a friendly smile. Customers sense when salespeople truly want to help them—or not. A company can improve customer satisfaction by paying attention to the following:

- *Give a good first impression.* Individuals decide within 4 minutes of meeting someone for the first time whether they want to continue the relationship. More importantly, this decision usually lasts a lifetime. If customer interaction is poor, the customer will not forget it.[21]
- *Listen to the customer.* Businesses use a variety of techniques, such as customer survey, focus groups, comment cards, and one-on-one conversations, to find out what the customer wants.
- *Hire a good sales force.* In a highly competitive market, fashion retail businesses rely on a sales team that is friendly, courteous, and customer-oriented.
- *Make service a core value.* Employees must know what is expected of them in situatuions related to customer service. Leonard Berry of Texas A&M University states, "By building the ethic of excellent service into the [organization's] core values, even without the rule book, your employees will know what to do." Management is responsible for embedding customer service as a core value.[22]
- *Empower employees to offer great customer service.* Has a customer ever walked into a retail operation to exchange an item only to find that the salesperson has to ask management if she or he has the authority to exchange the item? The employee is the point of contact between the retailer and the customer. Customers will be more likely to leave satisfied and return to purchase more merchandise if the salesperson can offer superior customer service.
- *Provide a customer training program for employees.* Often, employees do not arrive on the job knowing how to handle customers. Many companies allocate well-spent time and money training employees to provide good customer service. Entrepreneurs must make it a point to work on attracting, training, and retaining a good sales force that will provide quality customer service. When asked why they decided to buy from a particular salesperson or company, customers gave the following reasons: the reputation of the company, the level of service and support that the company offers, the reliability of the company and the salesperson, the responsiveness of the organization to complaints and requests, and the quality of the individual salesperson with whom they have been dealing. Price ranked seventh or eighth, if it came up at all in surveys.[23]

CONCLUSION

Developing a marketing strategy, as well as constructing and implementing a marketing plan, is key to the successful penetration of the market. Analyzing the marketing mix includes an examination of the interrelationship of product, price, placement, and promotion in a cohesive marketing plan. Setting the price of the product or service can help define and differentiate the marketing strategy and play a crucial role in the success of the business. Regarding promotion, several media options exist for getting the message to the target market about the product or service. It is important to recognize that not all forms of media work for all businesses. Determining the target market, selecting the right medium, and identifying promotional goals will help reach and penetrate the market. Effective customer service is a significant part of the marketing plan. Poor customer service will drive away customers. Good customer service will keep them coming back.

WRITING THE PLAN

Continue developing the marketing plan section of the business plan by using the following topics from Chapter 14 as a guide.

SECTION	TOPIC
Marketing	Pricing profile
Plan	Market penetration: Direct sales force
	Market penetration: Direct mail/telemarketing
	Advertising and promotion
	Guarantees
	Future markets

Business Mentor™ CD-ROM—Business Plan—Marketing Plan

KEY TERMS

advertising
below-market pricing
competitive pricing
flexible markup policy
four PS of marketing
incidental costs
initial markup
markup
objective and task method
odd pricing

operating costs
percentage of sales (or profits) method
price ceiling
price floor
price lining
price skimming
product
promotion
relationship selling
unique selling proposition (USP)

QUESTIONS

1. Define and discuss the five Ps of marketing. Why are they important to the company's marketing strategy?

2. Name the facts mentioned in setting the price of a product or service.
3. What does the price mean to a consumer?
4. What effect does pricing have on the image the company wants to project?
5. What are the four guidelines used in determining price? Discuss their impact on pricing strategy.
6. Discuss the implications of pricing a product too high or too low.
7. Give examples of the five pricing policies used in this text.
8. Define the difference between advertising and promotion.
9. Which factor(s) determine which advertising medium to use?
10. Discuss both advantages and disadvantages for the various advertising media.
11. How might customer service relate to the overall success of the business?

REFERENCES

1. Stanley Rich and David Gumpert, *Business Plans that Win $$$* (New York, New York: Harper and Row, 1983, p. 65)
2. John Grossmann, "Educational Retailer Learns Hard Lessson," *Inc. Magazine,* April 2000, p. 40
3. Jules Abend, "Jockey Colors Its World," *Bobbin,* www.findarticles.com, February 1999
4. Norman Scarborough and Thomas Zimmerer, *Effective Small Business Management: An Entrepreneurial Approach,* 6th ed. (Upper Saddle River, New Jersey: Prentice-Hall, 2000, p. 306)
5. Carolyn Z. Lawrence, "The Price is Right," *Business Start-Ups,* February 1996, p. 64
6. Sandra Dalbow, "Turner Eyes Still More for Polo Ralph Lauren," *Brandweek,* May 1, 2002, www.findarticles.com/cf_dmooBDW/18_41/62001169/print/jhml
7. Arthur DeThomas and William Fredenberger, *Writing a Convincing Business Plan* (Hauppauge, New York: Barron's Educational Series, Inc., 1995, p. 104)
8. Sandra Dolbow, "Rattling the Chains," *Brandweek,* October 16, 2000, www.findarticles.com
9. Arthur Lublow, "Wowing Warren," *Inc., Magazine,* March 2000, pp. 72–84
10. Television Bureau of Advertising, The Media Center, Bruskin/Audits and Surveys, www.tvbiorg/tvfacts/tvbasics/basics260.html, January 2001.
11. National Association of Broadcasters, "Frequently Asked Questions," www.nab.org/irc/virtualfaqs.asp
12. National Business Association Resource Guide, *Choosing the Right Advertising Medium for Your Business* (Dallas, Texas: National Business Association, 1998, pp. 4–5)
13. Scarborough and Zimmerer, *Effective Small Business Management: An Entrepreneurial Approach,* p. 346
14. Ibid., p. 353
15. Edmund A. Bruneau, "Advertising," *Marketing Series* (Fort Worth, Texas: U.S. Small Business Administration, p. 9)
16. National Business Association Resource Guide, *Choosing the Right Advertising Medium for Your Business,* p. 13
17. Millard W. Grubb, "Increase Profits Through Excellent Customer Service" (Cassopolis, Michigan: Edward Lowe Foundation, 1996, www.lowe.org
18. Gemmy Allen, "Customer Relationships," www.sales.about.com/careers/sales/library/weekly/aal/1200.htm
19. Ibid.
20. Business Editors, "Nordstrom.com Enhances Customer Experience Online During Busy Holiday Season; Company to Fulfill Customer's Wishes for Convenient Shopping and Comprehensive Selection," *Business Wire,* November 14, 2000, www.findarticles.com
21. Joan Fox, "How to Keep Customers from Slipping Through the Cracks," *The Small Business Journal,* 1995–2000, www.tsloj.com
22. Mark Hendricks "Five Best Customer Service Ideas: Don't Do Business Without Them," *Entrepreneur Magazine,* March 1999, www.entrepreneur.com
23. Brian Tracy, "Teaming Up with Your Customers," www.tsbj.com/editorial/03061304.htm

SUGGESTED READINGS

Jay Levinson, *Guerrilla Marketing: Secrets for Making Big Profits from Your Small Business,* 3rd ed. (Boston, Massachusetts: Houghton Mifflin Company, 1998)

Jay Levinson, *Guerrilla Advertising: Cost Effective Techiniques for Small Business Success* (Boston, Massachusetts: Houghton Mifflin Company, 1994)

Thomas Niagle, Reed K. Holden, Reed Holden, *The Strategy and Tactics of Pricing,* 3rd ed. (Upper Saddle River, New Jersey: Prentice-Hall, 2002)

Jody Hornor, *Power Marketing for Small Businesses* (Grants Pass, Oregon: Oasis Press, 1993)

CASE STUDY

Norman Childs knew he had to do something to set his company apart from the competition when Pearle Vision and LensCrafters started moving into the Pittsburgh area. Childs owns a company called Eyetique, a two-store eyeglasses operation. "Everyone was coming in at the low end or the middle of the road, like Pearle," says Childs, "I knew we couldn't compete with that."

So Childs went upscale—way upscale. He began carrying brands swankier than even Calvin Klein or Giorgio Armani. His average sale was about $450 and featured such fashion labels as Oliver Peoples, Lunor, and Matsuda. Such high-class products, however, were not enough. Childs had to get the word out.

To do that, he devised an advertising campaign that the national chains would not think to do: he featured local celebrities. The tough part was getting the right people to pose, especially since he wasn't going to pay them anything. Childs broke the ice with Delton Hall, a player for the Pittsburgh Steelers who happened to be the son-in-law of his photographer. The fashion editor of *Pittsburgh* magazine followed. Soon appearing in an Eyetique ad became a local status symbol. "Everyone wants their ego stroked," says Childs. "It's good publicity for them. Now it's become a sort of *Who's Who* of Pittsburgh."

Other ads have featured local musicians and journalists, as well as radio, television, and sports personalities. Childs runs the ads in about 15 periodicals. To further target his upscale audience, he also buys space in the printed programs of local symphony, ballet, and theater companies.

Child's photographer usually shoots four or five subjects at a time at a cost of about $1,000. Placing the ads costs anywhere from $250 for the local weekly paper to $2,500 for a *Phantom of the Opera* program page. During the campaign's second year, Eyetique's sales doubled. Since the ad program began in 1989, Eyetique has gone from 5 to 25 employees in its two stores, and sales have increased from $500,000 to about $2.5 million. (Christopher Caggiano, "Local Ads are Fresher," *Inc. Magazine,* July 1, 1999).

CASE STUDY QUESTIONS

1. Discuss ways in which Norman Childs could have penetrated the market had he not been able to get local celebrities to promote his products.
2. Who was Norman Childs's target market? How might he have determined this?
3. What role did the target market play in determining his approach to advertising?
4. Discuss the psychographics of the Childs's customer.

ENTERING THE WORLD OF THE ENTREPRENEUR

1. Contact a fashion retailer or manufacturer in your area and ask about its marketing mix: product, place, promotion, and price. How did the combination of these elements help the company penetrate the market?
2. What considerations are given to determining the price of the products? Does the company achieve the image it wants through its prices? How does the competition affect the pricing strategy? What is the percentage of markup? What pricing technique(s) is used (i.e., markup, price lining, or competitive pricing)?
3. Find out about the advertising program. Ask the entrepreneur the purpose or objective of the advertising campaign. Is it to get the consumer to buy? Is it to create awareness?

4. Find out what media option the fashion entrepreneur uses to penetrate the market. Why was this media option chosen?

5. Does the company itself design ads, or are outside consultants retained?

6. Contact several fashion entrepreneurs to determine how they arrived at their advertising budget. Does the size of the company influence the budget? What role does the size of the market play in determining the advertising budget?

7. Find out about the level of customer service. What steps does the company take to ensure quality customer service? Are the goals of establishing and retaining customer loyalty achieved?

8. What is the management philosophy of the company? Are employees made to feel a part of the driving force behind the company?

9. Has any consideration been given to taking the company global? Why or why not?

10. Does the company have a Web site? Who developed the Web site? How did the entrepreneur determine who was to be suited to help develop the Web site? What is the goal of the site? Does the site help in penetrating a larger market? How is the site maintained?

ENTERPRISING ENTREPRENEUR

Generation X entrepreneurs are cashing in on the fashion market for teens. These 25- to 35-year-old designers are creating products for the junior market. By 2010, the number of teens in the United States alone will rise to 35 million, more than at any other time in history, according to Teen.com, a Web site catering to the interests of teenagers. A Rand Youth poll estimated that teen girls spend $21.8 billion a year on clothes and beauty accessories.

Greg Herman is the 27-year-old president of Greg Herman Los Angeles Inc. Herman is the designer of funky, retro-looking handbags. Although he has a bachelor's degree in anthropology from the University of California, Herman was homeless, carting around two suitcases filled with his worldly goods and crashing on friends' sofas, when he started the company in 1997. He maxed out his credit cards and got $4,000 from an angel investor to make samples, which he then took to New York City.

"I put 40 handbags in a rolling suitcase and literally walked up and down the streets, stopping at showrooms," recalls Herman, who expects sales of $3 million this year and has recently added shoe, shirt, and scented-soap lines to his collection. Despite the company's unconventional beginnings, Herman, a benefactor of homeless causes, sells his bags to catalogers and major retail stores like Barney's and Anthropologie. Celebrities such as Jennifer Love Hewitt, Courtney Cox, Calista Flockhart, and Christina Applegate buy his bags, which retail for up to $50. (Adapted from Pamela Rahland, "Keep Your Cool," *Business Start-Ups* Magazine, August, 2000.)

Chapter 8

EXPLORING MANAGEMENT

INTRODUCTION

In the previous chapters, information on product, market research, market penetration, business location, and e-commerce have all been examined as they relate to creating the business plan. This chapter focuses on the importance of the management team and the key elements needed to complete the management plan section of the business plan. Leadership styles and company structure are significant components of management. Recruiting, hiring, training, and motivating employees are key activities that play roles in business management. This chapter also examines compensation for management and employees, as well as contracts that protect both the employer and employee.

THE MANAGEMENT TEAM

Managing a business involves planning, organizing, controlling, directing, and communicating. Being an effective manager and leader allows the entrepreneur to put together a good management team, which is essential to the successful venture. Managers of entrepreneurial companies experience a variety of issues and, subsequently, need the right team to make it all happen. They set the tone for the culture of the company. Forming a team through effective employees and/or an advisory council is critical to the success of the business.

Entrepreneurial companies recognize the importance of creating a management team because a team reduces risk. It ensures that the functions of a business such as sales, finance, marketing, and operations will be handled correctly. It is unlikely that one person will be competent in all aspects of the business. The strength lies in recognizing the limitations and strengths of each member of the team and bringing people onboard, either as employees or an advisory team, to compensate for limitations.

Management teams can fall into one of four categories, or levels, from most to least preferable, as follows:

- *Level 4: All members of the team are identified and fully committed.* This is the ideal situation. The management team is onboard and working. The business plan names all members, delineates their salaries and stock ownership, and describes their relevant business experience in a paragraph or so for each person. In addition, the business plan includes, as an appendix, a one-page biographical sketch or résumé of each team member. All have a good record of training and experience.

- *Level 3: All members of the team are identified, but not everyone is onboard.* It may be that two founders are working at the company full time, but a third member (and possibly a fourth), who was recruited for his or her special skills, is waiting for the financing to be completed before leaving an existing job. The third (and possibly fourth) member has reached an understanding about salary and stock in the new company. As in the previous situation, the team members, salaries and stock ownership, relevant experience, and résumés should be included in the business plan. There is always the danger that, despite commitment, the identified prospective management team members will decline to join. This possibility worries investors.

- *Level 2: One or more members of the team are not identified and are not yet with the company.* The situation may be the same as that described for level 3 except that the third and fourth members of the team with the necessary experience and education have not been found and identified. In such a circumstance, the business plan can describe the slots for the third and fourth team members in terms of experience, salary and stock ownership, and desired background. The missing people will have to be recruited, which can be a problem, rendering a level 2 management team less desirable to investors.

- *Level 1: The one-person team.* There is one founder, with no one else identified. This type of situation is usually unacceptable to investors. The one exception is if the founder has an outstanding previous track record and has brought several products from conception through to successful and profitable manufacturing and marketing.[1]

If given the choice, funders would rather see a first-rate management team and a second-rate product or concept than a second-rate management team and a first-rate product. The premise is that a good management team can turn the product or concept around. It is not unusual in the fashion industry for a successful CEO to be recruited by a competitor. Establishing that a good management team will be in place is critical to the business plan. Funders know that without such a team the venture often cannot succeed.

The management section of the business plan outlines key personnel and describes the contribution each member of the team will make. Additionally, it indicates where weaknesses exist and how the management team will compensate for those weaknesses. The management team section will clearly define job descriptions and include an organizational chart showing to whom each member of the team reports. It must also address any contracts between the company and its employees. The remainder of this chapter focuses on key issues related to developing an effective team.

Before determining job positions within the company and who will be hired for those positions, it is important to establish the culture of the company. Organizational culture is the personality of the business, its attitudes, values, and communication style.

Building an Organizational Culture

Organizational culture is the way things are done in a particular company. A company's culture is defined by its management and embodied by the employees. There is a system of shared characteristics that is valued within the organization among the employees and management. It has to do with how employees work together within the business. For example, Gap employees are casually dressed in khakis, jeans, tank tops, and T-shirts. Talbots, on the other hand, promotes the suit and blouse approach. Many companies nurture a culture whereby everyone's opinion is valued regardless of rank. In other companies, the culture dictates a more hierarchical approach. To be successful in creating an organizational culture that supports the goals of the company, entrepreneurs must persist in establishing beliefs and core values that are carried out on a day to day basis.

Hiring and maintaining quality workers often require creating an environment in which they want to stay. This has much to do with the culture of the organization. The fashion retail industry lends itself to offering a fun, creative, and well-liked culture. Companies have begun to embrace such concepts as casual dress, virtual teams, and flexible work schedules. Companies that have been successful in creating an employee-friendly and relaxed culture tend to rely on certain principles, which include:

- Respect for a healthy balance between work and life. They create an environment that is fun and respectful of the fact that employees have lives away from work.
- Sense of purpose that makes employees feel connected to the company's mission.
- Valuing diversity. They not only accept cultural diversity, but they also embrace and celebrate it. They seek out workers with different backgrounds.
- Honesty and integrity. Employees pride themselves on working for a company that is ethical and socially responsible. They expect the company to communicate openly and honestly about issues that are of importance to them.
- Participative management style. A participative management style encourages employees at all levels of the organization to be trusted and empowered to make decisions and to take the actions necessary to get the job done. Employee input is valued.
- Encouragement of lifelong learning among the employees.[2]

LEADERSHIP

"Effective entrepreneurial managers need to be especially skillful at managing conflict, resolving differences, balancing multiple viewpoints and demands, and building teamwork and consensus.[3] Entrepreneurs must recognize the importance of keeping up with innovation and responding quickly by anticipating changing environments and markets. Entrepreneurial managers thrive in an often chaotic environment and enjoy the challenge of keeping their team motivated and committed. The effective entrepreneur remains calm and possesses the confidence to turn adversity into opportunity.

According to Peter Drucker, "The real test of a leader is his or her followers—when you look over your shoulder is there anyone there following you?" According to one CEO, leadership is "not as much about what you need to know or what you need to do, as it is who you need to be."[4] Many definitions exist to define a leader. Leadership can be defined as the ability to create an environment in which others feel empowered to work together to achieve a common goal. Entrepreneurs must learn to be effective leaders if they are to take a company forward and help it grow.

As our culture changes, the skills needed to lead will change. In an entrepreneurial culture, certain leadership skills are needed to elicit certain behavior. Entrepreneurs must deal with the challenges of rapidly changing markets, innovation by technology, and starting and growing a company. Most employees are no longer interested in simply following a set of rules and focusing on one task. Today's generation is driven by the ability to be a part of the company. They want to be a part of the business. Today's workforce is more skilled and knowledgeable than those in the past.

Jeffry Timmons, in *New Venture Creation,* discusses interpersonal/team work skills or entrepreneurial influence skills needed by managers/leaders that exert influence over others. These skills involve:

1. The ability to create, through management, a climate and spirit conducive to high performance, including pressing for performance while rewarding work well done and encouraging innovation, initiative, and calculated risk taking.
2. The ability to understand the relationships among tasks and between the leader and followers.
3. The ability to lead in those situations where it is appropriate, including a willingness to actively manage, supervise, and control activities of others through directions, suggestions, and the like.[5]

Timmons goes on to expand on these interpersonal skills as shown below:

■ *Leadership/vision/influence.* These managers are skillful in creating clarity out of confusion, vagueness, and uncertainty. They are able to define who has what responsibility and authority. They do this in a way that builds motivation and commitment to cross-departmental and corporate goals, not just parochial interest. This is not perceived by other managers as an effort to jealously carve out and guard personal turf and prerogatives. Rather, it is seen as a genuine effort to clarify roles, tasks, and responsibilities, and to make sure there is accountability and appropriate approvals. This does not work unless the manager is seen as willing to relinquish his or her priorities and power in the interest of an overall goal. It requires skill in making sure the appropriate people are included in setting cross-functional or cross-departmental goals and in making decisions. When things do not go as smoothly as was hoped, the most effective managers work them through to an agreement.

■ *Helping/coaching and conflict management.* The most effective managers are very creative and skillful in handling conflicts, generating consensus decisions, and sharing their power and information. They are able to get people to open up, instead of clamming up; they get problems out on the table, and they do not become defensive when others disagree with their views. They seem to know that high-quality decisions require a rapid flow of information in all directions and that knowledge, competence, logic, and evidence need to prevail over official status or formal rank in the organization.

■ *Teamwork and people management.* Another form of entrepreneurial influence has to do with encouraging creativity and innovation and with taking calculated risks. Simply stated, entrepreneurial managers build confidence by encouraging innovation and calculated risk taking, rather than by punishing or criticizing whatever is less than perfect. They breed independent, entrepreneurial thinking by expecting and encouraging others to find and correct their own errors and to solve their own problems. They are perceived by their peers and other managers as accessible and willing to help when needed, and they provide the necessary resources to enable others to do the job.

The capacity to generate trust is critical. The most effective managers are perceived as trustworthy; they behave in ways that create trust. How do they do this? For one thing, they are straightforward: They do what they say they are going to do. They are open and spontaneous, rather than guarded and cautious with each word. They are perceived as being honest and direct. These entrepreneurial managers have a reputation for getting results.[6]

Management and leadership are not the same, although they are intertwined, and both are essential to the success of the business. Leadership deals with guiding and motivating people. Management is concerned more about logistics and meeting requirements.

Effective leaders are focused on certain activities. These activities include:

- *Treat Others As You Want To Be Treated.* Employees want to be treated as responsible professionals. Employees who are treated professionally are generally motivated and productive.
- *Become a Teacher.* A role model for the effective employee is the teacher who views any shortcoming as an opportunity for you to grow, someone who always focuses on your potential when he or she works with you. Such managers consistently support their employees, helping them discover the paths to success. As employees grow, reward them; nurture their careers and professional growth in every way possible.
- *Know and Communicate the Goals of the Company.* Effective leaders make the vision of the company part of everyone involved in it. It is communicated to employees and team members and is carried out.
- *Delegate, Never Dump.* The easiest way to become good at delegation is to surround yourself with subordinates whose abilities you respect; then you would be foolish not to use them to the best of their capabilities. When people sense that you expect great things from them, they tend to be challenged by that expectation and work hard to live up to it. Load your people with responsibility, provide them with the resources to do the job, and never be punitive when they make mistakes. Delegation crosses the line and becomes dumping when we delegate only the work we don't want to do ourselves; keep all the "glorious" fun projects for ourselves; fail to provide adequate resources for our subordinates to complete their work; delegate all the responsiblility and none of the authority for the job; or abandon our subordinates, failing to provide them with timing requirements, project guidelines, or our personal counsel when they need it.
- *Build a Team.* Similar to the teacher analogy, effective leaders strive to build cohesive teams, seeing themselves as the teams's captain. The team captain inspires excellence and earns loyalty, serving as a role model to be admired, not feared. The most effective teams comprise members with diverse skills and personalities. These are also the most difficult teams to manage. It can be frustrating work, but the rewards are tremendous when you watch the team become greater than the sum of its parts. In planning, you determined the goals of the team. To manage the team successfully, make sure everyone clearly understands his or her role in reaching those goals. Communicate the rules or norms for operating together. For instance, a rule that many successful teams adopt is, "When you have a problem with any team member, it is your responsiblity to discuss the problem directly with that team member. If you

appoach another team member instead, you will immediately be referred to the team member who has caused you difficulty."

- *Lead by Example.* People rarely learn from what we tell them to do. More often they learn from example. Start by living up to the rules you've already negotiated with team members. Treat each staff person with respect. Be kind and courteous. Keep your cool in crisis situations. Your calm will be just as contagious as your panic and temper flare-ups. Keep your word—to the letter. Nothing undermines trust in a professional setting more precipitously than a leader who breaks his or her commitments.
- *Listen to Employees.* Many managers talk about being good listeners, yet this skill often remains an area in need of substantial improvement. The benefits of good listening are numerous. Relationships improve, productivity and work performance are enhanced, team spirit is fostered, morale increases, and your staff gains better perspective and understanding of your mission. Good listening skills engender trust. And trust is what separates effective participatory leaders from autocratic managers.[7]

Effective leaders know that real leadership is earned. They recognize that they are only as successful as their employees. The business environment has changed over the years. Effective leadership is challenging. Employees must be inspired to achieve success; telling them to succeed is not sufficient. Effective leadership is based on good communication skills, hiring the right employees, training those employees, building a culture that promotes teamwork, and motivating employees to achieve a higher level of performance.

Open-Book Management

In the 1980s, many U.S. companies realized that they were losing their competitive edge and began to reexamine traditional management methods. The concept of open-book management began in the 1980s and was popularized by Jack Stack, CEO of Springfield Remanufacturing Company in Springfield, Missouri.

> For years, the message at Springfield had been: "When you come in here, leave your mind at the door." Jack saw the waste in human capital that resulted. He believed that if everyone understood the balance sheet and their impact on it, they could unleash unlimited productivity. He was right, and the result is what is now known as "Open Book Management." And what about the return on the employees' investment? Everyone at Springfield shares in a bonus plan based directly on company-wide productivity. To keep employees interested in ongoing improvement, bonuses are distributed quarterly. In addition, 32.5 percent of the company's stock is owned by the Employee Stock Ownership Plan.[8]

Open-book management (OBM) means sharing all company information with all employees, including financial data. This can prove to be very effective for a small company if it is handled properly and is reflective of the organizational culture. The objective of open-book management is to teach employees the financial basics of the business, trust them to make good decisions based on this knowledge, and treat them as responsible stakeholders in the venture. The premise is that as trusted and empowered members of the company, they will make significant contributions to its success.

According to some proponents of open-book management, successful companies that have implemented an open-book management policy experience a more solid performance by the company. Security is improved for the firm and its members. Employees are more satisfied with their work. And employees have the ability to build wealth. It allows the employees to participate in ownership in the company and have a stake in its success.

For this concept to work, employees must be able to align themselves with common goals that everyone understands. In order to do this, employees have to be informed and motivated. They need to know what makes a business viable and capable of sustaining a workforce. If management wants its employees to think and act like owners, then management has to treat its employees like owners. Using the concept of open-book management, everyone clearly has to understand the business plan. Employees are held accountable. They share in the risks and share in the rewards. Employees will take on the responsibility of supervising themselves and managing their own numbers when they have the following opportunities: (1) They become more skilled and employable through training and work experience; (2) they are rewarded psychologically and financially for making the organization more profitable; and (3) they have the opportunity to "learn business."

Open-book management implies a set of management practices: leadership, education, information, planning, involvement, rewards, and communication processes designed to involve all employees in creating, maintaining, and producing business goals. The following paragraphs outline the five elements needed to adopt an open-book management policy. Materials reproduced from the book, *Open Book Management, Your EZ Intro to OBM* by Donald F. Barkman, published by The Business Center, Knoxville, Tennessee, 1997.

1. *Leadership.* To operate an OBM organization requires a certain personal leadership philosophy. OBM is as much a matter of the heart as it is of the mind. The cornerstone of a leader's philosophy is his or her belief about sharing. Leaders must be eager to share three things with the employees of their organization:

    a. Information

    b. Decision making (control)

    c. Wealth

A leader must give people the real numbers about their firm's financial performance to achieve both credibility and motivation. Employees must have the opportunity to make a difference in a significant way. Not everyone gets to make the decisions of the CEO, but most employees will want and need more control over their work. Leaders must be willing to share the wealth created by the efforts of employees.

2. *Education.* Education means training and developing the knowledge and skills of employees to enable them to do everything their jobs require. It includes understanding the business context within which their work is done. This is where OBM adds its educational element. In OBM, everyone's job becomes larger because each person must understand how the business operates financially and how he or she can affect its financial results. Financial reports like the income statement, balance sheet, and cash flow statement become new tools for everyone to understand and use.

Education helps establish a "line of sight" between an employee's everyday actions and the larger operating and financial results of the business. A line of sight traces the effect of an individual's actions on the firm's financial preformance. Beginning with the key financial measure(s) the company uses, instructors can work backward through the measure's components until the line reaches the employee's department, team, and job.

3. *Information.* To be an informed and responsible business partner requires having access to pertinent financial information about the firm. Sharing financial information is the defining hallmark of OBM. Revealing confidential data about a company's financial performance has constituted "opening the books." While this is crucial to the success of OBM, it is hardly all there is to it.

Giving information to people who are not educated to properly interpret it can create problems, not solve them. Responsible business partners who act to achieve the mission of their enterprise must be both informed and educated. Managers who cite problems of information-sharing with employees usually describe situations where the employees were given the information without sufficient prior education. They argue against sharing information because it was misinterpreted or misused. This misses the point. They should argue for better education so that the shared information is properly understood and used.

Key financial and operating measures are carefully defined, measured, and intensely managed by all employees to produce results. These are called the firm's "critical numbers." OBM uses an information exchange system to track and achieve these critical numbers. This may turn traditional, hierarchically oriented, financial information reporting systems on their heads. Instead of being aimed at satisfying managers' needs for information, OBM stresses that the "troops" have information so they can make decisions to respond to changes. Information must loop quickly back to the people who contribute the data as well as move upward to inform managers.

4. *Involvement.* Involvement may be the least obvious of the five elements of OBM, perhaps because there have been so many employee involvement programs over the last 30 years. Involvement is, however, an indispensable element. Providing a structure for involvement and the mechanisms for it to occur are what turns motivation into action. Problem-solving teams and natural work teams are often used for this purpose.

OBM invites a high level of employee involvement with business affairs. The degree of involvement needs to be proportional to the degree of education and information possessed by those involved. It is like controlling the angle of a dive into a swimming pool based on the depth of the water. The more thorough the education and the more extensive the information exchange, the greater the involvement can be.

5. *Rewards.* Giving everyone a significant personal stake in the financial success of the firm is also characteristic of OBM. Educated and informed employees who are deeply involved with the business will produce results. It will no longer be a case of employees coming to work and just "doing a job." Employees gain a more tangible sense of accomplishment in an OBM operation. When everyone sees the company's numbers turn out well, a logical question arises—"What's in it for me?"

This is a question of long standing. Corporate America has not answered it well. Many "merit" pay programs don't really pay for performance. For most employees, the amount in the paycheck has little to do with their organization's current performance or their individual or team contribution. OBM stresses rewards linked directly to the critical numbers and profits. These rewards take a variety of forms.

    a. Short-term and long-term rewards.

    b. Cash and noncash rewards.

    c. Individual and group rewards.

    d. Operational and financial performance-driven rewards.

These choices are not either/or. Rather, they are both/and. All eight possibilities can be used simultaneously. Some firms focus on sharing profits, while others provide equity stakes in the firm through ESOPs (employee stock ownership plans). All firms must balance psychological and monetary rewards to create a balanced motivational climate. The secret is to keep it simple, easy to understand and administer, and on target for organizational performance.[9]

Information is communicated to the team as it evolves. By sharing information, employees are challenged to think differently about the company, their work, and their responsibilities. Financial information is no longer left to the owner or financial specialists. Employees are handed a set of financial statements and taught how those numbers can affect them.

Open-book management is not an answer to all issues companies face nor is it suggested that all companies benefit from implementing this policy. Implementing OBM does not necessarily mean all employees will suddenly "get along," that cash flow will increase significantly, or that customer service will necessarily take a giant leap upward. Not all companies have been successful in trying to implement this type of atmosphere. They failed in their ability to recognize that they were involving employees in too many things that did not add or create value. They were involving employees only to a point. Management would solicit suggestions from the employees, but not include them in the decision-making process. If implemented carefully, OBM is one way of encouraging employees and management to take on the challenge of running a business in a teamlike environment, thereby taking advantage of the team's diverse backgrounds, experience, and education.

Effective Communication

In the business plan the ability to communicate effectively can mean the difference between getting the venture funded or not. It is important to recognize the significance of written and oral communication skills when it comes to presenting the business plan internally and externally to funders. Communication is the process of transferring information and ideas from one person to another, with consistent understanding of the meaning. To make a business successful, leaders must communicate the vision, beliefs, and principles of the business effectively. They must ensure that all employees know and understand the mission and vision of the company and how to carry them out. A fashion retail business will require effective communication, not only internally, but between the business and its vendors and customers.

Communication may not always be effective. Often, employees fail to perform tasks or duties not out of lack of motivation, but out of a lack of understanding as to what to do or how to do it. The problem lies in communication between manager and employee. To perform the tasks, employees must hear and understand what they are being requested to do. They must also recognize that they have the authority to complete the task. They require feedback on their performance.

Barriers to communication can occur in both verbal and nonverbal communication methods. Verbal communication relates to what is said or written. Nonverbal communication relates to how one acts. It consists of gestures, expressions, body language, and tone of voice. Because messages are interpreted, they are not always received as they are intended. Both managers and employees must overcome verbal and nonverbal barriers in order to communicate effectively. A list of those obstacles to communication follows:

- *Insufficient knowledge of the topic.* The lack of sufficient knowledge of a topic by either sender or receiver will create a communication barrier. For example, in the business plan, the use of language or acronyms specific to the fashion industry will do the reader no good if he or she is not familiar with the field. If the sender knows the language, but the reader does not, a barrier in communication will result.
- *Ambiguity.* The same words can have different meanings to different people. For example, the business plan may include the following sentence: "We will carry high-end fashion merchandise." "High end" will mean different things to different people. Instead, the business plan may include the statement, "We will carry fashions produced by Donna Karan," giving the reader a better idea of the merchandise.
- *Selective listening.* Often, people hear only what they want to hear. The receivers in the communication process selectively see and hear based on their needs, motivations, experience, background, and other personal characteristics.[10]
- *Inability to be honest.* To a degree, people need to be given permission to say what they really mean and know that there will be no negative consequences for such openness. If the entrepreneur asks for honest feedback and then punishes the sender, the resulting environment will not be a culture where everyone tells the truth. The truth is important when starting a business. Managers need to know what employees and customers are feeling and thinking.
- *Distractions.* The lack of ability to concentrate on the message being sent will create a barrier to effective communication. People can be distracted in a number of ways. Someone trying to meet a deadline will not want to be interrupted to deal with another matter. By interrupting, the sender will not have the full attention of the receiver.
- *Communication via written documents.* Although effective in terms of getting the message out quickly, written communication can lead to misunderstandings. Often, people are in a hurry to get the message out and do not consider how it may be interpreted. Without the help of nonverbal communication, the message may be interpreted differently from what was intended. Written documents must be explicit to make up for the lack of nonverbal communication to reinforce the message.

Technology and Communication

The options for methods of communication have expanded over the years. Computers and technology have revolutionized communication. With the various forms of communication available now, one must be aware of more than just verbal and nonverbal communication. To become a more effective communicator and overcome the barriers of communication, entrepreneurs must focus on clarifying their ideas. They must consider the implications of their written communication. They must also assess the environment in which the communication occurs. Effective communicators stop and think about what is being written or said and how it may be interpreted. They encourage feedback from communication recipients.

Intrapreneurship

Today's workforce shows an increasing interest in "doing its own thing." Prospective employees want to be a part of the spirit, the creation process, the challenges, and the rewards of the organization. Many employees have the desire to take on more responsibility and to build something of their own. Lack of the ability to express themselves creatively in the organization may lead to discontent and, perhaps, the desire to seek employment elsewhere or start their own companies. Successful companies of today are recognizing the importance of instilling an entrepreneurial spirit among their employees. Intrapreneurship can be defined as thinking entrepreneurally within an existing business structure.

The intrapreneurial culture differs significantly from the traditional corporate culture. Intrapreneurial cultures are guided by creativity, flexibility, and independence. Intrapreneurs develop vision, goals, and action plans; are rewarded for actions taken; suggest, try, and experiment; create and develop regardless of the area; and take responsibility and ownership for their actions.[11] An intrapreneurial culture promotes a structure of teamwork, mentoring, and networking.

In the following statements, Hisrich and Peters discuss the factors and leadership characteristics they believe must be established in an organization to create an intrapreneurial climate:

> Intrapreneurs must have appropriate leadership characteristics. In addition to being creative, visionary, and flexible, the intrapreneur must be able to work within the corporate structure. Intrapreneurs need to encourage teamwork and work diplomatically across established structures. Open discussion and strong support of team members is also required. Finally, the intrapreneur must be persistent in order to overcome the inevitable obstacles inherent in a large organization.[12]

Top management must be willing to commit the time and resources to establishing the intrapreneurial environment. Incentives and rewards are needed to encourage team members to participate in this environment.

ORGANIZATIONAL STRUCTURE

Organizational structure is the way in which the organization defines job tasks, how these tasks are divided and grouped, and how they are coordinated. The organizational structure will define how employees interact with one another and will influence employee attitudes toward their jobs and other employees. When structure is used to clarify what is to be done, how it is to be done, and who is to do it, attitudes and relationships among employees will improve.

The way the organization is structured often depends on its size. A one-person entrepreneurial company will have a different organizational structure from a company with 20 employees. Many fashion retail businesses operate with a manager, or assistant manager, and sales associates. Each employee has a different role and is assigned different tasks, but all work together as a team.

Determining Key Roles and Tasks

Typically, a fashion retail business cannot be run by only one person. One individual cannot usually fill all the roles and handle all the tasks required to make the business successful. It takes a team of sales associates and management to ensure that all tasks have been completed. Funders reviewing business plans recognize the importance of designating responsibilities and tasks. They will review the business plan to ensure that the entrepreneur is aware of the roles employees must play and the tasks they must perform to make the company successful. Figure 8.1 gives an example of a divisional breakdown of job responsibilities for Garland Stores.

The first step in the management planning process is to evaluate the tasks that will need to be accomplished. This process is referred to as a job analysis. A job analysis is the "process of obtaining information about jobs by determining the duties, tasks, or activities necessary for those jobs."[13] The data obtained are used to develop a description for each position. Although job analysis is typically used in larger companies, it can be very beneficial to the small entrepreneurial company as well.

The first step in performing a job analysis is to determine the tasks required for each job. Data about the jobs or tasks required in a start-up company may be obtained from managers, supervisors, and employees of similar operations. A number of methods may be used to obtain these data. Some of the more common methods include interviews, questionnaires, observation, and diaries. Interviews may be conducted with employees and managers to obtain information regarding the tasks involved in doing the job. Questionnaires may be distributed to obtain data regarding the skills, education level, level of experience, and task requirements needed to fulfill the job. Another method of obtaining information, observation, can prove very effective. It allows the job analyst to learn about the jobs by observing and recording the activities of the jobholder. Using the final method of diaries, jobholders are asked to keep a journal detailing their work activities.

A job analysis defines in detail the requirements of the job. It goes beyond defining the specific tasks involved in the job to include a description of the conditions or environment in which the employees will work. For example, employment in the fashion retail industry requires working nights and weekends. It is not enough for the job description to state, "Must be available to work five days per week," while saying nothing about working on the weekends. Some people may not be able to work weekends. By conducting a thorough analysis, entrepreneurs can do a better job of screening potential applicants, and applicants can make more informed decisions about working for that company. (Figure 8.2.)

Once a job analysis is completed, the entrepreneur can begin the process of creating job descriptions. The job description outlines the tasks, duties, and responsibilities of the position. The job description will provide information needed to set skill requirements, physical demands, experience, education, knowledge, and abilities needed to perform the job. The job description also defines the working conditions of the position and who workers report to in the organization. The job description should clearly define what is expected of the person who will fill the position.

Figure 8.1 This Is an Example of a Divisional Breakdown of Job Responsibilities for a Retail Operation

GARLAND STORES

Division	Responsibilities
MERCHANDISING	• Merchandise development, selection, pricing, and selling • Controlling inventory (joint responsibility with Operations). • Sets merchandising policies: quality standards, price ranges, fashion leadership position, exclusivity. *The **Merchandising Division** is the only division that generates income for the store.*
CONTROL	• Payroll • Expense planning and control • Credit office • Internal auditing • Accounts payable • Inventory monitoring and reconciliation • Statistical: generates purchase journal *The **Control Division** initiates and monitors all areas covering finance and general accounting within the store.*
PROMOTION	• Advertising, copy, and layout • Catalog, radio, television • Display: interior and windows • Store design and decor • Public relations/Special events *The **Promotion Division** works closely with the **Merchandising Division** to generate customer traffic and a favorable store image.*
HUMAN RESOURCES	• Training • Employee selection and development • Rating and reviews • Termination • Job Analysis • Benefits *The **Human Resources Division** recruits, develops, evaluates, and manages the store's personnel.*
STORE OPERATIONS	• Customer service–sales, service desk • Telephone and mail order • Warehouse • Restaurants • Receiving and marking • General operations activities: security, housekeeping, delivery, alterations *The **Store Operations Division** provides general support services, internally and externally, that allow the store to function.* *The **Branch Store Division** operates as a microcosm of the other divisions— solely for branch store locations.* *Within each branch are offices for **Advertising, Operations, Personnel,** and **Control**. Branch department managers perform the operational and merchandising functions.*

M. Granger, *Case Studies in Merchandising Apparel of Soft Goods* (NY, NY: Fairchild Publications, 1996, p. 46)

Figure 8.2 Job Analysis Buyer/Manager

	D	W	M	O
1. Plan and monitor sales, inventory, and purchase budgets.	☐	☐	☐	☐
2. Project merchandise trends that will be preferred by target market.	☐	☐	☐	☐
3. Work with vendors on merchandise selections, to include reorders, timely delivery, purchase discounts, and exclusive stock.	☐	☐	☐	☐
4. Write purchase orders and monitor deliveries of goods on time.	☐	☐	☐	☐
5. Manage time efficiently to balance management and buying duties.	☐	☐	☐	☐
6. Educate sales staff on merchandise assortment (e.g., trends, vendors, and items).	☐	☐	☐	☐
7. Organize and process all paperwork to include payroll, merchandise receipts and sales, markdowns, and orders.	☐	☐	☐	☐
8. Install displays of merchandise with sales associates.	☐	☐	☐	☐
9. Motivate and review sales personnel.	☐	☐	☐	☐
10. Travel to markets in Dallas and New York.	☐	☐	☐	☐
11. Process all paperwork required to order merchandise.	☐	☐	☐	☐
12. Develop schedules for personnel.	☐	☐	☐	☐
13. Oversee receiving division for timely transfer of goods to sales floor.	☐	☐	☐	☐
14. Collaborate with store owner on personnel and merchandise performance.	☐	☐	☐	☐
15. Model high standards of motivation, team work, and flexibility.	☐	☐	☐	☐
16. Work nights and weekends, as needed.	☐	☐	☐	☐
17. Must be able to handle multiple tasks.	☐	☐	☐	☐

Creating Job Descriptions

The job description is beneficial to both employees and manager. With a job description, employees know what is expected of them. They recognize what their goals are and how to achieve them. To management, job descriptions provide a basis for evaluation. If the duties of the job are not performed by the employee, management has a basis for taking corrective action. Employees know how they must perform to be considered for promotion or rewards of other kinds.

Developing job descriptions should be done before applicant interviews begin. A job description typically includes the job title, whom the employee will report to, a brief statement regarding the major job duties, and any specific skills needed to fulfill the requirements of the job. Flexibility within a job description is necessary in smaller firms where employees typically act as part of team. Flexibility allows the manager to assign additional duties to employees to accomplish the goals of the company. Small companies may be too concerned with being specific in the job description and therefore may be limited in assigning different tasks to various employees. One way to avoid being too specific is to add a statement such as, "Other duties as may be assigned." Job descriptions should be reviewed and updated as the organization changes. No standard format exists for job descriptions. They vary in appearance and details from one company to another. Figure 8.3 outlines one job description that may be used for a fashion retail business.

When writing a job description for the potential employee, it is essential to use statements that can be clearly understood by the employee. Poorly written job descriptions will not provide enough guidance for the jobholder. As a company grows, the duties of the employees typically change. Determining the tasks and roles required of the position will go a long way toward hiring the right person for the job.

Figure 8.3 Job Description for a Retail Sales Associate

Job Title: Retail Sales Associate
Wage Category: Nonexempt
Supervisor: Manager, Retail Sales

Description
Assists customers in the purchase of merchandise. Must be able to describe a product's features, demonstrate its use, and show various styles and colors. Must be outgoing, polite, friendly, and patient. Must be able to work under pressure.

Tasks and Duties
• Displays clothing and fashion accessories.
• Greets customers as they browse through clothing.
• Advises customers on coordinating clothing and accessories.
• Collects payment and wraps clothing purchases.
• Keeps the store clean.
• May handle customer complaints.
• May keep account of inventory.
• May help to prepare the shop for special sales.
• Opens and closes registers.
• Is responsible for the contents of the register.
• Handles exchanges of merchandise.

Qualifications
High school diploma or an equivalent combination of education and experience from which comparable knowledge and abilities can be acquired.
Two to three years experience in retail sales preferable.

Fashion retail sales associates perform many tasks. Many associates are required to complete sales checks, receive cash, process charge payments, package merchandise, install displays, and maintain sales records. They may be held responsible for the contents of their registers, the handling of merchandise returns or exchanges, and counting inventory. Consumers spend millions of dollars every day on merchandise and often evaluate a store by its employees. Retail salespersons held over 4.6 million jobs in 1998 with the largest employers being department stores, clothing and accessories stores, and furniture and home furnishing stores.[14] Entrepreneurs of fashion retail companies should look for people who enjoy working with others, provide excellent customer service, and have the patience to deal with difficult customers.

Creating the Organizational Chart

Designing the organizational structure involves designating the "power relationship" between the owner, manager, and employees. The organizational structure is important to a business because the owner-manager cannot do all the tasks involved in making the business successful. Tasks, responsibility, and authority need to be articulated and delegated. The organizational chart defines how the business is organized and illustrates the relationships among the job positions. Management will want to assign individuals to positions that relate most directly to their skills and experience. Figure 8.4 is a sample organizational chart for a fashion retail business.

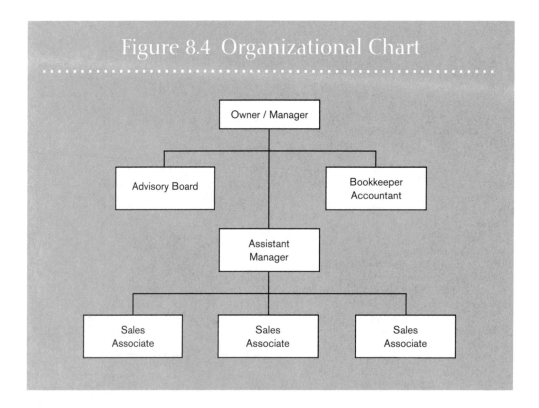

Figure 8.4 Organizational Chart

HIRING THE RIGHT EMPLOYEES

There are two qualifications to look for when hiring someone to join the team. First, the person must have the training and skills to do the job. Second, the person must have a track record that demonstrates his or her abilities. People are the most valuable asset of a company. The quality of the personnel determines the success of the company. Entrepreneurial management "involves recognizing the skills and know-how needed to succeed in a venture, knowing what each team member does or does not know, and then compensating for shortcomings, either be getting key people on board to fill voids or by an individual's accumulating the additional 'chunks' before he or she takes the plunge."[15]

Once the entrepreneur knows what to look for in an employee through the job analysis and job descriptions, the task of seeking the right person for the job can begin.

Sources for Recruiting Employees

Business owners have a number of avenues available to them to recruit employees. Sources for recruitment include personal recruiting or networking, classified advertisements, employee referrals, and employment agencies. Fashion retail businesses are fortunate in that they can usually recruit from a large pool of applicants. College students are always looking for part-time work; many look for an environment that promotes intrapreneurship in which they can use their creativity and skills. "A study conducted by Olsten Forum for Information Management found that while networking was the fastest-growing method of recruitment, help-wanted advertisements were the most frequently used—by 89 percent of respondents to the survey. Employee referrals were second (77 percent), followed by temporary help services (63 percent), networking (57 percent), and employment agencies (51 percent)."[16] Recruiting employees often requires using more than one approach. Hiring an employee is an investment in the business, and care should be taken to use as many sources as possible to recruit the best employees possible. Hiring an employee requires time and money. The process of finding and hiring employees has serious implications not only in time and money, but also in the future of the company.

The Job Interview

The interview process plays an important role in the selection of an applicant. It is rare that someone is hired without being interviewed. The interview process allows the entrepreneur to obtain information about a job applicant that will determine whether or not the candidate has the skills, education, abilities, and character traits necessary to fill the job. To make this determination, entrepreneurs will use such methods as application forms, background checks, employment tests, and personal interviews. Among these methods, the interview process typically carries the most weight in deciding who gets the job.

Planning for the Interview.
The interviewer should begin by collecting and reviewing résumés submitted by the applicants. Employers receive résumés from individuals who may or may not be good prospects for employment. The résumé summarizes the applicant's work history, education, and skills; it should include references. It will also be important to require the applicant to complete and sign a job application. By signing the application, applicants state that all facts contained on the application are true to the best of their belief. Simply submitting a resume does not give the business owner or company a signed statement. Screening job applicants ensures that candidates selected for the interview meet the minimum qualifications for the job. For example, if the job description states the candidate must have a bachelor's degree or several years of work experience, applicants without these qualifications would not be interviewed.

Once the pool of applicants has been determined, the entrepreneur will want to identify the goals of the interview. The entrepreneur should first review the job description and job analysis. Then the entrepreneur should develop a list of questions to ask each candidate. Asking open-ended questions, those that do not lend themselves to "yes" or "no" answers, gives the applicant the opportunity to expand on his or her experiences and abilities. For example, the interviewer may ask the candidate, "Give me an example of time when you had to deal with a dissatisfied customer. How did you handle the situation? What was the outcome?" These behavioral questions and hypothetical situations give the interviewer the opportunity to explore how the candidate will likely handle this situation if hired for the job. It will also help the interviewer assess the candidate's work habits and attitudes. It is important that each candidate be treated equally. Establishing a standard set of questions will help ensure that each candidate has the same opportunity.

Conducting the Interview.
It is likely that both the interviewer and applicant will be tense and nervous at the beginning of the interview. Easing into the interview through the use of icebreakers will lessen the tension. The interviewer may start by describing the culture of the business, the particular market niche the organization has, and the requirements of the job opening. Questions may be asked regarding special interests or hobbies

of the candidate. It may also be helpful for the interviewer to point out that he or she will be taking notes during the interview. Once both parties are relaxed, the formal interview process can begin. The interviewer will refer to the questions on the list compiled prior to the interview. Effective interviewers spend more time listening than they do talking. The goal is to find out about the job candidate.

At one time, interviewers could ask applicants almost any question they chose. Today, asking "any question" is a lawsuit waiting to happen. The Equal Employment Opportunity Commission (EEOC) is a government agency established by Title VII of the Civil Rights Act of 1964. It is designed to ensure equal opportunity in employment through administrative and judicial enforcement. Although this agency does not provide a list of questions not to ask in an interview, it will search for evidence of questions that have been asked that may have resulted in lawsuits. The burden of proof lies with the employer to prove all questions asked during the interview are job-related and nondiscriminatory. To avoid lawsuits, the entrepreneur must be certain the questions being asked are relevant to the position. As in all facets of hiring employees, it is important that candidates have not been screened out because they are in a protected class. Protected class may include race, national origin, sex, age, religion, and disability. State and federal laws protect individuals from discrimination based on these and other classes.

Once the interview is over, the entrepreneur should conduct background checks on all candidates being seriously considered. Résumés are easily fabricated. A background check may cover such things as credit reports, conviction reports, and calling previous employers listed on the applications or people listed as references. The intent of a background check is to determine the characteristics and work history of the candidate. It is important to know what type of work was performed in the past, how the job was performed, and whether the candidate would make a good employee. Conducting thorough background checks can avoid headaches for the employer down the road.

In an article published by *USA Today,* in January 1998, Del Still, author of *High Impact Hiring* (1998) and consultant to several Fortune 100 companies states, "One of the biggest mistakes when interviewing job candidates is making a hiring decision within the first five to nine minutes of the interview. Interviewers often base their decision on intuition or gut feelings rather than on data. Many respond to first impressions or physical appearance."[17] Through the job analysis, the completion of job descriptions, the screening of résumés, and the interview process, the entrepreneur will have the needed tools to hire the best employees for the positions. It is important to paint as complete a picture as possible of each candidate in order to make an informed decision. When the decision is made as to which applicant to hire, the job offer is made. It should include details of pay, work hours, holidays, employee benefits, working conditions, and job responsibilities. The job offer should be made in writing to prevent any misunderstandings.

SELECTING THE ADVISORY TEAM

Although fashion retail businesses may be set up as corporations (a separate legal entity), the board of directors may be the entrepreneur. A board of directors is a group of people elected by the stockholders of a corporation who will be responsible for overseeing the overall direction and policy of the corporation. The board then serves only a legal function. An individual entrepreneur will need a team of outside advisers such as accountants, bankers, lawyers, insurance agents, and marketing consultants. This group of consultants is known as an advisory team. To complement entrepreneurial weaknesses, the advisory team plays an integral role in the organization. It provides the entrepreneur with valuable knowledge and input to aid in decision making, particularly in areas where the entrepreneur has limited knowledge and expertise.

The advisers should be chosen in the early stage of the company, preferably before the business opens. They should be interviewed to determine whether they have the qualifications necessary to contribute to the success of the business. The fact that someone holds a marketing degree does not make him or her good at marketing. The entrepreneur may want to seek referrals from other entrepreneurs. Many professionals solicited to serve on an advisory board will do so with little or no compensation. The entrepreneur may consider providing benefits, such as in-store discounts to replace monetary compensation for their support.

Funders evaluating business plans will look for a solid advisory team to help drive the business to success. They recognize that entrepreneurs cannot do it all alone. They also recognize that most small companies do not have the capital available to hire a marketing team, a chief financial officer, and a human resources expert. Establishing an advisory team and indicating this in the business plan will not only ensure the entrepreneur that he or she has the tools necessary to run the business, but also let the funder know that a good foundation has been put into place.

MOTIVATING EMPLOYEES

To motivate employees, one must first understand what inspires or encourages them. Money is not the only motivator. Motivation is defined as the willingness to exert high levels of effort toward organizational goals, conditioned by the effort's ability to satisfy some individual need.[18] Employees often start a job highly motivated. Keeping them that way is difficult and challenging, but important. Motivated employees on staff reduce turnover and increase productivity. Motivated employees have positive morale that results in satisfied, well-served customers.

One of the ways in which employers can motivate employees is through empowerment. Employees are more motivated to make decisions and meet company objectives if they are given the freedom, responsibility, and authority to do so. Employees bring with them an array of skills, talents, and knowledge that they are ready to put to use. If business owners empower employees to use their talents and creativity, employees will feel challenged to use these attributes. To successfully empower employees, business owners must have the confidence to give their employees the authority and responsibility to grow in their jobs, must be willing to step back and let the employees do the job, trust that they can handle the empowerments, and acknowledge them for their contribution.

In addition to empowerment, employees can be motivated by other factors. Employees need feedback. Defining measurable goals is one way of providing feedback. The entrepreneur has the performance of the company to measure as well. By linking employee performance to the overall goals of the company, the entrepreneur can measure employees' performance against the progress of the company. Two factors improve the bottom line: increasing revenue or decreasing expenses. One way to increase revenue is to increase the customer base through effective sales personnel.

One of the more common ways in which employers provide feedback to employees is through the use of performance appraisals. The performance appraisal measures an employee's actual performance against the performance desired. Performance appraisals should be designed to provide the employee with measurable outcomes, to link the job description to the employee's performance, and to incorporate the goals of the employee. Employees are not always motivated solely by money. Today's generation is interested in being a part of a company. If designed and used properly, a performance appraisal can give employees feedback on how well they're performing in the company, which in turn can provide a source of motivation. It also provides the business owner and employee with the opportunity to set goals and create a plan for improving performance as well as a basis for rewarding employees for good performance. An employee evaluation form is illustrated in Figure 8.5.

Figure 8.5 Performance Appraisal Form

GARLAND STORES
EXECUTIVE PERFORMANCE EVALUATION MX 10535 (1/77)
BUYER/MANAGER

NAME _____   Spring / Fall

1 = Unacceptable   2 = Marginal   3 = Good   4 = Very Good   5 = Outstanding

MERCHANDISE RESPONSIBILITY
1. Initiates plans/actions to optimize sales.
2. Understands the importance of floor presentation by proper classification, color, or trend.
3. Understands the components of coordinated merchandise presentation by proper arrangement/assortment.
4. Understands the importance of proper stock levels relative to the business.
5. Sees that stock is filled in, labelled accurately as to price and size, counted per schedule, and is neat and accessible.
6. Department records are kept up to date correctly (turnover, etc.)
7. Plans actions and recommendations for assigned classification, which reflect an understanding of the department's current potential, trends, seasonal needs, and past experience.

MERCHANDISE KNOWLEDGE
1. Understands the Merchandise Budget.
2. Understands merchandising reports/information and effectively utilizes them.
3. Understands the flow of paperwork and related systems.
4. Able to project and forecast in a concise and precise manner (rates of sale, reorders, etc.)

LEADERSHIP RESPONSIBILITY
1. Constantly apprises and informs sales staff of merchandise selection and trends.
2. Is flexible and can adapt to the changing needs of the business within the context of the departments' goals and objectives.
3. Is well informed of the merchandise situations (on hand, on order, stock conditions); the action of the competition; department problems and recommended solutions.
4. Informs store owner about sales objectives (through communication, store visits, etc.).
5. Interacts well and deals effectively with store personnel.
6. Takes constructive criticism well and tries to correct shortcomings.
7. Is well motivated and a self-starter.
8. Maintains high standards for self and department.

PLANNING AND ORGANIZATION
1. Is well organized and apportions time constructively and wisely.
2. Meets deadlines and schedules.
3. Reacts to the changing needs of the business by taking actions which reflect a basic understanding of priorities.
4. Learns quickly and effectively.

ACCOMPLISHMENTS
What specific measurable results has this individual accomplished in the appraisal period (sales growth, profit):

....

....

....

OBJECTIVES
What specific business objectives are to be achieved by the next evaluation period:

....

....

....

....

....

....

....

....

....

FUTURE GROWTH AND DEVELOPMENT
What ideas and thoughts do you have for this individual's professional development:

....

....

....

....

....

....

....

....

....

....

....

....

1	2	3	4	5	**OVERALL EVALUATION**
☐	☐	☐	☐	☐	Performance as a manager
☐	☐	☐	☐	☐	Performance as a buyer
☐	☐	☐	☐	☐	Potential for merit increase

Discussed With Assistant Buyer:

Signature   Date

Owner's Signature   Salary Action

M Granger, *Case Studies in Merchandising Apparel & Soft Goods* (New York, New York: Fairchild Publications, 1996, p. 261)

It is important to review an employee's performance more than once a year. By frequently visiting the performance appraisal, the employee has the opportunity to correct and improve performance. The performance evaluation process, if done properly and often, can be a great motivational tool.

THE COMPENSATION PACKAGE

One of the challenges facing start-up and early-stage companies is the ability to hire and retain employees with a competitive compensation package. A compensation package refers to the monetary or other value an employee receives in exchange for services.

Often, start-up and early-stage companies do not have the luxury of giving large bonuses or other monetary rewards to employees. Compensation packages can come in many forms. Recognition, respect, feedback, and job security are a few elements that can make up a compensation package. Entrepreneurs can be creative when it comes to rewarding employees. A resourceful entrepreneur will determine what motivates the employee and what gives him or her a sense of reward. Fashion retail stores often offer employees discounts on merchandise or commissions on sales to compensate for good performance. Other rewards may come in the form of tickets to a concert, or dinner for two at a local restaurant. Some employees respond well to intangible rewards such as balance between work and home life, challenges in the job, and an exciting organizational culture. Others may feel that compensation in the form of company stock is rewarding. Creative compensation packages may ensure the keeping of productive, long-term employees. Whatever the compensation package, the goal is to recognize what motivates employees and reward them accordingly.

CONCLUSION

Management encompasses the processes of planning, organizing, controlling, directing, and communicating. Effective management is key to creating a successful venture. Funders would rather see a second-rate product with a first-rate management team than a first-rate product with a second-rate management team. The business plan requires defining the management and the advisory team. Successful entrepreneurs know and admit to their weaknesses and then bring in people to compensate for their weaknesses in order to move the company forward.

Effective management requires that the entrepreneur be an effective leader. Effective leaders have the ability to influence others to achieve a common goal and the power and freedom to achieve that goal. Effective leaders know how to create a vision for their company, to build a team, to respect their employees, and to lead by example. They provide the tools necessary for employees to carry out their jobs and goals, and they give credit where credit is due.

The organizational culture will define the ways in which things are done within a company. With an effective company culture, employees and management share a set of values and behaviors that govern the organization. Policies such as open-book management can be explored to determine whether they fit with the organizational culture.

Effective communication is important to any organization and good leadership. In a business plan, it can mean the difference between being funded or not. Effective communicators know their topic, say what they mean, listen, and give others their complete attention. Creating an intrapreneurial environment is another consideration of an organization. Intrapreneurship invites an entrepreneurial spirit among employees in an organization.

Defining the organizational structure—job tasks, how they are divided and grouped, and how they are coordinated—affects the management of the company. Knowing how to develop job descriptions and developing them before potential employees are interviewed, conducting background checks, and recruiting the right employees are invaluable to a start-up or an early-stage company. Conducting a job analysis and creating job specifications help both employer and employee know what is expected of them. Hiring the right employees and motivating these employees is key to the success of any venture.

WRITING THE PLAN

Develop the management plan section of the business plan by using the following topics from Chapter 14 as a guide.

SECTION	TOPIC
Management	Management team
	Compensation and ownership
	Board of directors/advisory counsel
	Infrastructure
	Contracts and franchise agreements
	Insurance
	Employee incentives
	Organization chart

Business Mentor™ CD-ROM—Business Plan—Management Plan

KEY TERMS

advisory team
board of directors
communication
compensation package
intrapreneurship
job analysis
job description
leadership
motivation

nonverbal communication
open-book management
organizational chart
organizational culture
organizational structure
performance appraisal
protected class
verbal communication

QUESTIONS

1. Explain the importance of the management team. Why would defining the team be important in the management plan?
2. What skills do effective managers need to bring to the table?
3. What is leadership? What are the differences between leadership and management?
4. What behaviors do leaders exhibit?
5. Why is determining the organizational culture important? What role does it play in the success of the company?
6. Define open-book management. Why would this work for some companies? Under what conditions might it not be successful?
7. What is the most important component of the communication process?
8. List some barriers to communication.
9. What is intrapreneurship? How does it differ from traditional organizational culture?
10. Discuss the process of conducting a job analysis.
11. What are the differences between a job specification and a job description?
12. What function does a job description serve in the hiring process?
13. Develop a number of questions to be asked in an interview.
14. Why is an advisory team important to the success of an organization? Which professions should be represented?
15. List several creative ways to motivate employees in start-up businesses.

REFERENCES

1. Stanley Rich and David Gumpert, *Business Plans That Win $$$* (New York, New York: Harper and Row, 1983, p. 65)

2. Norman Scarborough and Thomas Zimmerer, *Effective Small Business Management: An Entrepreneurial Approach,* 6th ed. (Upper Saddle River, New Jersey: Prentice-Hall, 2000, p. 306)

3. Jeffry A. Timmons, *New Venture Creation: Entrepreneurship for the 21st Century,* 5th ed. (Boston, Massachesetts: Irwin/McGraw-Hill, 1999, p. 246)

4. Marcia A. Reed-Woodward, "Lead, Follow, or Get Out of the Way," *Black Enterprise,* April, 2001

5. Timmons, *New Venture Creation Entrepreneurship for the 21st Century,* 5th ed. (Boston, Massachusetts: Irwin/McGraw-Hill, 1999, p. 246)

6. Ibid.

7. Adapted from Diane Eade, "Motivational Management Developing Leadership Skills," www.adv–leadership_grp.com./articles/motivate.htm

8. Brad Brown and Jack Stack, "Get Employees Involved in the Game of Business," *St. Louis Business Journal,* March 28, 1997, www.bizjournals. com/stlouis

9. Material reproduced from Donald F. Barkman, *Open Book Management, Your EZ Intro to OBM* (Knoxville, Tennessee: The Business Center, 1997)

10. S. Robbins, *Organizational Behavior,* 8th ed. (Upper Saddle River, New Jersey: Prentice-Hall, 1998, p. 323)

11. Robert Hisrich and Michael Peters, *Entrepreneurship,* 4th ed. (Boston, Massachusetts: Irwin/McGraw-Hill, 1998, p. 47)

12. Ibid.

13. A. Sherman, G. Bohlander, and S. Sneu, *Managing Human Resources,* 11th ed. (Mason, Ohio: South Western College Publishing, 1998, p. 90)

14. *Retail Salespersons, Occupational Outlook Handbook,* U.S. Department of Labor: Bureau of Labor Statistics, stats.bls.gov/ocos/21.htm

15. Timmons, *New Venture Creation Entrepreneurship for the 21st Century,* 5th ed. (Boston, Massachusetts: Irwin/McGraw-Hill, 1999, p. 246)

16. William Megginson, Mary Jane Byrd, and Leon C. Meggarson, *Small Business Management: An Entrepreneur's Guidebook,* 3rd ed. (Boston, Massachusetts: Irwin/McGraw-Hill, 2000, p. 224)

17. "Firms Can Avoid Costly Hiring Errors," *USA Today,* January 1998, www.findarticles.com

18. S. Robbins, *Organizational Behavior,* p. 168

SUGGESTED READING

Stephen R. Covey, *The 7 Habits of Highly Effective People* (New York, New York: Simon and Schuster, 1998)

Deborah Harrington–Mackin, *The Team Building Tool Kit: Tips, Tactics, and Rules for Effective Workplace Teams* (New York, New York: Americom, 1994)

Stephen R Covey, *Principle-Centered Leadership:* (New York, New York: Simon and Schuster, 1998)

John Schuster, Jill Carpenter, with Patricia M Kane, *The Power of Open Book Management: Releasing the True Potential of People's Minds, Hearts, and Hands:* (New York, New York: John Wiley and Sons Inc., 1996)

George Rimler, *Small Business: Developing the Winning Management Team* (New York, New York: Americom, 1994)

Ardella Ramey and Carl R.J. Sniffen, *A Company Policy and Personnel Workbook,* 3rd ed. (Grants Pass, Oregon: Oasis Press, 1996)

. . . .

ENTERING THE WORLD OF THE ENTREPRENEUR

. . . .

1. Schedule an appointment with an entrepreneur. Ask about his or her leadership style and what impact it has on the company. Ask about the leadership skills he or she possesses.

2. Ask the entrepreneur to define his or her organizational structure. What key positions are necessary to run the company? Ask whether job descriptions were developed before recruiting and hiring employees. What process is used to hire new employees? What questions are asked of applicants during interviews?

3. Ask the entrepreneur how the advisory team was selected. What did he or she look for in terms of qualifications for this team?

4. Ask the entrepreneur, "If you could go back and do anything different regarding hiring employees or conducting interviews, what would it be?"

ENTERPRISING ENTREPRENEUR

At 29, Malia Mills is one of American's hottest young swimsuit designers. Her lingerie-inspired creations have won kudos from all corners of the fashion world. Her creations have appeared on the cover of the *Sports Illustrated* swimsuit issue as well as on the pages of *Harper's Bazaar* and *Vogue*. Her curve-enhancing designs—which retail for from $120 to $160—are not for the bashful, but one cannot call them skimpy either. Her approach is so detailed that it is almost architectural. One top-and-bottom combination (each piece is sold separately) is crafted from 24 individual parts. To complicate matters, Mills frequently uses fabrics like oxford cloth, which has no stretch. "It's hard as hell," she says, "but it makes us different."

Mills grew up in Hawaii and traces her love of bikinis to her mother's prohibition of them. She never considered making them for a living until after her 1990 graduation from Cornell University, when she was working for a dressmaker. One day she received a call from a college classmate, Julie Stern, a newly hired assistant at *Sports Illustrated*. "Out of the blue, she called me and said, 'I'm working on the swimsuit issue and, I know it sounds insane, but you should make some bathing suits'."

Stern knew that Mills had stitched only a couple of purple bikinis for friends at school, but she had confidence in her pal's hardcore work ethic. "She used to sleep curled up on one of those huge pattern tables next to her sewing machine at school. I knew she had the drive and was excited to give her the opportunity."

Two weeks later, Mills overnighted six suits to Julie Campbell, who coordinates the swimsuit issue. "She called and said, 'They're great! We're taking them with us," Mills recalls. The suits never made it into the magazine, but a few encouraging words were all Mills needed to hear. She quit her job and two weeks later arrived at Campbell's New York office with sketches in hand, eager for some coaching on a new career. Never giving up, Mills resorted to showing her portfolio by day and working at a restaurant at night. In 1993, her designs made it inside the coveted *Sports Illustrated* swimsuit issue, along with the accompanying calendars and videos.

Mills's phone started ringing. Calls came in from women who do not like to be in the sun as well as men who appreciated the subtle sex appeal of covered arms. An editor at *Harper's Bazaar* wanted to feature the suits. Hugh Hefner's wife wanted to make a purchase. Someone from Vidal Sassoon called to give her an award for "excellence in new design." As orders began pouring in, Mills soon found out that designing dazzling suits was a cinch compared with manufacturing them, especially on a no-frills budget. One year, she and Stern (who became her business partner in 1994) hand-dyed fabric for

6,000 bikinis because they couldn't afford the minimum purchase of 1,000 yards in each of five colors. "I can't tell you how grueling it was," Mills recalls. "You might have a great idea and an amazing marketing strategy. You might be able to make the sale. But to truly execute it and make sure you bring money in, that's the hard part." Mills devotes most of her time these days to badgering manufacturers, negotiating with contractors, and courting investors, "To be successful in business isn't just a matter of how talented you are," she says. "It's how many times you can go to bat."

Adapted from F. Penn, www.maliamills.com/pr/features/pov.html, from P.O.V.

Chapter 9

MERCHANDISE PLANNING

INTRODUCTION

In the previous chapters, the entrepreneur examines the prospective business from a company, or holistic, perspective. The market potential of the company, its prospective customer and the product, methods of entering the market niche that will service this customer, and strategies for finding a location for the company were explored in terms of the business as a whole. In this chapter, a specific area of the business is examined. The entrepreneur is now ready to begin examining the business from an operational perspective, that of merchandising.

Merchandising refers to the buying and selling of goods. Merchandising is what separates a retail store with almost any product line from a fashion retail store. Fashion goods require unique policies and procedures in merchandising that other product classifications do not have. The reasons for a specific focus on fashion merchandising are diverse; however, they primarily include the following: seasonality of goods, limitations and localization of resources, and diversity of product life cycles. For example, the retail fashion buyer, for the most part, purchases goods at regional apparel markets or through manufacturers' representatives. These resources determine when new goods are available through the introduction of new lines, usually in relation to seasonal changes. Often, it is the merchandise selection that generates success or failure for the fashion retail business. It is the retail buyer's responsibility to locate, secure, price, and promote the merchandise assortment. Whether the entrepreneur takes on the role of the buyer or assigns this role to someone else, it is one of the most significant jobs within the fashion business.

THE ROLE OF THE BUYER

The merchandise found in a fashion retail operation has been purchased either by the entrepreneur, a buyer who is employed by the company, or a resident buyer who represents the retailer. In large operations, the buying tasks are performed by specialists who have acquired specific knowledge in preparation for the buying function. In small operations, the buying function may be one of many carried out by the company's owner. Whatever the size of the business, it is the purchasing of fashion merchandise, more than any other merchandise classification, that provides the greatest challenges. In nonfashion retail operations, the goods are considered to be staple or basic items, merchandise that is in demand for extended periods of time and that is not subject to rapid style changes. In contrast, fashion items are frequently available in a wide range of styles and have a life expectancy that is relatively brief.

Buyers are the individuals who determine the merchandise needs of departments or sometimes entire stores and, ultimately, make the purchases. The store buyer has a great number of responsibilities; these include: (1) purchasing the merchandise, (2) pricing it, (3) assigning floor space to items or lines, (4) selecting specific merchandise for visual presentation and advertisement, and (5) managing or collaborating with personnel in various areas of the business, such as sales, receiving, advertising, and visual merchandising. The most important task performed by the store buyer is merchandise selection. This responsibility encompasses determining which goods are needed, calculating the size of purchases, determining from whom goods should be bought, recognizing when merchandise should be ordered for timely delivery, and negotiating the prices and terms of sale. From a planning perspective, the buyer projects sales and inventory levels by month for each department and, subsequently, determines the amount of funding to be spent on inventory. Once the merchandise arrives at the store, the buyer's job is not over.

In order for the retail operation to make a profit, buyers must determine at what prices goods should be marked. Several factors are considered before pricing decisions are made, such as the level of competition in the trading area, the speed of inventory turnover, the perishability of the merchandise, and the buyer's judgment of the value of the individual goods. In some retail organizations, the manner in which merchandise is displayed on the selling floor and where it is actually placed are left to the buyer's discrimination. Selecting merchandise for promotions is yet another determination that the buyer makes. In addition to determining what to promote, the buyer decides how to promote the merchandise. The decisions related to products featured in window displays, newspaper or television advertisements, and fashion shows are frequently assigned to the retail buyer. While the buyer is not necessarily an expert in the technical aspects of promotion, he or she is considered the most knowledgeable in assessing which items should be featured to generate customer traffic.

THE RESIDENT BUYING OFFICE

Some entrepreneurs allocate funding to employ a resident buying office in order to gain support and assistance in buying and promotion. The resident buying office is a company that offers suggestions for merchandise suppliers and assists the entrepreneur and/or buyer by providing a significant number of services. Merchandise is generally not purchased by resident buyers, unless they have the company's authorization to do so. On occasion, some entrepreneurs will elect to use the resident buying office for all purchases. A resident buying office keeps the entrepreneur aware of occurrences in the marketplace without ever having to leave the retail operation. Located within the wholesale markets in the major fashion centers in the United States and abroad, these organizations provide different kinds of assistance to retail buyers. In the United States, resident buying offices are primarily located in New York, Dallas, Los Angeles, Chicago, and Atlanta. The primary function of the resident buying office is advisory. Some of the more typical services involve locating new resources, previewing collections, following up on orders that are to be shipped, communicating with buyers, preparing for market week visits, facilitating merchandise returns or markdown allowances, and analyzing market conditions.

More recently, the resident buying office has become critically important to the fashion retailer in the area of private label merchandise. The entrepreneur of a start-up business may not be able to finance the purchase of a large quantity of goods, as required for most private-label orders. Most manufacturers cannot, or simply will not, produce merchandise to specifications without a substantial commitment in terms of units purchased. The resident buying office can be instrumental in providing this service for specialty retailers. It can develop the specifications for the merchandise, then create a label that offers exclusively to its client fashion retailers. By combining the smaller orders of a number of these client stores, a large order can be placed with the manufacturer. This "combine and conquer" philosophy enables the entrepreneur of a specialty retail operation to have unique merchandise, exclusive to the trade area, at a reasonable cost and with acceptable profit margins.

Resident buying offices are owned and operated in a variety of ways. The majority of resident buying offices are independent. As independents, they have no affiliation with any specific company or group of companies. Rather, they represent retailers who are willing to pay a fee for their services. Retailers contract with the independent resident buying office, guaranteeing a flat fee for its services, a percent of the cost of merchandise ordered by the resident buyers, and/or a percent of the retailer's annual sales. Another type of resident buying office is one that is privately owned by the retailer. Such ownership is practical only for retailers with very large operations and where exclusive attention to their own needs is critical to the success of the business. Retailers, such as J. C. Penney, Sears, and Neiman Marcus, operate their own resident buying offices. In addition to the assistance these offices provide to the companies' buyers, the private resident buyers are primarily responsible for developing private label merchandise and reviewing foreign markets to secure exclusive merchandise for their own stores. In between independent and store-owned resident buying offices, the cooperative resident buying office represents a group of stores that operates under a corporate ownership. Companies, such as May Merchandising Corporation, which owns Famous Barr and Lord & Taylor, utilize the cooperative office arrangement.

THE BUYING AND MERCHANDISE PROCESS

The person responsible for buying merchandise for a fashion retail operation seeks out information sources to help identify the wants and needs of the company target market. Brand preferences, price ranges, sizing preferences, and colors are among the topics that the buyer will want to investigate.

Sources for Effective Buying

The entrepreneurs of fashion retail operations use a variety of sources within their own companies, in conjunction with numerous outside informational sources, to help them find key items and resources that will result in profits for their businesses.

Internal Sources **Internal Sources** that the entrepreneur of an established business may investigate are past records that are available most frequently through computers. These records may show merchandise performance by vendor, including markdowns, returns, and delivery performance. They may also illustrate unit and/or dollar sales by merchandise classification, as well as profit margins. Some retail software packages, such as Retail#Pro, allow the entrepreneur to examine the success or failure rates of each vendor, style, color, price point, and size allocation.

For the new business, internal sources are limited. Past sales records, for example, are nonexistent. As a result, the entrepreneur of a new operation may choose to develop questionnaires directed to potential customers seeking information on merchandise preferences. Additionally, the entrepreneur may choose to record observations. Exploring the merchandise assortments of competitive retailers and the buying patterns of customers of these retail operations will provide a great amount of insight on merchandise preferences. How many customers enter a competitor's store during a given period? How many of them exit with purchases? Which lines are carried? Which styles are featured in windows and on storefront fixtures? Which styles or vendors are heavily included on the markdown rack? Finally, the entrepreneur may decide to host meetings with employees or implement a "want slip" program as efforts to gain information about what the customer will be looking for once the business is open. A "want slip" program allows the sales associate to communicate customers' requests to the buyer. The sales associate fills out a form which indicates items customers are seeking that are not available in stock.

Employee feedback is an internal source that successful entrepreneurs often believe is of critical importance to the decision-making process for merchandise planning. Staff members can provide valuable information because of their close involvement with the customers or by virtue of the specialized fashion roles they play in the retail operation. What better resource is there than the sales associate when it comes to examining customer likes and dislike? While computer records can interpret the performance of merchandise that has been purchased, they fall short in terms of reporting customer requests that could not be satisfied. A particular designer line, a specific look or style, a hot color, or a significant price point are all merchandise assortment factors that may be described by sales associates and are not reflected in a computer-generated report. By involving the sales associate and management personnel in ways to improve sales and satisfy consumer needs, the entrepreneur and/or buyer accomplishes two goals. First, he or she can gain information that has come directly from the consumer. Second, these efforts can create a human resource team that is working a common mission, the successful and thriving business.

External Sources There are a number of external sources available to the entrepreneur. External sources are those available outside the business such as resident buying offices, fashion forecasters, and reporting services. They may be used to locate new vendors, to compare merchandise performance, or to identify fashion and consumer trends. The Donegar Group, based in Manhattan, is one of the largest resident buying offices in the country for specialty stores. Tobe, Color Association, and Cotton, Inc., are examples of fashion forecasters and reporting services used by fashion entrepreneurs.

Additionally, the entrepreneur may study any of the many trade and consumer periodicals that focus on specific fashion industries to learn about future trends and consumer preferences. Most merchandise classifications are represented by a trade journal. *Women's*

Wear Daily, *Daily News Record*, *Earnshaw's Review*, *Accessories*, *Stores*, and *Footwear News* are some of the trade periodicals available to the entrepreneur. Consumer publications, such as *Glamour*, *Mademoiselle*, and *YM*, also host seminars on seasonal trends and consumer directions for fashion retailers, as do fiber associations such as Cotton, Inc., Wool Bureau, and Mohair Council. Finally, the entrepreneur may seek trend and sales information from vendors, particularly during market weeks.

The entrepreneur will want to examine benchmark operations in noncompetitive geographic areas. A benchmark operation is one that reflects a vision similar to the one the entrepreneur has for his or her fashion retail operation, but is usually not in the same general location (therefore, not filling the market niche the entrepreneur hopes to capture). Many entrepreneurs will travel outside the locale where they intend to open their businesses to peruse retail operations around the country that are successful in similar market niches.

Market Week

There are traditional purchase periods, called market weeks, when buyers begin to make selections for the next season. Market weeks are predetermined times when buyers go to regional apparel markets to review new lines. The number of market weeks varies according to merchandise classification. Major apparel market weeks take place five to six times a year in New York City, Dallas, Chicago, Atlanta, and Los Angeles. Smaller regional markets are located throughout the United States, in such cities as Kansas City, St. Louis, Seattle, Boston, Denver, and Miami.

The apparel mart is a building or group of buildings that house showrooms in which sales representatives present apparel lines to retail buyers. The buyer can contact the market director of the apparel mart to obtain registration information, a calendar of market weeks, and a directory of vendors showing lines during the market weeks. Most of the apparel marts now have Web sites that provide this information, as well as dates of fashion shows, educational seminar schedules, and lists of special events that the buyer may want to attend. Some marts are devoted entirely to apparel or gifts and home furnishings; others house showrooms for all of these classifications. The marts contain permanent showrooms for sales representatives and companies that elect to lease the space on a yearly basis. Additionally, there are temporary booths in exhibition halls that the vendors can rent for each market week. Often, markets for men's, women's and children's wear are held during different weeks.

How important are market weeks to the buyer? Market weeks allow the buyer to review a significant number of lines in a fairly short period of time. As a result, the buyer has the opportunity to comparison-shop before actually ordering merchandise. By attending seminars held during market weeks, the buyer can acquire information about fashion trends, promotion and advertising, visual merchandising, and a number of other topics. Additionally, the buyer can locate new lines to purchase for the business. Finally, the buyer can develop a network of support systems during market week. Positive working relationships with sales representatives can result in timely deliveries, advertising allowances, and merchandise adjustments. Mutual respect, trust, and cooperation between the buyer and the vendor are necessary to ensure long-term profitability for both parties. Small, or start-up, businesses cannot overcome the edge that quantity purchasing power gives to the giants in fashion retailing (e.g., J. C. Penney, Macy's, and Sears). They can, however, improve their relative position by limiting their resources to a few key vendors and by building relationships with the sales representatives of these lines. Key vendors are lines carried in depth in a retail organization. These are the lines that the customer identifies with the retailer because of the broad style selection and large number of units. It is important, however, to strike a balance between developing key vendors and introducing new lines to the consumer. Herbert Seegel, former president of R. H. Macy & Company, states, "There is a certain synergy in having a combination of stars and rookies in a department's vendor mix."[1] The buyer can find them all during market week, new and old vendors.

A second important network available to the buyer during market week is other buyers. Market week allows buyers to meet buyers from different geographic locations who may be purchasing for similar businesses. Because the businesses are noncompetitive and the buyers share similar challenges, market week can be an ideal time to share successes and failures. Buyers of noncompetitive retail operations will often exchange the names of new vendors they have discovered, discuss lines with which they have had poor sales performance, and share insights on such topics as advertising, fashion trends, and travel bargains. Many of these buyers stay in touch between markets, using colleagues as sounding boards for new ideas and as sources of new information.

Resource Selection

With a seemingly limitless number of available resources, domestic and foreign, for every merchandise classification, the buyer must evaluate those companies from which purchases were made in the past and investigate the possibility of adding other vendors to the business's list of suppliers. A vendor analysis that summarizes sales, markdowns, and returns for each manufacturer can guide buyers after the opening season. The buyer for a new store, however, will have to rely on his or her perception of who the target market is, what this customer will likely purchase, and which lines will differentiate the business from the competition. Additionally, minimum orders specified by the various vendors often determine whether or not the buyer can purchase a line. Minimum orders refer to the dollar or unit amount that a vendor requires before accepting an order. For example, some vendors require a minimum opening order of $1,000, or, perhaps, 20 units. Other vendors may impose a minimum order of six pieces per style with a six-style requirement. There is no industry standard regarding minimum orders, and there are some vendors that have no minimum-order policy. The minimum order is, however, a common practice among fashion industry resources that buyers of small operations must consider.

If the minimum-order requirement does not eliminate a vendor for the buyer, then what factors should be considered in the selection of resources? There are a number of variables to consider such as merchandise offered, distribution practices, promotional policies, shipping and inventory maintenance, cooperation, competitive pricing, and adherence to the purchase order as it was written. Primarily, a vendor is selected when the merchandise styling, brand name, level of quality, and price point blend to match the customer's preferences. A designer label or brand alone, however, does not guarantee success. Distribution practices play a significant role merchandise desirability. Distribution practices refer to the manufacturer's policies concerning where a line is to be shipped. No buyer wants to carry the same merchandise that is found in a competitor's business.

Exclusivity, the limited availability of merchandise, is critical to specialty operations. In selecting vendors, the buyer should attempt to locate manufacturers that agree to limit sales of a particular style to a defined geographic area. Legislation makes this a difficult task, since manufacturers are not legally able to exclusively distribute merchandise at their discretion. If a retailer has the appropriate credit credentials, he or she cannot be denied the right to purchase from a company. Vendors deal with this problem in a number of ways. They may institute a large minimum-order amount for initial seasonal purchases, thereby eliminating retailers that are unable to meet this purchase requirement. Merchandise production may be limited so that orders are filled on a "first come, first served" or seniority basis. Additionally, many vendors have initiated policies that restrict specific groups within the lines to certain retailers. These vendors will offer specific merchandise groups to retailers located in noncompetitive trade areas. If two retailers are located in the same geographic location and target similar customers, each will have the opportunity to purchase a particular style grouping unavailable to the competition. With this option, retailers have some degree of exclusivity. The manufacturers are adhering to the law, as other merchants may still carry the line, but all retailers will not feature exactly the same style or colors.

Further, manufacturers' representatives will not call on more than one store in a locale. Unless the current account discontinues the line or reduces the amount of orders, the sales representative will not seek out competitive operations to sell the line to. In other cases, the sales representative may simply let a retailer know that there is a merchant in the area already carrying the line. Many buyers will decide to pass on a line that is featured at a nearby retail operation. Finally, the sales representative may work with more than one account in a given area, with the agreement that each will carry different styles within the line. An example of this type of negotiation is the former Crickett West specialty boutique located in the Country Club Plaza in Kansas City, Missouri. The store's claim to fame was its exclusive merchandise assortment. Although it carried top labels that other prestige stores on the plaza also featured, the buyers of Crickett West purchased the styles in colors that were not carried by the other retailers. Color, in this case, guaranteed exclusivity to the retail operation.

Another factor to consider in vendor selection is the manufacturer's promotional policies. Frequently, retailers have periodic sales to entice clientele. During these sale periods, markdowns are offered in conjunction with off-price merchandise, goods that the buyer has been able to purchase from the manufacturer at below the wholesale price. Through combining markdown merchandise with off-price goods, the buyer is able to achieve a higher markup and, ultimately, higher profits. Just as retailers need to reduce retail prices on merchandise that is slow to sell, manufacturers face the same problem. Some manufacturers dispose of such goods through their own factory outlets or through sales to companies that deal exclusively in off-pricing retailing. Others have promotional policies that allow their regular retail accounts the opportunity to buy closeout merchandise, which usually includes merchandise that has been overproduced or returned by retailers due to a lack of sales or shipment past the cancellation dates specified on orders. Often, closeouts are available in the middle of the retailer's selling season, when the manufacturer is moving on to the next season. As a result, the buyer has the opportunity to bolster the inventory with fresh merchandise, and possibly generate additional sales, at lower wholesale costs. The buyer offering special sales events must make certain that a number of vendors he or she works with will provide merchandise closeouts to ensure a more profitable business.

Another facet of the manufacturer's promotional policy is the availability of advertising allowances, funding provided to retailers by manufacturers for advertisements featuring their products. In today's retail environment, the cost of promoting the business is high. Many entrepreneurs find it extremely difficult to allocate the dollars necessary to effectively advertise their businesses. In order to add to the advertising budget, the buyer will want to negotiate with vendors for advertising allowances.

Cooperative advertising refers to a program in which the vendor shares the cost of advertising with the retail operations. The level of participation, dollar order requirements, and advertisement guidelines vary; however, the concept is fairly uniform among manufacturers. For example, a manufacturer may offer an advertising allowance based on 5 percent of the retail operation's total orders. If the buyer placed orders for the year totaling $10,000 at cost, then the advertising allowance for the retail operation from this particular manufacturer is $500. According to this manufacturer cooperative advertising plan, the retailer will pay 50 percent of the cost of the advertisement and the manufacturer will pay the other half. The retailer may decide to run two newspaper advertisements at $500 each, or one at $1,000. The size of the advertisement, the media used, and the style featured is often left to the buyer's discretion. It is, however, common for the manufacturer to impose some requirements for the advertisement. These requirements vary greatly from vendor to vendor. As an illustration, the manufacturer may require that its name and logo be featured in the headline of the advertisement, that the advertisement will not include merchandise from another vendor, and that the cooperative advertising monies be used only for full-price, rather than off-price, styles. An illustration of a cooperative advertising contract from an apparel manufacturer is shown Figure 9.1.

Yet another factor to consider in vendor selection is shipping and inventory maintenance. Some vendors ship merchandise in a timely manner, but will only ship large orders. Others, with limited resources, have difficulty with anything but small orders, and even these may not be shipped on time. It is critical that the buyer select manufacturers that are eager and able to ship current orders and future reorders, both on time and as specified. The buyer will want to be certain that the merchandise will reach the retail operation on the specified delivery date, the cancellation or completion date as specified on the purchase order. The cancellation date refers to the last day that the vendor is authorized to ship merchandise specified on a particular purchase order. The cancellation date is agreed upon by the buyer and the vendor at the time the order is placed. Lead time, the amount of time needed between placing an order and receiving the goods, is a critical shipping factor. Speed of delivery for orders and reorders is of particular importance for fashion merchandise. The longer it takes for fashion goods to reach the retailer, the less time they will be available to the consumer during the selling period. The customer may go elsewhere to purchase the item. Speed of delivery also affects financing for the entrepreneurial company. Being able to order small shipments, then reordering more merchandise as needed, not only reduces the risk of buying errors, but it enables the buyer to reduce large monetary outlays at the start of a season. Financing can be spread over a period of time in conjunction with the actual sales of the goods. Additionally, speed of delivery and space limitations can go hand in hand. More and more retail operations are decreasing nonselling space to increase the bottom line. They are eliminating excess office and storage space by changing it to selling space used to display merchandise. As a result, space is minimal for warehousing backstock, merchandise held off the sales floor until needed.

Figure 9.1 Cooperative Advertising Agreement

Bounce Intimate Apparel Co., Inc.

BOUNCE COOPERATIVE ADVERTISING PLAN

Because we recognize the value and importance of advertising as a mutually beneficial means of promoting increased sales of BOUNCE LINGERIE, LOUNGEWEAR, BODYWEAR, we offer to all our valued customers the following cooperative advertising plan.

This plan is in effect until further notice for all ads run on or after May 1, 2003.

1. BOUNCE AND CUSTOMER SHARES

Bounce will share 50% of the space-cost in accredited media vehicles, based on a store's lowest earned rate, up to an amount not to exceed 3% of first quality, branded net purchases at wholesale for each season.

This plan only covers first quality, branded net purchases and applies to all Bounce product lines.

2. CHARGES

NET COST IS LIMITED TO YOUR ACTUAL SPACE-COST ONLY. This agreement shall not include the cost of special preparation, art work, cuts or any other advertising or production costs.

We do not share in the cost of agency fees or special service charges. **WE WILL SHARE IN 50% OF THE COST OF NEWSPAPER COLOR CHANGE**. We do not share in mechanical or production costs for color reproduction.

3. ENCLOSURE ADVERTISING

Each season Bounce will make available attractive statement enclosures. Enclosures are to be ordered on the special forms provided by our Advertising Department. An adequate quantity of merchandise must be ordered to cover number of enclosures requested.

A fraction of the actual cost of enclosures, $3.00 per thousand has been established and this amount will be applied against the 3% Bounce cooperative advertising limit as set forth in this agreement.

4. MEDIA

This plan covers newspaper advertising in all daily, weekly and Sunday newspapers with recognized audited circulation and published rates. It does not cover souvenir programs, circulars, billboards, theatre programs or special editions.

We will participate in the cost of radio and television advertising under the same terms outlined in this plan for newspaper advertising. A notarized affidavit from the station itemizing specific time and commercial must accompany your invoice.

5. COPY REQUIREMENTS

a) The bounce product-logotype must appear prominently. The Brand Name must be large as the largest type in the advertisement exclusive of the store's own logotype. Company brand name must also appear in the heading or subheading as the use of the brand name in copy only will not meet requirements.

b) Competitive advertising cannot appear in the same advertisement with our brand. If the advertisement shows other merchandise, our portion must be separate and clearly defined. For newspaper: either by a rule around it or by a white space of not less than one-eighth of an inch.

6. PAYMENT

Claims (invoices) must be submitted within 30 days of promotion's debut. An advertising credit-memo will be issued for the Bounce share. No deductions are to be made for advertising prior to receiving our credit-memo authorizing the amount deductible.

Please submit bills (invoices) accompanied by tear-sheets for each newspaper advertisement to:

BOUNCE CO-OP ADVERTISING DEPARTMENT
BOUNCE INTIMATE APPAREL CO., INC.
640 FIFTH AVENUE
NEW YORK, NY 10019

We reserve the right to change or terminate this agreement at any time upon 30 days notice.

Another shipping concern that may be a determining factor in vendor selection is the vendor's adherence to the purchase order specifications. The buyer thoughtfully places a detailed purchase order that indicates style numbers, sizes, colors, delivery dates, and discount terms. The specifics of the order are based on the amount of money available for purchasing new merchandise and orders written for other manufacturers. Some vendors do not fill the order as it is written for a number of reasons. The vendor may not have the sizes or colors in stock and may substitute a different range of sizes and color. The manufacturer may not have received delivery of the fabric that was shown in the sample garment at market, shipping an alternative fabric instead. Deviations from the original order can seriously affect retail sales. The buyer does not have to accept what was not ordered; however, the sales lost from insufficient inventory, as well as the time and expense of returning the unwanted goods, can be costly in terms of revenue and customers. Manufacturers that ship the orders as specified and in a timely manner are likely to be used again.

If a large portion of the funding available for merchandise purchases is committed to a vendor that does not ship on time, sales goals will likely be missed because the merchandise is not there to be purchased. How does the buyer determine whether or not a vendor ships effectively? First, the buyer can ask the sales representative and hope to get an honest response. Second, he or she can talk with other buyers who have made purchases from the manufacturer. More often than not, actual experience with the vendor truly tells the tale. The buyer quickly learns which vendors can be depended upon for prompt and accurate delivery, as well as those that do not meet these standards. Assuming that the lines are successful at retail, those manufacturers that continually meet completion dates and provide the merchandise ordered should be given first consideration when new season orders are to be placed.

Finally, vendor cooperation is a key factor in the buyer's selection of lines. In what ways can the vendor provide the buyer with support and cooperation? While the buyer is the ultimate decision maker in style selection, he or she will (and should) seek the advice of the sales representative in terms of which styles to order. The manufacturer's representative has the vantage point of seeing which styles other buyers in the sales territory are selecting. The representative also receives selling reports from across the country. It is the buyer's mission to assess the sales representative's truthfulness. This assessment can usually be made only after the buyer has worked with the sales representative for a period of time.

In addition to style recommendations, the vendor may also provide financial and promotional assistance in the forms of fixtures, display materials, fashion show videos, in-store appearances, educational seminars, incentives for sales associates, and trunk shows. A **trunk show** is an event that features a designer or company representative who brings the line to the retailer's operation for the customers to see and learn about firsthand. In some cases, the customers can place special orders for the line during the trunk show. The buyer should look to vendors for cooperation. This not only enhances the retail business, but it can also increase the size of the orders the buyer places with the vendor. The relationship between key vendors and the entrepreneur can become true partnerships that will positively affect profits for both.

Purchasing in the Marketplace   The seasoned buyer rarely commits to ordering specific merchandise the first time he or she views manufacturers' lines. More often, the buyer takes notes on the merchandise that is available at each showroom in order to evaluate each item in terms of what she or he has seen at all the prospective resources. Once buyers have examined everything that is available for delivery during the specific time periods that merchandise is needed, they are able to choose those styles that are best suited to their retail business. Most frequently, buyers will want to write these orders on their company's order forms, rather than on those of the vendors. The company order forms should contain all the information needed for delivery, as well as company specifications regarding late deliveries and style substitutions. Using company order forms not only ensures the business of having its specifications honored, but it also speeds the accounting and receiving processes by the use of a uniform document. A sample order form for a fashion retail operation is illustrated in Figure 9.2.

Other Purchasing Places   While most buyers agree that there is no better place to view and purchase lines for a new season than at the apparel mart during market week, reviewing lines on the retailer's premises is another option. Sales representatives travel from city to city in a predetermined territory to show their lines to retailers they did not see at the market, or sell new items that have been added to the line. Buyers may welcome these sales calls since it gives them the opportunity to purchase goods that may have been overlooked at market, that are new to the line, or that they did not have the time to review. Many vendors offer catalogs or Web sites that feature their lines. Using the catalogs or Internet to view the lines allows the buyer to shop when he or she has the time and to solicit the opinions of sales associates and customers. The disadvantage to these selling tools are that the merchandise cannot be handled, quality is difficult to assess, and colors may not be represented correctly. Regardless of where the buyer views the line, the goal is to select the best merchandise in the right quantities, at the right price, and at the right time.

Managing Fashion Merchandise

Fashion merchandise is evaluated by the retail buyer in terms of seasons. Merchandise suppliers, or vendors, introduce new collections of styles each season for the buyer to preview and purchase.

Fashion Seasons   What are the fashion seasons? Although they vary by manufacturer, most manufacturers of fashion merchandise develop five seasonal lines. They include the following: fall I, fall II, holiday, spring, and summer. Some manufacturers, particularly those catering to designer customers, have an additional season—cruise—which is delivered between holiday and spring seasons. Other manufacturers, especially those with lines that do not reflect a high level of seasonal change, may present two lines a year; fall/winter and spring/summer. The two-season merchandise line presentation may be preferred by an active sportswear company or a home accessories producer.

6-Month Planning   One of the first steps the buyer must undertake is planning dollar purchases. In most retail operations, the merchandise plan is formulated for a 6-month period and is, subsequently, referred to as the dollar merchandise plan or, more commonly, the 6-month plan. The 6-month plan incorporates a number of quantitative categories for the business, designated in retail dollars for each month, as follows: planned sales, beginning of the month and end of the month inventory levels, markdowns, average inventory, and stock turn. A 6-month plan form is shown as Figure 9.3.

Figure 9.2 Purchase Order Form

PURCHASE ORDER

NO.

DEPT. NO.

MFG. NO.

1. Send separate invoice and separate packing slip for each store.
2. Ship this entire order in one package.

MFR.

ADDRESS

CITY

DATE | TERMS | EOM | FOB

STYLE	CLASS	DESCRIPTION	COLOR	BRANCH STORE							M QTY	BRANCH STORE							SP QTY	BRANCH STORE							L QTY	QTY TOTAL	UNIT COST	TOTAL COST	UNIT RETAIL	TOTAL RETAIL

S M L (column headers with size numbers: 12 14 16 18 20 22 24 / 3 5 7 9 11 13 15 / 6 8 10 12 14 16 18)

AUTOMATICALLY CANCELLED IF NOT SHIPPED BY

PREPAID FREIGHT?

TOTALS

ROUTING EXCEPTION ON THIS ORDER

NO ORDER VALID UNLESS IN WRITING ON OUR FORM & COUNTERSIGNED

VIA

BUYER

APPROVED

SHIPPING INSTRUCTIONS

Show order no. and dept. no. on all packages. Combine all pkgs. into one shipment. Unless otherwise stated on this order send all shipments from the Greater New York Area except furs and jewelry to National New York Packing and Shipping Co., 327 W 36th St., N.Y.C, N.Y. From points other than the Greater New York Area and all jewelry ship via: 0-50 lbs. under 200.00 value insured Parcel Post. Over 50 lbs. ship Roadway Express where available or other motor truck.

Furs-U.P.S.

BILLING INSTRUCTIONS

Mail all invoices to Rogers & Smith, Lincoln, Nebraska, 44503, Accounts Payable Dept. Indicate order no. and dept. no. on each invoice. Under EOM Terms, all goods received on or after the 20th of the month are dated as of the 1st of the following month. Invoices must be rendered by size, color, and style. This order is subject to price, terms delivery and conditions as stated.

In accepting this order, vendor agrees that he will furnish a guarantee rendered in good faith that the textile fiber products specified therein are labeled in accordance with the Federal Textile Fiber Products Identification Act.

Cumulative Markup %

This order is subject to the instructions and conditions stated this and on the reverse side which are made a part thereof.

Figure 9.3 6–Month Plan Form

MERCHANDISE BUDGET
(IN THOUSANDS OF RETAIL DOLLARS)

STORE _____ DEPT. TITLE _____ DEPT. NO. _____ YR. _____

	–SALES–					–STOCK–				–PURCHASES–		–MARKDOWNS–			
	PREV. YEAR ACTUAL	LAST YEAR ACTUAL	LAST YEAR PLAN	THIS YEAR PLAN	% INCR.	PREV. YEAR ACTUAL	LAST YEAR ACTUAL	LAST YEAR PLAN	THIS YEAR PLAN	LAST YEAR ACTUAL	THIS YEAR PLAN	PREV. YEAR ACTUAL	LAST YEAR ACTUAL	LAST YEAR MUC LY	THIS YEAR PLAN
EOM	XX	XX	XX	XX	XX					XX	XX	XX	XX	XX	XX
FEB															
MAR															
APR															
MAY															
JUN															
JUL															
TOTAL						XX	XX	XX	XX						
AUG															
SEPT															
OCT															
NOV															
DEC															
JAN															
TOTAL						XX	XX	XX	XX						
YEAR						XX	XX	XX	XX						

	–INITIAL MARKUP–				–MAINTAINED MARKUP–				–MARKDOWNS–				–TURNOVER–			
	PREV. YEAR ACTUAL	LAST YEAR ACTUAL	LAST YEAR PLAN	THIS YEAR PLAN	PREV. YEAR ACTUAL	LAST YEAR ACTUAL	LAST YEAR PLAN	THIS YEAR PLAN	PREV. YEAR ACTUAL	LAST YEAR ACTUAL	LAST YEAR PLAN	THIS YEAR PLAN	PREV. YEAR ACTUAL	LAST YEAR ACTUAL	LAST YEAR PLAN	THIS YEAR PLAN
SPRING	%	%	%	%	%	%	%	%	%	%	%	%				
FALL	%	%	%	%	%	%	%	%	%	%	%	%				

Sales Forecasting   One of the single most critical pieces of information contained in the 6-month plan is the sales forecast. Data gathered through industry analysis and market research are used to make a realistic sales forecast. Forecasting is the science of estimating what is likely to happen given an assumed set of conditions. A sales forecast is an informed estimate, based on a given set of assumptions about the future of sales volume for a specific target market and specific merchandise classification. Sales forecasting is based on a 4-5-4 calendar—4 weeks is indicated for one month, 5 weeks allocated to the next month, then back to 4 weeks. The purpose of the 4-5-4 calendar is to compare the same days of the week against one another from year to year in order to forecast sales accurately (Fig. 9.4). The buyer must evaluate the potential sales volume and use this

Figure 9.4 National Retail Federation 4-5-4 Calendar for Monthly Sales Releases 2003 vs. 2002

The 4-5-4 calendar provides retailers with an industry timeline used to coordinate the release of company same-store sales. It can also be used by retail entrepreneurs to compare same-day-of-the-week sales from one year to the next.

	Week	2003 Week Ending	2002 Week Ending		Week	2003 Week Ending	2002 Weak Ending
FEBRUARY	1	2/8	2/9	**AUGUST**	27	8/9	8/10
	2	2/15	2/16		28	8/16	8/17
	3	2/22 (Presidents')	2/23 (Presidents')		29	8/23	8/24
	4	3/1	3/2		30	8/30	8/31
Publish Date		**March 6**	**March 7**	**Publish Date**		**September 4**	**September 5**
MARCH	5	3/8	3/9	**SEPTEMBER**	31	9/6 (Labor Day)	9/7 (Labor Day)
	6	3/15	3/16		32	9/13	9/14
	7	3/22	3/23		33	9/20	9/21
	8	3/29	3/30		34	9/27	9/28
	9	4/5	4/6 (Easter)		35	10/4	10/5
Publish Date		**April 10**	**April 11**	**Publish Date**		**October 9**	**October 10**
APRIL	10	4/12	4/13	**OCTOBER**	36	10/11	10/12
	11	4/19	4/20		37	10/18 (Columbus Day)	10/19 (Columbus Day)
	12	4/26 (Easter)	4/27		38	10/25	10/26
	13	5/3	5/4		39	11/1	11/2
Publish Date		**May 8**	**May 9**	**Publish Date**		**November 6**	**November 7**
MAY	14	5/10	5/11	**NOVEMBER**	40	11/8 (Election Day)	11/9 (Election Day)
	15	5/17 (Mother's Day)	5/18 (Mother's Day)		41	11/15 (Veterans' Day)	11/16 (Veterans' Day)
	16	5/24	5/25		42	11/22	11/23
	17	5/31 (Memorial Day)	6/1 (Memorial Day)		43	11/29 (Thanksgiving)	11/30 (Thanksgiving)
Publish Date		**June 5**	**June 6**	**Publish Date**		**December 4**	**December 5**
JUNE	18	6/7	6/8	**DECEMBER**	44	12/6	12/7
	19	6/14	6/15		45	12/13	12/14
	20	6/21 (Father's Day)	6/22 (Father's Day)		46	12/20	12/21
	21	6/28	6/29		47	12/27 (Christmas)	12/28 (Christmas)
	22	7/5 (Independence)	7/6 (Independence)		48	1/3 (New Year's)	1/4 (New Year's)
Publish Date		**July 10**	**July 11**	**Publish Date**		**January 8, 2004**	**January 9, 2003**
JULY	23	7/12	7/13	**JANUARY**	49	1/10	1/11
	24	7/19	7/20		50	1/17	1/18
	25	7/26	7/27		51	1/24 (MLK)	1/25 (MLK)
	26	8/2	8/3		52	1/31	2/1
Publish Date		**August 7**	**August 8**	**Publish Date**		**February 5, 2004**	**February 6, 2003**

National Retail Federation, 2002

information to develop strategies for creating profits. Almost all business planning and operating activities revolve around anticipated sales figures. For purposes of this text, sales forecasting is approached for a start-up fashion retail operation.

Sales Forecasting Factors

The accuracy of sales forecasting revolves around several factors: the stability of the market, the experience of the entrepreneur, the type of business for which the forecast is prepared, and the age of the business. All play a role in the extent to which sales can be predicted. The more stable the market, the more experienced the entrepreneur, and the more established the business, the easier it becomes to forecast sales. The sales forecast is only as good as the underlying assumptions.

To prepare the business's sales forecast, the buyer will begin by compiling assumptions regarding the economy, the fashion retail industry, and the market. The entrepreneur will estimate sales potential for a particular segment of the market, a geographic target area, or a target market, and he or she will then estimate the share of that total that the company can hope to capture. Using data obtained from numerous trade, business, and government publications, the entrepreneur will look at what businesses in a similar market have done in the past and/or what potential businesses will most likely do in the future. To forecast sales for a new business, the entrepreneur will look at both qualitative data (informed estimates) and quantitative date (mathematical analyses of historical or estimated data). The *Merchandising and Operations Results* and Robert Morris and Associates reports contain these data by store type and merchandise classification.

Planning the Merchandise Assortment

A merchandise assortment is developed to ensure that the styles, colors, sizes, prices, and types or products offered satisfy the customer's needs, allow the retail operation to meet planned sales goals, and provide an adequate amount of merchandise to support these sales goals. Proper assortment planning is key to a viable 6-month plan. One of the techniques used to produce an effective merchandise assortment is the development of a model stock.

Model Stock for Staple Goods   A model stock is an inventory that includes an appropriate assortment of merchandise in terms of price points, styles, size ranges, colors, and fabrics. The buyer of fashion goods has a much more complicated task in the development of a model stock than buyers of hard goods and staple items. Since fashion merchandise is almost always seasonal in nature, the model stock is constantly changing. The model stock of a designer sportswear department, for example, must reflect merchandise assortment needs specific to the operation's customers. It will designate which lines will be featured, the depth and breadth of each merchandise subclassification (e.g., the proportion of tops to bottoms), the concentration on particular sizes, the price points that will be emphasized, and more. The buyer generally constructs a model stock that is viewed as a preliminary plan. It will likely change once the buyer visits the marketplace and peruses the offerings of the vendors.

To develop a realistic model stock, the buyer must examine four specific areas referred to as the *elements of buying*. They are the qualitative and quantitative considerations, fashion merchandise resources, and the timing of the purchase. Quantitative considerations are based on a single premise: how much money is available at any given time for new merchandise. The established limits for funding are based on sales forecasts for each department. The forecasts are based on past sales, economic conditions, and the entrepreneur or buyer's assessment of each department's relative contribution to the entire organization.

It is important to note that model stock development for staple goods is quite different from model stock development for fashion goods. Fashion retailers will be working with both types of merchandise, staple and fashion. Determining a model stock for staple goods, such as pantyhose, basic bras, and boxer shorts, is a relatively simple task. These are goods that have few fashion changes and that customers purchase on a consistent basis from season to season. The buyer's task is to calculate the level of stock and the assortment needed to provide continuity of the products to the consumer. Buying these goods usually requires an examination of the quantity, size, colors, and styles sold monthly. Often, the model stock for staple goods is developed and remains unchanged for a 6-month period before it is reviewed again. An example of a model stock for staple goods is presented as Figure 9.5.

Model Stock for Fashion Goods   Fashion merchandise, on the other hand, is a significantly more challenging area in which to determine a model stock. With each new season, the buyer will develop a model stock for fashion goods. Buyers use the following

Figure 9.5 Stock for Staple Goods

Basic Junior Dept. Sportshorts

Price Range	Percentage to Stock
$25	20
20	30
15	30
10	20
	100%

Colors	Percentage to Stock
Blue	30
Red	15
White	20
Fuschia	5
Green	10
Black	20
	100%

Sizes	Percentage to Stock
7	10
9	25
11	30
13	25
15	10
	100%

Fabrics	Percentage to Stock
Nylon	40
Cotton	20
Cotton/Polyester	20
Knitted	20
	100%

variables to construct a model stock: merchandise classifications and subclassifications, style, price, color, and size. Merchandise classification refers to the related group of items found in an area of the retail operation. A consumer may view a merchandise classification as the type of goods offered within a single department in a store. For example, men's wear is a merchandise classification. Within men's wear, there are a number of merchandise subclassifications, items with a specific merchandise classification. In men's tailored apparel, for example, suits, sports coats, and dress trousers are subclassifications. A merchandise classification of misses' sportswear will include subclassifications of sweaters, shirts, pants, skirts, jackets, and related separates. For each of these subclassifications, the buyer will determine a detailed breakdown based on the variables of price, color, size, and style.

Style refers to the specific looks within the subclassification. For example, in the skirt subclassification, there will be a number of style offerings that reflect the fashion trends of the season. Vendors may offer an array of fashion skirts for a particular season, such as miniskirts, culottes, knee-length slim skirts, and long-length full skirts. The buyer must determine which styles will be presented within the inventory in the highest proportion, which will be introduced in moderate quantities, which will be purchased in small, or test, quantities, and which will not be represented. These decisions are made based on the buyer's perception of the customer's taste, as well as past experiences with sales and markdowns, when available.

Merchandise Flow Planning   The buyer's task is to select a merchandise assortment that reflects the customers' needs and wants. Color trends will be prioritized, as will size selection and price points. Fashion trends, for example, may indicate that there are three color palettes or stories of importance for fall I season. The buyer may determine that the palette of blues will be preferred over browns and grays by the customers. As a result, the buyer will put a greater emphasis on blues while limiting browns and grays. The buyer may then decide that the customer is most likely to purchase skirts in a price range of $50 to $70. While the buyer may order some skirts that fall above or below this price range, the majority of skirts will be ordered in the preferred price range. The buyer will anticipate sizing needs by ordering the highest proportion of units in sizes the greatest number of customers will need. Finally, the buyer will plan a flow of merchandise deliveries that maximizes the sales potential of the inventory. For instance, blue skirts are going to sell, so blue blouses must be available to pair with them. If the majority of pants are purchased in sizes 12 to 14, then tops to match must be available in corresponding sizes. An illustration of merchandise classifications is illustrated in Figure 9.6 (page 216).

It is significant to note that the huge task of constructing a model stock becomes easier with each season that the business is in operation. The entrepreneur starting a new retail operation does not have the benefit of past sales data upon which to base decisions about fashion acceptance, sizes, and price points. Merchandise assortment planning for the new entrepreneur illustrates the critical importance of research, the information gathered to develop the business plan. The entrepreneur must review the data collected on competition and target market demographics in order to predict consumer preferences as closely as possible. Once the model stock is planned, the buyer is ready to prepare the open-to-buy in anticipation of purchasing merchandise for the business.

Figure 9.6 Merchandise Classifications in Women's Wear

Style Range	Styling	Age Range	Size Range	Figure	Price Range
Designer	Unique, top-name designer fashion	25 and up	Missy 4–12	Missy; mature, slim	Designer
Bridge	Designer fashion	25 and up	Missy 4–12	Missy; mature, slim	Bridge
Missy	Adaptations of fashion looks	25 and up	Missy 4–14	Missy; mature, 5'7" avg. height	Better to budget
Petites	Same as missy	25 and up	Petite 0–14	Missy; under 5'4"	Better to budget
Women's or large sizes	Same as missy, plus some junior looks	18 and up	16–26W or 16–26WP	Missy; large size + some petite	Better to budget
Contemporary	Trendy	20–40	Missy 4–12	Missy; slim	Better to budget
Junior	Youthful, trendy, figure-conscious	13–25	Juniors 3–15	Less curved	Better to budget

Preparing the Open-to-Buy

Open-to-buy (OTB) refers to the budget that dictates how much money the buyer will spend in each merchandise classification for each month of business. OTB is calculated in retail dollars; therefore, the order must be figured at retail before being included in OTB. Orders that have been placed with the vendors, but have not yet been shipped and/or received are referred to as on-order and are logged in a purchase journal. A purchase journal is a spreadsheet used to keep track of all orders that have been placed. Technically, OTB is the difference between how much the buyer needs in inventory at retail to reach sales goals less the merchandise that is currently available, referred to as on-hand stock. When calculating OTB, on-order is added to the on-hand stock, as the orders placed with the vendors represent a contractual agreement or commitment for the merchandise. Knowing how much money at any given time that can be spent on new merchandise is extremely important to the buyer. If the buyer discovers a new item and wishes to purchase it for stock, there must be money in the budget to do so. Successful buyers try to keep a portion of the OTB liquid. Liquid open-to-buy refers to unspent funds that allow merchandise to be bought to update inventories and to replenish items that have sold out. Most vendors add a few new items to their lines after the season's collections have been introduced. Often, these items are modifications of top-selling styles. As a result, a liquid OTB set aside for postmarket ordering can generate significant profits for the fashion retail operation. The formula for OTB follows:

1. Beginning of the month (BOM) inventory − Sales − Markdowns, discounts, and returns = X

2. End of the month (EOM) planned inventory − X = Planned purchases

Open-to-buy is based on the 6-month plan. The difference between them is that OTB carries the calculations one step further, by subtracting the retail dollar amount of the actual ending inventory from that of the beginning inventory of the following month. It tells the buyer the amount of retail dollars that must be spent to reach the inventory level planned in order to achieve planned sales during the following month. If sales are lower than anticipated, then the amount of OTB is proportionately decreased. If the sales are much lower than planned and/or if the buyer has purchased more than allocated, then the OTB will indicate that the merchandise classification, or department, is **overbought**.

It is important to note that OTB is a revolving figure. Sales are continually being made in the department; new merchandise is arriving; markdowns are being taken; and customer returns are being credited to the inventory. As a result, it is standard practice for the buyer to update OTB at midmonth to determine as closely as possible how much money is available for new merchandise.

The Markdown Policy

Most buyers find it helpful to anticipate markdowns with a plan that predetermines the dollar amount of inventory allocated to markdowns, the timing of markdowns, and the percent off retail prices. Because fashion merchandise is seasonal, markdowns are a fact of life for most apparel and soft good retailers.

Reasons for Markdowns
Every fashion entrepreneur must face the reality of markdowns. Unlike a fine wine, fashion trends do not improve with time. Instead, fashion merchandise ages; fashion items are, in essence, perishable goods. There are many reasons for reducing the prices of fashion merchandise. Some are attributable to buyer error, while others are caused by uncontrollable external factors. The various circumstances that contribute to merchandise markdowns include merchandise selection errors committed by the buyer, promotional errors, a lack of attention by the sales force and management, and too-high pricing. The buyer may place too great an emphasis on a potential fashion trend only to find that the consumer does not share this enthusiasm. The trend may also be presented to the customer too early. Overbuying a particular style or color palette may require markdowns to entice customer purchases. Incorrectly planning the proportion of private-label goods to designer labels, inaccurately timing the arrival of new merchandise, and placing too much emphasis on new and unproven vendors are other errors the buyer may make. When merchandise is not promoted properly, to include visual merchandising, the result can be markdowns. An inadequate sales force, disinterested management, or biased personnel may contribute to the lack of sales. If the selling prices of particular goods are not competitive, then markdowns are often necessary.

Finally, external factors affect the need for price reductions. The best merchandise can be carefully advertised, effectively displayed in the store, and presented to the consumer by knowledgeable, enthusiastic sales associates, yet it can still require markdowns to retail. Adverse weather conditions can affect the sales of seasonal goods. Snowstorms can deter customers from leaving their homes to shop. An unusually warm winter can destroy sales in the outerwear department. A rainy and cold summer can put the damper on swimsuit sales. The economy is yet another external factor that can influence the need for markdowns. A poor or declining economy can play a significant role in the decreased sales of fashion merchandise. While purchasing food and other essentials may not be affected, consumers generally pay less attention to fashion-oriented items during those times.

Timing of Markdowns   When a new line is purchased, retail buyers often use the time before delivery to clear out the prior season's goods through markdowns. The fashion industry is founded on the concept of intentional or planned obsolescence, the replacement of previously purchased merchandise resulting from the introduction of new styles. How many garments does a customer actually wear out? With planned obsolescence, the retailer encourages the consumers to make an emotional decision that they need something new and fashionable, such as a new color, fabric, or silhouette. A garment or accessory does not become obsolete because it is no longer functional; instead, it is no longer fashionable. This concept of planned obsolescence, in conjunction with changing seasons and fashions trends, creates the cyclical nature of fashion merchandising. Figure 9.7 illustrates the impact of fashion seasons on the introduction and clearance of merchandise lines.

The seasonal nature of fashion, and its unpredictability in terms of customer acceptance, make fashion goods more complicated to manage than any other. Product classifications that do not have to be replaced as frequently may be kept in inventory at full price for long periods of time, thus allowing the retailer to try different techniques to sell the merchandise. Fashion merchandisers do not have the luxury of time. Fashion entrepreneurs take a variety of approaches to timing their markdowns. Some fashion merchants, particularly those carrying higher-priced goods, subscribe to the semiannual markdown philosophy. With this markdown policy, merchandise is typically marked down after the Christmas holiday and after the Fourth of July. Other retailers take different approaches to markdown policies.

Today, many fashion retailers are electing to implement a perpetual markdown policy. Through this policy, retailers are reducing the prices on merchandise every month for a variety of reasons. Primarily, they believe that the quick disposal of less desirable goods will improve the retail operation's rate of turnover and, subsequently, enable the buyer to purchase new items that may have a greater profitability. Additionally, there will be more room on the sales floor, or in the inventory plan, for the new season's offerings. Markdowns can help clear the selling floor. Early markdowns may encourage the sale of goods at a lower markdown percent. If merchandise is held too long, its sale will require more significant markdowns. Merchants who carry this markdown philosophy may implement a markdown policy based on the date the goods were placed on the selling floor. Merchandise, for example, that is over 30 days old may be marked down 20 percent. At the 60-day-old stage, it may be reduced by 40 percent.

There are a number of factors that must be considered by the entrepreneur when establishing a markdown policy. First, the entrepreneur should consider that too many markdown periods might encourage the customer to wait for price reductions. Sometimes a decision to lower prices may be premature. Often, a few pieces of the best-selling merchandise may remain because of color or size irregularities. If the merchant has marked down these remaining leftovers, yet has reordered the style in the top-selling colors and sizes, then the new goods will be priced differently. Defining a markdown program is difficult, yet the entrepreneur needs a plan that can be modified.

Markup

What is markup? In retailing, the term markup may refer to one of the following three calculations: markup based on cost of goods, markup based on original selling price, or markup based on final selling price. The following example illustrates the differences.

Figure 9.7 Timing Calendar for Women's Apparel

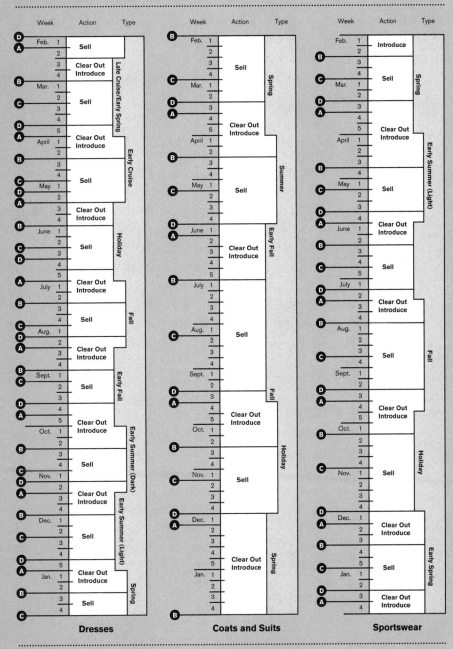

Buyer's Timing Calendar

Dresses

Coats and Suits

Sportswear

Ⓐ Begin receiving for new season
Ⓑ Major fashion promotion before this point
Ⓒ No reordering past this point
Ⓓ Begin markdowns

M Granger, *Case Studies in Merchandising Apparel & Soft Goods* (New York, New York: Fairchild Publications, 1996, p. 92)

An entrepreneur who owns a retail apparel store buys dresses that cost $40 each. These garments are priced at $80 each and are placed on the selling floor. The markup calculation on this retail price is referred to as initial markup. It is calculated as follows. From the retail price of $80, the markup amount of $40 is deducted, leaving $40. The remainder of $40 is then divided by the retail of $80, resulting in an initial retail markup of 50 percent. If markup is to be calculated on cost, it is figured by dividing the wholesale price of $40 by the difference between cost and retail prices, $40, resulting in markup based on a cost figure of 100 percent. Finally, let us assume that the dresses did not sell at full price. They did, however, sell after being marked down to $60. The resulting markup calculation is called maintained markup and is determined by dividing $20, the difference between the wholesale cost and the retail price, by $60, the actual selling price. The maintained markup is 33 percent.

Pricing Strategies for Fashion Merchandise

There are a number of pricing strategies that relate to the markdown and markup of fashion merchandise. Although some of these strategies are examined in Chapter 7, it is important to review them as they relate to markdown and markup planning. Introductory pricing is a strategy often used to gain entry into a market, by setting prices lower than the industry average markup. Skimming is yet another strategy in which the retailer sets a high initial price, usually through high markup, and then gradually lowers it. Price lining refers to grouping inventory into categories and then setting the same price for all items in each category. In this case, the buyer will usually determine an average markup for the lot of goods. A loss leader is selling one or few items at or below cost price in order to attract customers. A loss leader has little or no markup. The retailer assumes that the customer will purchase other items while in the store. All-in-one pricing refers to setting every item at the same price, resulting in some items at below-average markup, while others may be at above-average markup. Retailers use this strategy to simplify and strengthen advertising efforts while attracting clientele. Bundling is the term used for items that are grouped together and sold for less than if each item were purchased separately. Often, a manufacturer will group end-of-the-season merchandise, various styles in assorted sizes and colors, and sell the lot at a reduced price to the retailer as a special purchase to be used for a clearance event. In this case, the retailer has the opportunity to legitimately sell the items at a clearance price, while earning full markup.

In addition to determining markup, markdown, and pricing strategies, the retailer must establish other pricing policies and general pricing guidelines. Will the company match competitors' prices? Will it use coupons or multiple-purchase discounts? Will returned merchandise be accepted at the markdown price only, if a reduction was taken after the purchase? Will employees receive discounts on merchandise purchased? If so, will the employee discount increase with hours worked and /or years of service? Will the employee discount apply to clearance merchandise?

The buyer's work is not finished when the merchandise for the retail operation is purchased. The buyer has a pivotal role in the marketing and selling of this merchandise. By conveying the reasons for merchandise selection to the sales associates, the buyer increases the probability of retail sales. The buyer addressed a number of issues when the merchandise was purchased: "Why will the customer buy it? Why is it more appealing than that of the competitors? Is the price, fit, styling, or trend unique and appealing in specific ways?" When the buyer shares these questions and answers with the sales staff, the sales personnel have the confidence needed to approach the customer, as well as the information through a number of methods, such as sales floor interaction, telephone and e-mail contacts, and facsimile transmissions and memos.

VISUAL MERCHANDISING AND THE BUYER

Visual merchandising is an extremely important part of any retail operation's total sales promotional plan. The customer who is exposed to merchandise through visual merchandising techniques is a customer who has arrived at the store, either at its window or at its walls. When effective visual merchandising utilizes good display techniques, the display should be subordinate to the merchandise itself. This is where the buyer comes into focus. Whether an employee is assigned to visual merchandising or a sales associate is responsible for this duty, the buyer can be extremely helpful in selecting the items to be highlighted through interior displays, window displays, and/or signage. The buyer may want to feature a particular item that will generate customer traffic or one that was purchased in quantity, or both. Close cooperation between the buyer and the person installing the visual merchandising display can generate sales, enhance image, and encourage repeat business.

SALES PROMOTION AND THE BUYER

When the buyer wants to promote a key item in the inventory, it may be decided to advertise the item. In some retail operations, there is an advertising director to take care of the artwork, copy, and layout design needed for a print advertisement. For most start-up businesses, this responsibility belongs to the entrepreneur or the buyer. The buyer has the product knowledge to identify key selling points and the products' benefits to potential purchasers. Working within a promotional budget in an entrepreneurial operation, the buyer will usually work with media representatives to develop advertisements. The newspaper, television or radio station, and local magazine with which the product will be advertised will most often provide personnel to develop the advertisement, either for a fee or as a part of the advertisement's cost. It is the buyer who works with these representatives to make sure that the product is shown in its best light and in a way that the target customer will understand and desire.

SALES SUPPORTING SERVICES AND THE BUYER

The buyer will work with a variety of areas or functions within the retail operation. With the buyer's input, orders will be entered and processed through the accounting department. Inventory counts, whether annual or more frequent, are the buyer's responsibility. Merchandise will be received, ticketed, and moved to the sales floor, often with the buyer's supervision. Finally, the buyer may work on the scheduling of sales personnel when holidays or special events require additional sales support.

THE BUYER'S RESPONSIBILITY FOR PROFITS

The responsibility for profits is, by far, the buyer's most significant duty. Stockturn, stock-to-sales ratio, and inventory shortage are all terms that relate to the buyer's mission for profitability.

Stockturn

Stockturn, or turnover, is a statistical measurement that is formed as a simple fraction in which the numerator represents sales for a period and the denominator shows the average size of stock during that same period. Sales and stock are typically measured in retail dollars. Stockturn is a measurement of inventory performance; it guides the entrepreneur in assessing the productivity of inventory. Stockturn goals vary with the merchandise classification and the type of retail operation. A stockturn of four may be the objective for a specialty store featuring misses sportswear, while a stockturn of two may be more reasonable for a bridal boutique. There are a number of sources that can be examined for national stockturn data. The most widely used in fashion retailing is the *Merchandising and Operating Results*, published by the National Retail Federation.

Stock-to-Sales Ratio

Another measurement of sales and inventory performance is the stock-to-sales ratio which works together with stockturn. The stock-to-sales ratio is a calculation in which the inventory for a given period of time is divided by the sales volume for the same period. If, for example, the inventory for the month of December is $150,000 and the sales for December are $50,000, then the stock-to-sales ratio is 3 to 1, or 3:1. The figure indicates that the stockturn, at this particular time, is four, as the stock ratio of three is divided into the 12 months of the year. A stock-to-sales ratio helps the buyer see whether the stockturn goal is within reach. Table 9.1 illustrates the stock-to-sales ratio for clothing and accessories stores according to the U. S. Census Bureau.

Stockturn, markup, markdowns, and inventory shortages are all critical factors in the buyer's quest for profitability. It is not enough to simply buy the merchandise and place it on the selling floor. It must be priced, high enough at first to earn a profit and to offset markdowns. It must be secured adequately so that merchandise does not "walk off the floor." The buyer must have a creative eye for fashion and a quantitative mind for numbers.

BUYING FOR NONSTORE RETAIL OPERATIONS

E-tailing, cataloging, and television shopping are alternatives to the brick-and-mortar stores; they developed as a result of changes in consumers' lifestyle. Dual-career couples with less time to shop and new trends in customer buying habits have fueled an explosion of shopping alternatives. Catalogs, television shopping networks, and Web sites bring with them new challenges for the buyer working for these businesses. Nonstore retail operations are those that do not have a physical environment through which the customer can see, touch, and try on the merchandise, such as Web sites, mail-order brochures, and television shopping channels. They do not have a "home" in which the customer can get a feel for the business, its ambiance or personality, through a store visit. These nonstore operations serve a much broader market. In many cases, the buyer for these businesses serves a global clientele.

Catalogs can be distributed any place in the world. As a result, the buyer for a catalog firm must address a much broader market than do buyers employed by brick-and-mortar operations. The merchandise selection must appeal to consumers living in varying

Table 9.1. Estimated Monthly Retail Sales, Inventories, and Inventories/Sales Ratios, by Kind of Business (in millions of dollars)

NAICS Code	Kind of Business	Sales			Inventories 1			P???
		Aug. 2001 (p)	Jul. 2001 (r)	Aug. 2000 (s)	Aug. 2001 (p)	Jul. 2001 (r)	Aug. 2000 (s)	Aug. 2001 Jul.
442,3	Furniture, home furn., elect. & appl. stores	14,966	14,895	14,895	23,515	23,616	24,593	−0.8
448	Clothing & clothing access. stores	14,200	14,329	14,119	34,117	33,965	34,399	0.4
452	General merchandise stores	34,948	34,914	34,236	67,184	66,488	65,019	1.0
442,3	Furniture, home furn., elect. & appl. stores	15,473	14,299	15,299	23,045	22,955	24,126	0.4
448	Clothing & clothing access. stores	14,993	12,765	14,674	34,936	33,829	35,225	3.3
452	General merchandise stores	35,088	32,191	33,722	66,068	63,377	63,960	4.2

Source: *Monthly Retail Surveys Branch*, U.S. Census Bureau | Last Revised: October 15, 2001

climates and willing to pay a range of prices. Value pricing and exclusivity of goods are two of the merchandise criteria upon which a number of successful catalog operations have based their businesses. For some fashion retailers, the life span of a catalog can be quite long. Spiegel, J. C. Penney, and Sears, for example, publish two major catalog volumes annually, one for fall/winter and another for spring/summer. These issues must stand the test of time, as each of the vendors represented in these books must be able to provide the featured merchandise for a 6-month period. These retailers, as well as a host of other catalog businesses, publish smaller catalogs between the large seasonal issues. These catalogs must be planned well in advance and also require negotiation with vendors for timely and accurate deliveries.

Additionally, the buyer for a catalog operation will negotiate for exclusive styles or colors, discount pricing, and cooperative advertising allowances to offset the high cost of catalog production. For the most part, when the vendor's name appears in the catalog, cooperative advertising funds were solicited by the buyer to pay for that acknowledgment, Finally, the buyer for the catalog company will work more closely with the photographer, styles, and personnel in the promotion department than will the buyer of a brick-and-mortar operation.

As with catalog operations, the buyer for a television shopping network will serve a vast clientele, customers with few geographic or demographic limitations. The buyer for this type of retail outlet must have the skills to identify merchandise with vast market appeal and sufficient visual appeal. For this type of business, the buyer is often called upon to identify the selling points of merchandise that will convince viewers to buy. The buyer for a television shopping network is challenged to locate and secure merchandise that is unavailable elsewhere, that has a high price-value relationship, and that has broad appeal and characteristics (e.g., a wide range of colors and sizes).

One of the most debated issues in fashion retailing today is centered around e-tailing, Internet-based retailing. Can an entrepreneur start and successfully establish a business on the Internet? Is it more realistic to expect that the entrepreneur has more to gain by spinning off an Internet business from the core brick-and-mortar business? Should online sales be an adjunct to a physical store or an independent operation? Can an apparel retailer anticipate growth through a sales venue that does not permit the customer to touch, see, or try on merchandise? The buyer's role in e-commerce directly relates to the entrepreneur's answers to these fundamental questions. If e-tailing is an extension of an existing business, then the buyer will select goods for the Web site that reflect the merchandise assortment in the store. The buyer must keep making purchases. If the Web site is the business, then the buyer has a different task. The merchandise must be evaluated in terms of its appeal to a global audience, and a competitive price must be determined at which it will retail. With price competition and exclusivity as two key sales variables on the Internet, the buyer will need to be an effective negotiator to purchase goods at the lowest possible prices.

Timing is a primary factor in buying for the nonstore operation, whether it is catalog, television shopping, or e-commerce. The buyer must determine the potential fashion life cycle for each item in the merchandise assortment and be ready and able to make adjustments to the on-order if sales decline before anticipated. Some buyers place backup orders, shipments planned for later deliveries, with the vendor's agreement that a specific percent of the merchandise may be cancelled if necessary. This is not a common option, however, and is not offered to buyers placing small orders. Manufacturers are often cautious about going into full-scale production and then playing a waiting game. In some cases, the buyer must commit to a full purchase up front, warehousing the goods and shipping them to the consumer as ordered. The buyer's challenge is to locate vendors willing to share the risk or to guarantee a steady flow of goods within a specified time period.

Another challenge for the buyer of a nonstore operation relates to the item's visual presentation. The buyer will need to determine whether a photograph or a drawing best illustrates the product. If the buyer decides to use a photograph, he or she must determine which color to show and whether the item should be featured on a model or displayed flat. The buyer may work with copywriters of the Web site or catalog on the text that accompanies the image of the item. He or she may collaborate with the scriptwriter of the television shopping operation to develop a script for the show's host or hostess. Through nonstore retailing, the buyer's responsibilities in marketing the product are increased greatly. The format of a Web site, the layout of a catalog page, and the presentation of a television segment are new assignments to the buyer's realm of responsibilities. All these responsibilities result from a trend in retailing, a movement that has taken the buyer out of the store and into the customer's home.

CONCLUSION

Merchandising is the difference between an apparel and soft goods retail operation and those retailers offering all other product classifications. The resident buying offices, as well as internal and external sources of product information, are available to assist the buyer in determining which merchandise will best satisfy the target market's needs and desires. The resources for fashion goods primarily show new lines at apparel marts, located in market centers, during market weeks that are scheduled according to merchandise classification. Vendor selection is primarily based on the types and prices of goods and how these goods will match with the customer's preferences. Other significant factors in selecting vendors for the retail operation include exclusivity, timely and accurate shipping, reorder availability, promotional assistance, and vendor cooperation.

Once the buyer has reviewed the lines of vendors, the 6-month plan and its coordinating open-to-buy are the two tools used to calculate the amount of funds to be spent on new merchandise. These planning tools are also used to guide and register the amount of markdowns that will need to be taken on slow-selling goods.

The buyer's role in the marketing and selling process of the retail store is not limited to merchandise assortment selection and pricing. The buyer is responsible for disseminating product information to management and sales personnel. Additionally, the buyer shares this information with visual merchandising and sales promotion personnel and assists with sales supporting services, such as accounting, receiving, and inventory control.

The buyer's ultimate responsibility for profits is based on an understanding of stock-turn, as well as an understanding of the customer. Understanding the customer is bringing new challenges to buyers for catalog, e-commerce, and television shopping operations, as they are catering to a global market in the uncharted waters of nonstore fashion retailing.

WRITING THE PLAN

Develop the merchandising section of the business plan by using the following topics from Chapter 14 as a guide.

SECTION	TOPIC
Merchandising	Proposed lines
	Assortment of stock
	Vendor arrangements
	Market trips
	Markup policy
	Markdown policy
	Return policy

The Business Mentor™ CD-ROM, does not contain a merchandising section. It is not industry specific.

KEY TERMS

advertising allowances
all-in-one pricing
apparel mart
backstock
backup order
benchmark operations
exclusivity
external sources
fashion items
fashion seasons
forecasting

bundling
buyers
cancellation (completion) date
closeout merchandise
cooperative advertising
e-tailing
nonstore retail operations
off-price merchandise
on-hand stock
on-order
open-to-buy

initial markup
internal sources
introductory pricing
key vendor
lead time
liquid
loss leader
maintained markup
market week
merchandise assortment
merchandise classification
merchandise subclassification
merchandising
minimum orders
model stock

overbought
perpetual markdown policy
planned obsolescence
price lining
price skimming
purchase journal
qualitative data
quantitative data
resident buying office
sales forecast
6-month plan
staple (basic) item
stock-to-sales ratio
trunk shows
vendor analysis

QUESTIONS

1. What are the responsibilities and limitations of a resident buying office?
2. What are the differences in types of ownership of the resident buying office for the following classifications: independent, privately owned, and cooperative?
3. Define external and internal resources and identify a number of each, that the buyer can use to guide purchasing decisions.
4. List four product classifications in the fashion industry for which a model stock would be least difficult to develop and least likely to change on a seasonal basis.
5. What are the differences between a 6-month plan and an open-to-buy?
6. For which types of merchandise classifications are the changing fashion seasons less significant?
7. What should the buyer do to prepare for market week? List the steps necessary to maximize time and profitability on a market trip.
8. Locate the industry standards in children's apparel for the following financial calculations: initial markup percent, stockturn, and manufacturer's discount for timely merchandise payment (referred to as terms).

REFERENCE

1. Patrick Cash, *The Buyer's Manual* (New York, New York: National Retail Merchants Association, 1979)

SUGGESTED READINGS

Maurice J. Johnson and Evelyn C. Moore, *Apparel Product Development* (Upper Saddle River, New Jersey: Prentice-Hall, 2001)
Jeremy A. Rosenau and David L. Wilson, *Apparel Merchandising: The Line Starts Here* (New York, New York: Fairchild Publications, Inc., 2001)

CASE STUDY

If merchandising is the name of the game, then Hennes & Mauritz is the master player. Better known as H&M, the Stockholm-based company celebrated the opening of its first United States store on Fifth Avenue in the heart of Manhattan's shopping district in 2000. H&M has built a reputation in Europe for offering trendy apparel, inspired by couture runways and street fashions, at affordable prices. Founded in 1947, it now has more than 600 stores in Europe and is planning an aggressive expansion in the United States. Presenting the merchandising genius of "cheap and chic," customers will find Burberry-inspired plaid skirts for $12 , and 1950's nostalgia printed T-shirts for $6 on the first floor of the Manhattan store. On this level, featuring H&M's "Clothes" line, the merchandise reflects the most current junior trends for both young women and men. The entire second floor houses the men's wear departments. This is not the traditional Savile Row look. Instead, there are suits and sports coats in fashion colors with quality tailoring, and attention to detail that contradict their price tags. The third floor features a variety of H&M's private labels, such as Hennes, L.O.G.G. (Legion of Graded Goods), and BIB, a plus-sized line.

How does this merchandising master conduct its business? A team of over 60 designers collaborates with the store buyers in studying international runway and street wear trends. Next, they develop and design the affordable clothing that stocks H&M stores for the cost-conscious, fashion-conscious shopper. The stock is kept fresh with almost hourly deliveries of new merchandise. It is as though H&M views the year as having 52 fashion seasons, one for every week.

H&M offers ideas and designer-inspired merchandise at reasonable prices for the mass market. If the long lines queued up in front of H&M are any indication of its growth potential, H&M may play out the Gap phenomenon with a store on every corner. As H&M plans to add 100 more stores in the United States over the next 2 years, merchandising may be the Swedish key to global fashion success.

Pat Doran and Colleen McCarthy, "ChicCheap," May 9, 2001, www.fashionplanet.com

CASE STUDY QUESTIONS

1. How does H&M manage to stock its stores with new goods so quickly? How does its stockturn compare to that of a traditional fashion retail store in the United States?
2. How does vendor selection play a part in the H&M merchandising strategy? Are there U.S. retailers that have similar merchandising philosophies?
3. Review the Gap's merchandising strategies and compare them to those of H&M. What are the similarities? The differences?
4. In what ways do the buyers and product designers work together at H&M to maintain its strong position?
5. What are your predictions for the future of H&M in the global market? Why?

ENTERING THE WORLD OF THE ENTREPRENEUR

1. A number of entrepreneurs will identify a market niche and assume that it is unfilled because no one else has discovered it. In truth, the market niche may be available at retail due to lack of resources for manufacturing the types of products needed to fill this void. One of the first steps a prospective entrepreneur can take in merchandising is to conduct a comparison survey of vendors that supply merchandise for the business concept.
2. What sources are available for a comparison survey? Catalogs, company Web sites on the Internet, fashion Web sites (e.g., WGSN and Fashion Planet), and existing retail operations are excellent sources for a vendor survey. Additionally, apparel market centers publish directories of merchandise resources that show during their particular market weeks. Trade publications, such as *Women's Wear Daily*, *Apparel News*, and *DNR*, as well as consumer publications, such as *Lucky* and *W*, feature new vendors and photographs or illustrations of the merchandise for these lines, often with retail prices, sizes, and colors.
3. After creating a comparison survey of vendors that may fill the niche for the business concept, the next step is to comparison shop the retail competition in the prospective location of the business. Are there nearby retailers carrying these lines? If so, the profit potential is reduced.

4. What can the entrepreneur do if the label merchandise resources do not exist? If this is the case, then private label merchandise (as discussed in Chapter 2) is the most common solution to the problem. The entrepreneur must ask the following questions: Do resources exist that will produce this product line to specification in the quantities that can be profitably sold? Are these resources reliable? Is the markup potential there? Will a resident buying office be a cost-effective liaison between the manufacturer or private-label goods and the entrepreneur?

. . . .

THE ENTERPRISING ENTREPRENEUR

. . . .

Schooled in Prague and Vienna, Georgette Klinger launched the concept of customized skin treatment and custom-created beauty products in the United States 60 years ago. When the first Georgette Klinger salon opened on Madison Avenue in Manhattan in 1941, it introduced to American women the European concept of luxurious pampering and beauty maintenance. Until that time, only society women who toured the European continent were treated to customized skin and beauty services, as well as natural beauty products. Klinger was among the first to use herbal treatments, botanical extracts, and even seaweed body treatments to rejuvenate and relax her clientele. In 1972, she pioneered the area of men's care products with her line, Klinger for Men. Today, Georgette Klinger salons have taken on a spa atmosphere and offer such services as advanced oxygen facials, collagen treatments, makeup services, hairstyling, and manicures and pedicures. The salons offer an extensive collection of skin and makeup products that can be purchased for at-home pampering. Georgette Klinger salons are located in the prestigious shopping districts of Manhattan, Palm Beach, Costa Mesa, Chicago, Washington, D.C., Dallas, Short Hills, and Beverly Hills.

Chapter 10

SELECTING A BUSINESS ENTITY

INTRODUCTION

The previous chapters have dealt with establishing the company in terms of its product, location, management, and how it will enter and penetrate the market. Now a decision must be made as to the kind of legal entity the business will be. This chapter examines the various legal forms of businesses and the pros and cons of each form. It should be noted that an attorney and accountant should be consulted before any final decisions are made. Laws vary from state to state.

CONSIDERATIONS IN CHOOSING A LEGAL ENTITY

Entrepreneurs must take many factors into consideration before they make a decision about what kind of legal entity their business will operate as. A legal entity is an individual or organization that is legally permitted to enter into a contract or be sued if it fails to meet its contractual obligations. Such factors include the type of business the venture is, tax considerations, liability concerns, and accessing capital. Once a business is set up, changing from one entity to another can be difficult and costly.

Each form of ownership has its advantages and disadvantages. Understanding the characteristics of each and how those characteristics affect the entrepreneur's business and personal circumstances will help guide the entrepreneur in making the right decision.

In the process of choosing a form of ownership, the following factors should be considered:

- *Tax considerations*. Tax rates, income, and how expenses can be deducted all play a role in determining the legal structure of a business. The entrepreneur should calculate the tax implications under each form of ownership before making the final determination.
- *Liability issues*. Certain forms of ownership limit personal liability more than others. Entrepreneurs must consider the extent to which they are willing to assume

personal responsibility for their business's obligations. Problems can arise due to financial difficulties, disgruntled customers and employees, and numerous other issues. Choosing the right legal entity can help limit personal exposure.

- *Cost of forming the legal entity.* Forming a corporation can be more costly than setting up a sole proprietorship. The benefits and costs of a particular entity must be carefully weighed.

- *Control of the business.* Certain forms of ownership take some of the control away from the entrepreneur. The entrepreneur must decide how much control he or she is willing to give up in order to expand the company.

- *Transfer of ownership.* The entrepreneur must consider how difficult it will be to transfer ownership when the business is sold or when it is passed on to other family members. With a sole proprietorship, when the owner dies, the business dies. It does not continue as an ongoing entity. The corporate structure allows for much easier transfer of ownership. A corporation is a "fictional" entity which will continue even after the death of all the original shareholders.

- *Obtaining funding.* Depending on how much capital is needed and from where the funding will come, some forms of ownership make it easier to obtain funding than others. For example, with a corporation, shares of stock may be sold to bring money. Venture capitalists are not likely to be enthusiastic about investing in a sole proprietorship.

The initial choice of ownership does not have to be final. However, it is easier to move from a sole proprietorship to a corporation than from a corporation to a limited liability company. As the business grows, it may be necessary to change the form of ownership. The change in ownership may be necessary to attract additional capital or to bring in staff or employees to help the business grow. Evaluating the needs of the company on an ongoing basis will help make the determination as to which form of ownership is best suited for the entrepreneur's venture.

There are basically three forms of ownership from which to choose: the sole proprietorship, the partnership, and the corporation. Variations of these have emerged: the s-corporation and the limited liability corporation.

THE SOLE PROPRIETORSHIP

A sole proprietorship is a business that is owned and operated by one individual. A majority of small businesses in the United States are operated as sole proprietorships. A sole proprietorship is not actually a separate legal entity under the law. It is merely an extension of the individual who owns it. A sole proprietorship can exist as long as the owner is alive and desires to continue the business. Should the owner die, the sole proprietorship ceases to exist. The assets and liabilities then become part of the owner's estate.

Advantages of a Sole Proprietorship

Electing to operate the business as a sole proprietor has certain advantages over other forms of ownership.

- *Easy to create and not costly.* Most sole proprietorships can be formed in a day. A sole proprietorship may be started simply by the owner beginning to conduct business. It may be necessary in some states, counties, or cities to file for the necessary business license to begin operation. A business license permits a company to conduct business in that jurisdiction. The fees are usually nominal. A sole proprietorship may be operated under the name of the individual owner, although other names may be used. If the name of the business is different from that of the owner, a fictitious name registration may be required by the secretary of state's office in the state in which the entrepreneur's business lies. The fictitious name registration will inform the entrepreneur whether or not the name chosen is being used by another company. It will also notify the state of who the owner of the business is. Note that registering a fictitious name is not the same as trademarking the name. As a sole proprietorship, the owner is the business.

- *Absolute control.* The owner of a sole proprietorship controls the business in every way. Although employees may be hired to help run the business, legal responsibility for decisions made by the employees lies with the business owner. The sole proprietor has authority over all decisions made in the company. Because of this, the business owner can respond quickly to changes in the market. As discussed in Chapter 7, markets can change rapidly, and response time can be critical to a business.
- *Profit incentive.* One advantage of the sole proprietorship is that once the owner has paid all expenses, the entrepreneur can keep the remaining profit (less taxes).
- *Easily dissolved.* The sole proprietorship is one of the easiest forms of ownership to dissolve. Once all outstanding debts and obligations have been resolved, the entrepreneur can simply discontinue the operation.

Although the sole proprietorship has many advantages in terms of being inexpensive to start, being simple to run, and being able to be started quickly, this form of ownership also has its disadvantages.

Disadvantages of a Sole Proprietorship

Operating as a sole proprietorship has its disadvantages.

- *Unlimited personal liability.* In a sole proprietorship, the business and the owner are one and the same. There is no separate legal "person." This means that as a sole proprietor, the business owner will have unlimited personal responsibility for the business's liabilities, including its debt. The sole proprietor is *personally* responsible for all the assets of the business as well as the liabilities. For example, if the business cannot pay for merchandise ordered, the owner may be sued as an individual. Creditors may be able to seek payment by going after both the business and personal assets. Often sole proprietors use personal assets to secure debt financing. Should the business get into financial trouble, the lender may require the owner to liquidate personal assets to cover the debt of the business. Some states may provide protection under the law by enabling an individual to protect personal assets by owning them jointly with a spouse or by transferring them to a spouse or the children of the individual. Some states may also require creditors to leave some equity in a home, or automobile, or some other asset.
- *Inability to access more capital.* Often sole proprietorships use personal assets as collateral to secure funding, and personal assets are limited. As the business grows and expands, it may become necessary to access more capital. Without the ability to issue

shares of stock, as can be done with a corporation, or by offering more collateral to secure another loan, sole proprietors are limited in their ability to generate additional funds.

- ▪ *Limited life.* The sole proprietorship ceases upon the death of its owner or the inability of the owner to carry on the business. When the owner dies, the business dies. It cannot be passed on to a relative or sold as an ongoing entity. The business owner *is* the business.
- ▪ *Inadequate management skill.* Large companies have the ability to attract individuals with the skills and education necessary to keep the business going. Often sole proprietors possess many, but not all, of the skills that may be needed to run a successful business.
- ▪ *Inability to attract and retain good employees.* Sole proprietorships cannot ensure advancement and the opportunity for secure employment. Therefore, recruiting good employees can be a challenge.

The sole proprietorship may be the right decision for an individual wanting to start a company and keep it small. It can be started easily at very little cost, control can be maintained by the business owner, and it allows for flexibility to make changes quickly in a rapidly changing market. To overcome some of the disadvantages of forming a sole proprietorship, business owners can and may choose to form a partnership. Partnerships allow the entrepreneur to recruit one or more individuals to share in the management and capital needs of the company. Partners may bring the addditional skills, education, and experience necessary to make the business a success. They may also have the additional capital necessary to take the business forward.

THE PARTNERSHIP

A partnership is formed when two or more individuals join together to create a business to make a profit. In a partnership, the partners jointly own the assets, profits, and losses of the business as set forth by the partnership agreement. There is no limit to the number of partners or types of partners a business may have. A partnership can consist of individuals, other partnerships, or corporations.

A partnership can be formed though either an oral or a written partnership agreement. The partnership agreement dictates the details of operating the partnership. It does not have to be in writing, although a written agreement is highly recommended. Too often, entrepreneurs form partnerships with unrealistic expectations that everything will go smoothly, without dispute. The reality is that, every year, thousands of partnerships end in "divorce" over disagreements in how the business should operate. The written partnership agreement is a document that will define, in writing, the rights, duties, obligations, and liabilities for each partner, except for what is covered by state law. It outlines how the business will operate. "Discussing a partnership agreement forces partners to face issues up front and see if they are compatible in resolving those issues. If they aren't, then it's a whole lot better and easier to walk away at that point than to go on and face a costly and emotionally draining breakup in the future," says Gerald Cayer, a partner in the accounting firm of Cayer, Prescott, Clune & Chatellier of Providence, R.I.[1]

A partnership agreement should specifically address the areas of organization, operations, and how the business will be dissolved should the want or need arise. Each area should address what each partner is contributing and expected to contribute to the business, and what each part will get in return.[2]

Partnership agreements typically cover the following:

1. The name of the partnership.
2. The duration of the partnership. The number of years until the partnership is dissolved.
3. The purpose of the business.
4. The names of each partner and his or her address.
5. The location of the business.
6. The contribution of each partner. The agreement should outline the capital contribution of each partner at the present time and in the future. It may also address the level at which capital accounts of the partners must be maintained.
7. The participation of each partner regarding profits and losses.
8. The salaries or "draws against profits" that will be paid to each partner.
9. The duties, responsibilities, and activities expected of each partner.
10. The agreement should clearly define who is to be the *managing partner* and whose decision will prevail in case of a tie or a dispute. It should also define when partners can make decisions on their own, and when the other partner or partners must be involved.
11. The procedure for admitting new partners.
12. The method of determining the extent to which the partners will be able to participate in outside business activities that would be or may be in competition with the partnership business.
13. The method that will be used to determine the value of goodwill contributed by each partner in the business, in case of withdrawal, death, or dissolution of the partnership.
14. The person(s) who will be the authorized signor(s) on checking accounts and who has authority to sign legal documents in the business.
15. The prohibition of partners to pledge, sell, or transfer their interest in the partnership except to other partners. Can a partner sell his or her interest to an outside person without first approaching the other partner for a buyout?
16. The way a business partner is to be compensated should he or she have to leave the business for a period of time. What if the partner is disabled or cannot continue his or her activities in the business?

The ultimate goal of a partnership agreement should be to address any and all issues that may be cause for disagreement. Taking the time to work through these matters before starting the business can save a lot of time and money. The agreement can be discussed by the partners before they hire an attorney to draft the legal document, thereby saving money. The agreement should delineate what each partner is contributing to the business and how that contribution will be measured. What will each partner get for his or her contribution? Contributions to a business can be made in the form of cash, real property, "goodwill," trademarks, clients, or other assets.

The list above includes some of the more common issues that must be addressed in establishing a partnership. Each and every business is different. The business should be researched and reviewed with the other partners to determine whether any additional issues should be covered in the partnership agreement. The partnership agreement should be reevaluated as the business grows. Just like a business plan, it should be revisited often.

In the absence of a partnership agreement, the Uniform Partnership Act (UPA) governs the operations of the partnership. This act may vary from state to state. It is important to consult an attorney on the matter. The Uniform Partnership Act was established to try to reduce controversy in integrating the laws relating to partnerships.

Under this act each partner has common ownership and shares in the management and operation of the business. Each partner is responsible for the actions of all the other partners. All partners, then, are liable for all debts of the business as well as the assets. Each partner has the right to share in the profits of the business, receive interest on additional advances made to the business, and be compensated for expenses incurred in the name of the business. Each partner has the right to review the business's books and records and to receive a formal accounting of the partnership's business affairs. Each partner must also share in any losses sustained by the business and work for the partnership without salary.

A partnership exists as long as the partners agree it will and as long as all the general partners remain in the partnership. Unless the partnership agreement specifies differently, the death of one partner or the decision by one partner to leave will dissolve the partnership. If this occurs, the assets of the partnership must be sold or distributed to first pay the creditors of the partnership, and then the partners.

Like a sole proprietorship, the partnership has both advantages and disadvantages.

Advantages of a Partnership

The entrepreneur contemplating the establishment of a partnership will find the following advantages.

- *Low cost; easy to establish.* Like a sole proprietorship, the partnership can be formed at minimal cost and relatively quickly. As stated earlier, although it is not advised, a partnership does not need a formal written agreement. Some states require that a fictitious name registration or a certificate for conducting business as partners be signed if the business is operating under a trade name. The secretary of state's office in each state has this information.
- *Access to more capital.* Every new venture faces the issue of raising enough capital to give the business an opportunity to succeed. Bringing in a partner may increase the availability of capital. Assets may be combined to make it possible for the partners to borrow enough money to carry the business through its initial start-up phase.
- *Permits ownership by more than one individual.* Partnerships allow for more than one individual to run the company. If the partners seek complementary skills, the business has a better chance of success. If one partner is good at merchandise and the other at financial issues, the business increases its chances of success.
- *Profits.* Unless established otherwise in the partnership agreement, each partner shares equally in the partnership's profits and each owns an equal portion of the business. No restrictions exist on how profits are to be distributed among the partners.
- *Partnerships allow for limited partners.* Limited partners take no part in the management of the business, but rather are investors in the company. Provided the limited partners do not spend more than 500 hours in the day-to-day operation of the business per year, they are limited in their personal liability for the company's debts and obligations. Should the business fail, they lose only the amount they have invested.

- *Ability to react rapidly to a changing market.* The partnership, like a sole proprietorship, has the ability to react quickly to a changing market.
- *Taxes.* The partnership itself is not taxed on the income generated by the business. A partnership tax return is filed for informational purposes only. Each partner is taxed on his or her share of the business income. The profits and losses "flow down" from the partnership to the individual partners. It is best to consult with an accountant on tax issues pertaining to any form of ownership of a business.
- *Few legal formalities.* Like a sole proprietorship, the partnership has very few governmental regulations.

Disadvantages of a Partnership

Forming a partnership can also hold many disadvantages.

- *Unlimited liability.* The biggest disadvantage to a partnership lies in the liability of its partners. Under this form of ownership, the general partners are "jointly and severally" liable for the partnership. This means that all of the partners are jointly liable and each partner is individually liable for all the obligations of the partnership. Creditors have the right to require an individual partner to pay all the money the creditor is owed. Even if a partner has a small percentage of ownership in the company, he or she can be held responsible for 100 percent of a partnership liability. "A partner can be held liable for partnership liabilities due to contracts, debts, taxes, employment, or claims arising from product liability, accidents, services rendered by the business, or even acts of other partners on behalf of the business."[3] Unless specified otherwise in the partnership agreement, each partner can hire and fire employees, accept orders, extend credit, and so forth. Poor decisions made by one partner affect the other partners and expose all partners to significant liability.
- *Difficulty in decision making.* The partners may not agree on how to run the business. They may think they do in the beginning, and, once the business has been established, the disagreement begins. One partner may begin to make decisions without the consent of the other partners. This can lead to "partnership divorce" and, ultimately, the failure of the company.
- *Difference in values.* For a partnership to work, all partners must strive to achieve the same goals. They should have the same goals, ethics, and general business philosophy. One partner may have difficulty dealing with employees, vendors, customers, or others, thereby harming the reputation of the business. One partner may not have the capability or competence he or she seemed to have before the business was begun.
- *The partnership may be dissolved upon death of a general partner.* Unless specified in the partnership agreement, the death of one partner may dissolve the partnership. As stated earlier, the assets would be liquidated to first pay the creditors of the partnership, then the partners.
- *Profits insufficient to support more than one partner.* The business may be too small or not generate enough profit to support more than one partner. How will each be compensated in this circumstance? What if one partner is working harder than the other partner or if the other partner's efforts are less effective? Will both be compensated equally?
- *Difficulty in transfer of ownership.* General partnership interest may not be sold or transferred without the consent of all partners.

Partnerships are difficult at best. The issue of personal liability for the actions of all partners can make a partnership a very undesirable form of ownership. The bad decisions of one partner will affect all the other partners. Every entrepreneur goes into a partnership assuming that everyone will get along, value the same business practices, and never be forced to address conflict. Conflicts do arise. More times than not, these conflicts result in the dissolution of the partnership.

Limited Partnerships

In a limited partnership, the partnership is composed of at least one general partner and one or more limited partners. Limited partners do not make day-to-day management decisions in the company. Their risk is limited to the amount of their investment. To form a limited partnership, the partners must file a certificate of partnership with the secretary of state's office in the state in which the limited partnership will conduct business. In addition to the name of the limited partnership, the address of the business, and the name and business address of each partner, the certificate of limited partnership should also indicate which partners are general partners and which are limited partners. It should specify when a limited partner may withdraw from the company and how, when financial contributions will be made by any of the partners, and what it will take in terms of funds for a partner to withdraw from the company. An attorney should be consulted before any limited partnership agreements are made final since the partnership agreement can be very complex.

THE CORPORATION

A corporation (also known as a c-corporation) is a separate legal entity under the authority granted by state law. It is "an entity used to facilitate a business association among its owners (known as its shareholders or stockholders), created by charter under state or federal law and treated by law as a person independent of its owner."[4] It has its own legal rights and liabilities. Corporations may sue and be sued.

The corporation has a life independent of its owners, shareholders, and directors, or officers. Because of this, it shelters its owners from any personal liability provided that the owners do not do anything that would "pierce the corporate veil." A common way in which the corporate veil is sometimes pierced is when the owner intermingles private and corporate funds. The funds of a corporation should be kept completely separate from those of the personal accounts of the owners. As an example, the owner of the corporation should not write a check from the corporate account to pay a personal bill. The "veil" could be pierced if the officers fail to follow corporation formalities such as electing officers and conducting annual meetings.

Corporations may be closely held corporations or publicly held. Closely held corporations are more common among small businesses than are publicly held corporations. The shares of a closely held corporation are typically owned by a small number of people. These individuals are often investors, friends, and family who invest small amounts of money in the corporation. Publicly held corporations have a large number of shareholders and are traded on one of the large stock exchanges. Laws and tax issues vary from state to state with regard to corporations and other legal entities.

Forming a Corporation

Forming a corporation is more complex than forming a sole proprietorship or a partnership. Corporations are established by filing articles of incorporation with the secretary of state in which the corporation will be headquartered. If the secretary of state finds that the articles of incorporation conform to applicable legal requirements and the required incorporation fee has been paid, then the original articles of incorporation will be filed in the secretary of state's records and a certificate will be issued by the secretary of state informing the applicant that the corporation has been organized.

The following information is typically contained in the articles of incorporation:

1. The name of the corporation. The name of the corporation must include a term such as corporation, incorporated, or company so people are aware they are dealing with a corporation. In choosing a name, care should be taken to make sure the name is not so similar to that of another that it is confusing and leads to deception.
2. The names and addresses (residence) of the incorporators. The incoporators are able and must attest that all information in the articles of incorporation is correct.
3. The address of the corporation's office in this state and the name of its registered agent(s). A registered agent is an individual designated by the corporation to act as a contact and to receive formal and legal notices. An example may be the corporate attorney.
4. The capital requirement at the time the business is incorporated. Some states may require the corporation to deposit a percent of the stocks par value before incorporating.
5. Any restrictions on preemptive rights. Shareholders will be entitled to preemptive rights (meaning they protect the interests of shareholders by giving them the right to maintain their percentage of stock ownership) unless expressly limited or denied in the articles of incorporation.
6. The duration of the corporation's existence (which may be perpetual).
7. The purpose of the corporation (which should be broad enough so as to not limit its activities).

The articles of incorporation must be signed by all the incorporators, and their signatures must be notarized.

The selection of the state in which the corporation chooses to do business is referred to as its domestic state. A corporation is referred to as a domestic corporation in its domestic state. If a corporation's offices and business activities are located in a single state, then choosing that state as its domestic state reduces the number of states in which the corporation must comply with corporate and other laws.

If a corporation conducts business in a state other than its domestic state, then the corporation is considered a foreign corporation by that nondomestic state. It must obtain a certificate of authority stating that it is "qualified" to transact business in the other state as a foreign corporation. The standards for what constitutes transacting business vary from state to state and an attorney should be consulted.

Corporate Name   A corporation's name must include one or more of the following words: *company, corporation, limited,* and/or *incorporated.* It may not include any word or phrase that would suggest it is a government agency or organized for a purpose other than that stated in its articles of incorporation, or permitted by the corporate law. The name must be distinguishable from the name of other corporations in the state. This lessens the possibility that people will perceive the owner as trying to be deceitful with its name. A **name search** can be conducted through the secretary of state's office in the corporation's domestic state. Once the business name has been cleared through the name search, the name should be registered immediately.

The importance of registering the business name is illustrated by the following: An entrepreneur named his jewelry company Unique Treasures after conducting a name search. He neglected, however, to register the company name. After several years of doing business, a new competitor entered the area and named her company Unique Treasures. Although he hired an attorney and took the competitor to court, the original creator of Unique Treasures lost his company name because he had failed to register it.

Operating a Corporation

Once a corporation has been formed, the business must be appropriately organized and operated in order to obtain the benefits and protections of being a corporation. For example, authorized signers for the corporation should always sign as officers of that corporation (e.g., Jane Doe, President). The corporation should be kept separate from any personal ventures.

Certain organizational steps must be taken in order to implement the appropriate corporate structure and procedures. The first step is to elect and hold the first meeting of the corporation's directors. Many states permit a corporation to have only one stockholder, one director, and one officer. These positions may be held by the same person. If the initial directors have not been identified in the articles of incorporation, then they must be appointed by the incorporators. The first meeting of the board of directors should be held promptly after the corporation is formed for the purpose of taking the following actions, together with any other necessary organizational or business actions:

1. Adopt bylaws to govern the procedures by which shareholders and director meetings will be called and held, officers will be elected and will function, and stock will be issued.
2. Elect the officers of the corporation.
3. Establish a fiscal year. Not all entities start their accounting period on January 1. An accounting period of 365 days, but not necessarily started on January 1, can be designated as a fiscal year.
4. Adopt the form of corporate seal. An insignia representing the company is referred to as a corporate seal.
5. Approve the form of stock certificate and authorize the issuance of shares of stock for the initial capitalization. (Start-up capital or funding for the business).
6. Approve resolutions to establish a banking account and other banking relationships.
7. Approve payment of any organizational expenses and ratify preincorporation actions of incorporators on behalf of the corporation.

Different Roles: Shareholders, Directors, and Officers

The corporation's articles of incorporation and bylaws establish the various roles in the corporation's business by allocating rights and duties among its shareholders, directors, and officers.

Shareholders   A shareholder is an owner with right to very little participation in the management of the corporation. A shareholder is entitled to participation by voting on the election and removal of directors, the ratification or rejection of voidable acts of the corporation, any amendments to the articles of incorporation and (unless otherwise provided in the articles of incorporation or bylaws) the bylaws, and other fundamental changes to the corporation.

Directors   A corporation must have at least three directors unless otherwise provided in the articles of incorporation. Directors are elected annually by the shareholders and are subject to removal by the shareholders with or without cause and/or by a majority of the other directors. Directors are generally responsible for managing the business of the corporation. Directors also choose the corporation's officers.

Officers   Officers are chosen by the board of directors and may be removed if the directors believe the best interests of the corporation would be served by this change. The rights and duties of the officers are flexible and are established by the bylaws and the directors. Usually, officers carry out the decisions of the directors and are authorized to conduct the business of the corporation between meetings and in the absence of action by the directors. The corporation must have a president and secretary. More than one office may be held by the same person, unless otherwise provided in the articles of incorporation or bylaws. Typically, the officer positions and related duties are as follows:

- *President.* Manages and controls the corporation's business as chief executive officer (CEO) of the corporation.
- *Vice president.* Serves in the president's absence. The vice president, as with other officers, performs any other duties assigned by the board of directors.
- *Secretary.* Attends all meetings (e.g., shareholders and directors) and gives notice of meetings; maintains a list of shareholders and addresses; maintains a stock ledger; and generally serves as custodian of the corporation's records.
- *Treasurer.* Maintains custody of the corporation's funds and securities; keeps the corporation's financial records; and make disbursements as directed by the board of directors or president.

Issuing Stock

Stock is evidence of the value of money or other property invested in the corporation and is considered to be the equity for the corporation. Owning stock represents ownership in the corporation. The equity invested in the corporation is at risk. If the corporation does not succeed, amounts paid for stock may be lost. Stock is treated as personal property in that it can be transferred, and unless the transfer is restricted, it can be sold, bought, mortgaged, or given away. Most corporations hold one class of stock known as common stock.

Shares of stock may be issued only for money paid, labor done, or property actually received. Services that may be rendered in the future are not a proper basis for issuing stock. Shares of stock are evidenced by the issuance of stock certificates, typically signed by the corporation's president and secretary with the corporate seal impressed on them. The stock certificate indicates the number of shares and the name of the registered shareholder. When (1) the issuance of shares of stock has been duly authorized by the board of directors, (2) the proper consideration has been paid to the corporation, and (3) the stock certificate has been properly completed, signed, sealed, and delivered to the shareholder, the shares of stock are then "fully paid." As a result, the shareholder is entitled to exercise all rights of a shareholder and is not subject to any further assessment by the corporation.

Annual and Other Regular Meetings

Corporations are required to hold annual meetings of shareholders for the purpose of electing directors. In addition, the board of directors typically holds an annual meeting at the same time to elect officers. The board of directors also may establish regular meeting times between annual meetings.

Certain corporate actions may be required by law or a corporation's articles of incorporation or bylaws to be specifically approved by the directors or shareholders. If such action is required and a regular or annual meeting is not scheduled at an appropriate time, then a special meeting may be called for such a purpose following procedures established in the bylaws.

Reporting Requirements

A corporation is required to file certain reports with the secretary of state and other appropriate government authorities in order to remain in good standing. The corporation is required to file such reports as an annual registration report, franchise tax report, and income tax returns. Additionally, any changes in registered agents or offices, or changes in the number of directors, must be reported. Provided the corporation files the necessary reports and is in compliance with the law, the secretary of state or other government agency may issue a certificate of good standing. A certificate of good standing is a document issued by the state that certifies the corporation has complied with all laws and regulations to remain a separate legal entity. In addition to the credibility the certificate of good standing provides for the corporation, it is required by most lenders prior to fulfilling a loan request for the company. For a corporation to legally conduct business, it must be in good standing. A corporation that has not complied with the necessary requirements to remain in good standing is no longer a legal entity and therefore can no longer conduct business as a corporation. If a bank loans money to a corporation that is not in good standing, the bank is loaning to an entity to which it cannot enforce payment should the borrower default on the loan.

Advantages of a Corporation

A corporation can provide substantial benefits. There are four primary advantages to forming a corporation. They include limited liability for shareholders, directors, and officers; continuity; transferability of ownership; and accessibility of capital.

- *Liability.* The corporation is its own legal "person" and is separate from its owners. The shareholders are not personally liable for the losses of the business as long as the corporation does not pierce the corporate veil in some manner. Liability of the shareholders is typically limited to the amount they have invested in the company. Creditors will look to the corporation to repay the corporation's debt. There is an exception to this. Most lenders require that the major shareholders of the corporation personally guarantee any debt incurred by the corporation. Doing so makes the shareholders personally liable for the amount of the debt. The lender may find it necessary to liquidate personal assets should the corporation fail to satisfy its obligation to the bank.
- *Continuity.* The continuity of the corporation is advantageous to the shareholders in that it does not cease to exist if one or more of its owners dies or leaves the corporation.
- *Transferability.* Ownership of a corporation can be transferred simply by the sale of all or a portion of stock. More owners may be added by selling stock directly from the corporation or by having the current owners sell some of their stock.
- *Access to capital.* Corporations have the ability to attract capital from investors because they can sell stock. Corporations can sell their stock to a small number of investors or through a public offering. The decisions to issue shares of stock should not be taken lightly. Both public and private offerings could be subject to certain Securities and Exchange Commission (SEC) restrictions. The SEC is a federal agency for the securities industry that is responsible for protecting investors against fraudulant and manipulative practices in the securities market. It is important to get good legal advice prior to issuing stock.

Disadvantages of a Corporation

Forming a corporation also has its disadvantages.

- *Double taxation.* The corporation pays taxes on its profits, and the shareholders must pay taxes on the dividends they receive from the profits. The corporate tax rate is typically higher than that of the sole proprietorship or partnership.
- *Loss of control by founders.* Owners of corporations can sell enough of their stock to lose control of the company. Even minority shareholders have certain rights. Often entrepreneurs find themselves selling stock to raise enough capital to get or keep the business going.
- *Reporting requirements.* The corporation is the most labor-intensive of all forms of ownership. Annual meetings must be held, minutes must be kept, reports must be filed with the state, and managers may be required to submit some major decisions to the stockholders for approval.

ALTERNATIVE FORMS OF OWNERSHIP

For many years, small business owners operated their businesses as sole proprietorships, partnerships, and corporations. Now, business owners have alternative forms of ownership.

The Limited Liability Company

The limited liability company (LLC) offers the advantages of a corporation and a partnership. The LLC is advantageous over an s-corporation in that it is not subject to many of the restrictions imposed on an s-corporation such as limited shareholders. It is not limited in the number of owners it can have. The owners are refered to as members. All members may participate in the day-to-day management of the company without the restrictions enforced on a limited partnership. As in a corporation, personal assets of members are protected from debts and lawsuits related to the business. It is critical to note that banks often require the personal guarantee of the owners to secure financing for the business. Limited liability companies do not face the issues of double taxation as does a corporation. Business income is reported on the members' individual tax returns and not on both the company and individual returns. The income and loss reported by the LLC is passed through to the members and reported on their personal tax returns. Members' finance liability is limited to their investment in the company.

Limited liability companies provide a great deal of flexibility with regard to management and business organization. Very little paperwork is required to form an LLC. In most states, LLCs have an operating agreement or contract that dictates the company's organizational structure, describes internal policies, and specifies how the profits will be shared. Owners are required to file articles of organization, which are similar to a corporation's articles of incorporation. The company is typically required to use "limited liability company" or "LLC" in its name. The articles of organization include the company's name, names and addresses of the organizers, the purpose(s) of the organization, and whether or not the company is run by one or more managers. The operating agreement governs the way in which the company will conduct business. It specifies who has authority to sign for the company, and the contributions of each member of the LLC. Because of their flexibility and the capacity to be formed relatively quickly and inexpensively, LLCs have become very popular among business owners.

The S-Corporation

The s-corporation is an IRS designation made in terms of its federal tax issues. The s designation is an Internal Revenue Service designation. To be eligible as an s-corporation, the business must meet the following requirements:

1. It must be a U.S. corporation.
2. The corporation may not have more than 75 shareholders.
3. All shareholders must be U.S. citizens or residents.
4. The corporation cannot have more than one class of stock. The exception is that the s-corporation can issue both voting and nonvoting stock.

Violating any of these requirements will automatically terminate the s status. Election to operate as an s-corporation requires the filing of Form 2553 with the Internal Revenue Service.

The s-corporation has the advantages of a reagular corporation in that it provides the following: ability to easily transfer ownership, limited liability for its owners, and the continuation of the company should the original owners die or decide to leave the company. The s-corporation avoids double taxation in that the profits of the company are passed through to the individual owners. The profits are then reported on individual tax returns at the individual rate. Should the company remain profitable by year-end, the owner has the authority to withdraw any of these profits.

SELECTING A LAWYER

Because of the complexity of business today, entrepreneurs need the expertise and advice of lawyers. Just as doctors specialize in different fields of medicine, lawyers specialize in different areas of the law. The entrepreneur should seek an attorney who practices business law and whose law firm is known for its expertise in this area. There are various avenues for finding a competent attorney. First, the prospective entrepreneur can ask other entrepreneurs already in business. The attorney should have the experience and knowledge needed to provide competent legal assistance. The *Martindale-Hubbel Law Directory*, found in most public libraries, provides information about lawyers and their credentials. It includes detailed information on the background of law firms, areas of specialization, and, sometimes, includes major clients. It assigns "ratings" to lawyers based on their legal ability, ethical standards, professional reliability, and diligence. Additionally, local bar associations provide lists of lawyers practicing corporate law and other forms of law. It is also important for the entrepreneur to know the lawyers' level of expertise, how many years they have been in practice, and whether or not they are interested in working with smaller companies.

Larger law firms typically charge more for their services than do smaller firms. In contrast, they have the ability to provide a wide range of services with numerous attorneys specializing in various areas of the law. This can be important for a fashion retail company considering that they may conduct business overseas or take the company public.

SELECTING AN ACCOUNTANT

Like attorneys, accountants may specialize in different areas. Some work only with tax returns, while others provide a full range of accounting services for the start-up company. Initially, an effective accountant will make sure that the entrepreneur is making an informed decision as to the type of ownership the company should operate under to receive the greatest tax advantage. Later, a good accountant will take the time to explain the financial information of the company to the entrepreneur. The entrepreneur will want to know how many years of experience the accountant has, particularly his or her experience in working with start-up companies. To a start-up company, the availability of the accountant is important. The entrepreneur will want to know that the accountant has the time and will be available to address accounting issues as they arise.

CONCLUSION

When forming a new venture, the entrepreneur must make an informed decision about the form of ownership under which the business will operate (Table 10.1). Understanding the characteristics of each form of ownership will help ensure that the entrepreneur is making the right decision. Choosing a form of ownership involves reviewing tax considerations, liability issues, cost of forming the legal entity, control of the business, the ease with which ownership, can be transferred, and how easily the company can obtain capital.

Table 10.1   Characteristics of the Major Forms of Business Ownership

	Sole Proprietorship	Partnership/Limited Liability Partnership	Limited Liability Company	S-Corporation	Corporation a/ka (C-Corporation)
Investor Called	Proprietor	General partner Limited partner	Member	Shareholder	Shareholder
Legal Liability	Unlimited	General partner—unlimited Limited partner—limited	Limited	Limited	Limited
Number of Owners	1	2 or more (at least 1 general partner required)	1 or more	Maximum of 75 stockholders (restrictions on who they are)	Unlimited
Organizational Structure	None	Partnership agreement/Limited partnership agreement, filing of certificate with state	Organized by charter issued by state; governed by articles of organization and operating agreement	Corporate charter issued by state; governed by articles of incorporation, by-laws, and shareholder agreements	Corporate charter issued by state; governed by articles of Incorporation, by-laws and shareholder agreements
Organizational Documents	Maybe Fictitious Name Registration	Partnership Agreement (oral, writing, or state law)	Articles of Organization	Articles of Incorporation; corporate records (cf. close corporation)	Articles of incorporation; corporate records (cf. close corporation)
Transfer of Interest	Easy. All assets are owned by the proprietor	Assets and right to management cannot be transferred without consent of other partners	Management rights transferable with consent of other members	Easy transference of stock unless restricted by agreement, articles of incorporation, or by being statutory close corporation	Easy transference of stock unless restricted by agreement, articles of incorporation, or by being statutory close corporation. Fully transferable
Acquisition of Capital	Limited to what the owner can secure	Generally limited to what the partners can raise collectively	Generally limited to what the members can raise	Transfer of stock is relatively easy unless articles of agreement, or by being statutory close corporation	Easier to raise capital. Stock may be sold but capital is not generally raised this way

Cost of Formation	Low	Low to moderate	Relatively low	High	High
Management	Proprietor	Partners	Manager	Board of directors, corporate officers with legal requirements	Board of directors, corporate officers with legal requirements
Continuity of the Entity	Limited to life of proprietor or upon termination of proprietor	Limited. Death or retirement of a general partner, unless provided for in partnership agreement	Dissolve date/may be perpetual	Perpetual life	Perpetual life
Taxation	All income and expenses reported on proprietor's individual tax return. No double taxation	Divided among partners in accordance with investment or partnership agreement and reported on partners' individual returns	Divided among members in accordance with investment or operating agreement and reported on members' individual returns	Passed directly through to the shareholders according to the amount of stock held. Generally no income tax paid by corporation	Taxed separately at the corporate level, again at the shareholder level if distributed as a dividend. Double taxation

Adapted from a joint project of Missouri Department of Economic Development, Outreach & Extension, University of Missouri & Lincoln University and Missouri Small Business Development Centers. Editor Sharon Gulick, Missouri Department of Economic Development, May 2000

There are basically three forms of ownership from which to choose: the sole proprietorship, the partnership, and the corporation. Variations of these entities have emerged, two of which are the s-corporation and the limited liability corporation. The emergence of these new forms of ownership gives the entrepreneur more options.

Selecting an attorney and an accountant are just as important as selecting the right entity for the business. Today's business world is complex. The laws and tax regulations are complicated. The laws vary from state to state. The entrepreneur is well advised to consult with both an attorney and an accountant prior to selecting a form of ownership.

WRITING THE PLAN

Use this chapter to address the form of ownership.

The form of ownership is not a seperate section in the business plan. The form of ownership is referred to throughout the plan.

KEY TERMS

articles of incorporation	members
articles of organization	name search
business license	operating agreement
certificate of good standing	partnership
corporation	partnership agreement
director (for a corporation)	publicly held corporation
domestic state	s-corporation
fictitious name registration	shareholder
foreign corporation	sole proprietorship
limited liability company (LLC)	Uniform Partnership Act
limited partnership	

QUESTIONS

1. What key factors play a role in determining form of ownership for a business?
2. What is a sole proprietorship? Discuss the advantages and disadvantages of a sole proprietorship. Why is it a popular form of ownership?
3. What is a partnership? Discuss the advantages and disadvantages of a partnership. How can an entrepreneur reduce the risk of conflict in a partnership?
4. What is the role of a limited partner in a partnership?
5. What is the Uniform Partnership Act?
6. What is a limited partnership? How does it differ from a partnership?
7. What is a corporation? Discuss the advantages and disadvantages of a corporation.
8. What is double taxation?
9. What steps would an entrepreneur take to avoid "piercing the corporate veil" and prevent losing corporate status?
10. Discuss the benefits and drawbacks to a limited liability company.
11. Discuss the advantages and disadvantages of an s-corporation.

REFERENCES

1. Steven Riggs, "Breaking Up Is Hard to Do," *Self Employed Professional*, September/October 1996, p. 32

2. Ibid.
3. Mary Hanson, *Business Articles Partnership: The Pros and Cons*, www.bizadvisor.com/pshp.htm
4. Philip Krause, "Forming a For-Profit Corporation" (Missouri: conference handout)

SUGGESTED READING

Corporate Agents, Inc., *The Essential United Liability Company Handbook: The Newest Alternative in Business* (Grants Pass, Oregon: Oasis Press, 1995)
Carl F. Sniffen, *The Essential Corporation Handbook* (Grants Pass, Oregon: Oasis Press, 1995)

. . . .

ENTERING THE WORLD OF THE ENTREPRENEUR

. . . .

1. Make an appointment with a fashion retail entrepreneur. Ask the entrepreneur why he or she chose the form of ownership for the business. What tax and legal considerations were made in the decision?
2. Ask the entrepreneur if he or she consulted with an attorney and accountant prior to choosing the form of ownership. If not, how does the entrepreneur perceive that this has affected the business?
3. Contact the secretary of state's office in your state and find out what the requirements are for forming the various legal entities. Contact your local, city, and county governments to find out about local laws and business license requirements. What documentation is required in your state, city, and county to start a business?
4. Talk with business owners who operate as a partnership. Do they have a formal written partnership agreement? What happens if conflict arises? How do they handle disagreements? Does each partner have an exit strategy?

. . . .

ENTERPRISING ENTREPRENEUR

. . . .

Sam's Club is the nation's leading members-only warehouse. Sam's Club offers its 43 million members brand name merchandise at "member's only" prices. In addition to its current offerings in merchandise, Sam's Club has added striking black jewelry display cases and a product offering to include some stunning jewelry pieces. In 1999, it featured dozens of items priced at several thousand dollars in approximately 25 clubs.

> The changes to the jewelry department are the result of Sam's decision in April 1999 to not renew its contract with Jan Bell Marketing, the company that previously operated the jewelry departments. Jan Bell staffed the approximately 270 square foot departments, managed the inventory, and paid Sam's tenancy fee of 9 percent of net sales. The typical merchandise offerings consisted of 300 jewelry items, 100 watches, and 200 other items such as fragrances, figurines, sunglasses, and writing instruments.
> M. Troy, "Sam's Club Adds Luster to Jewelry Department," *DSN Retailing Today*, November 2000.

Sam's Club is changing the appearance of its jewelry department by changing the overall appearance and including some high-end brands and higher price points.

The Sam's Club in Springdale, Arkansas, featured watches by Cartier, Tag Heuer, Breiting, and Omega. Prices ranged from $1,749 to $3,444. Previously, Movado brand watches in the $500 to $800 range were the most expensive watches found at Sam's.

Sam's decision to operate its own jewelry department ends an affiliation with the club industry that goes back to 1984 and Price Club. When Price Club and Costco merged in 1990, the combined company decided to operate its own jewelry departments. Jan Bell still had deals with Pace and Sam's, but when Sam's bought the Pace division from Kmart in 1994, Jan Bell was left with one customer who accounted for 93 percent of its revenue.

With so many eggs in one basket and perhaps sensing that Sam's would eventually decide to directly operate its own jewelry departments, Jan Bell acquired the Mayor's Jewelry chain of 24 stores in July 1998. Less than a year later, Sam's said it didn't plan to extend its contract with the company. Jan Bell has since changed its name to Mayors Jewelers and operates 32 stores.

M. Troy, "Sam's Club Adds Luster to Jewelry Department," *DSN Retailing Today,* November 2000.

Chapter 11

CREATING AND UNDERSTANDING THE FINANCIAL PLAN

INTRODUCTION

We have addressed the issues of sourcing the correct products, marketing and advertising the business, determining the best way to enter the market, deciding where to locate the business, and hiring the people necessary to run the business. All these issues have costs attached to them. This chapter focuses on understanding and constructing financial statements. It also looks at what variables affect the numbers in financial statements. Key ratios are examined, since these are the tools that are used to determine how well a business is doing. The chapter also explains how to calculate the break-even point for the business, how cash flow affects the business, and how to access capital. It is important to note that many scenarios exist for each business. It is beyond the scope of this text to address every scenario. Accountants should be consulted when preparing financial documents.

THE IMPORTANCE OF THE FINANCIAL PICTURE

The financial plan is one of the most critical elements of the business plan. Most entrepreneurs also find it one of the most frightening. The financial plan helps determine the amount of financing that will be needed to make the business feasible, the type of financing that will be needed, and when the financing needs to be there. The numbers tell a story about the condition of the business. Without them, the entrepreneur would make uninformed decisions, usually wrong ones, about the company's operation. The financials are a reflection of the decisions that will be or have been made. To determine which numbers go into the financial plan, information is pulled from other parts of the plan. For example, if the management plan states that the business will employ three full-time sales associates, then the financial statements will reflect salaries and benefits for three full-time sales associates. The entrepreneur will want to look at such sources as the *Annual Statement Studies*, published by Robert Morris and Associates, for financial statement data obtained from other fashion retail businesses throughout the country. Doing so enables the entrepreneur to compare projected numbers with industry averages. This is especially important to a start-up company for which there is no historical data to compare the numbers.

In addition to serving as a tool for determining the capital that will be needed to launch and run the business, the financial plan also serves as a management tool in helping the entrepreneur run his or her business. It can affect decisions concerning inventory, hiring more sales staff, or changing the mix of merchandise. The financials can indicate whether or not pricing may be too low or too high. They can indicate whether or not the business is suffering from theft or lack of sufficient labor.

While all activities are important in running a business, none is more important than ensuring the financial well-being of the business. Competition is fierce for a start-up company, and resources are limited. Maintaining good financial records will help prevent catastrophes. They will provide the entrepreneur with the opportunity to stop failure before it happens. For a start-up company with limited resources, good information counts.

It is wise to collect cost and income information before calculating the financial section of the business plan. This is needed, not just for location decisions, but also for personnel, equipment, and inventory decisions as well. The costs related to planning a business are similar to pieces in a jigsaw puzzle. They all must fit together to make one cohesive image. Estimating the potential sales volume of the business is the first step to fitting a piece into the puzzle.

Faced with developing a business plan, the majority of prospective entrepreneurs ask the same question, "How do I know how much money my business will make?" The answer is often one the entrepreneur does not want to hear. He or she cannot or will not know for certain. What kind of an answer is that? It is an honest response; however, there are a number of ways to logically estimate the performance of a specific type of business. The most common method of determining annual sales volume is through **application of industry averages.** There are two key sources for this information. The first is the Robert Morris Associates (RMA) data, published annually and located in most libraries and small business support organizations. The second is specifically geared toward retailers of apparel and soft goods. It is entitled *Merchandising and Operating Results* and is published annually by the National Retail Federation, most often available for a fee.

THE FINANCIAL STATEMENTS

Sound and reliable information about the financial performance of a business is required to effectively manage the day-to-day operation. The entrepreneur must know the answers to such questions as:

- Is the business generating cash flow sufficient to be profitable?
- Is the rate of inventory turnover sufficient to maintain satisfactory profit margins?
- Are operating costs under control?
- What is the break-even point for the business?

These questions can be answered through well-researched financial information. The budgeting process helps with this information. The budget answers such questions as:

- What can the business achieve in sales during the first year?
- How much inventory will the business need on hand to achieve this sales volume?
- What expenses will be incurred in order to achieve this amount in sales?

The more detailed the information, the more accurate the data will be. Although the entrepreneur's accountant often prepares the basic financial documents of cash flow, income statement, and balance sheet, it is still necessary for the entrepreneur to understand how to read and interpret these documents. To do this, there must be an understanding of what each document is and where the numbers come from.

The entrepreneur preparing financial documents to open a business will prepare a pro forma set of financial statements. Pro forma, a term commonly used in the business and accounting industry, means projected. These pro forma financial statements will help determine the amount of funds needed to open the doors and to keep them open. The three basic financial documents of cash flow, income statement, and balance sheet correspond with one another. A pro forma cash flow statement can be no more than an estimate of the business's sources and use of funds. It is a management tool that is updated as the business continues. Once the business is open, it is strongly advisable for an entrepreneur to take the time to compare actual numbers to those that were projected. This should be done monthly for at least the first year of business. Doing this will enable the entrepreneur to catch major cash problems before they get out of hand. Following is a description of the three basic financial statements used by businesses, and how to prepare these pro forma documents. For purposes of this text, the company BeTwixt, Inc., is operating on a cash basis versus accrual method of accounting. The cash basis method of accounting recognizes income and expenses when income is received or expenses are paid. The accrual method of accounting recognizes income and expenses when they are incurred and not necessarily when they are actually received and paid.

The Cash Flow Statement

Cash flow is defined as the amount of cash that flows in and out of the business during an accounting period. The cash flow statement serves as a cash flow management tool for the business. The cash flow statement is probably the most important financial document used for a start-up company. It will determine the cash needs of the business on a month-to-month basis. If the employees cannot be paid, merchandise cannot be bought, or bills cannot be paid, then the entrepreneur will not be able to stay in business. The cash flow statement is an important tool in managing the operations of the business. It is used as a management tool by allowing a comparison of the projected amount in revenues and expenses with the actual amount. It is particularly important for a fashion retail business that will have large inventory purchases, which will be seasonal in nature.

Working Backwards

In a nutshell . . . your sales need to cover the cost of goods sold and your monthly expenses . . . with money left over to realize a profit or simply pay back your small business loan.

How do you work backwards, as they say?

1. Calculate how much money you must spend each month to pay the bills on a monthly basis. Plan for rent, insurance, utilities, advertising, telephone, taxes, etc. See the Monthly Cash Flow Projection form provided. Don't forget payroll, taxes, and loan payments as expenses.
2. Calculate how much money you will need to open your doors for the first day of business. Include your opening inventory and opening promotional fees as start-up expenses. Don't forget your rent deposit, business license, name search fee, remodeling costs, fixtures expenses, market trip to purchase goods . . . what else?
3. Add the total monthly fixed expenses per month. Deduct this amount from your retail sales for the month. Where do you stand?
4. Plan to have a 3 to 4 stock turn. This means that every 3 to 4 months you will need to purchase more goods. Think retail dollars for everything, except writing your orders for market.

Can you calculate your break-even point? You are figuring how much you need to make just to cover your costs.

The cash flow statement is a document that reflects all cash flowing into the business and all cash going out of the business on a monthly basis for a time period of not less than 1 year. While the cash flow statement shows the amount of cash the business will have in the bank; it is not about the amount of profit the company will show at the end of the year. Cash is the money that flows through the business in a continuous cycle without being tied up in any other assets. Profit (or net income) is the difference between a company's total revenue and its total expenses. For example, assume that BeTwixt fashion retail store sells uniforms to high schools for their teams (Table 11.1). BeTwixt takes orders for jerseys with the school logo to be placed on the merchandise. Because the school is placing an order and the school will be invoiced for payment, BeTwixt has now generated an account receivable. An account receivable is money owed to the store for merchandise sold on credit. The store will place an order with the manufacturer. The manufacturer will deliver the product to BeTwixt; the store will then deliver it to the school; and the school will be invoiced for payment. At the time the school is invoiced, it creates an account receivable for BeTwixt. The school typically pays the invoice within a 45-day period. Cash will not flow into the business until the invoice is paid on or before 45 days. At the point of sale, the cash flow statement will not reflect the money being received. Subsequently, the net profit will be different from the cash shown by the business.

The cash flow statement is divided into two sections: cash in and cash out. The cash received is totaled for each month in the line labeled Total Cash. This figure also includes beginning cash, in addition to any loan proceeds (money borrowed from a bank, individual, or other funder if applicable); and any cash generated from sales. The total cash received for the year is reflected in the Totals column on the far-right side of the document. This indicates total amount of cash that will come into the business for the year.

Expenses are added and totaled by month. The Total Cash (Revenue) figure is not included in this total. Remember, this is cash. When an expense is generated is not important; it is important to know when the expense is paid for and when cash is deducted from the the bank account. For example, if BeTwixt receives a bill for rent, until the rent is paid, the bill is not reflected on the cash flow statement. Total expenses by month are reflected on the line labeled Total Expenses (line 37). The owner's draw, the amount of money the owner is taking out of the company, is then deducted from this line to reflect total cash payments (outgoing). By subtracting Total Cash (line 7) from Total Cash Payments (line 39), the result is cash on hand at the end of each month ($90,464 [December] − $84,738 [December] = $5,726). (See Table 11.1.)

The following steps guide students through preparing a pro forma cash flow statement.

Step 1: The first step in preparing a cash flow statement is to develop a chart of accounts. A chart of accounts is a listing of the accounts used to track business transactions. In a fashion retail business, this list would include such items as sales, inventory, rent, and utilities. This is a list of all transactions the business has. In researching the product, the industry, marketing strategies, and other aspects of the business, the entrepreneur will discover the types of costs and sources of revenue for the business. This will be translated into the business's chart of accounts. Once the chart of accounts has been established, numbers can be input for a spreadsheet.

Step 2: Now that the chart of accounts has been established, the entrepreneur will want to refer to the research that was conducted in order to determine the amount of funding the business will need for start-up costs. Start-up costs are those costs that will be incurred to get the doors open. The start-up column of the cash flow statement shown in Table 11.1 contains a range of start-up costs. Such items will include leasehold improvements, furniture and equipment, opening inventory, signage, advertising, travel expenses to purchase merchandise, loans, and so on. Start-up costs will vary depending on the nature of the business. Cash on hand is the amount of cash the entrepreneur has to inject into the company. Banks will require the entrepreneur to have some capital in the business. This is discussed later in the chapter.

Step 3: Next, the entrepreneur will need to estimate the ongoing costs of running the business and revenue for the first year. He or she will begin by determining the amount of sales the business will generate for a 1-year period. This number can be estimated by looking at other fashion retail stores of approximately the same size, in the same type of geographic location, carrying the same type of inventory. If sufficient research has been done, it will be a good estimate. To use this data as a comparison to projected financial information compiled for your business, you would read the study as follows:

If you were a company that anticipated sales of 0–$1MM and wanted to know how close you projected financial information in relationship to other companies in your industry, you would look in column D (Current Data Sorted by Sales) for comparison.

Table 11.1 Cash Flow Statement

BeTwixt, Inc.
Pro Forma Cash Flow
12 Months 2002

#		Start-up	Jan.	Feb.	Mar.	Apr.	May	June	July	Aug.	Sept.	Oct.	Nov.	Dec.	Totals
1	Cash On Hand	30,500	900	274	348	7,117	583	2,449	9,338	3,137	886	11,253	525	464	
2	Loan Proceeds	60,000	0	24,000	1000	12,000	0	0	21,000	8,000	0	10,000	5,000	0	141,000
3			0	0	0	0	0	0	0	0	0	0	0	0	0
4	Cash Sales		15,000	20,000	21,000	27,000	32,000	22,000	17,000	32,000	27,000	22,000	55,000	90,000	380,000
5			0	0	0	0	0	0	0	0	0	0	0	0	0
6			0	0	0	0	0	0	0	0	0	0	0	0	0
7	Total Cash	90,500	15,900	44,274	22,348	46,117	32,583	24,449	47,338	43,137	27,886	43,253	60,525	90,464	
8															
9	Expenses														
10	Rent	2,500	2,500	2,500	2,500	2,500	2,500	2,500	2,500	2,500	2,500	2,500	2,500	2,500	30,000
11	Direct Labor		3,000	3,000	3,000	3,000	3,000	3,000	3,000	3,000	3,000	3,000	3,000	4,000	37,000
12	Payroll Expense		690	690	690	690	690	690	690	690	690	690	690	920	8,510
13	Inventory	50,000	0	33,000	0	34,000	0	0	28,000	30,000	0	30,000	47,000	0	202,000
14	Repairs/Maintenance		25	25	25	25	25	25	25	25	25	25	25	25	300
15	Office Supplies	500	25	25	25	25	25	25	25	25	25	25	25	25	300
16	Travel Expense	3,750	3,750	0	3,750	0	0	3,750	3,750	0	3,750	0	0	0	18,750
17	Advertising	3,000	1,000	1,000	1,000	1,000	1,000	1,000	1,000	1,000	1,000	1,000	1,500	1,500	13,000
18	Bad Debts		50	50	50	50	50	50	50	50	50	50	50	50	600
19	Bank Charges		300	350	350	400	400	350	300	400	400	350	600	1,000	5,200

#	Item	Start-up												Total
20	Contributions		0	250	0	250	0	0	0	250	0	0	250	1,000
21	Dues & Subscripts	175	0	0	0	0	0	0	0	175	0	0	0	175
22	Insurance		250	250	750	250	230	750	250	250	750	250	250	4,980
23	Meals & Entmnt		50	50	50	50	50	50	50	50	50	50	50	600
24	Office & Postage		0	180	0	180	0	0	0	180	0	0	180	770
25	Security	3,500	30	30	30	30	30	30	30	30	30	30	30	360
26	Accounting & Legal	250	250	250	250	250	250	250	250	250	250	250	250	3,350
27	Taxes & Licenses	125	0	0	0	0	0	0	0	0	0	0	425	425
28	Telephone/Comm.	1,000	231	231	231	231	231	231	231	231	231	231	231	2,772
29	Utilities	750	200	125	50	75	125	150	110	110	110	110	110	1,515
30	Interest & Principal		0	200	208	19,308	150	150	325	392	392	475	62,517	84,117
31	Amortizing Loan I & P	0	1,275	1,275	1,275	1,275	1,275	1,275	1,275	1,275	1,275	1,275	1,275	15,300
32	Leasehold Improve.	10,000	0	0	0	0	0	0	0	0	0	0	0	0
33	Furniture/Equip/Racks	8,950	0	0	0	0	0	0	0	0	0	0	0	0
34	Income Tax	0	0	0	0	0	0	0	0	0	0	0	7,150	7,150
35	Sign	3,600	0	0	0	0	0	0	0	0	0	0	0	0
36	Grand Opening	1,500	0	0	0	0	0	0	0	0	0	0	0	0
37	Total Expenses	89,600	42,926	14,231	44,534	29,134	14,111	42,201	40,251	14,633	40,728	58,061	82,738	438,174
38	Owners Draw	0	1,000	1,000	1,000	1,000	1,000	2,000	2,000	2,000	2,000	2,000	2,000	18,000
39	Total Cash Payments	89,600	43,926	15,231	45,534	30,134	15,111	44,201	42,251	16,633	42,728	60,061	84,738	456,174
40	Cash (End of Month)	900	348	7,117	583	2,449	9,338	3,137	886	11,253	525	464	5,726	
41														
42	Operating Line of Credit	0	24,000	25,000	37,000	18,000	18,000	39,000	47,000	47,000	57,000	62,000	0	0
43	Amortizing Loan Bal.	60,000	0	0	0	0	0	0	0	0	0	0	0	0
44														
45														

You would then look at the first column in this section and note that 19 statements have been used for comparison (10 compiled statements, 6 tax returns, and 3 others). For this size company, the statement indicates that inventory is 62.1% of total sales. So, if your company's financial data exceeded or was less than this percentage, you would want to know why. The industry standards per this report are at 62.1%. The study provides the same information for cash and equivalents, trade receivables, etc. Moving down this sub-column, you note that for a company with sales of 0–$1MM, operating expenses are 37.7% of sales. Again, if your company's operating expenses were above or below the industry average, you would want to know why.

The *Statement Studies* also provide information on ratios calculated for the industry. Each ratio gives an upper, middle, and lower quartile for comparison. The Robert Morris Association *Annual Statement Studies* is a compilation of industry averages for specific industries. It enable bankers, entrepreneurs, and others to compare the financial information of their business, to the financial information of other businesses in the same industry. Figure 11.1 is taken from the Robert Morris Associates *Annual Statement Studies*. Men's & Boy's Clothing & Accessory Stores is being used as an example to explain what the information means.

For each industry, financial data are collected and compiled in this format (Figure 11.1). Financial data for each industry are sorted by both assets (column A) and sales (column D). Columns B (Historical Data by Assets) and C (Historical Data by Sales) provide a comparison of historical data for both assets and sales respectively. The comparative historical data is sorted by year, with totals given for the number of statements reported for each type of statement (i.e., in column B, 19 unqualified statements were collected from 4/1/96–3/3/97, 31 reviewed, 66 compiled, 7 from tax returns, and 45 from other sources. For this time period, a total of 168 statements were used). Note that in columns A and D, information is also sorted by the size of the company (0–$500M, 0–$1MM, etc.). Type of Statement for Assets, and Type of Statement for Sales represent the types of information provided.

It is important to note that in the fashion retail industry, sales are based on the total square footage of the facility used for selling merchandise. In the sample business plan used in Chapter 14, the business is estimating $380,000 in sales for the first year. The assumption for this plan is that the store has 3,000 square feet. The store has 2,500 square feet of selling space and 500 square feet of nonselling space. Sales are calculated at $152 per square foot. Sales per square foot will vary depending on the type of merchandise in the store. It is not a hard and fast rule to have $152 in sales volume per square foot. The annual sales figure must then be broken down monthly. Chapter 9 provides an illustration of monthly sales projections that reflect seasonality in the fashion industry. Next, the entrepreneur will determine the amount of inventory that must be purchased as start-up (or core) inventory to have on hand when the doors open. This number is inserted in the Start-up column under the account Inventory (line 13) on the cash flow statement. In Table 11.1, this number is $50,000.

Step 4: It is extremely rare that a retail business can open without a loan and a line of credit. As illustrated in Table 11.1, total expenses (line 37) for the start-up are $89,600. The entrepreneur is investing $30,500 (line 1) into the company (i.e., cash on hand). As a result, a loan will be needed in the amount of $60,000 (line 2) to get the doors open. ($89,600 − $30,500 = $59,100). Once a business has opened, the actual expenses and sales rarely end up the same as the estimates. The entrepreneur should secure an operating line of credit with the bank to cover expenses when sales do not meet projections or

Figure 11.1

RETAIL-MEN'S & BOYS' CLOTHING & ACCESSORY STORES   **SIC# 5611 (NAICS 44811, 44815)**

Ⓐ **Current Data Sorted by Assets**   Ⓑ **Comparative Historical Data**

						Type of Statement		
		8	2	4		Unqualified	19	18
1	6	9	3			Reviewed	31	29
15	14	6				Compiled	66	58
7	5					Tax Returns	7	8
3	8	6	2	1	2	Other	45	34
	28 (4/1-9/30/00)		74 (10/1/00–3/31/01)				4/1/96–3/31/97	4/1/97–3/31/98
0-500M	500-2MM	2-10MM	10-50MM	50-100MM	100-250MM		ALL	ALL
26	33	29	7	5	2	NUMBER OF STATEMENTS	168	147
%	%	%	%	%	%	**ASSETS**	%	%
8.2	11.9	12.1				Cash & Equivalents	7.4	9.1
4.9	12.2	7.5				Trade Receivables–(net)	8.9	8.6
61.9	54.4	48.4				Inventory	54.8	53.0
1.2	.9	.7				All Other Current	2.5	.8
76.2	79.4	68.6				Total Current	73.7	71.6
16.6	12.5	19.2				Fixed Assets (net)	17.8	18.2
2.1	2.1	2.6				Intangibles (net)	2.5	2.5
5.1	5.9	9.6				All Other Non-Current	6.0	7.7
100.0	100.0	100.0				Total	100.0	100.0
						LIABILITIES		
8.4	8.4	14.7				Notes Payable-Short Term	11.9	13.0
4.9	2.8	2.6				Cur. Mat.-L/T/D	2.2	3.0
18.4	16.3	19.3				Trade Payables	18.3	18.7
1.0	.3	.2				Income Taxes Payable	.2	.4
19.0	10.2	7.8				All Other Current	10.1	9.3
51.8	38.1	44.7				Total Current	42.7	44.5
10.2	10.4	13.9				Long Term Debt	11.2	12.3
.0	.0	.1				Deferred Taxes	.2	.3
3.8	5.0	2.7				All Other Non-Current	4.0	5.3
34.1	46.4	38.6				Net Worth	41.9	37.6
100.0	100.0	100.0				Total Liabilities & Net Worth	100.0	100.0
						INCOME DATA		
100.0	100.0	100.0				Net Sales	100.0	100.0
41.6	46.5	42.9				Gross Profit	41.6	49.1
37.9	44.5	40.5				Operating Expenses	39.0	40.0
3.6	2.0	2.3				Operating Profit	2.6	3.1
.8	.4	1.1				All Other Expenses (net)	.9	1.2
2.9	1.6	1.2				Profit Before Taxes	1.7	1.9
						RATIOS		
3.5	3.7	3.1				Current	3.0	2.5
1.7	2.1	1.6					1.8	1.7
1.0	1.4	1.1					1.2	1.1
.6	1.2	1.0				Quick	.8	.7
(25) .2	.7	.3				(167)	.3	.4
.1	.1	.1					.1	.1
0 UND	1 402.4	1 533.1				Sales/Receivables	1 549.6	0 999.8
0 UND	6 60.2	5 75.7					4 100.2	4 85.0
4 96.6	27 13.7	11 32.1					23 16.1	23 15.6
79 4.6	86 4.2	85 4.3				Cost of Sales/Inventory	83 4.4	91 4.0
123 3.0	151 2.4	115 3.2					140 2.6	130 2.8
188 1.9	203 1.8	200 1.8					228 1.6	203 1.8
12 31.0	14 26.7	25 14.3				Cost of Sales/Payables	18 20.1	20 18.1
26 13.9	30 12.0	45 8.1					29 12.4	42 8.6
46 7.9	71 5.2	68 5.3					68 5.4	70 5.2
4.8	4.5	5.1				Sales/Working Capital	4.3	4.5
9.4	5.4	10.4					8.0	8.7
NM	9.1	41.0					22.5	33.6
10.3	7.2	6.1				EBIT/Interest	5.5	5.3
(22) 3.4	(31) 2.8	(27) 1.2				(138)	2.0	(125) 2.2
1.0	1.2	.4					1.0	.7
						Net Profit + Depr., Dep., Amort./Cur. Mat. L/T/D	6.6	5.5
							(36) 2.0	(34) 1.5
							.9	.4
.0	.1	.2				Fixed/Worth	.1	.1
.3	.2	.5					.4	.4
5.2	.6	.9					.8	1.0
.4	.5	.6				Debt/Worth	.7	.8
1.8	1.3	1.5					1.6	1.7
59.1	2.2	5.1					3.4	3.9
46.2	19.7	13.2				% Profit Before Taxes/Tangible Net Worth	27.8	34.3
(21) 17.3	(32) 5.4	(27) 6.6				(159)	13.1	(137) 12.9
.0	.3	−1.4					1.3	.0
17.0	9.7	6.6				% Profit Before Taxes/Total Assets	10.9	11.6
6.5	3.5	1.3					4.1	4.0
.0	.2	−1.3					.0	−.4
352.5	79.7	29.1				Sales/Net Fixed Assets	48.1	48.7
57.3	29.1	14.3					20.8	21.5
15.8	16.7	9.1					9.7	9.0
5.2	3.2	3.3				Sales/Total Assets	3.1	3.2
3.2	2.7	2.7					2.4	2.5
2.1	2.2	1.9					1.8	1.6
.2	.2	.7				% Depr., Dep., Amort./Sales	.5	.5
(21) .5	(27) .6	(24) 1.4				(143)	1.1	(121) 1.3
1.1	1.6	2.0					1.9	1.9
5.2	3.8	1.9				% Officers', Directors', Owners' Comp/Sales	2.8	3.3
(19) 9.5	(16) 6.5	(12) 3.1				(78)	5.3	(63) 5.1
15.1	13.2	5.3					9.2	8.5
21357M	93518M	363083M	316831M	984281M	681658M	Net Sales ($)	3487804M	3602835M
6133M	33014M	132937M	131900M	370846M	349327M	Total Assets ($)	1636705M	1597266M

© RMA 2001   M = $ thousand   MM = $ million
Used with permission–"2002" by RMA Time Risk Management Association

(continued)

257

RETAIL–MEN'S & BOY'S CLOTHING & ACCESSORY STORES SIC$ 5611 (NAICS 44811, 44815)

© Comparative Historical Data   Ⓓ Current Data Sorted by Sales

			Type of Statement	0–1MM	1–3MM	3–5MM	5–10MM	10–25MM	25MM & OVER
14	13	14	Unqualified				1	7	6
24	30	19	Reviewed		2	5	4	4	4
48	53	35	Compiled	10	16	4	3	2	
6	12	12	Tax Returns	6	5	1			
36	28	22	Other	3	7	2	3	2	5
4/1/98–	4/1/99–	4/1/00–		28 (4/1–9/30/00)			74 (10/1/00–3/31/01)		
3/31/99	3/31/00	3/31/01							
ALL	ALL	ALL							
128	136	102	NUMBER OF STATEMENTS	19	30	12	11	15	15
%	%	%	**ASSETS**	%	%	%	%	%	%
7.8	9.4	11.0	Cash & Equivalents	8.8	6.3	15.1	9.8	20.6	11.3
7.5	9.4	8.0	Trade Receivables–(net)	5.7	7.5	16.6	15.3	2.9	4.7
58.2	54.8	53.7	Inventory	62.1	60.7	40.6	53.3	48.0	45.6
1.1	1.3	1.1	All Other Current	1.2	.9	.5	.8	1.0	2.3
74.7	75.0	73.8	Total Current	77.8	75.3	72.8	79.2	72.6	64.0
17.1	15.8	17.2	Fixed Assets (net)	16.0	15.0	14.8	12.7	18.9	27.0
2.7	3.0	2.2	Intangibles (net)	1.3	3.4	1.4	.0	1.9	3.5
5.5	6.2	6.7	All Other Non-Current	5.0	6.3	10.9	8.1	6.6	5.5
100.0	100.0	100.0	Total	100.0	100.0	100.0	100.0	100.0	100.0
			LIABILITIES						
11.4	9.8	9.7	Notes Payable–Short Term	10.5	6.1	10.1	14.3	15.2	7.1
3.1	3.6	3.1	Cur. Mat.-L/T/D	2.6	4.9	3.0	1.9	1.9	2.5
19.4	17.1	17.6	Trade Payables	17.3	16.3	16.6	21.3	19.2	17.5
.4	.3	.5	Income Taxes Payable	1.3	.3	.2	.2	.3	.4
9.2	9.6	11.7	All Other Current	17.4	13.0	8.5	8.2	8.6	10.5
43.6	40.5	42.8	Total Current	49.0	40.6	38.3	45.9	45.2	37.9
12.7	14.6	11.3	Long Term Debt	12.5	12.0	12.0	8.4	11.1	10.5
.1	.2	.0	Deferred Taxes	.0	.0	.0	.2	.0	.1
4.6	5.3	3.9	All Other Non-Current	4.5	4.5	3.7	4.0	1.6	4.1
39.0	39.4	42.0	Net Worth	34.0	42.9	46.0	41.4	42.2	47.3
100.0	100.0	100.0	Total Liabilities & Net Worth	100.0	100.0	100.0	100.0	100.0	100.0
			INCOME DATA						
100.0	100.0	100.0	Net Sales	100.0	100.0	100.0	100.0	100.0	100.0
44.2	43.3	43.5	Gross Profit	41.9	46.8	44.5	44.0	38.2	43.3
41.0	39.8	40.9	Operating Expenses	37.7	44.5	42.4	42.8	35.4	40.3
3.1	3.5	2.7	Operating Profit	4.2	2.3	2.1	1.2	2.8	3.0
.3	.9	.8	All Other Expenses (net)	.9	1.1	.2	.2	.5	1.3
2.8	2.6	1.9	Profit Before Taxes	3.3	1.2	1.9	1.0	2.3	1.7
			RATIOS						
3.4	3.4	3.4	Current	3.2	4.4	3.1	3.0	3.2	3.6
1.9	1.9	1.9		2.1	1.8	2.7	2.4	1.3	2.1
1.2	1.3	1.2		1.3	1.3	1.4	1.1	1.1	1.4
.7	.9	1.0	Quick	(18) .7	.7	1.7	1.1	1.1	.6
.3	.3 (101)	.3		.2	.3	1.2	.5	.2	.4
.1	.1	.1		.1	.1	.2	.3	.1	.1
0 999.8	1 516.5	0 999.8	Sales/Receivables	0 UND	1 722.5	1 278.0	3 120.6	0 UND	2 190.2
5 73.9	7 55.5	3 116.7		0 UND	3 117.6	13 27.9	6 61.2	2 170.1	3 106.6
17 21.3	21 17.3	17 21.6		8 43.4	22 16.4	39 9.4	35 10.4	6 58.0	6 58.1
102 3.6	92 3.9	84 4.4	Cost of Sales/Inventory	85 4.3	109 3.3	56 6.6	106 3.4	70 5.2	79 4.6
157 2.3	147 2.5	125 2.9		159 2.3	160 2.3	89 4.1	119 3.1	92 4.0	119 3.1
219 1.7	223 1.6	187 2.0		256 1.7	216 1.7	184 2.0	203 1.8	129 2.8	162 2.3
22 16.6	21 17.3	15 24.3	Cost of Sales/Payables	14 26.9	13 29.1	19 19.2	24 15.2	12 29.5	21 17.5
41 8.8	36 10.1	31 11.7		30 12.2	28 13.0	29 12.8	41 8.8	30 12.0	41 8.9
76 4.8	78 4.7	67 5.4		52 7.0	67 5.4	51 7.2	77 4.8	67 5.4	67 5.4
4.0	3.9	4.7	Sales/Working Capital	4.3	4.5	5.0	3.9	7.4	4.5
6.8	6.5	6.7		6.3	5.8	6.0	6.1	19.8	7.7
21.9	14.8	25.5		29.7	22.7	12.1	24.9	51.9	15.7
		9.0	EBIT/Interest	(16) 9.8	(27) 6.5	5.0	(10) 10.2	(14) 18.3	(14) 10.9
(109) 6.5	(116) 5.6	2.7		2.3	2.8	2.6	3.5	1.1	2.7
3.4	2.8	.8		.8	1.1	.9	1.0	.3	-2.2
1.4	1.4								
		4.4	Net Profit + Depr., Dep.,						
(31) 5.3	(29) 3.2	(23) 1.8	Amort./Cur. Mat. L/T/D						
2.2	1.8	.7							
.9	.8								
.1	.1	.1	Fixed/Worth	.0	.1	.1	.2	.2	.3
.3	.3	.3		.3	.2	.3	.3	.5	.5
.7	1.0	.8		2.7	2.2	.6	.5	.9	1.1
.7	.7	.5	Debt/Worth	.4	.5	.6	.6	.5	.4
1.4	1.7	1.4		1.9	1.3	1.5	1.2	1.5	1.1
3.6	4.5	3.2		20.7	5.0	2.3	4.1	6.4	1.8
33.9	35.8	26.1	% Profit Before Taxes/Tangible	(16) 41.0	(27) 19.5	23.5	(10) 18.3	67.3	(14) 26.2
(117) 15.1	(125) 12.4	(94) 9.3	Net Worth	14.3	6.9	2.9	10.8	5.2	14.1
3.0	2.9	-1.5		-2.1	1.4	-.3	4.7	-14.1	-7.6
12.5	10.0	10.1	% Profit Before Taxes/Total	21.6	9.7	9.0	7.0	22.7	13.7
5.2	4.9	4.4	Assets	4.7	4.3	1.6	4.9	1.3	6.1
1.0	1.2	-.7		-1.1	.7	-.2	1.0	-2.5	-10.1
56.2	57.2	73.0	Sales/Net Fixed Assets	302.3	81.3	29.3	34.2	80.5	12.1
18.6	25.5	23.1		47.1	37.1	25.4	24.0	14.3	8.9
9.8	10.0	11.1		14.5	16.0	14.5	11.9	12.7	6.7
3.0	3.1	3.3	Sales/Total Assets	3.5	3.5	3.7	3.1	3.7	2.9
2.4	2.3	2.7		2.4	2.7	3.0	2.4	3.3	2.6
1.7	1.7	2.0		1.7	2.1	2.0	1.8	2.7	1.9
.5	.4	.4	% Depr., Dep., Amort./Sales	(16) .3	(24) .2	(10) .4	(12)	.4	(14) .7
(109) 1.2	(115) 1.0	(85) .8		.6	.5	.8		1.2	1.7
1.9	1.7	1.7		1.2	1.6	1.1		1.9	2.9
4.0	3.3	3.4	% Officers', Directors',	(12) 3.7	4.4				
(48) 5.6	(70) 5.6	(48) 6.2	Owners' Comp/Sales	7.4	(20) 9.1				
8.5	8.2	11.2		11.0	16.5				
3929213M	2860443M	2460728M	Net Sales ($)	11018M	53920M	46503M	79176M	260923M	2009188M
1669281M	1272257M	1024157M	Total Assets ($)	4383M	24788M	18961M	33440M	81270M	861315M

© PMA 2001   M = $ thousand   MM = $ million
See Pages 9 through 18 for Explanation of Ratios and Data

Financial Hints . . .

- Markdown as a percent of sales for women's apparel—15 to 20%
- Average sales per square foot for a women's specialty apparel store— $140 to $180
- Payroll as a percent of sales for a women's specialty apparel store— 7 to 8%
- Advertising as a percent of sales—3%—BUT your grand opening will be higher AND your first year of operation may require a greater percent!
- Stock turn—3 times a year is average; 4 times a year is superior
- Start-up costs as loan amount is acceptable; repayment of loan as a monthly expense
- Don't forget interest as part of your loan repayment amount! Call a bank and ask for an amortization schedule.
- Calculate these three categories separately: start-up expenses, monthly expenses (cost of inventory is monthly expense), monthly sales
- Next, deduct each month's expenses from that month's revenue . . . how much money do you have remaining? That's your monthly cash flow.

Advertising and Promotion
1. Develop a promotional plan for your first quarter (3 months) of business operation. Grand opening, promotional activities such as fashion shows, radio spots, newspaper ads, magazine ads, billboards, trunk shows, publicity, etc.
2. Budget by month for the first three months, then show as a percent of sales.
3. Use a blank calendar to show specific activities for each month!

when additional capital will be needed for the purchase of inventory. A line of credit is a loan that operates much like a credit card. Funds may be advanced on an as-needed basis when the business's expenses exceed the amount of cash generated from sales. Loans are discussed in greater detail later in the chapter.

The financial plan for BeTwixt presented in this chapter and again in Chapter 14 shows the business as having cash on hand of $5,726 (line 40, December) at the end of the first year. Although in this scenario the numbers would be very close, profit and cash are not the same. This business is showing a core inventory on hand of $50,000 (line 13) at wholesale when it opens. The owner has accounted for seasonality factors and months in which more merchandise should be purchased. The scenario assumes the inventory at the end of the year will be $50,000.

Use the worksheet in Figure 11.2 to help determine the amount of cash needed to staff the business. Estimates will be based on research conducted in previous chapters.

The Income Statement

The income statement is also referred to as a profit-and-loss statement. It is a comparison of expenses and revenue over a certain period of time, usually 1 year. The income statement reflects the company's net profit or loss for this determined period of time. Figure 11.3 shows the income statement for BeTwixt for the year ending December 31, 20XX.

Figure 11.2 Management/Staff

Employee Needs	Year 1	Year 2	Year 3
Management No. of employees Salary/wages Benefits Payroll taxes Total costs			
Sales/Marketing No. of employees Salary/wages Benefits Payroll taxes Total costs			
Administrative Support No. of employees Salary/wages Benefits Payroll taxes Total costs			
Other No. of employees Salary/wages Benefits Payroll taxes Total costs			

Adapted from Rhonda M. Abrams, *The Successful Business Plan: Secrets & Strategies*, Running 'R' Media, Palo Alto, California, 1999, p. 214.

The top portion of the income statement is known as the *revenue section*. It includes all income from the sale of merchandise throughout the year. If a fashion retail store incurred returns and provided refunds for those returns, this amount would be deducted or subtracted from gross revenue to reflect net sales for the year. In addition, any markdown taken would reduce gross revenue to reflect net sales for the year.

The next item on the income statement is cost of goods sold. Cost of goods sold represents the total cost of the merchandise that was sold during the year. This figure should include the beginning inventory, plus all purchases for the year, less ending inventory. This number will also include shipping charges to get the merchandise in the store. In a fashion retail store, cost of goods sold also reflects any markdowns taken during the year. In the example given, BeTwixt, Inc., reflects 30% markdown on 15% of the total merchandise sold during the year. Cost of goods sold is subtracted from net sales to arrive at gross profit, which is the profit the company will generate before deducting operating expenses and other expenses including interest. It is important that a company does not let the cost of goods sold get out of control because it will cut into the gross profit of the company. Operating expenses include those costs that are related to maintaining the operations of the business such as rent, telephone, meals and entertainment, and office supplies. The exception to this is depreciation. Depreciation is the allocation of the cost of an asset over the term of the asset's useful life. Interest is usually reflected in other expenses. Depending on the format used for the income statement, interest may be included under the operating expenses.

The start-up company should review its income statement at least quarterly. Sometimes an increase in cost of goods sold or an additional expense can greatly affect the bottom line of the business. For example, if cost of goods sold increases, it may affect the amount of operating capital the business has to borrow, which will then affect the interest expense. It may affect the cash flow of the business because more money is being paid out for inventory.

Let us see how the income statement and cash flow statement from BeTwixt, Inc., flows to one another.

Step 1: *Sales*. The sales figure (all cash sales) (line 1) on the income statement is taken from line 4 (cash sales) on the cash flow statement.

Figure 11.3 Income Statement

Profit-and-Loss Statement
For
Year ended December 31, 20XX

	Revenue	
1	Sales	$ 380,000
2	Cost of Goods Sold	202,000
3	**Gross Profit**	**178,000**
	Expenses	
	Operating Expenses	
4	Rent	$ 30,000
5	Direct Labor	37,000
6	Payroll Expense	8,510
7	Repair/Maintenance	300
8	Office Supplies	300
9	Travel Expense	18,750
10	Advertising	13,000
11	Bad Debts	600
12	Bank Charges	5,200
13	Contributions	1,000
14	Dues & Subscriptions	175
15	Insurance	4,980
16	Meals & Entertainment	600
17	Office & Postage	770
18	Security	360
19	Accounting & Legal	3,350
20	Taxes & License	425
21	Telephone/Communications	2,772
22	Utilities	1,515
23	Depreciation/Amortization	4,510
24	**Total Operating Expenses**	**$ 134,117**
	Other Revenue and Expenses	
25	Miscellaneous Income	0
26	Interest Expense	8,679
27	Total Expenses	$ 142,796
28	Income Before Taxes	35,204
29	Income Tax	7,041
30	**Net Income**	**$ 28,163**

Step 2: *Cost of goods sold.* To illustrate the flow of numbers, the assumption has been made that beginning inventory and ending inventory will be the same. The formula for cost of goods sold is beginning inventory plus purchase minus ending inventory. The assumption has also been made that all inventory will be purchased and paid for in a 12-month period. Many new fashion retail stores buy merchandise on a cash basis or cash on delivery (COD). Very few are able to purchase on credit until they establish a positive credit rating. Cost of Goods Sold is shown on the income statement and is taken from line 13 (inventory) on the cash flow statement.

Step 3: Cost of goods sold is subtracted from sales to arrive at gross profit. ($380,000 (line 1 of profit and loss statement) − $202,000 (line 2 of profit and loss statement) = $178,000 (line 3 of profit and loss statement).

Step 4: *Operating expense.* Year-end totals for each account, flow to the profit and loss statement (income statement). For example, Rent (line 10 of the cash flow statement) flows to Rent (line 4) on the profit and loss statement, and Advertising (line 17 on the cash flow statement) flows to Advertising (line 10) on the profit and loss statement. There are exceptions. The cash flow statement reflects payments of both principal and interest on the amortizing loan and the line of credit. The profit and loss statement will reflect only the interest paid for the one year period. These figures may be obtained from an amortization schedule that is provided by the bank or other source. An amortization schedule is a breakdown of the amount of payment that goes to principal and the amount of the payment that goes to interest.

Step 5: *Depreciation.* Depreciation is reflected only on the income statement and not the cash flow statement because a check is not written for depreciation. Using our example, depreciation is calculated by determining the total of all assets that can be depreciated. Those assets include the sign (line 35 of the cash flow statement), furniture and equipment (line 33 of the cash flow statement), and leasehold improvements (line 32 of the cash flow statement). We then calculate $3,600 + $8,950 + $10,000 = $22,550. Assuming a useful life of 5 years ($22,550 divided by 5), the annual depreciation would be $4,510.

Step 6: *Total expenses.* Total expenses equal total operating expenses (line 24) plus the interest expense (line 26) ($134,117 + $8,679 = $142,796 [line 27]).

Step 7: *Income before taxes.* The total of all expenses including the interest expense is subtracted from gross profit (line 3) ($178,000 − $142,796 = $35,204). Once this figure has been determined, the accountant will calculate the company's tax rate. This number is then subtracted from income before taxes to arrive at net income ($35,204 [line 28] − $7,041 [line 29] = $28,163 [line 30]).

It is important to note that the information in the income statement does not reflect principal payments on the loan. The principal portion of the note is the payment excluding interest. Principal payments are not a taxable expense. The income statement serves as a tax document which is used to calculate the amount of taxes the company will pay based on earnings before taxes (EBT).

The Balance Sheet

The balance sheet is a "snapshot" of the business at a given point in time. It reflects what the company is worth on paper (book value) at a given time. It shows what the company owns (assets) and what it owes (liabilities). Figure 11.4 shows the balance sheet for BeTwixt, Inc., for the year ending December 31, 20XX.

The balance sheet is based on the following formula: Assets = Liabilities + Owner's equity. The balance sheet must balance; hence the name. An increase or decrease on one side must be offset by an equal increase or decrease on the other side. The balance sheet will let the entrepreneur know how assets, liabilities, and net worth are changing.

Assets and liabilities are divided into two sections on the balance sheet. Assets are typically on the left side of the page, while liabilities are listed on the right side. An alternative method is to list assets at the top of the page with liabilities listed below them. Assets are divided into current assets, those items that can be converted into cash within 1 year or within the normal operating cycle of the company, and fixed assets, those assets that were acquired for long-term use in the business. Assets include such items as cash, accounts receivable, inventory, equipment, land, and buildings.

The second section of the balance sheet shows liabilities. A *liability* is a claim a creditor has against the company's assets. Current liabilities are those debts that must be paid within 1 year or within the normal operating cycle of the company. Current liabilities may include accounts payable, notes payable (within 1 year), and interest payable. Long-term liabilities are those debts that will come due beyond the 1-year period.

Figure 11.4 Balance Sheet

Balance Sheet
BeTwixt, Inc.
December 31, 20XX

ASSETS		LIABILITIES AND OWNER'S EQUITY	
Current Assets:		**Current Liabilities:**	
Cash & Marketable Securities	$ 5,726	Notes Payable–Bank	$ 0
Accounts Receivable	0	Notes Payable–Other	0
Inventory	50,000	Accounts Payable	397
Prepaid Expenses	0	Accruals	212
		Income Tax Payable	0
		Current Portion of LTD	9,736
		Other Current Liabilities	0
Total Current Assets	**$ 55,726**	**Total Current Liabilities**	**$ 10,345**
Fixed Assets:		**Long-Term Liabilities:**	
Fixed Assets	$ 22,550	Long-Term Debt	$ 39,508
Less Accumulated Depreciation	(4,510)	Subordinate Officer Debt	0
Notes Receivable	0	Total Liabilities	49,853
Intangibles	0	Common Stock	18,000
Deposits	4,250	Capital Surplus & Paid in Cap.	0
Other Assets	0	Retained Earnings	10,163*
Total Net Fixed Assets	22,290	(Less) Treasury Stock	0
		Total Net Worth	28,163
Total Assets	**$ 78,016**	**Total Liabilities & Net Worth**	**$ 78,016****

Note * = Net income ($28,163) minus owner's draw ($18,000)
** = Total Liabilities & Net Worth equal Total Liabilities ($49,853) plus common stock ($18,000) plus retained earnings ($10,163)

The final section of the balance sheet is owner's equity. Owner's equity refers to the value of the owner's investment in the business. It represents all capital contributions the owner has made to the business in addition to all accumulated earnings not distributed to the owner. This calculation is the balancing figure on the balance sheet.

The current assets on a balance sheet are defined as follows:

- *Cash and marketable securities.* This is the amount of cash in the bank plus any highly liquid items such as marketable securities. In this scenario, cash and marketable securities is taken from line 40 (December) of the cash flow statement. Highly liquid items are those items that can be turned into cash almost immediately. There is no rule as to the amount of cash availability a business should have on hand to open its doors. There is, however, a rule of thumb that states that a business's cash balance should cover its operating expenses (less depreciation) for one inventory turnover period. The entrepreneur will either need cash in the bank or a line of credit from the bank to cover the operating expenses. For example, using the examples of BeTwixt, the formula would read as follows:

Cash requirement:

$$\frac{\text{Cash expenses (taken from the income statement)}}{\text{Average inventory turnover}} = \text{Amount of cash or cash availability}$$

Using this formula, BeTwixt's cash requirement is calculated as follows:

Cash requirement = $138,286 (total expenses [$142,796] including total operating expenses [$134,117] and interest expense of $8,679 minus depreciation $4,510)

(For a start-up company, with no historical data, the entrepreneur would refer to the Robert Morris Associates *Annual Statement Studies* to determine the average inventory turnover rate for the industry.) In this example, the inventory turns at a rate of 4.04 times per year.

Cash requirement: $\dfrac{\$138,286}{4.04} = \$34,229$

The formula is stating that the business should have $34,229 in cash or availability of cash on hand on average over a 12 month period. In a business with large seasonal inventory requirements, this number may be higher for a brief period of time. In the case of BeTwixt, Inc., a line of credit was advanced in the amount of $62,000 (Table 11.1, line 42, November). If the business had $62,900 (highest loan balance and beginning cash, line 1, January) in the bank at the time it opened, there would have been sufficient cash to cover the expenses. This business required a large inventory purchase in November (line 13 of the cash flow statement) of $47,000 as illustrated in Table 11.1.

- *Accounts receivable.* Accounts receivable refers to those items that are owed to the business by other persons and/or firms. Accounts receivable for a fashion retail store are often minimal, but it is necessary to show this item on the balance sheet. A business that takes orders and is then invoiced for payment has accounts receivable.

Examples of fashion retail operations that have accounts receivable are fashion forecasting firms and public relations companies.

■ *Inventory.* The amount of merchandise available at the end of the period to meet the sales needs of the business is referred to as inventory (or stock). It is possible to calculate a rough estimate as to the amount of inventory a store should have on hand, as follows:

Average stock turnovers:

$$\frac{\text{Average monthly inventory (in retail dollars)}}{\text{Total annual sales (in retail dollars)}} = 4.04 \text{ times/year}$$

(In this calculation the 4.04 turnover rate above is used.)

The inventory level, then, would be calculated using the following numbers:

$202,000 \div 4.04 = \$50,000$ (inventory level)

■ *Prepaid expenses.* Prepaid expenses represent payments in advance for services that will benefit the business in the future. An example would be payment of an insurance premium that will provide coverage over several accounting periods.

Accounts receivable and inventory do not provide dollars to keep the business going. Therefore, it is important to keep these items under control since they provide no money to pay debts, purchase new assets, meet ongoing expenses, and so on until they are collected or sold.

Fixed assets are valued on a balance sheet at book value. Book value is the value of an asset as it appears on a balance sheet equal to cost minus accumulated depreciation rather than market value. This is important because the amount an asset was purchased for and what it can be sold for are often two different amounts. Land, buildings, vehicles, deposits, and equipment are self-explanatory on the balance sheet. Depreciation, however, warrants discussion.

Assume you buy a new vehicle for your business at a cost of $18,000, and your accountant determines it will provide value to the business for three years. Because the assumed life of the asset extends beyond one year, your accountant does not write off the $18,000 cost as an expense of doing business on the income statement for this period. Rather, the cost of the vehicle is recorded as a fixed asset at the time of purchase. During each year of the vehicle's three-year life, that portion of the original cost or value that is lost is recognized as an expense of doing business. The expense write-off appears on the annual income statements as depreciation expense, and the difference between original cost and total depreciation taken on the asset appears on the balance sheet as book value of the asset for that year.

To calculate this, assume that you will spread the cost of the asset equally over the three-year period. If so, the annual depreciation expense would be $6,000 ($18,000 divided by 3). At the end of each year the value of the vehicle would appear on the balance sheet as $18,000 less all depreciation charged to date. This latter amount is referred to as accumulated depreciation.[1]

Depreciation is a noncash item. There is no check written for depreciation.

Liabilities and Owner's Equity

Current liabilities on a balance sheet include the following:

- *Notes payable.* Notes payable are obligations owed to creditors that have loaned the company money, such as a bank.
- *Accounts payable.* Accounts payable represent obligations owed to creditors for merchandise or for services purchased on credit.
- *Accruals payable.* Accruals payable are obligations the company has incurred but has not yet paid. They can include payroll, taxes payable, or interest payable. It is the differences between the date a debt has been incurred and the date it will be paid for. For example, assume that an employee has worked for 2 weeks and is paid every 2 weeks. Assume as well that the accounting period in which the books will be closed falls within this 2-week period. Wages have been earned by the employee for 1 week, but since the pay period will not occur for another week, the employee is still owed for 1 week's work. The wages for the 1 week are treated as a current obligation or an accrual payable.
- *Current portion of long-term debt.* In the case of BeTwixt, Inc., the current portion of long-term debt is the portion of the loan that will be paid in 1 year. It is the balance of the loan that is owed for that 1 year.

Long-term liabilities can include mortgage payments, if applicable, and any long-term installment loans. They can also include long-term debt, which is the balance of the loan—the amount that will not be paid within a year.

Owner's equity is the owner's claim to the assets of the business after all obligations have been accounted for and satisfied. Owner's equity is made up of any capital stock and retained earnings. Retained earnings is net income kept within the business.

The balance sheet is a historical statement. If the entrepreneur knows how to extract information from it, the balance sheet can provide valuable information about the status of a particular asset or liability or the general health of a company. Changes in the balance sheet provide a good picture of how the finances within the company are being handled. Later in this chapter, ratio analysis is used to interpret the financial statements. The financials tell a story. Ratio analysis can be a very useful tool in understanding the story.

The Assumptions

Accompanying any good set of financial statements is a good set of assumptions. Assumptions provide an explanation of the source and thought processes behind the numbers, especially in the cash flow statement. They provide the reader with an explanation of how the entrepreneur arrived at the numbers presented. The numbers are meaningless without an explanation. If the financials do indeed flow through with the rest of the business plan, the plan will explain the source of the numbers; however, bankers and funders will not want to sift through pages of information to reconstruct the financial plan. The financial assumptions for BeTwixt, Inc., are provided below. It is not necessary to explain all accounts listed on the cash flow statement because some items are self-explanatory.

- *Cash on hand.* Principal will inject gift from parents in the amount of $30,000.
- *Loan.* A loan for start-up expenses is requested in the amount of $60,000. For projection purposes, the loan has been calculated at an interest rate of 10 percent for a period of 60 months. The loan injection will be used as follows:

    $50,000—core inventory.
    $3,000—advertising.
    $3,500—security system.
    $1,500—grand opening expenses.
    $2,000—secure lease on building.

- *Revolving line of credit.* A line of credit in the amount of $62,000 has been requested. For projection purposes, interest accrues at the rate of 10 percent and will be paid monthly.
- *Rent.* Landlord has agreed to a 1-month deposit of $2,500. The facility is 3,000 square feet. The facility has 2,500 square feet of sales floor space and 500 square feet of office/storage space.
- *Travel expense.* Travel includes buying trips to market five times per year and includes initial buying trip. Travel expenses include hotel, meals, and transportation.
- *Advertising.* Management will advertise through local newspapers and radio ads. Advertising will increase in the months of November and December to promote the holiday season. Newspaper ads will run 2 times per month at a cost of $3,900 plus. Radio ads will run 2 times per week for 28 weeks, at a cost of $9,100.
- *Accounting and legal.* Professional fees of $250 per month have been allocated for accounting services. Legal services will be engaged on an "as needed" basis. An allocation of $600 has been made for start-up and first-month legal expenses.
- *Leasehold improvements.* Leasehold improvements include painting, lighting, new floor covering, two dressing rooms, and remodeling of the bathroom, which will cost $10,000. And $8,900 will be spent on furniture, display racks, tables, and office equipment.
- *Direct labor.* BeTwixt will employ one assistant manager at a salary of $25,000 per year and two part-time sales associates at $8 per hour for 25 hours per week. Wages for part-time employees are based on 50 working weeks per year with rotation for time off.
- *Inventory.* BeTwixt, Inc., will have a core inventory of $50,000 and will maintain an inventory level of $50,000 (at cost).
- *Insurance.* Insurance includes casualty, hazard, and liability insurance. Health insurance is calculated at $250 per month for the owner and assistant manager.
- *Bank charges.* Bank charges are based on a 2.5 percent service charge for credit card transactions and standard account service fees of $60 per month.
- *Taxes/licenses.* The business license is $125 (start-up) and $425 is for property tax on business assets.
- *Owner's draw.* The owner will receive a draw of $1,000 a month for the first 6 months with an increase to $2,000 per month beginning in month 7.
- *Tax rate.* Taxes have been calculated based on a tax rate of 20 percent.

ANALYZING THE FINANCIALS

Financial analysis allows the entrepreneur to check the "heartbeat" of the company. Just as the instruments in the cockpit of an airplane let the pilot know how the plane is flying, the financial statements of a company let the entrepreneur know how well the business is operating. If the pilot never checked the instruments in the plane, he or she would not know whether or not the plane was operating as it should. If the entrepreneur never checks the financial statements of the company, he or she will never know how it is operating and whether adjustments need to be made.

Getting the business open and running is one thing. The entrepreneur then has to focus on keeping the business running profitably. Without the financial statements to guide the decision-making process, the entrepreneur is almost destined to make bad business decisions. The entrepreneur who establishes a system for analyzing the financials and using that information to make informed decisions has a much greater chance of survival and success.

One way in which the entrepreneur and his or her accountant and banker evaluate the performance of the company is through ratio analysis. Ratio analysis allows the entrepreneur to examine the relationship between one financial value and another. Ratio analysis enables the entrepreneur to spot trends in the business and compare its performance and condition with the average performance of similar businesses in the same industry. Through the use of financial analysis, the entrepreneur can determine the answers to such questions as whether the business is carrying too much inventory, whether operating expenses are too high, and whether enough cash is on hand to pay short-term debt if the need arises.

Key financial ratios are used to evaluate ways to run the business more efficiently and effectively. The following section focuses on the ratios that could be used to determine the heartbeat of a fashion retail store. As the ratios are explained, it is important to keep in mind that all financial numbers represent one point in time. For example, in the case of BeTwixt, Inc., a calculation of the ratio in December will tell a different story from the same calculation done in September. Ratio analysis, in this context, is meant to create an awareness and understanding of how the numbers in the business affect one another.

Understanding Key Financial Ratios

Financial ratios are broken down into four categories: liquidity, profitability, risk, and operating ratios. Liquidity ratios measure the ability of the business to pay its current obligations as they come due. These ratios measure the amount of cash or investments the business has in relationship to its obligations. There are two types of liquidity ratios: *current* and *quick*. Profitability ratios measure how efficiently a business is being managed. Profitability ratios are classified as *gross margin ratios* and *net profit on sales ratios*. Risk ratios measure the extent of the company's debt and includes the amount of financing extended by creditors against the amount of funding supplied by the company's owners. Risk ratios show the extent to which the entrepreneur relies on debt, as opposed to equity capital, to finance the operations of the business. Risk ratios are categorized as *debt to equity ratios* and *debt ratios*. Operating ratios measure how effectively a company utilizes its resources. The more effectively a company operates, the less it will need to access capital. An operating ratio is also referred to as an *inventory turnover ratio*.

The following section breaks down the four categories of financial ratios and provides an explanation of the ratio that would commonly be used for a fashion retail business. The financial statements of BeTwixt, Inc., are used to illustrate the various ratios. An assumption has been made that the numbers represent what the company did in its first year of business and are not pro-forma. The examples use industry standards from the

Robert Morris Associates *Annual Statement Studies,* to illustrate how BeTwixt, Inc., compares with the national average.

Liquidity Ratios   Liquidity ratios measure the ability of the business to meet its current obligations as they come due.

1. *Current ratio.* The **current ratio** measures whether or not the company has enough liquidity from its current assets to pay its short-term obligations or current liabilities. It determines whether or not there is enough cash or near cash assets to pay the bills. **Near cash assets** are those assets that can easily be converted to cash. A rule of thumb for an effective current ratio is 2:1. This means that for every dollar in short-term obligations, the company has 2 dollars in current assets to pay its obligations. Current assets include such items as cash, marketable securities, accounts receivable, and inventory. Current liabilities include notes payable, accounts payable, taxes payable, and accruals. Generally speaking, the higher the company's current ratio, the stronger it is financially. However, this does not always hold true. A fashion retail business with too much non-marketable inventory will show a good current ratio, but the business may not be able to quickly turn the inventory into cash to service its short-term obligations.

   Formula for current ratio: $\dfrac{\text{Current assets}}{\text{Current liabilities}}$

   Here is an example from the balance sheet of BeTwixt, Inc.:

   Current ratio: $\dfrac{\$55,726}{\$10,345} = 5.39{:}1$

   BeTwixt is way above the rule of thumb of a 2:1 ratio. This suggests that the store has no problem paying its short-term obligations.

2. *Quick ratio.* The quick ratio conservatively calculates whether or not the company has enough liquid assets, or cash, to cover its short-term obligations. This ratio is sometimes referred to as the acid test. A rule of thumb for the quick ratio is 1:1. This means that for each dollar the company has in short-term obligations, it has 1 dollar to pay those obligations. The quick assets used in this calculation include such items as cash, marketable securities, and accounts receivable. They do not include inventory, because it may not be possible to sell inventory and turn it into cash within a short period of time. The quick ratio takes only cash into account. Current liabilities include notes payable, accounts payable, taxes payable, and accruals. A ratio below 1:1 would indicate that the company is depending on turning its inventory and on future sales to satisfy its short-term debt. The higher the quick ratio, the more liquid the company is, and, subsequently, the more financially stable the company is.

   Formula for quick ratio: $\dfrac{\text{Quick assets}}{\text{Current liabilities}}$

   Here is an example from the balance sheet of BeTwixt:

   Quick ratio: $\dfrac{\$5,726 \text{ (total current assets minus inventory)}}{\$10,345} = .55{:}1$

   BeTwixt is below the rule of thumb for having enough cash to service its short-term obligations.

Profitability Ratios   Profitability ratios measure how efficiently a business is being managed. Gross margin ratios and net profit on sales ratios will be used to calculate the profitability of BeTwixt, Inc.

1. *Gross margin ratio.* The **gross margin ratio** measures the amount of profit after the direct costs are deducted. This ratio measures the overall profits of the business. If cost of goods sold is increasing at a rate faster than sales, then the direct costs of the business may be out of control. An analysis of the business would then need to be conducted to determine why the cost of goods sold is increasing at a higher rate. In the fashion industry, the net profit margin typically runs 100 percent with a gross margin ratio of 50 percent.

   Gross profit is calculated by deducting the cost of goods from sales in the income statement. **Net sales** refers to the sales figure on the income statement. Net sales is the dollar amount of sales made during a specific time period excluding sales tax and returns or allowances. Using comparative data, the gross margin ratio indicates whether or not the cost of goods sold is too high. This ratio is a more effective measurement when there are at least three years of historical data to allow a comparison of changes in the gross margin ratio. For example, if in year 1 the gross margin ratio was 30 percent, in year 2 it was 40 percent, and in year 3 it was 50 percent, this suggests an improving trend. Cost of goods sold is declining in relation to gross profit. Conversely, if the trend were to change direction and gross profit began to decline, it would be necessary to determine the reason for the change.

   Formula for gross margin ratio: $\dfrac{\text{Gross profit}}{\text{Net sales}}$

   Here is an example:

   Gross margin ratio:
   $\dfrac{\$178{,}000 \text{ (gross profit on the income statement)}}{\$380{,}000 \text{ (sales on the income statement)}} = 47 \text{ percent}$

   Note that BeTwixt does not show any returns of damaged goods the first year. Any returns of damaged goods would be subtracted from sales on the income statement to arrive at net sales. The industry standard for a fashion retail store is 50 percent before markdowns. BeTwixt's cost of goods sold is in line with industry standards.

2. *Net profit on sales ratio.* The **net profit on sales ratio** measures the company's profit per dollar of sales. The ratio shows the number of cents of each sales dollar remaining after all expenses and income taxes are deducted. It is important to know the industry average in order to make a realistic comparison. For example, a grocery store has a profit margin of approximately 2 percent; however, its inventory may turn over as many as 20 or 30 times per year. This ratio must take into account the asset value of the company, how often it turns its inventory, and how efficient it is at collecting its accounts receivable. Net profit, in this calculation refers to income before taxes found on the income statement. Net sales are sales found on the income statement.

   Formula for net profit on sales ratios: $\dfrac{\text{Net profit (before taxes)}}{\text{Net sales}}$

For example:

Net profit on sales ratio: $\dfrac{\$35,204}{\$380,000} = 9.3$ percent

If the industry standard for the fashion retail industry is 12.5 percent, then we know that the net profit margin is less than industry average. A low ratio says one of two things: either the gross profit margin is too low, or expenses are too high.

Risk Ratios   Risk ratios measure the extent of the company's debt. They show the extent to which the entrepreneur relies on debt to finance the operations of the business.

1. *Debt to equity ratio.* The debt to equity ratio measures the proportion of assets that are financed by creditors with assets that are contributed by the owners. It is a comparison of how much the business owes with how much it owns. It helps determine whether or not a company has the ability to sell its assets and have enough money to meet its obligations. The higher the debt to equity ratio, the less chance the business will have of obtaining financing; that is, the higher the number, the weaker the company. The acceptable debt to equity ratio varies from industry to industry. Over the years, norms have been developed that serve as guides as to the "right" amount of debt to include in the capital structure of the business. Different industries face different risks. Therefore, what is appropriate for one industry may not be appropriate for another. The fashion industry is typically a cash industry, which would allow a higher debt to equity ratio. The debt to equity ratio takes into account total liabilities and total owner's equity. Total liabilities and owner's equity are taken from the balance sheet.

   Formula for debt to equity: $\dfrac{\text{Total liabilities}}{\text{Total owner's equity (total net worth)}}$

   For example:

   Debt to equity: $\dfrac{\$49,853}{\$28,163} = 1.77{:}1$

   BeTwixt, Inc., shows a debt to equity ratio of 1.77:1. The higher the ratio, the lower the degree of protection afforded creditors. The higher the debt to net worth, the less capacity the business has to borrow capital.

2. *Debt ratio.* The debt ratio measures the portion of total assets that are financed through debt. The higher the debt ratio of a company, the more debt financing the business has incurred. Creditors prefer smaller debt ratios. The smaller the number, the less likely the creditor is to lose money should the business need to be liquidated. High debt ratios are an indicator of a business with a high chance of default on the debt. The debt ratio takes into account total liabilities and total assets. Total liabilities include all current liabilities. These may also be any outstanding long-term notes payable. Total assets include the total of the company's current assets, fixed assets, and intangible assets.

   Formula for debt ratio: $\dfrac{\text{Total liabilities}}{\text{Total assets}}$

Here is an example:

Debt ratio: $\dfrac{\$49,853}{\$78,016} = .64{:}1$

BeTwixt, Inc., is showing a debt ratio of .64:1. For every $1 in assets, the business owes creditors 64¢.

Operating Ratios   The inventory turnover ratio measures how many times the company's inventory is sold during a year. It is calculated by dividing the cost of goods sold by the average level of inventory on hand. The average inventory figure is determined by taking the average of the beginning and ending inventory figures. The average number of days it takes to sell the entire inventory one time can be calculated by dividing 360 by the inventory turnover figure. Financial institutions treat every month as having 30 days. Using 360 days is standard in the financial industry. While grocery stores turn inventory very quickly, the fashion industry turns much more slowly. If the inventory is turning more slowly than the industry average, the business may have merchandise that will not sell or the business has excess inventory. By the same token, if inventory turns too fast, the inventory level may not be high enough.

Formula for inventory turnover ratio: $\dfrac{\text{Cost of goods sold}}{\text{Average inventory balance}}$

For example:

Inventory turnover ratio: $\dfrac{\$202,000}{\$50,000} = 4.04$ times

Average sales period: $\dfrac{360}{4.04} = 89$ days

In the example of BeTwixt, Inc., the beginning and ending inventories are the same. Inventory turns at a rate of 4.04 times per year and turns over completely every 89 days (360 divided by 4.04 = 89).

Ratios are a starting point for understanding the story about the business. Ratios alone are not sufficient to adequately evaluate the health of the business. Ratios will, however, provide a set of questions to enable the entrepreneur to begin analyzing the business. Other factors such as industry trends, changes in economic factors, and changes within the company itself play roles in how well the business is performing.

While performance varies among industries, it also varies within the same industry. A jewelry store will perform differently from a store that sells junior sportswear. Each entrepreneur must determine which ratios are important to understanding his or her business. It is also possible to create ratios that measure unique circumstances within an industry. A business owner can calculate ratios not only on his or her own data, but also for other businesses similar in size, geographic location, and merchandise.

The Break-Even Point

All entrepreneurs must recognize the point where the business breaks even. The break-even point is the point at which the company shows neither a profit nor a loss but simply covers all its costs. It is the point at which total sales revenue equals total expenses.

The break-even point lets the entrepreneur know exactly the level of business he or she will need to generate to keep the doors of the business open. Lenders and investors will want to know that the entrepreneur has identified the break-even point of the business. For example, if costs indicate the store must do $75,000 in sales per day to meet its total fixed expenses and the store is only 1,500 square feet, it will never sell enough merchandise to break even and keep the doors open. For a break-even point to be correct, the estimates of revenue and expenses must be as accurate as possible.

To begin to look at the point at which the business will break even, the entrepreneur must first distinguish between fixed costs and variable costs. Fixed costs are those costs that will be incurred whether a sale is made or not. They remain constant regardless of changes in levels of activity. For a fashion retail store, such costs include labor, rent, interest expenses, and utilities. Variable costs are expenses that vary in proportion to changes in the level of activity or in proportion to sales. Such items include inventory, income tax, and travel to market. Each time a sale is generated, the business automatically incurs a certain percent to variable cost. Determining the difference between a fixed and variable cost is not always obvious. For example, if the business is not selling its inventory, and, therefore, does not need to purchase additional inventory, then costs of travel to market will not be incurred. On the other hand, if inventory is selling and marketing trips are needed, the business must incur travel expenses to maintain the inventory level. In the case of BeTwixt, Inc., break-even is calculated on a yearly basis, because of the seasonality of the business. Break-even in the month of July would be different from break-even in December. Given this assumption, all expenses are treated as fixed costs. The company will incur these costs regardless of the amount in sales throughout the year. Inventory is treated as a variable cost. If the inventory is not sold, no additional costs are incurred. Start-up costs are not used in the calculation because they are not an ongoing cost.

The contribution margin affects the calculation of a break-even point. The contribution margin is equal to sales less variable costs. This figure represents the "amount remaining from sales revenues after variable expenses have been deducted that can be used *to contribute* toward the covering of fixed expenses and then toward profits for the period."[2] If the contribution margin is greater than zero, the business is generating a contribution to fixed costs. The contribution margin is calculated as follows:

Formula for contribution margin: $\dfrac{(\text{Sales} - \text{Variable costs})}{\text{Sales}}$

The contribution margin represents a portion of the formula to calculate break-even.

The break-even for BeTwixt, Inc. is calculated as follows:

Break-even (sales): $\dfrac{\text{Fixed cost}}{(\text{Sales} - \text{Variable costs}) / \text{Sales}}$

For example, using BeTwixt, Inc., the contribution margin is calculated below:

Contribution margin: $\dfrac{(\$380,000 - \$202,000)}{\$380,000} = 47\%$ or .47

Break-even (sales): $\dfrac{\$147,274 \text{ (fixed costs)}}{.47 \quad \text{(contribution margin)}} = \$313,349$

The figure $313,349 represents the amount of sales BeTwixt must generate in 1 year to break even. This figure does not include the owner's draw because the owner does not have to withdraw money. It excludes the travel expense, inventory, principal repayment on the line of credit, and income tax.

UNDERSTANDING CASH FLOW

Cash is king. This statement is heard often by entrepreneurs. Lack of cash can send a business under in a hurry. As a result, developing procedures and a plan to manage and understand cash is crucial. The entrepreneur must focus on the amount of cash it takes to open the doors and to keep the business going. By managing cash efficiently, the entrepreneur can pay bills, pay employees, and invest in income-generating accounts. As the business grows, the entrepreneur will have to invest more cash into hiring more employees and increasing inventory.

As stated earlier in this chapter, there is a difference between cash and profit. Profit is the difference between the business's total revenue and its total expenses. Cash is money that flows through the business in a continuous cycle.

There are three areas in which a business will encounter cash problems. One is not managing accounts receivable. It is necessary for some businesses in the fashion industry to sell merchandise and services on credit. They run a risk, although a necessary risk, in doing so. Carrying an account receivable is the same as making a loan to someone. The money is owed to the business. If and when the account is paid becomes an issue. A background check should be done before granting credit to anyone. A credit policy should be put in place to let every customer know the credit terms that have been established. Often a business will not receive payment on its accounts receivable because it fails to send an invoice. Without sending an invoice in a timely manner, the business cannot expect payment. Overdue accounts require immediate action. An account receivable due for over 90 days is practically impossible to collect.

The entrepreneur must also watch accounts payable. It is just as important for the business to pay its bills on time and maintain a good credit rating as it is to be paid on time. Waiting too long to pay bills may push the suppliers to require that merchandise be paid in cash on delivery, or alienate vendors. This can greatly affect the cash flow of a business. It can also reduce the number of vendors willing to conduct business with the company.

The final issue in managing cash flow is managing inventory. For a fashion retail business, lack of inventory means lack of sales. It is important to monitor inventory closely so that the business does not maintain too much stock yet has enough to generate sales. Inventory is not a liquid asset. It cannot be turned into cash easily. It is important not to tie up too much cash in inventory. Carrying inventory is expensive.

ACCESSING CAPITAL

Accessing capital can be a major challenge for a start-up company. The entrepreneur does not have the historical data to prove that the company is likely to survive. Additionally, new companies typically start with very little in assets. Lenders and investors consider start-up companies to be very high risk. Although they are high risk, numerous start-up companies seek and find funding each year. The more informed the entrepreneur, the more likely he or she is to obtain the capital needed for launching the venture.

There are two types of funding: debt financing and equity financing. Debt financing involves securing funds by borrowing money that must be repaid. The other type of financing, equity financing, means sharing ownership of the business. It is the personal investment of the owner or other source of capital in the business. (Equity financing through venture capital is discussed later in this chapter.) It is important to be aware of all options available to businesses. Very few entrepreneurs have the funds in place to open a business without the need to access additional capital.

Debt Financing

Businesses borrow money for a number of reasons. Among them are the need to increase sales staff or increase inventory, to purchase new equipment, to take advantage of cash discounts offered by suppliers or to secure funds before the business takes a downturn and accessing capital would become more difficult. Very few entrepreneurs have the ability to cover all the cash requirements of a business without borrowing money.

Businesses need three types of capital: seed capital (or start-up capital), working capital, and growth capital. Seed capital is the amount of money the business needs to open the doors. It is typically money earned and saved by the entrepreneur. Working capital is the money needed to operate the business on a short-term basis. Working capital is typically the difference between current assets and current liabilities. It is needed for the times in the business when cash flow is an issue. Growth capital is money needed to help a business grow and expand.

Debt financing is more common than equity financing for small companies. This is due in part to the amount of money that a small start-up company needs. As is discussed later in the chapter, venture capitalists rarely consider deals of under $1 million. Debt financing allows the owner to maintain complete control of the business. Although smaller companies typically borrow at a higher interest rate than more established businesses, it is still less than the cost of obtaining funds from a venture capitalist. Venture capitalists are individuals or organizations that purchase an equity position in the company in exchange for a return of their investment. In other words, they own a part of the business.

Many options are available to the small business owner seeking debt financing. Before applying for any type of financing, it is important to research and explore all sources available. A program not suited to the business now may prove to be the answer to funding down the road.

Family and Friends   Family and friends can be an accessible source of financing to provide the funds necessary to start a venture. Caution should be taken to ensure that family and friends will be paid back just as a bank or outside investor would be. It is a common theme among business owners that one does not do business with friends and family. Everything is fine until something goes wrong in the business, and money becomes scarce. If family and friends are going to be funding sources, it is advisable to put written agreements in place that outline the expectations of the lenders and the entrepreneur.

Credit Cards   Credit cards can be a convenient source of funding when other avenues have failed. Banks are quick to grant credit via credit cards. Credit cards, however, have downsides. They carry high interest rates and are difficult to pay off. The manner in which they are structured leaves the entrepreneur struggling to meet the payments.

Commercial Banks   Commercial banks represent the greatest source of funding for entrepreneurs. Entrepreneurs ready to start a new venture typically begin by visiting with their local bankers. Of all business loans 80 percent come from banks. There is a difference between a conventional commercial loan and a guaranteed loan issued by the bank.

Bankers are conservative in nature. They loan money based on the bank's deposits. In other words, they are loaning the money that is deposited by their customers. Because of this, they have an obligation to make sound lending decisions. They are often skeptical of new ventures because of high failure rates. They typically want to see a 3-year history of the business before they will grant a traditional, or conventional, commercial loan. Traditional commercial loans are loans made without a Small Business Administration (SBA) guarantee. Obtaining a bank loan without a guarantee by the Small Business Administration can be challenging.

U.S. Small Business Administration   The U.S. Small Business Administration (SBA) is designed to help obtain financing for both start-up and existing small companies that do not qualify for traditional loans because of the risk of failure or lack of a good asset base. It was established in 1953 to provide financial, technical, and management assistance to small businesses. The SBA has a portfolio of more than $45 billion in loan guarantees and disaster loans.[3]

A misconception among borrowers is that the SBA lends money. With the exception of disaster loans, the SBA does not make a direct loan. The SBA guarantees loans for banks and other institutions. The potential borrower applies for a loan through a commercial bank that is a certified SBA lender. The lender then makes a determination as to whether or not to loan money with an SBA guarantee. If an application is approved with an SBA guarantee, the bank sends the application to the SBA office for approval. With an SBA guarantee, the SBA is saying that if the person or company receiving the loan defaults, it will step in and guarantee up to 80 percent of the loan balance. This greatly reduces the risk for the bank. The SBA has enabled many entrepreneurs to access capital who would not otherwise qualify for funding.

For a bank to make SBA loans, it must be certified by the SBA to do so. Lenders are certified as either regular certified lenders or preferred lenders. These certified lending and preferred lending programs were established to help speed up the process of obtaining an SBA loan. Previously, an SBA loan could take anywhere from 24 hours to 6 months for approval. The bank was responsible for part of the problem, but the lack of information provided by the entrepreneur also contributed to delays. In an effort to streamline the process, the SBA created the certified and preferred lender programs. As a certified lender, a bank can process and get approval for a loan in 3 to 10 days. As a preferred lender, the bank makes the final lending decision with an SBA review. The lender can approve the loan without preapproval of the SBA. The SBA can then review the loan at a later date. Under this process, a bank can often approve a loan in 24 to 36 hours.

Businesses must meet SBA requirements to be eligible for an SBA loan. The business must show that it is not able to obtain financing through any conventional sources without

SBA's help. It must also be a business that qualifies in terms of its type. The SBA will not guarantee loans made to gambling institutions, pyramid sales schemes, or illegal activities.

The SBA has several programs available to help entrepreneurs access capital. Below is a listing of those programs that are most likely to be utilized by a fashion business.

- *Microloans.* The microloan program was designed to provide financing to start-up and early stage companies that do not yet qualify for conventional bank financing. Microloans are administered through community-based not-for-profit lenders such as economic development companies. The program was designed to target minorities, women, and people with a low income, although these are not its only market. It requires that the borrower not be able to obtain financing through any other conventional source. The program is designed to loan up to $35,000 for working capital or the purchase of inventory, supplies, furniture, fixtures, and machinery and/or equipment. The interest rates are typically high, and the financing period usually cannot exceed 6 years. Under the SBA microloan program, the loans are not guaranteed by SBA. This is important to an entrepreneur who cannot qualify under traditional methods. Turnaround time for these loans can be as fast as 24 hours or they can take months, depending on the lender. They are typically much easier to obtain than a traditional loan. In addition to loans, under this program, intermediary lenders receiving grant dollars from the SBA are required to provide technical assistance to their microloan borrowers. Technical assistance is designed to help the entrepreneur with marketing issues, financial issues, growth strategies, and management issues. A list of microlenders can be obtained through the Small Business Administration Web site at www.sba.gov.

- *Minority and Women Prequalified Loan Program.* The Minority and Women Prequalified Loan Program was designed to help minority and women entrepreneurs prepare loan applications and "prequalify" for SBA loan guarantees before applying through a bank or other lending institution. By prequalifying for an SBA loan, the entrepreneur increases his or her chances of obtaining a loan through the bank. The guarantee is already in place. To qualify under the Minority and Women Prequalification Loan Program, the business must meet the following criteria: it must be minimally 51 percent owned, operated, and managed by women or minorities; annual sales cannot exceed $5 million; and it must employ fewer than 100 workers. The maximum loan amount is $250,000 and can be repaid over a period of 7 to 25 years, depending on the purpose of the loan. The loan proceeds may be used for working capital or for purchasing equipment, inventory, and real estate.

- *504 Loans.* The basis of the 504 loan program is to recruit businesses in order to create jobs and expand facilities. The program provides long-term, fixed rate financing to small businesses to help them acquire real estate, machinery, or equipment for expansion or modernization. Although this loan would not work for a fashion retail business that leases its space, it would be an option for a retail business that is located in its own building. The process of obtaining a 504 loan involves three lenders; the bank, the SBA, and a certified development company (CDC). A CDC is a nonprofit organization designed to promote economic growth in a community. The entrepreneur is generally required to invest 10 percent of the total project cost into the venture. The CDC will loan 40 percent at a long-term fixed rate, with an SBA guarantee. The bank will then provide the other 50 percent financing which is guaranteed by the

SBA. For every $35,000 the CDC loans, the business must create at least one new job. The machinery and equipment must have a useful life of at least 10 years. Other restrictions apply and a list of qualifications can be obtained through the SBA or the local CDC.

- *7(a) Loans.* The most common type of SBA loan is the 7(a) loan. This program serves as the SBA's primary loan program. Loans are granted by commercial banks and are guaranteed up to 80 percent for loans up to $100,000 and 75 percent for loans over $100,001. The maximum the SBA will guarantee is up to $750,000. Under this program, banks are more likely to loan to start-up companies because the SBA is reducing their exposure or risk. Again, the SBA is simply guaranteeing the loan. It does not actually loan the money. The proceeds of these loans can be used to purchase inventory, machinery, equipment, and real estate and can be used for working capital. The interest rate generally cannot exceed 2.75 percent over the prime rate in effect on the day the SBA receives the application. For loans under $50,000, the rate may be slightly higher. The loans may be financed for up to 25 years depending on their purpose.

Lines of Credit A **line of credit** is a short-term loan that provides cash flow for the day-to-day operations of the business. With this type of loan, the bank establishes a specified amount of money that is available to the business to withdraw as needed, much like a credit card. It is expected that the line of credit will be used and paid back in a very short period of time and the money will be there to use again. It is advantageous to the entrepreneur in that the unused portion of the line of credit does not accumulate interest. Interest is only charged on the amount outstanding.

Many types and sources of financing exist for small companies. This chapter has listed only the most common sources of funding. Before attempting to secure any type of financing, it is important for the entrepreneur to explore all the options available. Many government agencies such as the Department of Economic Development and Small Business Development Centers exist in part to help locate various programs.

The Mind-set of the Banker

Bankers expect that the entrepreneur has done his or her homework. They want to know that the entrepreneur knows what he or she is talking about when it comes to the financial plan for a business. If the entrepreneur has done the homework, he or she will be able to discuss the amount of money or funding that is needed, why it is needed, the impact the loan will have on the business, and how the business will operate at a profit. An entrepreneur ready for financing will be able to discuss the financial plan in detail. The entrepreneur will be able to explain how the sales figures were developed, how expenses were determined, and what pitfalls may occur that would prevent the business from meeting projections.

Bankers make lending decisions based on the five Cs of credit: capacity, collateral, credit, character, and capital. *Capacity* is the ability of the entrepreneur to pay the loan as agreed. Banks determine this by reviewing the financial plan within the business plan and the entrepreneur's personal finances. It is advisable for the entrepreneur to have explored a number of situations before approaching the bank. Bankers will look to the business as the primary source of repayment. They will look to the entrepreneur to determine the secondary source. How will the entrepreneur repay the debt if the business does not meet projections?

The second criterion for lending is collateral. *Collateral* represents the assets the business is willing to pledge to the bank as security for repayment of the loan. If the borrower defaults on the loan, the bank has the right to sell the collateral and use the proceeds from the sale to satisfy the loan. It is very unlikely that a bank will loan dollar for dollar. This means that if a computer costs $5,000 at the time of purchase, the bank may be willing to loan only 50 percent of the cost of that computer. Banks want their loans to be fully collateralized. For every dollar borrowed, they want 1 dollar in collateral.

The third criterion for lending is *credit*. The borrower must have a good credit history before the bank will loan him or her money. Often, borrowers own homes and automobiles. They have credit cards or other forms of financing that have established a credit history for them. For a student, a credit history can be established in other ways. Paying utility bills on time, paying credit cards as agreed, and paying phone bills or rent on time all serve as a history of how the student repays debt. Credit reports provide information on a person's credit history. It is advisable for an entrepreneur to request a credit report from one of the three credit reporting agencies in the United States before approaching a bank. Credit reports may be obtained by contacting Experian, Equifax, or Transunion— the three primary credit reporting agencies. The report will reveal any negative information. Addressing the issue of "derogatory credit" before the bank brings it up can serve the entrepreneur well, if applicable.

The fourth C of credit is *character*. To obtain funding, the banker must be convinced that the borrower is of good character. To make this evaluation, banks rely on intangible factors such as honesty, determination, intelligence, organization, and competence. If the entrepreneur does not have it together going into the business, he or she will most likely not do well once the business is opened. The borrower can help present himself of herself successfully by making sure he or she knows and understands the business plan thoroughly. The borrower should make an appointment with the lender, arrive on time, and dress appropriately.

The fifth C is *capital*. The banker does not want to be the only one at risk. The entrepreneur will be expected to invest anywhere from 20 percent to 30 percent in capital into the business. The banker will also look to see that the business is not opening its doors with too little capital. According to the U.S. Small Business Administration, lack of capital is one of the three more common reasons for business failure.

In addition to the five Cs of credit and a solid business plan, the banker will want to see supporting documentation in the loan package. The banker will look for such documentation as licenses, articles of incorporation, lease agreements, noncompete agreements, contracts, and other legal documents. The banker will also want to see a proposed list of collateral, to include the amount of collateral the business has to offer and the value of that collateral. The banker will want to review tax returns covering the previous 3 years, personal financial statements on all the principals of the company, bank statements, and pay stubs (if applicable). The banker will also expect to see a detailed list itemizing the use of loan proceeds. Although the banker may be able to ascertain this information from the business plan, he or she will not want to have to look for it.

Equity Financing

Equity financing refers to the owner's equity in the business. Equity financing can come in the form of an investment by the entrepreneur and/or an investment of capital from an outside source. This type of outside funding is the most difficult to get for a number of reasons. Venture capitalists are private persons or organizations that purchase an equity position in a company in exchange for a return on their investment. This is difficult to set up in a very small company. Most venture capital firms will not look at a deal worth under $1 million. They also tend to prefer high growth companies.

Angels are a more likely source of outside capital. Angels are wealthy individuals who invest in start-up companies in exchange for an equity position in the company. Angels have a tendency to invest funds at the local level. They are often entrepreneurs themselves. They earn their money as the company increases in value. There is really no source that lists angel investors. The SBA has developed an Angel Capital Network (ACE-Net) that lists small, fast-growing companies in which angels would be interested. It can be accessed on-line.

CONCLUSION

The financial plan is one of the most crucial elements of the business plan. A good financial plan helps determine the amount and type of financing that will be needed to make the plan feasible. The financial plan can also serve as a valuable management tool in helping the entrepreneur run the business efficiently.

The entrepreneur can rely on three key financial documents to provide information about the business: the cash flow statement, the balance sheet, and the income statement. Together, all three provide insight into the availability of cash, the book value of the business, and where the money is going. Through a set of ratios, the entrepreneur can evaluate ways in which to run the business more efficiently and effectively. The key financial ratios and break-even analysis allow the entrepreneur to measure the performance of a business against like businesses in the industry. The entrepreneur can then begin to make adjustments as needed to ensure the success of the business.

The financial plan provides the opportunity to access capital through either debt or equity financing. A number of programs exist that provide financing to start-up and early-stage companies. Knowing the key areas bankers and investors examine in a financial plan is a critical factor for entrepreneurs to be able to access credit.

WRITING THE PLAN

Develop a financial plan by referring to the financial plan topics in Chapter 14.

SECTION	TOPIC
Financial Plan	Cash flow statement
	Assumptions
	Profit and loss statement
	Balance sheet

Business Mentor™ CD-ROM—Business Plan—Financial Plan

KEY TERMS

accounts payable	growth capital
accounts receivable	income statement
accruals payable	inventory
angels investors	inventory turnover ratio
assets	liabilities
assumptions	line of credit
balance sheet	liquidity ratios
book value	long-term debt
break-even point	long-term liabilities
cash	near cash assets
cash flow	net sales
cash flow statement	notes payable
cash on hand	operating expenses
certified development corporation	operating ratios
chart of accounts	owner's draw
contribution margin	owner's equity
cost of goods sold	prepaid expenses
current assets	principal payments
current liabilities	profit
current portion of long-term debt	profitability ratios
current ratio	pro forma
debt financing	quick ratio (acid test)
debt ratio	ratio analysis
debt to equity ratio	retained earnings
depreciation	risk ratios
equity financing	seed capital
fixed assets	variable costs
fixed costs	venture capitalists
gross margin ratio	working capital
gross profit	

QUESTIONS

1. Why is the financial plan important to a company?
2. What is the purpose of a cash flow statement? Income statement? Balance sheet?
3. Why are pro forma financial statements important to the financial plan?
4. How do key ratios help an entrepreneur understand the business?
5. How does knowing the break-even point of the business help the entrepreneur in the start-up phase?
6. Why is it necessary to concentrate on effectively managing cash flow?
7. What is the difference between cash and profit?
8. Discuss the 5 C's of credit.
9. Discuss the various lending programs available to small businesses.

REFERENCES

1. Art DeThomas, *Financial Management Techniques for Small Business* (Grants Pass, Oregon: Oasis Press/PSI research, 1999, pp. 16–17)
2. Ray H. Garrison, *Managerial Accounting; Concepts for Planning Control, Decision Making*, 5th ed. (Plano, Texas: Business Publications, Inc., p. 89)
3. "Learn about SBA," www.sba.gov/aboutsba

SUGGESTED READINGS

William G. Dioms, *Finance and Accounting for Nonfinancial Managers: All the Basics You Need to Know,* 4th ed. (Cambridge, Massachusetts: Perseus Books, 1997)

Robert N. Anthony, *A Review of Essentials of Accounting*, 5th ed. (Reading, Massachusetts: Addison-Wesley Publishing Company, 1993)

Bruce Blechman and Jay Conrad Levinson, *Guerrilla Financing: Alternative Techniques to Finance Any Small Business* (Boston, Massachusetts: Houghton Mifflin Company, 1991)

James O. Gill, *Understanding Financial Statements: A Primer of Useful Information* (Menlo Park, California: Crisp Publications, Inc., 1990)

Art DeThomas, *Financial Management Techniques for Small Business* (Grants Pass, Oregon: Oasis Press, 1991)

Jose Placencia, Bruce Wedge, and Don Oliver, *Business Owners Guide to Accounting and Bookkeeping* (Grants Pass, Oregon: Oasis Press, 1997)

David H. Bangs, *Mastering Your Small Business Finances* (Chicago, Illinois: Upstart Publishing, 1996)

Robert J. Low, *Bottomline Basics: Understand and Control Business Finances* (Grants Pass, Oregon: Oasis Press, 1995)

CASE STUDY

Lidia Backer opened her clothing store, Lidia's Boutique, in 1994 with the help of her mother and sister-in-law. With $25,000 in the bank and a commitment from her mother and sister-in-law to invest an additional $30,000 in the company, Backer found a prime location for the business and began negotiations on the lease. While searching for a location for the business, Backer and her investors began the process of developing the business plan and determining the merchandise the store would carry. Backer had worked in the clothing industry for over 15 years and wanted an opportunity to own a store of her own.

According to the business plan, Backer would need a loan in the amount of $75,000 in addition to her initial capital injection of $45,000 to finance start-up costs. Backer would also need an operating line of credit in the amount of $10,000. "I was anxious, yet optimistic," Backer recalls. The bank approved a loan in the amount of $75,000 for start-up costs and a $10,000 operating line of credit. With the investment of $30,000 from her mother and sister-in-law, Backer has planned to purchase $50,000 in core inventory to start the business.

A family emergency occurred and Backer's mother and sister-in-law could no longer invest their $30,000 capital into the company. Backer was determined to open the business. She went to market and purchased $20,000 in inventory, $30,000 worth of inventory short of the projected level. The business opened in March of 1994 and was a success. It was such a success, that Backer found herself short on merchandise to sell. Though the business went through a rough time, the bank was able to loan her an additional $30,000 for inventory.

Lidia's now boasts over $400,000 in sales per year. Backer has plans to expand her store within the next 2 years. She paid her outside investors in full and is anticipating the loan to be paid within the next 36 months.

CASE STUDY QUESTIONS

1. What factors caused Lidia's Boutique not to meet cash flow projections?
2. What could Lidia have done to determine the amount she needed for core inventory?
3. What caused the decline in the gross profit margin?

ENTERING THE WORLD OF THE ENTREPRENEUR

1. Ask an entrepreneur to discuss how often he or she reviews the financial statements. Ask whether she or he uses key ratios to analyze the business. Has it helped in making management decisions?
2. Ask several accountants and bankers to discuss their experiences with small business owners and their understanding of the financial aspects of such businesses.

3. Visit two to three bankers to discuss the criteria for financing a start-up company. What do they look for and why? What percent of the loans the bank makes is made to small businesses?

. . . .

ENTERPRISING ENTREPRENEUR

. . . .

Mary Jane Nesbitt, 51, opened her consignment clothing shop, Nine Lives, in Los Gatos, an upscale community in California's Silicon Valley, in February 1993. Before opening the shop, Nesbitt had worked for many years in the legal department of a commercial real estate brokerage. Her decision to leap from employee to entrepreneur came during a soul-searching walk with her husband, David Butcher.

"I was unhappy and frustrated," Nesbitt recalls. "We had talked about the possibility of my opening a consignment shop for maybe six months. We got to this end of town, and my husband pointed across the park and said, 'Look, that space is for rent. This is it. You're doing it.'"

The storefront to which Butcher pointed is ideal for a consignment shop, Nesbitt says, because there's plenty of regular foot traffic. The next-door neighbors are a bakery and a dry cleaner. Down the block is a U.S. Post Office, and across the street is a park where community functions are held.

Nesbitt started the business by taking $17,000 out of her retirement plan to cover initial lease costs, racks, hangers, shelves, bags, printing costs, lighting, and other necessities. Her husband, a Webmaster for a large networking company, wrote the shop's custom financial and inventory management software.

Nine Lives grossed $180,000 last year. More important, Nesbitt is doing something she loves: "My satisfaction in life is so much greater."

Marcie Geffner, "Rags to Riches." *Business Start-ups* magazine, May 1998, www.entrepreneur.com

Chapter 12

DEVELOPING OPERATING AND CONTROL SYSTEMS

INTRODUCTION

In Chapter 8, the principles of management are presented and discussed, with emphasis on leadership and organizational structure. In Chapter 9, merchandising is examined from an organizational perspective. The job description, sources of information, and responsibilities of the retail buyer are presented and discussed. In this chapter, management and merchandising are explored from a very different perspective. The procedures and policies that an organization needs to develop and implement for merchandising and management functions to succeed are referred to as operations and control. Operations, simply defined, are the procedures put in place to actually run the business. Control refers to the point in the strategic planning process where results are compared to the goals and objectives. Operations are concerned with how to do things. Control is concerned with what can be done to do things better, and what obstacles to quality performance can be removed. An operations and control plan regulates the day-to-day functions of the business, from the receiving of new merchandise to following up on the customer's purchase. A good operations and control plan facilitates a number of goals for the organization. It communicates and coordinates the activities within the business. It acts as a control and monitoring tool by providing continuity. It summarizes information about the organization's infrastructure.

Where will the entrepreneur begin in developing an operational plan for the new business? Reviewing the operations and procedures manual of an existing business can give the entrepreneur a head start in recognizing the operational plans needed. In this chapter, operations and control systems are examined as they relate to the facility, the merchandise, the employees, and the customers. An emphasis is placed on security, as well as on legal issues associated with operations and control.

OPERATIONS AND THE FACILITY

In Chapter 5, factors are examined as they relate to the decisions the entrepreneur must make in choosing a specific location for the business. In that use, the decision-making process focuses on external factors. Decisions are made to determine the placement of the business, rather than how the location will be managed. In this chapter, the facility is examined from an operational perspective. There are a number of operational issues that relate directly to the facility. These include space allocation, staff efficiency, hours of operation, fixturing and supply needs, customer mobility, energy requirements, construction and material costs, and business security.

Space Allocation

The area within a retail operation can be divided into the following four types of space: sales, customer service, merchandise warehousing and handling, and staff or personnel areas. Customer service areas include dressing rooms, lounges, rest rooms, coffee or juice bars, restaurants, checkout stations, credit departments, and merchandise return stations. Merchandise is handled in receiving areas, warehouses, and alteration departments. Retail staff members may utilize such spaces as offices, lounges, lunchrooms, conference rooms, and training areas. Not every business needs each of these kinds of space allocation. One of the managerial tasks of the retail entrepreneur is to determine which business operations will take place in which spaces. The amount of square footage to be allocated for displaying merchandise to be sold is referred to as **selling space**. The remaining areas are called **nonselling space**.

The entrepreneur must decide how much selling and nonselling space to allocate. This decision will affect the estimated sales per square foot of the business, as this calculation is generated solely by the amount of square footage dedicated to selling space. Typically, a store dedicates from 65 percent to 85 percent of its space to the actual selling of merchandise. Based on national industry averages compiled by the National Retail Federation (2000), sales per square foot in women's apparel are $145 in retail dollars; in men's apparel, they are $200; and, in children's apparel, sales per square foot average $100. These calculations vary by geographic location, as well as by the kind of store such as a specialty store versus department store. The *Merchandising and Operating Results* published by the National Retail Federation can provide more specific data for the entrepreneur.

Staff Efficiency

Staff efficiency works hand in hand with the business layout. For example, if the dressing rooms are located far from the selling floor, the sales associate will run a marathon by the time the workday is over. If the merchandise is so congested on the selling floor that sales associates cannot monitor the inventory, then merchandise losses due to theft may be high. If the telephone is located in the office, then the sales associate will have to leave the floor to answer it. A primary goal in designing the facility layout is to accommodate the duties of the staff in order to make the operation run more smoothly.

Customer Mobility

Like staff efficiency, the layout of a facility can affect customer mobility. **Customer mobility** refers to the ease with which clientele can find a parking place, enter the establishment, and move about the business. Additionally, it refers to accessibility for clientele with physical limitations. Can a customer with physical restrictions move through the aisles, comfortably use a dressing room or rest room, and write a check at the cash desk?

Hours of Operation

In certain locations, the hours of operation are predetermined for the business. In most malls, for example, the lease agreement includes designated hours of operation by which the businesses must abide. If the entrepreneur has located the business in a facility that does not require specific hours of operation, there are several factors that may influence which hours are chosen. First, the entrepreneur will want to examine what neighboring businesses are doing in terms of opening and closing times. Second, the entrepreneur will want to explore the times that the organization's customer will most likely prefer to do business. For example, if a fashion retail operation appeals to a target market dominated by college students, it is unlikely that an 8:00 A.M. opening will elicit much customer traffic. Third, the entrepreneur will want to consider external factors, such as safety, parking, and transportation options for the business's location.

Lease and Improvements

Operational concerns related to the leasing of the facility include the length and terms of the lease, particularly whether or not it is a straight lease or rent plus a percent of sales. These issues must be incorporated into financial plans. Improvements and additions, such as signs, wall fixtures, or utility hookups, must be considered within the operational plan. Will the entrepreneur pay these costs directly, split them with the landlord, or make payments to the landlord for these investments? In most cases, permanent improvements, such as paint, wallpaper, and track lighting become the property of the landlord once the lease is terminated. The rule of thumb is that if it will require repairs once it is removed, it is likely that it must remain.

Utilities and Maintenance

The costs of gas, water, and electricity may be covered as part of the lease; however, it is more frequent that the entrepreneur will be required to pay them directly to utility providers. An objective of the entrepreneur should be to estimate and anticipate these operational costs for the financial section of the business plan. Additionally, the entrepreneur will want to identify energy-efficient measures to control these expenses. Janitorial, trash removal, and other ongoing facility maintenance expenses must also be incorporated into the monthly financial plan, if they are not part of the monthly lease payment.

Security

Protecting the facility may include a security system, or a security guard, depending on the business location and the type of business. The cost of installing a security system, if one is not in place, may be negotiated as part of the lease agreement. If there is a security system in place, the entrepreneur will likely have monthly costs associated with operating the system. These costs should be included in the financial plan. Additionally, procedures for operating the security system need to be developed for personnel who open and close the business.

OPERATIONS AND THE MERCHANDISE

Operational procedures need to be established for receiving, marking, and placing goods for sale. The accuracy and timeliness of paying vendors, pricing merchandise, and keeping records are dependent upon these processes. Cost and time efficiencies are significant goals for the entrepreneur when addressing receiving and ticketing of merchandise.

Receiving Goods

Merchandise is processed from the purchase order. The completion, or cancellation date is the last day that the buyer has authorized the vendor to ship the merchandise. It is the buyer's decision whether to accept or return goods shipped past the cancellation date. In some cases, the buyer will contact the vendor to negotiate a reduced price on merchandise shipped late. In other cases, the goods will be returned to the vendor. If the completion date is acceptable, the invoice is compared to the purchase order and the correct style, color, size, number of units, and price are checked. The invoice is the vendor's detailed shipment listing with prices. Next, the packing slip, the vendor's listing of merchandise in a particular carton or container, is compared to the invoice. Some orders may be shipped in a series of cartons, each with an individual packing slip and with one invoice for the total shipment. Once the paperwork provided by the vendor has been reconciled with the purchase order, the merchandise can be checked into inventory. Any discrepancies, such as shortages or overages, are noted on the purchase order for adjustments by the employee responsible for accounting.

Marking Goods

Once the merchandise is checked in, tickets with the appropriate data are prepared and attached to the goods. Some entrepreneurs use a specialized ticket-making machine; others use computer software to generate tickets; and a few prepare the ticket by hand. The entrepreneur will want to predetermine the data that will be included on the ticket. Commonly, a department number indicating the merchandise classification number, a vendor identification number, style number, size, color or color number, and retail price are included. Additionally, some operations include the date the merchandise will be ticketed. Often, a code is used for the ticketing date so that this is not obvious to the customer. For example, the month of the year may be indicated by letters of the alphabet (e.g., A for January, B for February, C for March, etc.), while the actual day of the month is indicated by the corresponding number. In this case, February 26 would be represented by B26. Dating merchandise is extremely helpful in locating merchandise when it is time to take markdowns. Example of merchandise tickets are illustrated in Figure 12.1.

Placing Merchandise on the Sales Floor

After the merchandise has been ticketed, it is folded or hung, steamed or pressed, and delivered to the sales floor. In most cases, new merchandise is highlighted at the front of the

Figure 12.1 Examples of Merchandise Tickets

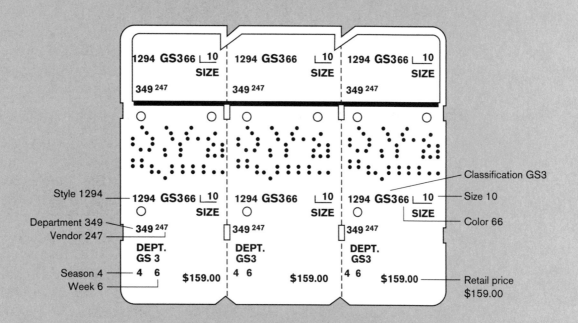

Style 1294
Department 349
Vendor 247
Season 4
Week 6

Classification GS3
Size 10
Color 66
Retail price $159.00

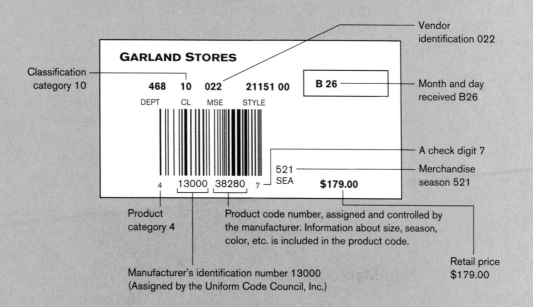

Classification category 10

GARLAND STORES

468   10   022   21151   00   B 26

DEPT   CL   MSE   STYLE

4   13000   38280   7   521
                        SEA $179.00

Vendor identification 022
Month and day received B26
A check digit 7
Merchandise season 521
Retail price $179.00

Product category 4
Product code number, assigned and controlled by the manufacturer. Information about size, season, color, etc. is included in the product code.
Manufacturer's identification number 13000 (Assigned by the Uniform Code Council, Inc.)

Source: Michele M. Granger, 1996, *Case Studies in Merchandising Apparel and Soft Goods* (New York, NY: Fairchild Publications, Inc., page 204) store to attract new customers and entice repeat clientele. Visual merchandising efforts are important when it comes to newly arrived merchandise, which is what the entrepreneur will want to feature in windows, on mannequins, and on key fixtures. The physical placement of merchandise in selling space is significant. The location of goods and fixtures can discourage or encourage shoplifting. High fixtures and tall displays provide visual protection to the thief. The layout of the inventory and displays should be designed so that employees are able to see all sections of the business. Merchandise placement is key to security and sales.

Paying the Suppliers

Once the merchandise has been received, the purchase order, invoice, and packing slip(s) are filed together for payment. In most cases, the retailer has 30 days in which to pay the bill. When the buyer has a solid business relationship with the vendor, she or he may attempt to negotiate **dating,** which is an additional amount of time in which to pay the vendor. Dating usually means an additional 30 days before payment is due, or 60 days in total. This is noted on the purchase order as "30X." When the bill is paid, the check number and date of mailing are noted on the invoice.

If an employee pays bills and handles checks, it is important to note that these two areas provide an opportunity for theft. The employee can make out checks to nonexistent companies for goods or services, and then personally cash the checks. To prevent this type of theft, a procedure should be established in which different employees are in charge of authorizing and issuing bank checks for all payments from payroll to inventory. Additionally, each check should be verified against a corresponding invoice.

Tracking Merchandise

Tracking merchandise refers to monitoring the performance of items in inventory. A computerized system simplifies and speeds this process. When goods are sold, they are entered into the computer by department number, vendor number, style, size, color, and retail price. A **point-of-sale** (POS) system refers to a computerized cash register that generates a customer receipt while adjusting the retail dollar inventory level. In addition to maintaining a record of merchandise that is sold, POS systems keep track of items that are returned or exchanged. The result is a complete analysis of sales and stock by unit. By analyzing these data, the entrepreneur, or buyer, can determine which merchandise should be reordered and which should be reduced in price to encourage sales.

Taking Markdowns

Taking **markdowns** refers to the process of marking and recording a reduction in the selling price of an item. Markdowns are a fact of life in fashion retailing. The entrepreneur will want to establish a policy and procedure for taking markdowns. The policy may include what to markdown (e.g., merchandise that is over 30 days old) and when to take the markdown (e.g., the first of every month). The policy should also indicate how to take markdowns. For example, the entrepreneur may determine that the first markdown will be a reduction of 30 percent off the initial price. He or she may decide that this price change will be noted on the merchandise ticket in red pen and that all markdowns will be processed in the computer, according to department and vendor. Precise records of markdown amounts are necessary to generate an accurate inventory result. Additionally, a detailed record of markdowns enables the buyer to determine which vendors provided the best sales and profit performance, and which vendors should be eliminated from the merchandising mix.

Returning Goods to the Vendor

When does the retailer find it necessary to return merchandise to a vendor? There are a number of reasons for an **RTM (return to the manufacturer)**, also referred to as an **RTV (return to the vendor)**. First, goods shipped past the cancellation date may be designated by the buyer as returns. Second, defective merchandise may need to be returned to the vendor. Third, the buyer may negotiate with the manufacturers' representative to return styles that did not sell for an exchange of merchandise credit toward future purchases. In any case, the retailer cannot simply mail the merchandise back to the manufacturer. Instead, the buyer must request a **return authorization label** from the vendor. This label, which is attached to the carton containing the return, ensures that the shipment will be accepted at the receiving dock of the manufacturer. It is important for the entrepreneur to calculate returns as a reduction in inventory by deducting the cost and retail price of the RTM from the stock figure. If this not done the amount of the RTM will appear to be a shortage that may be interpreted as a loss from theft.

OPERATIONS AND THE EMPLOYEES

The number of employees the business will require is dependent upon a number of factors, including the size of the facility, the need for merchandise security, how busy the operation will be, the level of assistance customers will require, and the amount of funding that will be allocated for payroll. Once funding for payroll has been calculated, the next step is determining the number of employees, as well as the hours each employee will work.

In Chapter 8, the focus is on recruiting, interviewing, and hiring effective employees. While there is no fail-safe system for hiring perfect employees, the entrepreneur can improve the probability of finding and keeping good employees by following a few simple procedures, such as adhering to job descriptions when determining training strategies. From an operations perspective, the entrepreneur will want to have established policies and procedures to motivate, manage, and maintain effective employees.

Training Employees

There are three key pieces of advice for entrepreneurs when it comes to hiring effective employees while minimizing the level of training they will likely require. First, the entrepreneur should look for actual accomplishments, or outcomes, by carefully interviewing candidates and reviewing job applications, résumés, and comments of references. Second, the entrepreneur should look for the personal attributes that will benefit the position. Finally, the entrepreneur should look for people with good contacts. The entrepreneur needs employees who can hit the floor running and, subsequently, produce revenue quickly. If the position is, for example, that of a sales associate, then the applicant who has an established clientele at a similar organization nearby will be a preferred candidate, assuming that all other factors are positive. Because the entrepreneur will be in a race to reach the break-even point, there is often not enough time to develop a sales force from square one. Additionally, employees with work experience in receiving, purchasing, and promotion not only provide expertise in these areas, but they also bring with them contacts. These contacts can prove helpful in pricing and shipping of supplies and merchandise.

As the entrepreneur prepares a training plan for employees, he or she will want to assess the job candidates in terms of how they will get along with each other. The entrepreneur will also want to evaluate which tasks will require training for all employees. Will staff members be able to function cooperatively and interdependently? Will differences in personalities and job descriptions require several types of training programs?

Even if the new employees the entrepreneur will hire have previous work experience in a similar retail operation, they will need to be trained on the methods of the particular business. Whether the job is assisting a customer, processing shipments, arranging merchandise, or operating the computer, there should be a procedure to follow. Many entrepreneurs compile an employee procedures manual that lists business policies and procedures.

Some entrepreneurs prefer to work individually with each employee. Others believe in a more informal approach to employee training. These business leaders encourage interaction by asking for their input on how to do things in a better way. Robert Price, chairman of the board of the Price Club, states:

> We don't believe in procedures manuals: we don't have a lot of detailed directions on how people should do things. We teach our people the principles and give them lots of room to develop. This is true at all levels, not just for managers, but also the person who stocks merchandise. If properly taught, they will feel responsibility and will have an understanding of what needs to be done (Abrams, 1993, p. 140).

Regardless of the diversity in style, there is a six-step training technique that many employers have found to be effective in formal and informal training situations. First, the employer describes the task and explains how it should be accomplished. Second, the employer demonstrates the task. Third, the employee is asked to explain how the task should be done. Fourth, the employee actually does the task. When the employee is finished, the employer provides feedback (step 5) to include praise, as well as areas in which the employee may improve. As the employee continues the task, the sixth step is the employer's periodic checking to confirm that the job is being accomplished in the appropriate manner. The objective in coaching employees is to guide them fairly, consistently, and tactfully. Employees need to know what is expected and how they are doing. Regular employee reviews help communicate this information.

Compensation and Incentives

Most employees need compensation and incentive programs to provide the consistent motivation needed to keep them pushing forward. Compensation is the employee's payment for services rendered. The most common form of compensation is fixed-rate compensation, which is pay that is not tied exclusively to performance. It is set at a specific level for a specified time period, such as an hourly wage or a monthly salary. In the fashion industry, there are variations on fixed-rate compensation that may motivate employees to work harder and to remain employed with the organization. These compensation methods are referred to as variable-rate, or merit, compensation programs, as they tie pay directly to the performance of the individual or group (e.g., department, area, organization, or some combination of all three). One method of variable-rate compensation that is common in fashion entrepreneurial organizations is sales commission. There are a number of variations to a commission plan. The simplest form is that of straight commission. Through this plan, the sales person is paid a percent of his or her sales volume. In most situations, returns are deducted from future commission payments. Another commission alternative is quota plus commission. In this case, the sales person is assigned a sales goal (i.e., hourly, weekly, or monthly sales volume performance) by management. The sales person receives a specified percent of commission on sales generated above the quota. Yet another commission alternative is referred to as hourly plus commission, or base plus commission. In this situation, the sales person earns a set amount for each hour, week, or month worked, as well as a percent of his or her sales volume.

A word of warning is necessary when the compensation plan includes a form of commission, particularly straight commission. The sales person receiving commission may go to any length to make a sale. The result can be pushy sales people who see little return business. Additionally, customers who do not appear to be making a purchase (in the view of the commissioned sales person) may not be serviced at all. Stanley Marcus, chief emertitus of Neiman Marcus, tells the story of a woman who was not being waited on by the sales associates in one of his stores. She did not resemble a usual Neiman Marcus customer; in fact, she looked as though she did not have two dimes to rub together. Mr. Marcus proceeded to assist this customer himself. It turned out that oil had recently been discovered on her family's land. The customer had the desire and the money to purchase everything needed to furnish a new mansion and several walk-in closets. The "sell or starve" aspect of commission is not appealing to some highly capable sales people. There is not an easy answer to motivating sales personnel. Commission can be counterproductive if improperly designed and managed.

Finally, the employer may offer compensation packages unique to that particular business. A share of the profits of the business, or stock options, may be offered by the entrepreneur as compensation and incentive rolled into one. The possibility of increased future earnings and the opportunity to own a piece of a thriving business may attract exceptional employees when highly competitive salaries are difficult to offer in the start-up business.

It is important for the entrepreneur to identify a number of incentives in order to keep employees motivated. Incentives are methods developed to generate high performances by employees. Successful retail managers agree that the more immediate the reward, the more effective it is. Some managers will offer a cash prize, a special merchandise discount, or an item from stock as a reward for top sales on a given day. Incentives are not restricted to cash prizes; they can vary from preferred days off to recognition awards. Merchandise discounts are one form of incentive that the majority of fashion retailers use to recruit and reward employees. Merchandise discounts are mutually beneficial, and they encourage the sales person to purchase and wear merchandise carried by the business. Sales people are, in essence, walking advertisements for the company.

A bonus, a lump-sum payment on performance over an extended period of time, can also provide motivation for employees. For example, the entrepreneur may offer employees a percent of the sales volume achieved over the annual sales goal, to be divided according to hours worked. Sam Walton, an entrepreneurial star, offered Wal-Mart employees a bonus for keeping losses generated from shoplifting, employee pilferage, and clerical errors under control. As a result, the Wal-Mart shortage percent was at an all-time low, while employees gained a sense of pride, ownership, and responsibility. An attractive compensation and incentive program is needed to attract and maintain the best employees possible. This includes offering a competitive salary, with the possibility of future increased earnings, in a thriving work environment where expectations are known and possible to be accomplished.

Reprimands and Terminations

Negative aspects of being an entrepreneur include reprimanding employees who are not doing their jobs well and, even worse, terminating employees who do not improve after reprimands. Selection procedures are not perfect. Sooner or later, someone who seemed right for the job will not work out. The need to terminate an employee may be very clear, as in cases such as theft or excessive absences. In some cases, however, the reason to fire an employee may be less clear-cut. Before an employee is fired, the entrepreneur will want to be certain that everything possible has been done to help him or her succeed at the job. The entrepreneur will want to have clearly articulated the problems, suggested ways to improve, and provided a time limit for improvements to be visible. Along the way, the entrepreneur will want to document efforts to help the employee succeed. The entrepreneur should compile a written record of the dates of reprimands and related discussions, the desired outcomes, the deadline for improvements, and the consequences of no improvement. If, after a final warning, there has been no improvement, then the entrepreneur has a responsibility to the business to terminate the employee.

Communication with Employees

Communicative supervision is the key to a satisfied staff and a profitable business. Accountability by the employee and the entrepreneur is necessary for a flourishing business. Staff meetings, memos, and meetings between an employee and the entrepreneur represent important communication efforts. The job description assigned the employee to his or her direct supervisor. This supervisor should be available to answer questions, discuss problems, and suggest solutions when the employee needs assistance and direction.

OPERATIONS AND THE CUSTOMER

Operational plans must be designed for the business to effectively interact with its customer. Procedures may be established for approaching and assisting the customer, ringing up a sale, processing a return, or following up on a purchase. What are the advantages to developing operational plans for customer interaction? Such strategies help ensure that the customer will receive consistent and efficient service. Additionally, these efforts aid in building the confidence of sales associates and in generating repeat business.

Approaching and Assisting the Customer

There is a selling strategy that has been passed on from sales person to sales person for generations. There are variations of this actual plan. In some, the steps are in a different order, while, in others, two steps may be condensed into one. But basically, the techniques for selling are the same. According to most, the ten steps to a successful sales transaction are as follows:

1. Approach the customer and gain his or her attention.
2. Establish rapport with the customer.
3. Find out what the customer's needs are through active listening.
4. Explain how the product will fill those needs by emphasizing its benefits.
5. Deal with customer concerns.
6. Gain commitment and close the sale.
7. Try suggestive selling to make the "extra sale" of an accessory or an additional service.
8. Ring up the sale and package the merchandise.
9. Reinforce the purchase decision and thank the customer.
10. Walk the customer to the door, invite him or her to return soon, and follow up on the sale.

How do these steps influence the operational plan of a business? For many of the steps, procedures need to be developed and implemented to enable the sales person to do his or her job and to ensure that the business runs smoothly. What if, for example, the sales associate closed the sale, but did not know how to ring it up? In many cases, the customer would be headed for the door, empty-handed, before the sales associate could figure out how to process the sale.

Writing Up the Sale–Transaction Flow

Most businesses, including small ones, operate on a computerized system. A customer transaction refers to a cash or credit sale, an exchange, or a return. Some businesses also offer a layaway plan, in which the customer has an item held by making a deposit and then making weekly or monthly payments on the merchandise until the merchandise is paid off. Layaway has become less prevalent in recent years because of the increasing speed of fashion cycles, which generate quicker markdowns. Frequently, the customer who places an item in layaway will find it at a reduced price by the time the payments are made in full. The customer will then want to receive the clearance price on the layaway merchandise. As a result of this problem, as well as limited warehousing space, a number of fashion retailers have eliminated the layaway option.

Cash and credit transactions require different procedures and policies, all of which need to be determined before the company actually opens for business. Cash transactions are the simplest. The customer's purchase is entered in the computer, or cash register, and a customer receipt is generated. The merchandise stockkeeping unit (SKU) refers to the identification numbers used to tag each item. The SKU and corresponding retail price should be processed for inventory reconciliation, whether cash or credit. The process for accepting bank checks must also be clarified. Will out-of-state checks be accepted? Which types of identification will be required? Are second-party checks acceptable; company checks? Will the business use a company, such as Tele-Check, to approve customer checks? If the business accepts major credit cards, then the procedure will be explained by a representative of the bank or banks providing this service to the business. The appropriate forms, telephone contact numbers, and employer identification number are tools the sales associate must have to make this transaction run smoothly.

Handling Returns

The entrepreneur must decide who will be authorized to accept returns and under what circumstances returned merchandise will be accepted. Return policies often identify a time limit (e.g., up to 30 days after purchase), whether or not a receipt will be required, whether or not the item must have the ticket attached, and whether or not the item is refundable for cash or a company credit. Retailers are finding that liberal return policies are expected by most customers. As accommodating customers with returns is viewed as a component of good customer service, a number of entrepreneurs are embracing a philosophy of "the customer is always right" and developing ways to deal with returns without losing clientele or profits. For example, a customer brought a child's dress she purchased back to the retail store because the neckline frayed when the garment was washed. Rather than immediately refunding the customer's money, the storeowner offered to have the garment repaired by an alteration service. The customer was satisfied; the repair cost as much as the shipping fee to return the garment would have.

Following Up on Sales

It takes just a moment to thank a customer, yet the memory of the thank you lingers far longer. If an entrepreneur truly contemplates how many places the customer can purchase similar goods, it would be quite a long list. Direct competitors, indirect competitors, catalogs, Web sites, and discount retailers are all enticing the customer to buy from them. Employees should be trained to consistently and sincerely thank their clientele. A spoken word, a thank-you note, or a follow-up call can help generate repeat business and encourage word-of-mouth promotion. Again, the employees should be provided with the tools to do this job successfully. One entrepreneur provided employees with stamped postcards to use as thank-you notes. She rewarded those employees who faithfully sent these cards to customers along with a merchandise gift certificate.

Another method of following up on the sale is maintaining a client file. Employees are asked to complete customer profile forms that contain information about the customer, contact information, size, brand preferences, past purchases, and personal information. An example of a customer profile form is shown in Figure 12.2. Such forms enable the sales associate to preselect newly arrived merchandise for the customer, and to contact the customer for an early look at the items. In essence, it encourages the sales associate to be a personal shopper for the customers.

Handling Customer Complaints

Some people avoid conflict. Some take it personally. Others resolve the problem and use the experience to improve and grow. Employees need to be educated on how to handle complaints. The entrepreneur should clarify how employees should handle disgruntled customers. Additionally, the entrepreneur should let employees know when and to whom they should refer complaints they feel they cannot resolve themselves. Personnel, merchandise, and general business complaints need to be communicated to the supervisor by the staff in order to effectively resolve problems. Additionally, the entrepreneur may want to implement procedures to allow employees to make suggestions or voice

Figure 12.2

CLIENT PROFILE

NAME Irene Magnin		TITLE or NICKNAME Mrs.	
DATE ENTERED 1/20/02	☐ CASH ☐ CHARGE	CUSTOMER NUMBER 160 01 7872	
CHARGE ACCOUNT Visa		OTHER CHARGE TYPE ☐ AE ☐ MC	VALID/EXP. DATE 10/03

ADDRESS (Billing Address)
1000 Broadway

CITY San Francisco	STATE CA	ZIP CODE 94109

SECOND ADDRESS
2600 Park Avenue

CITY Palm Desert	STATE CA	ZIP CODE 92260

HOME PHONE (415) 555-1212	OFFICE PHONE (415) 555-0821

OCCUPATION
Owner of Fragrance Company

CONTACT PREFERENCE ☐ PHONE ☐ HOME ☐ WORK ☐ MAIL ☐ EMAIL	PREFERRED CONTACT TIME No Weekends–10-12 AM (M-F)

BIRTHDAY 4/14	OTHER SPECIAL DATES 2/22–anniversary, 10/18–daughter's birthday

SIZE INFORMATION
6–jacket, pants, skirt, dress
4 or 6–shirt

VENDOR AND STYLE PREFERENCES
Likes updated, Armani-ish styles, lightweight, quality fabrics, subtle, pulled together, combos.
Travels–packable coordinates

PERSONAL INFORMATION
Approximately 5'6", slender
Age–late 40s/early 50s
Demanding, sense of humor
ASK ABOUT DAUGHTER (a new SF attorney)

concerns. It is better for the employee to discuss business problems with the supervisor rather than to share them with other employees or customers.

INVENTORY AND OPERATIONS

The inventory is one of the business's most significant assets. Too much or too little of it can undermine the best sales associates, the best promotional campaign, and the best location. In order to carry the right amount and type of merchandise, certain information must be available. Data on how much stock is on hand, which vendors are selling or are not selling, and what customers are or are not buying, can be accurately accessed if operations and control strategies are put into place.

Methods of Inventory Management

Careful inventory management is one of the most important contributing factors to a successful fashion business. Each piece of merchandise simply hanging around, whether on the sales floor or in the stock room, represents money that has been spent and is losing value because of the perishability of fashion goods. On the other hand, if there is an inadequate amount of inventory, then the entrepreneur cannot expect to reach sales goals. Often, not only are sales lost, but customers who did not find what they were looking for will not return. Maintaining the right level of inventory is a balancing act. Information is the key to finding the right balance.

The type and amount of information shared about the customer, the sales staff, the buyer, and the vendors can directly affect the quality of inventory management. If the buyer has access to information about what exactly is and is not selling and has relationships with vendors that allow him or her to respond to this information, the inventory will be what the customer wants when he or she wants it. **Just-in-time inventory control** is dependent upon the vendor-buyer relationship and adequate communication systems. Just-in-time refers to the system in which inventory is shipped as it is sold. Hanes, for example, provides a just-in-time inventory replenishment system. The retailer provides sales data to Hanes as soon as the merchandise is sold, most often through the computer system. As the retailer has established a model stock with the vendor, Hanes can automatically ship fill-ins for sold merchandise. As a result, the stock is maintained, the customer does not find that what they are looking for is out of stock, and the buyer does not spend time counting inventory and placing reorders.

Inventory Control

There are two primary methods for valuing and recording inventory. The first, referred to as "last in, first out" (LIFO), places a higher value on most recently received merchandise. The second, "first in, first out" (FIFO), applies higher value to goods according to the order in which they were received. As these methods can have significantly different tax implications, depending on the business, most entrepreneurs consult with an accountant before determining which valuation method to apply.

Shrinkage is the industry term for inventory losses resulting from employee theft, shoplifting, and clerical errors. A **physical inventory count** is a formal, item-by-item analysis of the operation's stock on hand. The vendor, style number, and selling price of each item are recorded, and then all prices are totaled to create a physical price inventory dollar valuation. The physical inventory is usually conducted at the end of a selling season when the stock level is at a low point, either annually or biannually. The result of the physical inventory is compared to the book inventory, the financial record of the stock. If there is less physical inventory than book inventory, the difference is referred to as a shortage. Shortages are caused by theft and bookkeeping errors, such as not recording markdowns or employee discounts. In contrast, if the physical inventory is greater than the book inventory, the difference is called overage. An overage indicates that there are clerical errors in one of the accounting functions, such as recording merchandise receipts, posting markdowns, or returning goods to the manufacturer.

Merchandise Fulfillment and Customer Needs

Finding the right product for the customer is the first step. Making certain the customer receives this product, in good condition, and in a timely manner, is the critical follow-up step. Training employees, from those responsible for shipping to those responsible for selling, in customer services can pay dividends in repeat business and referrals. The entrepreneur will want to develop policies and procedures that allow employees to accommodate customer special orders or special requests. Employees should be empowered to make certain decisions on their own, such as exchanging merchandise, rather than requiring the customer to wait for management assistance.

How does the entrepreneur assess merchandise fulfillment processes as they relate to customer service? Merchandise fulfillment refers to the process of filling customers' orders. In most cases, it encompasses mail, phone, and Internet ordering, rather than on-the-floor sales. The entrepreneur will want to develop a process and assign herself or himself, or a staff member, to hear customer feedback, from complaints to congratulations. In purchasing, the buyer will want to assess vendors in terms of who can provide special orders or rush deliveries. In the inventory area, management will want to evaluate the presentation and accessibility of merchandise. In the sales area, service provided to customers after purchases are made should be examined. Are alternatives, repairs, returns, and warranties adequately provided to the customer? In the receiving area, the level of accuracy and amount of lead time between receipt of new shipments and availability on the selling floor should be examined. Supply chain management is a trend in merchandise fulfillment that enables the entrepreneur to provide customers with goods in a timely manner.

Supply chain management (SCM) refers to an integrated approach to all the activities of channel members. Certain activities are performed by the channel member who can do them most efficiently. For example, if a vendor is able to ship merchandise tagged and on hangers more efficiently than the retailer can, then the vendor will take over these operations in SCM. Additionally, the vendor may ship a special order directly to the customer to save the retailer and the consumer time and money. The vendor may also service products as part of SCM. For example, a customer may purchase a watch with a manufacturer's warranty from a retail operation. If the watch needs repair, rather than returning it to the retailer, the customer may send the watch directly to the vendor for repairs or replacement. As the manufacturer has the equipment and knowledge to most effectively satisfy the customer, it takes on the responsibility of repairs. Channel partnerships that benefit all members are the primary objectives of SCM.

RESEARCH AND DEVELOPMENT

Change is an unchanging part of operation. The entrepreneur who views his or her business with an eye toward the future has a greater probability for success than one who does not. A business's target market is always changing; it is growing older, developing new tastes, and seeking new products to satisfy new needs. Research and development refers to an ongoing analysis of trends and issues that may affect the products, services, operations, promotional efforts, competitors, and customers of the business. Some companies establish relatively large research and development areas because they deal with constantly evolving technology, rapidly changing fashion trends, or a target market with a great need for new products. Research and development activities may encompass running a complete department staffed with personnel inventing or experimenting with new products, promotional techniques, and equipment. Research and development may also be spearheaded by one person, usually the entrepreneur, who attends conferences and subscribes to publications that focus on the future of the industry or the product classification(s) of the business. Regardless of the scope of the efforts, research and development must be a goal in the operational plan of any type of business.

In research and development, the business examines its product types and industry trends from a futuring perspective. Some of the questions that may be asked by the person responsible for managing research and development include the following:

- What new products and services are currently in development?
- What percent of the staff's time, including the entrepreneur's, is dedicated to research and development?
- What resources, such as publications, seminars, and Internet resources, are used by the business as sources for research and development data?
- What equipment and supplies, such as software and merchandise samples, are needed for effective research and development?
- What costs are associated with research and development activities in the business?
- How are research and development findings disseminated within the business?

Research and development may reveal that change provides new opportunities for growth.

OPERATIONS AND THE COMPUTER

Nowhere has change had more impact and speed than in the area of technology. The microcomputer was created by entrepreneurs. It is as though it was designed for entrepreneurs. The right computer, with the right software, can make all the difference in a business. It takes orders, handles details, files, cross-checks files, prints, copies, calculates payroll, determines vendor performance, keeps the entrepreneur in touch with business information that will help the company survive, and analyzes the future of profit and cash flow. An electronic spreadsheet, a computer generated chart, simplifies this daunting task and increases accuracy. Entrepreneurs have found the computer to be extremely useful in maintaining not only financial records, but also databases on target customers.

Through **cross-filing,** a reference system in which the same information is listed in two or more categories, customer files can be used to generate mailing lists for promotional fliers and newsletters. For example, the entrepreneur of a children's apparel store can download the names of all customers who have purchased merchandise from a specific vendor, in order to send these particular clients invitations to a trunk showing for the line. From a different operational perspective, retail buyers can gain invaluable information through computerized reports. Through point-of-sale software, the buyer can see what customers purchased in terms of item, size, color, cost, retail price, frequency, and vendor. On the flip side, the buyer can see how each vendor has performed in all of these variables. The result is better job of planning purchase orders, placing reorders, and taking timely markdowns.

How does the entrepreneur choose the right computer for the business? The computer selection process consists of three steps. First, the entrepreneur should identify problems that need solving and tasks that need to be done. Once the entrepreneur has developed the operations and control systems for the business, the problems and tasks to be executed will become clearer. Next, the entrepreneur will need to review software that can solve the problems and do the tasks. Third, the entrepreneur needs to locate the hardware that will accommodate the software and the company's budget. Computer consultants recommend budgeting at least 50 percent of the total system cost for software. It is important to buy a system that is expandable. The business will expand, so should the computer. Finally, the entrepreneur should invest time in computer education, either through on-line training or a computer course, in order to maximize computer capabilities and, ultimately, its productivity.

CONCLUSION

Planning operations and control for a business means determining how the actual day-to-day functions of the company will be run. These are the fundamentals of the business, its foundation. Without a clearly laid-out foundation, the business will have difficulty thriving. In operations and control, each internal function is analyzed; every step is evaluated. From facility layout to merchandise receipts to product sales, operational mechanisms are needed to provide staff and customers with consistency, accuracy, and quality. The first area requiring operational and control standards is the facility. Next, the entrepreneur must develop procedures to make certain the staff is effectively trained. Inventory management and control strategies help ensure that the right products are available to the customer. Research and development strategies are planned as part of operations to ensure business growth. Finally, computer operations are developed to support the facility, employees, inventory, and research and development.

In the business plan, the operation and control section is not thoroughly detailed. In it, discussion is limited to those operational and control issues essential to the nature and success of the business. The focus is on the operational and control strategies that provide the business with a competitive advantage, such as how this business will overcome a problem that similar businesses have not. The primary results of careful analysis in operations and control are the policies and procedures that will actually run the company after it is open for business.

WRITING THE PLAN

Develop the operating and control section of the business plan by providing brief procedure statements using the following topics from Chapter 14 as a guide:

SECTION	TOPIC
Operating and Control Systems	Receiving orders
	Paying suppliers
	Reporting to management
	Staff Development
	Inventory Control
	Handling returns
	Company budgets
	Security systems
	Documents and paper flow
	Risk Analysis
	3 planning charts: product availability, financial requirements, and marketing flow

Business Mentor™ CD-ROM—Business Plan—Operations and Control Section.

KEY TERMS

base plus commission
bonus
book inventory
client file
compensation
completion date
control
cross-filing
customer mobility
dating
employee procedures manual
FIFO (first in, first out)
fixed rate compensation
hourly plus commission
incentives
invoice
just-in-time inventory control
layaway
LIFO (last in, first out)
markdown
merchandise discount
merchandise fulfillment

nonselling space
operations
overage
packing slip
physical inventory count
point-of-sale
quota plus commission
return authorization label
research and development
RTM (return to the manufacturer)
RTV (return to the vendor)
sales commission
selling space
shortage
shrinkage
spreadsheet
stockkeeping unit
straight commission
supply chain management (SCM)
tracking merchandise
transaction
variable-rate (merit) compensation

QUESTIONS

1. Describe the difference between operational and control procedures and policies.
2. List the operational considerations that relate to the location of the business.
3. What are the four classifications of location space?
4. Provide an example of applying space efficiency for sales associates in a fashion retail business.
5. Research the legal requirements defined by the federal government for providing customer mobility for disabled persons in retail establishments.
6. What is the significance of a completion, or cancellation, date for a purchase order to the retail buyer?
7. What are the differences between the packing slip and the invoice provided by the manufacturer?
8. Describe the procedure for tracking merchandise sales and returns through a point-of-sale computerized system.
9. What is the process for returning merchandise to a vendor?
10. What are the important topics to be included in an employee procedures manual?
11. Consider the various forms of employee compensation including the following: fixed-rate, variable-rate, straight commission, quota plus commission, and base plus commission. Which form of compensation would most significantly benefit the entrepreneur? The sales associate of a fashion service organization? The shipping clerk in a mail-order business? The alteration person in a fashion retail store?
12. Contrast LIFO and FIFO methods of inventory control. Which is preferable and why?
13. What is the difference between book and physical inventory?
14. What is meant by the term, supply chain management? Provide an illustration of how the entrepreneur can motivate channel members to work as a team.
15. In what ways can the entrepreneur of a fashion specialty store operation conduct research and development?
16. List the three steps recommended to the entrepreneur who is selecting a computer for the new business.

CASE STUDY

We assume that your desire to open an apparel store is not because you want to prove to your old high school friends that you are actually hip and happening or that you are so confident of your style that you need to share that good taste with the community. We instead assume that you have an acute business sense, a sincere interest in the clothing business, and more than a little cash in the bank. Opening an apparel store is serious business. For some, it may mean giving up the safety of a corporate job with its steady income, paid holidays, fringe benefits, and opportunities for advancement. It may mean giving up all this in order to take on 12- to 14-hour days. "Running an apparel store is more than a full-time job," stresses Nancy Stanfort, professor of merchandising at Oklahoma State University. "Running an apparel store is something you do all day everyday."

Fortunately, there is always room for the right kind of apparel store. Although one might not guess it by the number of malls and outlet centers cropping up, we are mostly a nation of small, independent merchants. In fact, most retail stores, and that includes apparel stores, are small, both in size and in sales volume, compared to a Gap or Old Navy. The typical apparel store is a small operation, usually run by the owner alone or by a husband and wife team. Here is handy set of questions that will help you determine whether fashion in indeed your forte.

1. *Is this a business in which you have experience?* Maybe you have taken those merchandising classes; maybe you've watched your father, mother, or grandparents run a business; maybe you spent a summer selling makeup over the counter at Macy's. In any case, your experience and business sense are as important as your interest in clothes.
2. *Can you live with the risk inherent in the apparel business?* This is not meant to scare you; it is meant to present a balanced picture. If you are serious about an apparel store, you need to know that, like the restaurant business, the apparel business is risky. You may pour your life savings into a business that goes bust within a year. "Nothing is sure-fire, and there are risks attached to starting any

kind of business," says Fred Derring, president and owner of D.L.S. Outfitters, a New York City–based apparel marketing and consulting company, "but you've really got to love the clothing business because you can make more money doing almost anything else. Even in the restaurant business—if you're successful—you can make more money in five years than you can in 15 years in the apparel business."

3. *Do you believe strongly in the apparel industry?* You really need to think why you've decided to open an apparel store, as opposed to a homeopathic pharmacy or an organic grocery store. Whatever your particular fashion passion, it has to be enough to carry you through the yearly holiday rushes as well as the slow summer lulls. It is like marriage: When times get tough, you need to remember why you took those vows in the first place.

4. *Is your niche overcrowded or dominated by a few?* It doesn't take a Ph.D. to see that the apparel industry is crowded. All you need to do is save all those catalogs stuffed in the mailbox or visit your local mall on the weekend. However, there always seems to be room for more, particularly if the retailer is offering consumers something they feel they are lacking.

5. *Can you become a specialist?* If you are opening an apparel store for the right reasons, you probably think you have got something someone else in your professional community does not. Maybe it is surf clothes; maybe it's chic plus-size fashions; maybe it's leather and jewelry imported from Turkey. Specializing, or finding your niche in this business, is crucial to your success. In many cases, all it takes is a little common sense. As Kira Danus, a buyer from D.L.S. Outfitters in New York City, says, "No apparel store should be stocking twill khaki shorts if there's a Gap within ten miles."

6. *Do you have a competitive advantage?* In a word, this is called "marketing." For now, hear this collective quote culled for every apparel entrepreneur in the country: "Today the competition isn't two doors down the block; it's at the local mall. People can get everything we sell at their local mall, so we have to set ourselves apart in other ways Pay attention to the demographics in your area, to the location and available foot traffic, to television and movies and what people are wearing on the street."

Compiled by Laura Tiffany, *How to Start an Apparel Business, an Entrepreneur Start-up Guide* (Irvine, California: Source: Small-BizBooks.com, 2000)

CASE STUDY QUESTIONS

1. What have you done, in terms of work experience, cocurricular activities, and community service, that will help prepare you to be an entrepreneur in the fashion retail business? What do you plan to do to build your portfolio of pre–entrepreneurial knowledge?

2. Why would you choose fashion entrepreneurship? Do you agree with Mr. Derring's comparison to the restaurant industry? Gather current data—facts and figures and their sources—to support your position.

3. What is your passion in the fashion industry? Is it a service, e-commerce, a particular merchandise classification, or a designer?

4. What is an area of expertise, a specialty niche, that you believe you can conquer? Describe successful entrepreneurial firms that made their fortunes in niche merchandising. How does your work experience support your future endeavors in the niche you have chosen?

5. What will separate your business from its competition? How will you market it to create an image and a customer following?

6. How do consumer demographic trends look in the next decade? How does your business concept and its merchandise offerings fit with this picture?

ENTERING THE WORLD OF THE ENTREPRENEUR

1. Talk to an entrepreneur about the operating and control systems in place for the retail operation. How has this system helped in staff efficiency, customer mobility, and inventory control?

2. What systems are in place to monitor customer service?
3. What systems are in place to monitor quality of goods received?
4. Provide a list of the operating and control systems for a local fashion retail store.
5. How do the control systems of a franchise differ from those of a "mom and pop" fashion retail store?
6. How does customer services within a franchise operation differ from that of a local retail operation? Give examples.

ENTERPRISING ENTREPRENEUR

Judy George is the founder and chief executive officer of Domain Home Fashions. George started Domain because, she states, "I had a vision. Wanting to share my vision with others, the best way I knew to do that was to develop my brand. If people could recognize the name, and associate it with a quality product, then they'd come into my stores, and we'd be successful. Sounds easy enough, but it's not. Building a brand should not be your end goal. It's merely one step on the path toward a thriving business. I learned that the hard way. But having a name people can identify with doesn't hurt!" George gives five sound pieces of advice to prospective entrepreneurs. First, she encourages them to carefully do their homework. Second, she suggests that entrepreneurs work to create brand identity, rather than another store. Third, she recommends that entrepreneurs recognize the importance of both promotion and public relations. Fourth, she stresses the need for a management team that can cover all the bases. Finally, George reminds prospective entrepreneurs to maintain their individual visions.

Homework was a two-decade assignment for George. During her 20 years of experience in the furniture industry before creating Domain, George used that time to learn everything she could about the industry. George states, "Before spending one single cent establishing my brand, I did my homework." She constantly attended furniture fairs, conducted research, and developed the "look" that ended up being the cornerstone of Domain's business. George recognized a market that she did not believe was being attended to properly. People had been reading lifestyle and home-related magazines for decades, but they could never find a store that matched what they were reading. She set out to change that. Traveling across the country, interviewing customers of furniture stores as they came out, she listened, asked questions, and spent as much time as possible determining what they wanted in a furniture store. Her investigation covered three primary topics: what they liked, what they did not like, and what they felt could be done better. Combining her industry experience with what these potential customers were saying, she realized she could create something unique and truly special. The end result was Domain, a store that catered to the individual—providing a beautiful place for a customer to explore his or her own individuality and creativity when it came to furnishing one's home. George explains, "Inventing a catchy name is not the key to branding success. Homework, research, and preparation are the real secrets. It made me realize that my customers were women brought up on reading glossy lifestyle magazines. They saw all these lovely homes on the pages, but could never find a store to live up to those magazines. I set out to give them that place."

Building the business's identity was the next step. Once she had the idea, George set out to tell people about it. It was her mission to create a store that catered to everyone, no matter his or her age, or social and economic background. The goal was to create a lifestyle brand, a place where people could explore their individuality. Cohesive product lines in an appealing environment that allows for changing looks form the foundation for a lifestyle brand. George describes the task, "Building a brand for everyone isn't so easy. I opened my stores in shopping malls and spent a lot of time creating nice window displays. They were changed frequently, just like a clothing store. I wanted people to see something fresh every time they walked by. If you can spark someone's imagination, then you increase the chances of her walking in and buying something."

Visual merchandising was not the only key to reaching the consumer. A promotional campaign was implemented to herald the message. When the first stores were launched, George ran full-color advertisements in all the major newspapers to show the public what was being offered. Advertisements were designed with particular attention to image. The objective was to give the customer a small taste of the experience that would be provided in the stores. George also hired a traditional public relations company. She believes that paid professionals helped tell the customers that she was offering a decorator look at reasonable prices. The messages needed to imply that Domain wasn't going to be the cheapest store in town, but she was determined to offer high-quality items that were also attainable. It did not take long for the media to pay attention.

The power of the press soon became apparent, as the media began to show interest in Judy George. Right from the start, she made herself available as the person behind the brand name. People like to know who is responsible, as well as who the person is behind the idea. George explains, "Life is about relationships and so is brand loyalty. Wanting my customers to connect with the store's concept, I had to let them know the buck was stopping with me, and that I had their best interests at heart." Of course, it helped that George is a rare commodity, a female CEO of a retail chain. She did not hide from the media; she enthusiastically answered their requests. She went on radio, conducted press interviews, and then national television programs. George believes that an entrepreneur cannot hide behind the business's name if he or she wants it to be successful because "no one likes dealing with a faceless organization." She made the decision to become more of a public figure. In fact, at that point, her investors wanted to call the store "Judy George," but she resisted. People within the furniture industry knew her, she insisted, while her customers did not. Judy states, "The name would've been terrific for my ego, but a failure in the marketplace. The name Domain gives a greater sense of my goals—to make the customer feel she is in charge of her own space. Setting ego aside is an important part of the process too."

The hardest part of building a brand is delivering on the promise. George's idea almost died because she did not initially get that part right. After several years, it was clear she was getting people to come into the stores, but was far from perfect on the delivery side. The company struggled for a couple of years after that before it reorganized, refocused on infrastructure, and moved forward. George describes this process, "You can have the most well-known brand in the world, but if you can't back it up with a quality product, you'll fail very quickly. I can't say this strongly enough. Do not get too focused on the name and the image—spend even more time on the product and the consistent delivery." Customers were coming into the stores and enjoying their experiences, until it was time for the furniture to be delivered. George had hired a whole crew of Judy Georges, people like her with great passion and vision, when she really needed people focused on the details and the infrastructure. It was all part of the learning experience. She listened as customers told her that having a nice brand and a nice store is terrific, but "if you can't get my furniture to me in one piece, at the time you say, then I'm not coming back." George worked to build a solid core of people with different skills.

Finally, Judy George advises that the entrepreneur keep sight of his or her vision. Once all the research has been completed, all the foundations have been laid, a solid team has been built, and the market niche has been identified, only then does the entrepreneur have a true vision. Next, when the entrepreneur truly starts building the brand, he or she must stick to that vision. George elaborates on this concept, "You'll hit some tough times. During these tough times, plenty of people will suggest ways to improve your business; however, stay the course. Know who you are and what you're trying to achieve." George reminds the entrepreneur that this does not mean he or she should be inflexible. The entrepreneur needs to continue to listen to the customer, but to try to be proactive instead of reactive. Sometimes it will be a real struggle to maintain one's vision, but it's the only way to survive The entrepreneur has spent all this time building a brand and building a company, so why risk all of that for short-term gain? In terms of her own work as an entrepreneur, she concludes, "Creating this company—this brand name—has been the most satisfying thing I have ever done in business. I am so proud now of my stores and of my people. It is a wonderful feeling to know that people appreciate the brand and enjoy my stores. But I have to keep working, keep listening, and keep learning, so that Domain can continue to make people happy for years to come."

Source: www.entreworld.com

Chapter 13

PLANNING GROWTH STRATEGIES

INTRODUCTION

Many businesses become successful and then require a strategy for growth. Growth strategies refer to the plans that enable the entrepreneur to build and expand upon the initial business. Growth strategies should be examined before the business actually opens. In the previous chapters, the business was conceived and developed as though it would open, become established, grow, and profit. In the final part of the business plan, the growth plan is covered. It addresses the resources needed to take the business to the next level.

STRATEGIC GROWTH PLANNING

It is tough deciding to start a business. Once the decision is made, the entrepreneur must devote the time, energy, and money needed to guide it through its beginning life stages. When the business reaches the growth stage, it will either stall or move forward. Either way, the entrepreneur will want to minimize risk by having a plan in place. The preferred plan is, obviously, to guide the business into a growing, thriving company. Strategic growth planning is needed to meet this objective.

Success catches the eye of competition. The business that survives its initial growth stages and flourishes enters a new strategic arena in that new competitors frequently enter the market. This competitive environment presents new challenges. For example, Ralph Lauren established an extremely successful business with his Americana fashion lines. Soon, Tommy Hilfiger entered the scene and targeted the same market at a lower price point. Later, Abercrombie and Fitch opened its retail stores with private label merchandise aimed to take a bite out of the same target market. Still later, American Eagle followed as a direct competitor with lower priced goods. New competitors of successful companies emerge at a frenetic pace. Competition is a fact of life in the fashion retail world. Unless a company has a competitive advantage that is protected by patents, trade secrets, and proprietary skills, competition can be expected to emerge, increase, and ultimately threaten market share. Growth strategies can be classified in the following three ways: strategies for facing new competition, strategies for becoming a market leader, and strategies for creating a niche.

Strategies for Facing New Competition

How does the entrepreneur anticipate this emerging competitive environment? There are three primary strategies that can reduce the negative impact of new market entries. First, reduced costs of merchandise, distribution, and overhead can provide the entrepreneur with options that may maintain or increase market share. Through these savings, the entrepreneur may decide to decrease the retail price of goods, either on a regular basis or during clearance periods. The entrepreneur may use this pool of funds to increase promotional endeavors such as a greater number of advertisements, additional media channels, and in-store events, such as fashion shows. Additionally, the entrepreneur may elect to use the money to increase customer services, such as free alterations or free shipping. The goal is to maintain the current customer's interest, while adding new patrons to the market share.

Second, the entrepreneur can work, from the start, to create a successful transition from product introduction to the creation of value for the customer. If the customer is convinced that if he or she could purchase the product elsewhere the level of service and breadth of selection would be less satisfactory, then the entrepreneur has accomplished this task. A significant number of specialty stores are thriving as a result of their successful implementation of this strategy. While department stores may carry the same lines, perhaps even the identical styles, many customers prefer the personalized attention and intimate atmosphere of a well-operated specialty store. The attributes of service, environment, and convenience add value to the actual product lines. Another important component of creating value for the consumer is establishing positive brand identity, which is the third strategy for facing an influx of new competitors.

Through positive brand indentity, the entrepreneur can work to establish relationships with vendors that offer critical, exclusive goods. Through this plan, the entrepreneur can negotiate with manufacturers to limit competitors' access to these lines and to ensure timely, complete deliveries. How does the entrepreneur accomplish this task? One method is to commit to purchasing future lines. For example, the entrepreneur may agree to place a specific amount of money on next season's line in order to maintain an exclusive arrangement. Another option is to procure private label merchandise for the business, from a private label vendor, a manufacturer, or through a resident buying office. Additionally, the entrepreneur may seek out new, undiscovered vendors that will provide unique merchandise with limited distribution resulting from limited production capabilities. The ultimate goal of all three strategies is to develop and maintain a high level of customer loyalty to stave off the competition.

Strategies for Becoming a Market Leader

If the business has the largest market share as its market enters a growth stage, it is referred to as a market leader. Market leaders face different challenges from the entrepreneurial businesses that may be significant market players, but that are not market leaders. While most entrepreneurial businesses cannot lay claim to the market leader position, it is important to examine the strategic options for the market leaders. Market leaders often increase promotional efforts in order to firmly establish their names in the marketplace. They turn up the sound, tooting their own horns through national advertising, often with status messages. These messages imply that it is popular and prestigious to purchase the market leader's products or to shop at his or her retail operation. Market leaders may fortify their position by purchasing suppliers and/or distributors, thus blocking competition from entering the market. An example is Neiman Marcus and its purchase of the handbag company, Kate Spade. As part of its strategic growth plan, Neiman Marcus allocated funds to purchase key vendors. This strategy provides the specialty store chain with exclusive goods, the earliest deliveries, and the best possible prices. From the manufacturer's perspective, it was a win/win situation. Kate Spade was a privately owned entrepreneurial business. The sale of the company has allowed its principals to expand into new merchandise categories, such as home accessories. (The case studies at the end of this chapter provide the details on this business arrangement.)

Strategies for Creating a Market Niche

Many entrepreneurial businesses enter the growth stage in a strong market position while not being market leaders. The majority of entrepreneurial businesses, often small companies, simply do not have the resources necessary to compete directly with market leaders. They can, however, find ways to grow substantially, particularly through niche retailing. Niche retailing identifies and fulfills the specific merchandise needs of a specific customer group. There are two main strategies for niche retailing. First, the entrepreneur can aggressively identify and develop a market niche whose needs most closely match the company's capabilities and distinctive competencies. Through niche marketing, the entrepreneur focuses on specific product lines geared toward a particular group of customers. The entrepreneur must know in detail who this customer is and what he or she is wanting to purchase. The critical element in niche marketing is accurately determining the strategic and operational fit between the company and the market segment's needs. Mail-order retailers provide excellent illustrations of niche marketing. There are shoe catalogs for those with narrow feet, catalogs for people who love to dress their dogs, and catalogs for persons who prefer jewelry with a Southwestern look.

Second, the entrepreneur can establish a niche in fashion retailing by developing a "follow the leader" strategy. This certainly contrasts with the market leader position; however, it can be an extremely successful plan in strong economic conditions. If, for example, there are a number of major retailers succeeding in selling large-sized fashions, then the entrepreneur may focus on this niche in similar looks, at a lower price, and in a specific merchandise classification, such as sportswear. When price compensates for the designer label, then the specialty retailer has an opportunity to tap into this profitable market segment.

Entrepreneurs who succeed in getting through the growth stage face a new challenge, one of transformation. They must transform their businesses to remain competitive and, subsequently, to maintain success. Organizational competitiveness results when companies consistently and continually improve their product lines, services, and operations. One of the current trends and issues in growth planning for businesses is that of global expansion.

GOING GLOBAL AS A GROWTH STRATEGY

Taking a company global has become a growth strategy for small businesses as well as large corporations. Until recently, only those corporations with financial resources to reach foreign markets and withstand a failed venture could tap into the global economy. Entrepreneurs have begun to look beyond national borders for market opportunities. Small companies have the ability to react to changes in the market faster than giant corporations do, thus giving them an edge in competing with larger companies. "The Organization for Economic Cooperation and Development (OECD) projects the growth rate of global business to be 3.5 to 4 percent per year over the next two decades. At that rate of growth, global trade will double by the year 2020."[1]

The fashion industry relies on the global market to manufacture textiles, develop products, and produce clothing and accessories. Fashion businesses in the United States both import and export fashion products. With the creation of the World Wide Web, fashion manufacturers, designers, and retailers can more easily promote and sell their products throughout the world. U.S. companies, such as Gap, Inc., and The Limited Corporation, have opened retail stores abroad. Conversely, H & M and Sephora, European retailers, are opening their doors in the United States.

Businesses of any size must recognize that, in a global economy, the competition increases. Careful consideration and extensive research should be done before an entrepreneur enters the international marketplace. Managing an international business is quite different from managing a domestic business. Economics, politics, culture, and technology are often uncontrollable factors that influence the decision to take the company global. There are many opportunities and benefits to taking a company global. A list of these follows:

- While a market for a particular product may be declining in the United States, it may be thriving in another country.
- Dealing with another country forces the business owner and his or her employees to be open to cultural differences. The owner and employees learn to be sensitive and respond to various customs, preferences, and unique tastes. They learn to become more customer-oriented.
- The demand to export goods to other countries has increased. This demand can help a company increase sales, and profits.
- Customers in other countries may be more difficult to satisfy than those in the United States. This can force a U.S. company to raise the standard of quality to a level that can compete in the global market.

In addition to benefits, taking a company global presents a set of challenges. Any company contemplating a global presence must first be aware of the purchasing habits and attitudes of customers in other countries. It may be important to employ multilingual people or to contract with a firm that offers language interpreting and cultural advice. Companies must continually look for innovative ways to deliver goods faster and better than their competitors. They must consider the capital requirements of taking a company global from financial and personnel perspectives. There is no point in taking a company global unless the business can make a profit in the currency in which the headquarters is located. The exchange rate for currency may make the overseas venture too costly. The successful global entrepreneur will understand the differences between international and domestic business, and then take the necessary steps to research the venture.

Avenues to Global Growth

Many strategies exist for entering the global market. This section provides an overview of some of the most common avenues to global growth. (For an in-depth look at all the variables that must be considered in determining the avenue through which to take the company's product into the international markets and the ways in which to enter international markets, investigate specific organizations and Web sites.) The four primary avenues of growth in the global marketplace are the World Wide Web, exports, international locations, and foreign licensing.

Using the World Wide Web   Perhaps the most inexpensive and simplest way for a small company to enter international markets is by using the World Wide Web (WWW). Access to a well-developed Web site allows potential and existing customers around the globe access to products 24 hours per day, 7 days per week. Web sites can be developed at very little cost. Access to the World Wide Web provides not only a means of communication, but also an avenue to research other markets. Communicating through e-mail provides entrepreneurs with the ability to reach customers quickly and easily. Technology also provides the entrepreneur with opportunity to purchase goods on the WWW via a secure line.

Exporting   For most small companies, a barrier to exporting goods is a lack of understanding of the process of exportation. To begin, a company should first assess its readiness to export. What does the company want to gain from exporting? Is exporting consistent with other company goals? What demands will exporting place on the company's key resources, management and personnel, production capacity, and finance and how will these demands be met? Are the expected benefits worth the costs, or would company resources be better used for developing new domestic business?[2]

Next, key management issues need to be addressed in order to analyze the impact exporting will have on the company in terms of human resources, as illustrated in the shaded box (page 314). Exporting requires a commitment of resources and time to develop markets abroad. As stated earlier, many organizations, mostly governmental agencies, exist to help entrepreneurs assess the feasibility of taking their products into markets outside their own country.

The next step is to research the market and define which foreign market(s) provides the most opportunity and/or place the most constraints on entering that market. Research will also help identify prospective buyers and customers.

Market research can be conducted through libraries and governmental agencies. Just as important is to stay informed about world events that may influence the international marketplace. This can be done through various media or by visiting the countries in question. Products may have to be modified to be accepted by foreign customers. Lifestyles, body types, cultures, and economics vary from country to country.

Next, it is necessary to determine how the product or service will be distributed—which channels of distribution will be used. Two types of exporting exist. Direct exporting, where selling goods to another country takes place through the parent company, or indirect exporting, where companies sell products to another country through another company in the entrepreneur's home country. In the fashion industry, a company may sell directly to foreign retailers, although products are generally limited to consumer lines. Many U.S. retailers maintain overseas buying offices and use these offices to sell abroad when it is practical.

Management Issues Involved in the Export Decision

1. Experience:
   - With what countries has business already been conducted, or from what countries have inquiries already been received?
   - Which product lines do foreign customers mention most often?
   - Are any domestic customers buying the product for sale or shipment overseas? If so, to what countries? Develop a list of these customers indicating which products they are buying.
   - Is the trend of sales and inquiries up or down?
   - Who are the main domestic and foreign competitors?
   - What general and specific lessons have been learned from past export attempts or experiences?

2. Management and personnel:
   - What in-house international expertise does the company have (international sales experience, language capabilities, etc.)?
   - Who will be responsible for the export department's organization and staff?
   - How much senior management time (a) should be allocated and (b) could be allocated?
   - What organizational structure is required to ensure that export sales are adequately serviced?
   - Who will follow through after the planning is done?

3. Product capacity:
   - How is the present production capacity being used?
   - Will filling export orders hurt domestic sales?
   - What will be the cost of additional production?
   - Are there fluctuations in the annual workload? When? Why?
   - What minimum order quantity is required?
   - What would be required to design and package products specifically for export?

4. Financial capacity:
   - What amount of capital can be committed to export production and marketing? Where will the needed capital come from?
   - What level of export department operating costs can be supported?
   - How are the initial expenses of export efforts to be allocated?
   - What other new development plans are in the works that may compete with export plans for the company's dollars?
   - By what date must an export effort pay for itself?

Adapted from *A Basic Guide to Exporting* (Washington, DC: U.S. Department of Commerce, 1998)
www.unzco.com/basicguide/table1.html.

The final steps required in exporting include financing the venture, shipping the product, and collecting payment from the foreign accounts. Loan programs exist through the Small Business Administration to assist entrepreneurs with financing. It is, however, still difficult to obtain financing. Bankers may not be comfortable initially financing a business exporting goods and services. Exporting is generally considered high risk. A good business plan, including a section within the marketing plan, on how the company will penetrate the foreign market and make money doing it, will help eliminate some of the discomfort.

Establishing an International Location   Establishing an international location may be challenging. Setting up a company in another country may require a significant amount of capital—sometimes more than the average small company budget would allow. Careful planning and research will help the entrepreneur create a realistic budget to approach funders for money. In some countries the infrastructure of the business world would present a challenge. Paperwork, lack of a good management pool from which to choose, and licenses and permits may make an international location prohibitive. Once an international location is established, however, a small company can often reap the rewards of lower labor costs.

Most companies "test the waters" in international markets by implementing one or more of the other six methods of global market entry before planning for the establishment of an international location. Establishing a site in an international location can require a significant investment that surpasses the financial resources of many small firms. There are, however, a number of fashion service operations that have found success through an international presence. Companies, such as fashion or color forecasting services, modeling agencies, and public relations firms, have realized that the addition of an office in London or Paris provides the image, exposure, and new clientele needed to generate profits that exceed the cost of operating the foreign office.

Foreign Licensing   Foreign licensing provides an opportunity for a company to enter foreign markets quickly and easily with almost no capital investment. Foreign licensing refers to a domestic company allowing a company overseas to license its patents, trademarks, technology, or products. In return, the domestic company collects a percent of the sales of products under its foreign licenses. For example, Gucci USA may allow a Swiss manufacturer to produce and retail watches under the Gucci label in exchange for a percent of all watch sales. In the foreign licensing agreement for a retail operation, the business is often exporting product and marketing knowledge to international markets rather than actual products.

Textile and apparel export efforts have brought special attention to international commerce. A program has been created to encourage and assist U.S. manufacturers in initiating or expanding export sales and to improve foreign market access for these products. The program provides information on overseas markets and counseling on entering those markets. It also facilitates the exchange of information between industry and government relative to improving exports of U.S. textile and apparel products. The program provides such vehicles as trade fairs and trade missions to improve exposure for U.S. textile and apparel firms, and it attempts to influence policy to identify and negotiate away foreign trade barriers and to examine other methods by which the environment for U.S. textile and apparel exports can be improved. The program is administered by the Market Expansion Division, Office of Textiles and Apparel.[3]

Entry Strategies for Global Avenues

Regardless of the selected global avenues, small retail companies interested in establishing a global operation have four methods of entry available. They are as follows: (1) collaborating with trade intermediaries, (2) establishing joint ventures, (3) franchising, and (4) countertrading and bartering. The simplest way of gaining entry to international markets is by using a trade intermediary. A trade intermediary is a business that serves as a distributor in foreign countries for domestic companies of all sizes. Trade intermediaries rely on networks of contacts, an extensive knowledge of local markets and customs, an understanding of currency exchange rates, and experience in international trade to market products effectively and efficiently around the world. Trade intermediaries can be classified as agent and merchant intermeditaries. Agent intermediaries sell the products of domestic companies in foreign markets without actually taking ownership of the merchandise. Essentially, they function as merchandise brokers, working on a commission basis. Merchant intermediaries actually purchase the goods at a discount from domestic companies and resell it abroad.

In a domestic joint venture, two or more U.S. businesses form an association for the purpose of exporting their goods and services abroad. These businesses share the costs, responsibilities, and risks of securing export licenses and permits. Additionally, they share the profits and losses. Franchising, discussed previously in Chapter 4, provides another entry opportunity for global expansion. Through foreign franchising, the U.S. entrepreneur sells the rights to his or her business concept and practices to a buyer who will open the retail operation overseas.

Due to the difficulty that some countries have in exchanging currencies, entrepreneurs of large firms may choose to sell products globally through a countertrade or barter system. A countertrade is a transaction in which a company selling goods and services in a foreign country agrees to help promote investment and trade in that country. Bartering, on the other hand, refers to finding a business with complementary needs in order to exchange some goods and services for others. While countertrading and bartering are not commonly used by entrepreneurs of small businesses to enter the global market, some creative entrepreneurs have used these options successfully. The owner of a home furnishings and accessories business in the United States for example, established a bartering arrangement with the owner of a similar operation in France. The two entrepreneurs trade American and European antiques, providing a supply of highly sought goods for the tastes of target markets on each side of the ocean.

Opening the Doors to Global Growth

Attitudes toward free trade among countries have changed over the last several years. In 1947, the General Agreement on Tariffs and Trade (GATT) was established as the first global tariff agreement. A tariff is a tax, or duty, that a government imposes on products and services imported into that country. Tariffs serve two purposes. They raise the prices of imported goods, making them less competitive with those offered by the host country. Additionally, they protect the producers of comparable products in the host country. A quota is a nontariff or a restriction on the amount of product that can be imported into a country or exported out of a country. Quotas can be classified by fabric type or product type. For example, one country may limit the poundage of cotton products imported, while another nation may restrict the quantity of women's sweaters that are allowed into its borders. Another form of nontariff is the embargo, a ban on imports of specific products. The objective of GATT was to make trade easier by eliminating or reducing tariffs and import quotas. Originally, the agreement was signed by the United States and 22 other nations. Today, GATT has over 124 member countries. A recent round of GATT negotiations, called the Uruguay Round, lasted from 1986 to 1993. Remaining industrial tariffs were reduced by 40 percent. Each round has shown more reductions in tariffs among member nations.

The North American Free Trade Agreement (NAFTA) created a free trade area among the United States, Canada, and Mexico. This agreement eliminated trade barriers among these three nations, but each remained free to set its own tariffs on imports from non-member nations. The agreement opened doors for small companies wanting to conduct business within these three countries.

The attitude of the entrepreneur can play a key role in determining whether to enter foreign markets. As discussed earlier, companies face not only domestic issues, such as financing and lack of information, but also political and cultural barriers as well. To be successful in an international market, the entrepreneur must have an understanding and respect for the belief system, values, views, language, and philosophies of the country in which he or she wants to conduct business. The entrepreneur must be aware of the politics involved in other countries. High-risk countries, in terms of government regulations, government takeovers of private property, and violent acts, threaten businesses and their employees.

For the entrepreneur considering global growth, an examination of the domestic, cultural, and international barriers that may inhibit international expansion is critical. The most prevalent domestic barrier is a lack of financing. Many banks are hesitant to fund international business transactions. Another domestic roadblock is the entrepreneur's mind-set toward global retailing opportunities. The entrepreneur of a small or new business may consider global growth as an option only for the "big hitters." Finally, a lack of information about foreign target markets, marketing strategies, currency exchanges, importing and exporting laws, among other topics, may dissuade the entrepreneur from contemplating global retailing. Information on these topics is available; the Small Business Administration and the U.S. Government Printing Office are two excellent sources of information on global retailing.

Cultural barriers refer to the differences in civilizations, the disparity in values and lifestyles among nations. Languages, work philosophies, business practices, etiquette, and traditions vary greatly from country to country. There is an extensive selection of books, as well as business courses, that analyze cultural differences as they relate to global business transactions. An understanding of cultural differences can often lead to recognition of international barriers to global retailing.

PLANNING FOR GROWTH

Once the entrepreneur has examined and defined specific strategies for growth, whether domestic or international, the next step is to analyze the estimated costs and potential revenues associated with implementing the growth plan. Expansion through starting additional sites, franchising, and/or enlargement of the original operation through new lines and departments are alternative growth strategies that entrepreneurs often consider. A current business trend by entrepreneurs who are expanding their companies is to add a manufacturing site to the business. The Limited Corporation, Zara, and H & M are fashion retail giants with the inventory flexibility and profit margins that come only from owning one's own manufacturing plants. Smaller firms are purchasing or building smaller manufacturing plants to follow their lead. Growth can also be generated through the purchase of another business. For example, the entrepreneur of a successful monogramming service in a college town may purchase the retail operation that sells T-shirts and other products to sororities and fraternities. The options for business growth are many and varied, depending on the type of business and its location. It is the entrepreneur's challenge to determine which growth alternatives will be most financially beneficial for the business, when they will be implemented, how much will it cost to implement them, and how much profit can be anticipated from each.

In the business plan, the growth strategies should be identified in the order they will be implemented. For example, the first phase of the growth plan may be expansion of the initial site. The second phase may be the addition of a second location, followed by the third phase which may be franchising the business. For each phase, the entrepreneur should identify the revenues that must be achieved before the business can move into that stage. In the growth section of the business plan, these options, as well as others the entrepreneur may develop, are referred to as new offerings to the market.

New Offerings to the Market

First, new offerings to the market must be examined in terms of new retail locations and merchandise offerings. Will the entrepreneur decide to open an additional location if the company's revenues warrant expansion? If so, the costs of opening a new site, staffing the location, promoting the new business, as well as filling it with merchandise, must be estimated. Where will a new business be located? Will there be additional costs associated with procuring and distributing merchandise? The entrepreneur will need to consider whether or not a new location will mean additional market trips, the hiring of a buyer, or a larger warehouse and distribution center. All these elements require capital that is currently not included in the company's cash flow needs.

In designing a growth plan, the entrepreneur should identify the levels of profits needed to support the various phases of the plan. For example, the entrepreneur will need to answer the following question in the business plan: "What are the financial requirements for pursuing a new product line or business location?" The ongoing cost of the growth strategy must be identified in terms of capital and personnel. Sometimes, the funds may be accessible to support the growth plan for an operation. If the personnel to run the expanded operation are not available or affordable, then the expansion will be destined to fail. Personnel needed to implement the growth strategy must be identified in terms of job titles and descriptions, as well as anticipated payroll and benefits costs. Additionally, the entrepreneur will want to investigate the labor market for such positions. As an illustration, an entrepreneur of a swimwear boutique determined that, as a growth strategy, she would offer custom swimwear by opening a small production facility. She leased the building, bought the machinery, and located skilled personnel to operate the sewing machines. She did not, however, investigate the availability and cost of finding a skilled pattern maker for swimwear in the Midwest. The cost of recruiting an experienced pattern maker from New York to Kansas was prohibitive. Planning for personnel was the weak link in her growth strategy.

Steps to Planning the Growth Stage

There are a number of strategies that the entrepreneur can put into place to avoid disasters during the growth stage of the business. First, the entrepreneur can clearly identify and prioritize the significant new products, services, and/or sites planned for continued growth. Second, he or she can be cautious not to overestimate the revenue these growth plans will likely generate. Third, he or she can prepare to have a management team and support staff available to execute the growth plans. Fourth, the entrepreneur can accurately identify the capital expenditure costs needed to implement the growth plan. Fifth, he or she can develop an effective system to control operations during the growth phase. Finally, the entrepreneur can plan ahead to have an exit point identified in the growth plan.

CONCLUSION

Strategic growth planning is developed before the business is actually opened. Growth strategies are described in the business plan to ensure that prospective funders see the potential for the proposed fashion retail operation. There are three primary strategies for growth planning: strategies for dealing with new competition, strategies for becoming a market leader, and strategies for developing a market niche. Entrepreneurs are finding that global expansion provides a significant opportunity for business growth. Whether domestic or international, growth strategies require careful analyses of product offerings, personnel requirements, and funding needs. Once these requirements are determined, the entrepreneur must develop a step-by-step plan to implement the selected growth strategies.

WRITING THE PLAN

Develop the growth section of the business plan using the following topics from Chapter 14 as a guide.

SECTION	TOPIC
Growth Plan	New offerings to the target market
	Capital requirements
	Personnel requirements
	Exit strategy

Business Mentor™ CD-ROM—Business Plan—Growth Section.

KEY TERMS

agent intermediary
bartering
countertrade
direct exporting
embargo
foreign licensing
General Agreement on Tariffs and Trade (GATT)
growth strategies
indirect exporting

joint venture
market leader
merchant intermediary
niche retailing
nontariff
North American Free Trade
  Agreement (NAFTA)
quota
tariff

QUESTIONS

1. What are the three primary types of growth strategies? Provide an example of a major fashion retailing operation that has successfully implemented each growth strategy.
2. List three retail entrepreneurs who started small, yet became market leaders in the fashion industry.
3. List consumer variables that a retailer may consider when determining a market niche.
4. Define the "follow the leader" strategy and explain how a small retailer would implement such a plan.
5. Is global expansion a realistic option for many entrepreneurs? What support systems ar available to small companies considering a global presence?
6. Of the seven methods of global entry, which do you believe is the most effective at the lowest cost for the largest number of entrepreneurs?
7. List the three most significant barriers to global expansion for entrepreneurs.
8. What are the options for expansion for the entrepreneur whose business is in a growth stage?
9. Construct a list of financial considerations for the entrepreneur planning expansion through the addition of a new retail store.

REFERENCES

1. Renato Ruiggiero, "The High Stakes of World Trade," *Wall Street Journal*, April 28, 1997, p. 21.
2. *A Basic Guide to Exporting* (Washington, D.C.: U.S. Department of Commerce, 1998) www.unzco.com
3. Ibid.

CASE STUDY 1

From a modest launch of six different boxy nylon totes in 1993, kate spade has now catapulted into a multimillion-dollar business in less than a decade. The company was founded by college sweethearts Kate Brosnahan and Andy Spade, who combined their names, talents, nest egg, and unpretentious belief in themselves to swiftly transform an idea into a collection of savvy and functional accessories. The couple met at Arizona State University. "It was love at first sight," Andy Spade remembers, "but neither one of us said anything about it. We were great friends and let it build slowly." After graduation, Kate Spade knocked around Europe by herself while Andy embarked on a successful career at an advertising agency in New York. When Kate returned to the United States, she headed for the Big Apple. "I didn't have a résumé or anything," she recalls with a laugh. "I was hired by *Mademoiselle* as a temp." She quickly proved herself and, within a couple of years, rose to the position of senior fashion editor/accessories.

"After being with the magazine for five years, Andy and I decided that we wanted our own business, and he came up with the idea of handbags. We didn't do any market research; we just looked around and saw what wasn't there. I couldn't find a wonderful bag that would assume a woman's personality instead of making a big statement. I couldn't find a bag that I just had to have."

So, Kate bought some tracing paper and began to fold and cut patterns for the types of handbags that she would want to own—timeless, simple shapes, but a bit playful. "I grew up in Kansas City, Missouri," she explains, "and there are things I remember, such as my father's tweed coats and our canvas beach umbrellas, that have the kind of practicality and style that inspire our designs."

In 1993, she left the magazine and, from the loft they shared, the couple launched kate spade. (However, Kate herself officially became Kate Spade when she married Andy three years later.) In the beginning, the business was a hands-on proposition. The night before her first trade show, Kate looked at her totes and decided, at the last minute, that they still needed something. "I wanted to keep a clean look, but I felt there should be some sort of visual." With only hours to spare, she hit upon the idea of displaying her small, black label on the outside of each bag. Then she spent the rest of the evening sewing with a friend "until our fingers hurt."

The bags were an immediate hit, but the couple wisely decided to grow their fledgling business in a deliberate, controlled manner. "We used our own money," says Andy. "Basically, I worked two jobs for two years, before joining kate spade full time. Kate and I wanted to be independent. We were clear about our company's point of view and didn't want pressure from investors to go too fast."

In 1999, the company had grown to the point that it attracted the attention of a major player in the fashion retail industry, Neiman Marcus, which offered to pay 56 percent of the selling price that the Spades had established for the business; they agreed. The rest is retail history. Today, their factory and corporate offices are housed in an old warehouse in the flower district of Manhattan, and Kate and Andy still oversee every aspect of the operation. Andy continues to guide the positioning of the product in the marketplace, while Kate remains in charge of design. What is new for kate spade? The company has added a line of shoes, rain wear, and stationery featuring whimsical illustrations and agendas for the fashionable executive. Kate's late venture is a collection of intimate apparel, "kate spade lounge," that includes simply elegant pajamas for relaxing in style. For men, her husband Andy recently launched a line of vintage-inspired accessories under the label, jack spade.

Christopher Palmeri, "Retailer's Revenge," *Forbes Magazine*, May 3, 1999

CASE STUDY 1 QUESTIONS

1. Identify the benefits of the business arrangement for Kate and Andy Spade. For Neiman Marcus?
2. Discuss the potential disadvantages of the business arrangement for each of the parties.
3. Some analysts describe the kate spade/Neiman Marcus business transaction as a merger, while others define it as an acquisition. How do you describe it? Why are there multiple definitions for this business agreement?
4. What options for growth are available to the Spades following the purchase by Neiman Marcus?
5. If you were in the Spades' position, how would you explain the business arrangement to other retail clients in order to retain their accounts?

CASE STUDY 2

You are shopping at the 4-story Neiman Marcus store in Houston's Galleria mall. You want to buy a Gucci suit, a piece of luggage, maybe even a pair of those flowery, 1970s style pants that Gucci has been advertising in magazines lately. You have come to the wrong place. To find some of Gucci's hottest-selling products, try the bustling little Gucci boutique at the other end of the mall.

"I used to wish they weren't opening stores next to us," says Burton Tanksy, president of the Neiman Marcus Group, "but we lost that battle." Indeed, all manner of designers have been copycatting Ralph Lauren, who opened his smashingly successful store on New York's Madison Avenue in 1986. Gucci Group N.V. now gets two-thirds of its sales from its company-owned and franchised stores. By capturing both the retail and the manufacturer's markup, Gucci earns glamorous profits. Other high-fashion companies like Prada and Louis Vuitton Moet Hennessy (LVMH) are stepping up their retailing efforts by opening company-owned or franchised boutiques.

Neiman Marcus still carries plenty of Gucci, Prada, Ralph Lauren, and Louis Vuitton merchandise, but the company, like other retailers, is in a constant battle to offer something that's different not only from traditional competitors like Saks Fifth Avenue but also from designer-owned stores that have an inside track. Says Neiman Marcus Group's chief executive, Robert Smith, "The line between retail and wholesale gets blurrier every day."

One traditional point of differentiation for retailers is the house brand or private label. But those brands don't command the highest prices because of a lower level of brand status recognition. At the company, private labels make up less than 10 percent of sales. Neiman's Tanksy indicates, "Our customer wants designer clout. She wants something easily recognizable so that people will know she paid a lot for it."

Neiman Marcus may have found its method of counterattack. The company has begun taking stakes in some of the up-and-coming brands sold at Neiman's and its sister store Bergdorf Goodman. In December, for $6.7 million, Neiman Marcus Group bought 51 percent of Gurwitch Bristow Products, the $9 million a year maker of Laura Mercier cosmetics. In February 1999, Neiman paid $34 million for 56 percent of kate spade LLC (1998 revenues, $27 million), known for its sleek nylon handbags.

Smith says he envisions making half a dozen such investments over the next few years, spending as much as $200 million. "We've seen a lot of value created [by designers] over the years," he explains. "We should have some of that value." Smith notes that at the prices Neiman Marcus paid for kate spade and Laura Mercier, the company can't afford to turn off any customers. Smith is leaving day-to-day management to the design company founders, who continue to own nearly half of each of the firms.

www.neimanmarcus.com/pressrelease

CASE STUDY 2 QUESTIONS

1. What are the advantages to kate spade in agreeing to a 56 percent ownership by Neiman Marcus? The disadvantages?
2. What are the positive and negative aspects of this acquisition from the perspective of Neiman Marcus?
3. Which trends in fashion retailing parallel the kate spade/Neiman Marcus business deal?
4. If you were the chief executive officer of a major competitor of Neiman Marcus, how would you react to the news of Neiman's acquisition of kate spade? Would there be any implications to the way your company does business?
5. Which firm, kate spade or Neiman Marcus, will carry the highest level of risk as a result of the business arrangement? Why?

ENTERING THE WORLD OF THE ENTREPRENEUR

1. Conduct research about entrepreneurs who have successfully expanded their businesses. Generate a list of when, how, and where expansion was implemented. Look for a pattern of successful growth strategies in fashion retailing.
2. Research entrepreneurial companies that failed over the past few years. Construct a summary of reasons for failure, determining why and when these firms found it necessary to close. Again, observe consistencies among the companies that failed.
3. Examine the financial implications of expanding a business. What new expenses would be incurred? Which expenses would be one time, monthly, or other?
4. Ask an entrepreneur who has expanded his or her company to discuss the product lines, the location, facility, or other factors that were an issue in the expansion.

ENTERPRISING ENTREPRENEUR

Donna Karan International Inc. and Fossil, Inc. finalized a strategic licensing alliance to produce and distribute Donna Karan New York, DKNY, and DKNY Active watches worldwide. "By combining the design vision of Donna Karan International and Fossil's expertise in product development, manufacturing, and distribution, we will be able to provide our customer with the best product," states John Idol, chief executive officer of Donna Karan International. "We are extremely pleased to have finalized this agreement with Fossil and look forward to creating an exciting watch collection."

"Our watch designs are creative, innovative, and have a real fashion/lifestyle look to them," comments Gary Bollinger, Fossil's senior vice president, Donna Karan Division. "Fossil's objective in creating the DKNY watch line is to leverage the DKNY and DKNY Active brands into strong watch categories that will enhance Fossil's top-line revenue and bottom-line profit and also enhance the DKNY and DKNY Active portfolio of products," concludes Bollinger. The DKNY watch collection consists of approximately 100 styles for both men and women with retail prices from $75 to $195. Styles range from contemporary bracelets and classic stainless steel to athletic watches.

Fossil is a design and marketing company that specializes in consumer products predicated on fashion and value. In addition to watches, Fossil leverages its development and production expertise in other merchandise classifications such as handbags, personal leather goods, belts, and sunglasses. Fossil products can be found in department stores and other upscale retailers in over 80 countries around the world.

www.donnakaran.com/pressrelease

Chapter 14

CONSTRUCTING THE BUSINESS PLAN—CREATING THE ROADMAP

Note: The business plan template located in this chapter was adapted from FastTrac,™ *Venture Planning Workbook*, 2001, Kauffman Center for Entrepreneurial Leadership at the Ewing Marion Kauffman Foundation. Used with permission.

INTRODUCTION

The basis of this text has been to provide guidance and the framework necessary to help in the understanding and development of the business plan. Throughout the text, the key components that must be addressed in a well-written business plan have been reviewed. The chapters have provided information concerning different sections of the plan. This final chapter of the text shows how each prior chapter has provided the information needed to complete an actual business plan. It provides the key elements and preferred format. It defines the business plan, its purpose, and how it is analyzed by investors, funders, and key management personnel within the company. A sample business plan for a fashion retail business is presented at the end of this chapter. This sample plan is fictional and does not relate to any existing company.

THE REASONS FOR DEVELOPING A BUSINESS PLAN

To an entrepreneur in today's fast-changing environment, the business plan is the most critical document. The answer to the question "Why is it necessary to develop a business plan?" is simple. The process of gathering the information needed to prepare the plan minimizes the possibility of failure. It is the roadmap that guides the entrepreneur through the business. One would ordinarily not get into a car to travel to a new city without a map to provide direction. A business plan guides the entrepreneur's concept from an idea to reality. No entrepreneur can expect to be taken seriously by investors, bankers, accountants, or others without a well-written plan. Bankers will not consider funding new companies without a written plan. The plan will help the banker or investor analyze the conceptual and analytical skills possessed by the entrepreneur. The business plan reflects on the entrepreneur. A plan that is written with little or no objectivity, lacks research and analysis, or does not indicate the sources that back up the research can send the banker running. Bankers receive numerous business plans and spend time only on those they feel have merit. It will help the funder determine whether or not the entrepreneur has a good understanding of the fashion retail industry and the ability to manage that business. Additionally, funders reviewing the business plan may have recommendations of changes that will improve the company's chances for success.

Business Plan Myths

Myth #1: Business plans are boring. Not so, says Vicki L. Helmick, a CPA and business consultant in Orlando, Florida. "If you're excited about your business, you should be excited about doing the planning that will make it a success," Helmick points out. "Your business plan is where you articulate your vision of what you want your company to be, and then outline a strategy to make it happen."

Myth #2: Business plans are complicated. A good business plan doesn't have to be formal or complicated, Helmick says, but it must be thorough and in writing. "For a simple business, you may only need a page or two," she says. "Or you may take 20 or 30 pages and include charts and graphs. The key is to make it as detailed as necessary to give yourself a road map."

Myth #3: I don't need to write my plan down. Many solo operators don't bother putting their plans in writing, but it's not enough to just have the information in your head. Besides making it easier to remember, committing the plan to paper forces you to think through each step of the process, consider all the consequences, and deal with issues you might prefer to avoid. It also increases your sense of accountability, even if it's just to yourself. After all, once you've written the plan down, you have an obligation to either follow it or come up with a good reason for doing something different. Plus, if you have partners, a written business plan reduces the risks of misunderstanding or conflict.

Myth #4: I only have to do it once. Writing a business plan is not a one-time exercise. "Don't write your plan, pat yourself on the back, and then stick it on the shelf," Helmick says. "This should be a tool you use to run your company every day. If you want to obtain loans or attract outside investors, either in the start-up stage or down the road, you'll need to show them a strong plan that you've kept current to demonstrate the viability of your company."

(Jacquelyn Lynn, "What's the Plan?," *Business Start-Ups*, March 2000)

Entrepreneurs are self-motivated people who are determined to reach a goal. They understand that, in order to do so, they must have a plan in place. A good business plan is essential for determining which resources are needed and from where those resources will come, at the time of start-up and in the future. Lack of a written plan takes away the tools necessary to make sound business decisions. Many businesses fail because the owners went into the venture without ever having thought about what it would take to succeed.

As the entrepreneur puts together the various sections of the business plan, he or she has the opportunity to look at the business and determine its viability. This can be done only if the plan is written objectively. Too often entrepreneurs use the plan to confirm what they are thinking, rather than to find the true answer to the question, "Will this concept work in this market?" While unexpected incidents will occur with a good plan in place, no written plan increases the chances of failure.

The research needed to write a good business plan to open a fashion retail operation provides the entrepreneur with the opportunity to learn about the industry and the market. Additionally, it allows the entrepreneur to "comparison shop" in terms of expenses relating to location, merchandise, operations, and personnel. A well-thought-out business plan can save the entrepreneur money. By taking time to understand the needed capital, the management team, the target market, and other factors, the entrepreneur can get off to a good start. It is easy to get caught up in the excitement of the potential new venture and want to jump in immediately. Good entrepreneurs step back and evaluate.

DEFINITION OF THE BUSINESS PLAN

The business plan is a written document that describes the business concept, the goals of the company, how management will reach those goals, and why the business will be successful. It is a living document to be reviewed over and over. The plan will change as the business grows and new information is obtained. It provides the entrepreneur with the opportunity to formulate a strategy for success. It will allow the entrepreneur and his or her management team to know whether or not they have all the elements necessary to succeed. It is a communication tool that will be used between management and the entrepreneur, and between the entrepreneur and the banker or investor.

The business plan will do the following:

- Define the company, its goals and objectives.
- Serve as a guide to help the entrepreneur stay focused on the direction of the company.
- Serve as a management tool in measuring whether or not the company is on target with its projections and goals.
- Provide an understanding of the financial considerations of the business.
- Encourage research and the need for knowing the fashion industry and intended market thoroughly.
- Summarize the information needed to make critical business decisions.
- Provide an opportunity to understand both the internal and external forces that can affect the business.
- Define a strategy for exiting the business when the time is right.
- Provide an opportunity to understand the competition and to position the company in relationship to that competition.
- Highlight the strengths and weaknesses of the business.

ANALYSIS OF THE BUSINESS PLAN

The evaluation of the plan depends on the reader. The plan may be read by potential employees, bankers, suppliers, venture capitalists, consultants, and the board of directors or advisory council. Each person will read the plan with a different perspective, concern, and purpose. It is important then for the entrepreneur to be prepared to address the various issues and concerns of each.

Evaluation of the business plan by the entrepreneur should be based on whether or not the plan clearly explains the business and what it is about. Can the entrepreneur, through the use of the business plan, clearly articulate the business concept and the key elements of that concept? Can the entrepreneur clearly support the premise that there is a potential market for this product or service? It should help the entrepreneur look at the business opportunity objectively. What is the competition? Are the people in place to manage this company?

Potential employees may want to review the business plan prior to giving up another job to work for this new company. The plan will enable the potential employee to become familiar with the business, its goals, and objectives. It will help validate the plan for success. It is common knowledge that start-up companies often struggle financially. A good business plan can help alleviate concerns of potential employees.

Funders, such as bankers and venture capitalists, will review the business plan thoroughly to determine whether or not the entrepreneur possesses the management skills and thought processes needed to succeed. They will pay particular attention to the cash-flow projections and cash requirements. Although part of the plan is based on assumptions, they will look at whether or not the entrepreneur has a contingency plan in case projections are not met. Investors want a return on their investment. Bankers want loans to be repaid. The entrepreneur must be able to convince this group that these things will happen.

HOW THE PLAN TAKES SHAPE–COMPONENTS OF THE PLAN

There is no one correct way to write a business plan. Various textbooks and other books on the market outline business plans in different ways. The order of the content should flow logically. Some issues may repeat in more than one section of the plan. Following is the organization selected for the text:

- Cover letter
- Cover page
- Table of contents
- Executive summary
- Product/service plan
- Management and organization plan
- Marketing plan
- Location
- Merchandising plan
- Financial plan
- Operating and control systems plan
- Growth plan
- Appendix

Cover Letter

The cover letter is the vehicle through which the entrepreneur's concept is introduced to the reader. It should state the reason the business plan is being presented and introduce the documents that are included in the package. It should be precise and to the point—no longer than one page.

Cover Page

The cover page should identify the document. It should include the name of the company; its address; contact information of the business (including an e-mail address, if applicable); the date; and the name, title, and address of the contact person within the company (if the address is different from that of the business). The reader should not have to search within the plan to determine whom to contact, nor does the reader want to search to determine the name of the company. Information on the title page may be arranged in any format deemed appropriate by the writer.

Often, business plans contain confidential information, such as the finances of the entrepreneur, that should not be distributed. It is advisable to include a confidentiality statement on the cover page. It should state that the plan is confidential and the property of the company about which it was written. It can state that the business plan may not be duplicated without the written consent of the company's contact person.

Table of Contents

The table of contents should list each section of the plan and the page number on which it first appears. The reader will not necessarily start at the beginning of the plan and read through it front and back. It is not uncommon, for example, for a banker to begin with the financial plan. Remember, the banker initially wants to know that the business will have a positive cash flow. Bankers will want to know at what point the business will break even. Readers will want to access information as easily as possible.

Executive Summary

This is the first opportunity the entrepreneur has to get the reader's attention. The *executive summary* provides a sketch or overview of the business. It should contain key points relating to each section of the plan. It should include information about the business concept, the financing needed, how the entrepreneur intends to penetrate the market, the competitive advantage, the management team, and the business operations.

The executive summary may be written first or last. It is not uncommon for it to be written first, to serve as a synopsis of what is to come. It can then be rewritten once the final business plan is complete to reflect any changes. The summary should be written in a narrative form to tell a story about the business. It should not be longer than two pages. The writer will want to avoid using the summary to hype the business. Sophisticated readers will pick up on this immediately. For an unknown entity such as a new business, the entrepreneur must be convincing and use factual information to support claims. Readers will be looking for the why and how of the business, as well as the factors that will contribute to the success of the venture.

The executive summary should cover the following:

1. The name of the business and the form of organization under which it will operate. Forms of organization include sole proprietorship, partnership, limited partnership,

corporation (i.e, s-corporation, c-corporation), or limited liability company. State where the business will be located.

2. The type of business. Indicate whether the business is retail, wholesale, or service. The current stage of development for the venture (e.g., concept stage or start-up) should be identified.

The executive summary should answer the following questions:

1. What will be unique about the business? What proprietory rights will the business have? Trademarks, licenses, franchise agreements, and a niche market should be included.

2. Who will be the key management personnel, and what skills will they bring to the business? Who will be the key support groups for the management team? For a start-up company, the name of the person to be hired for the position may not yet be established. Although a funder may want to know who it is, the entrepreneur may give the title and a brief description of the skills and qualifications needed. Key support groups for the management team may include accountants, attorneys, consultants, and a board of directors or advisory council members.

3. What is the market like in terms of the industry, the customer, customer needs, product benefits, the target markets, and the market penetration plan? Provide a specific description of the market and the potential customers.

4. Who will be the major competitors, and what are their strengths and weaknesses? Give the reader an overview of the marketing plan. Identify whom the venture is going up against as direct competition. Be sure to use specific facts and figures from the market research.

5. How much money will the venture need for start-up costs? How will the money be spent?

6. What kind of financing will the company need? Who will provide start-up capital?

In the closing paragraph, the writer should thank the reader and encourage him or her to read further. The readers need to feel free to contact the entrepreneur if they have any questions. The writer should state that he or she looks forward to meeting with them after they have had the chance to review the business plan.

Product/Service Plan

The reader must have a clear picture of the product. It is important not to make the assumption that the reader will know, for example, what a Ralph Lauren jacket looks like or what it costs. The writer must adequately explain the product so that the reader will understand it. What will the reader need to know to understand and appreciate the venture? The focus should be on the benefits or value the product creates for the customer. It is a good idea to include photos or drawings of the product in the appendix. Many fashion entrepreneurs use storyboards to visually present concepts to funders.

In the fashion retail industry, it is important to convince the reader that the inventory can and will be delivered. Some manufacturers will not supply their product to a start-up company, even if the entrepreneur stands at the door waiting with cash in hand. The supplier may require the business be open 1 to 2 years before getting its merchandise to ensure that the business will be there, able to pay its bills, and will not close in 6 to 12 months.

1. *Purpose of the product.* Describe the product and the product mix. How will it benefit the customer? Will it solve a problem or address an opportunity? Provide a list of the products that will be offered. Consider using catalogs of merchandise with percentages of sales to describe the product mix. If available, include testimonials, results from market surveys, focus groups, and the like.

2. *Unique features.* Is there anything unique about the merchandise or product, such as cost, design, or quality? Describe each feature in terms of the benefit the customer receives. Focus on the benefits or a value the product or service creates. Describe the unique features of the store, such as, store design and layout, or exclusivity of the merchandise. Include any available photographs or drawings of the exterior and signage and the layout of the store interior.

3. *Proprietory property.* Are there licenses or royalty agreements that will be associated with the product/service, and what plans are there for future agreements? In the fashion industry, perhaps this will be the only retail operation to provide a certain line of clothing in this market.

4. *Government approvals.* Identify any governmental approvals that are necessary. Such approval may include licenses at the federal, state, or local level. Examples of governmental approvals may include a local business license or planning and zoning commissions.

5. *Product limitations.* Will there be any limitations of the product? For example, a bridal store has "dead inventory" in that all stock will not be sold at full price. The entrepreneur, in this case, will want to explain how this merchandise will be moved.

6. *Product liability.* Discuss any insurance requirements and costs. Will the product pose any liability? Include the name of the insurance company, contact person, kind of insurance, and premium cost.

7. *Related products.* Will there be any related products? How will they increase or enhance the profitability of the business? What new products could be developed to meet the changing market needs in the industry? How will the company be flexible in meeting changing trends and fashions?

8. *Facilities.* What are the plans for the retail facility? Describe the need for facilities. Discuss the capital that will be required to either build the facility or improve on an existing building.

9. *Suppliers.* From where will the merchandise come? Who will be the major suppliers? Will there be backup suppliers?

Mangagement and Organization Plan

The management and organization plan is the section of the plan that must establish the credibility of the management team. It must reflect the team's ability to successfully operate the business and achieve its outlined goals and objectives. If any member of the management team lacks the needed credentials or experience, then the entrepreneur must explain how these deficiencies can be overcome with assistance from members of the support groups, such as the board of directors, advisory council, consultants, attorneys, and accountants. The entrepreneur must be able to prove he or she has access to the management expertise needed to operate the business profitably.

This section of the business plan lists the key management positions, along with a description of primary job duties and responsibilities. It should include a summary of each person's prior business experience, since this explains how the person's skills will contribute to performance. If the person has not yet been hired, the writer must still include a brief description, as well as the types of business skills and experience needed for the position. Additionally, the entrepreneur should describe how he or she intends to recruit and hire such a person to meet the needs of the management team.

To develop a good management plan, the entrepreneur should address the following issues:

1. *Management team.* What will be the role of the entrepreneur? Who will be the key management personnel, and what are their job descriptions and prior experiences? Provide a list of the key members' titles and job descriptions of the management team members. List their experience, talents, training, and special expertise. The writer should indicate that copies of résumés are included in the appendix. Key members might include the entrepreneur, floor manager, sales manager, and buyer. Descriptions should include key members' job duties, such as buying, selling, advertising, and marketing.

2. *Compensation and ownership.* What will the compensation package be for the entrepreneur and management team? List in chart form their salaries, benefits, bonuses, and stock options, if any. Describe the ownership of the company and whether it will be a corporation (s-corporation, c-corporation), limited liability company, partnership (limited or general), or sole proprietorship. Indicate if a fictitious business name will be registered and used.

3. *Board of directors/advisory council.* Who will serve on the board of directors or advisory council? List in table form the board of directors and advisory council members, including names, titles, addresses, and phone numbers. List their potential contribution, salary, benefits, and any ownership in the company. Identify the officers who will hold the position of chairperson, vice chairperson, secretary, and treasurer. Highlight their qualifications that relate to the fashion retail business.

4. *Infrastructure.* Who will be selected as the team of outside advisers, such as accountants, lawyers, or consultants, and what will their compensation package be (if any)? Consultants may include buyers from noncompeting companies, computer technology consultants, or marketing specialists. Include in chart form the key adviser's name, address, phone number, and any compensation, along with a brief description of his or her expertise.

5. *Contracts and franchise agreements.* Discuss any management contracts, noncompete agreements, franchise agreements, or other contractual agreements. Briefly describe each of the contracts and include copies of the contracts in the appendix.

6. *Insurance.* List the insurance policies for key personnel for which the company will be the beneficiary. List the insurance company name, buy-sell agreements, disability insurance, and owner's insurance. Other types of insurance such as fire and theft should be listed under operating control systems.

7. *Employee incentives.* What employee incentive plans will be in effect? Explain the incentive plan using performance goals tied to projected revenues. Define various incentive programs including special recognition awards and commissions. Summarize key points and put any supporting documents in the appendix.

8. *Organizational chart.* Prepare an organizational chart showing how the company will be organized by person and job title. If a person has not been selected for hire, list job title only.

Marketing Plan

The marketing section of the plan is divided into four parts: an industry profile, competition analysis, pricing structure, and market penetration. The *industry profile* is an in-depth look at the internal and external factors that affect the fashion industry. It will help determine the major competitors in the industry, as well as the demographics and psychographics of the industry's customers. It will give an indication of the economic trends in the fashion industry in terms of sales and profits, as well as factors that affect these trends.

The *competition profile* looks at and compares pricing, quality, unique features, distribution systems, advertising avenues, and strengths and weaknesses of the competition. It looks at market share of competitors. The *pricing profile* examines industry norms to include gross margin, markup percent, markdown percent, and stock turn. It also articulates how the business may or may not differ from industry standards and why. The pricing profile looks at the break-even point for the product or service.

The *marketing plan* describes the target market and how that market will be penetrated. It must convince the reader that there is a large enough market to make the venture successful. It describes the promotional efforts that will be implemented to reach the customer. It should also discuss any future markets that may be sought.

To develop a good marketing plan the entrepreneur should address the following questions:

1. *Industry profile: current size.* Describe the current size of the industry at national, regional, state, and local levels. Indicate the amount of money spent annually in the industry. Cite the sources of information.
2. *Industry profile: growth potential.* Is the industry growing, declining, or remaining stable? How many new businesses have entered this industry in the past 3 years?
3. *Industry profile: geographic locations.* Are there any geographic limitations? Are there seasonal changes that will affect sales? Indicate trends in distribution and production. Cite the sources of information.
4. *Industry profile: industry trends.* What are the trends in the industry? Who are the primary customers from an industry perspective? What common buying characteristics do they share? What factors influence their purchases? What are the major economic, competitive, and demographic factors that drive this industry? What are the trends and outlooks for these factors? Is there any evidence that the key industry factors are changing?[1]
5. *Industry profile: seasonality factors.* What are the special seasons in the fashion industry? It is important to remember that the funder will most likely know little about the fashion industry. The writer must help the reader understand the seasonal buying patterns, such as fall I, fall II, holiday, and so on.
6. *Industry profile: profit characteristics.* What are the profit characteristics of the fashion retail industry?
7. *Industry profile: distribution channels.* Who are the industry's major suppliers? Will the business be able to get the merchandise as needed? Where are markets located and goods produced?
8. *Industry profile: basis of competition.* Does the industry compete on the basis of price, quality, promotion, service, or a combination of factors? Cite the sources of information.
9. *Competition profile.* What is the profile of the competition? What is this business's competitive advantage? Prepare a competitive analysis chart and summarize key

points. Compare prices, quality, unique features, distribution system, marketing/advertising, geographic location, strengths/weaknesses, and market share. Use the competitive analysis matrix. (Figure 14.1).

10. *Customer profile.* What is the profile of the targeted customer? Describe the customer in terms of age, gender, profession, income, geographic location, and other demographics. Include customer psychographics—attitudes, values, belief systems, and social status. Incorporate any testimonials, results from market surveys, focus group studies, and the like.

11. *Target market profile.* What is the size of the target market? Define the number of potential customers or the potential dollar volume.

12. *Pricing profile.* What is the pricing structure? What are plans for negotiating a price for large orders or for special price deals? How is the pricing structure sensitive to the customer's buying points? Defend the pricing profile in terms of customers' price limitations, competitors' prices, and the market's perceived values. Explain how the pricing structure is sensitive to customer buying points. What is the gross margin potential? How does this compare to industry standards? Include the gross margin percentage (margin/prices). Use merchandise categories if there are many products. Compare pricing policies and gross margin potential to traditional markups and discount structures in the industry.

13. *Break-even analysis.* What is the break-even point for the business?

14. *Market penetration: direct sales force.* Will a direct sales force be used for selling the merchandise to the end user? If so, how many salespeople will be hired? Describe their compensation package (e.g., salary plus bonuses, commissions, and draw plus commissions), amount and type of training, and support staff members. Project costs of meeting and training, if applicable.

Figure 14.1 Competitive Analysis Matrix

	Price	Product/ Quality	Unique Features	Distribution System	Marketing/ Advertising	Geographic Location	Strength/ Weakness
Product							
Competitor A							
Competitor B							
Competitor C							
Competitor D							
Competitor E							

15. *Market penetration: direct mail/telemarketing.* Will direct mail or telemarketing be used as means of selling the product or service to the end user? If so, list the size of the mailing list, schedule for mailings, and estimated response rate. Include an example of a mailer in the appendix. Project costs of mailing lists, print materials, telemarketing costs, e-tailing, brochures, assembly, and postage.

17. *Advertising and promotion.* What advertising and promotion media will be used for the distribution system and end users? Include media channel costs and projected response rate.

18. *Guarantees.* What guarantees will be offered? Consider the industry standards for returns and service costs for the merchandise.

19. *Future markets.* What opportunities could occur in future markets? This would be a good place to discuss e-commerce, if it is not in the start-up plan for the business.

Location

Location plays a key role in the success of any fashion retail business. In developing the location section of the business plan, the entrepreneur must be careful to address the following topics:

1. *Region, state, and city.* For a retail store, address the location of the business in terms of the region of the country in which it will be located. Why does this area have the greatest number of characteristics necessary for the business to succeed? How accessible is the regional, state, and city location to suppliers? How does the location affect the business in terms of workforce?

2. *Demographic and psychographic characteristics.* How does the location help the business in terms of its psychographic and demographic characteristics for the proposed target market? How many people reside per square mile in the given area in the city in which the business will be located.

3. *Competition.* Describe the number, quality, and locations of competing firms. Explain why this business can capture a market share large enough to earn a profit at this location.

4. *Site.* Will the business be located near a central business district, in a neighborhood, near a shopping center or mall, in an outlying area, or at home? How will this location contribute to the success of the business? Describe the location in terms of image and why it fits with the target market.

5. *Location factors.* What qualities are necessary to the success of the business? Describe the location in terms of how the product will be sold.

6. *Physical visibility.* Is the location visible to the target market? Is visibility necessary to the success of the business? Why?

7. *Finances and location.* Will the building (if applicable) be purchased, built, or leased? Define the terms of the purchase lease. Discuss potential for future growth. Describe the number of square feet and how much will be allocated for office space, warehouse, and retail space.

8. *Facilities and layout.* Describe the location in terms of its exterior design, signs, approach, and display windows. Describe the interior of the location. Describe the size of the store, colors, displays, the fixtures and mannequins, lighting, fitting rooms,

and placement and look of the cash desk. Help the reader to visualize the facility. This is most concisely communicated through the floor plan.

Merchandising Plan

In this section, it is important to recognize that the reader most likely will not have an in-depth understanding of the fashion industry. All industry terms must be clarified for the reader. Following are key topics for the merchandising section:

1. *Proposed lines.* List lines to be carried by the business. Give the name of the manufacturer and indicate where the lines will be sourced.
2. *Assortment of stock.* Describe the merchandise classifications (e.g., dresses, sportswear, accessories). Indicate the percentage of the total merchandise assortment that will be represented by each classification.
3. *Market trips.* In table format, list the destination and dates of market trips, the objective of each trip, and the projected cost. Note whether or not the cost includes airfare, car rental, and so on. Specify for which fashion season each market trip will provide merchandise.
4. *Markup policies.* Discuss the markup policy on merchandise for initial and maintained markups.
5. *Markdown timing and percentage.* Discuss the markdown policy.
6. *Return policy.* Discuss the return policy that will be offered by the business. There are two perspectives for returns. The first policy should refer to returns to vendors. The second should refer to returns made by customers.

Financial Plan

The financial plan section should include a monthly cash flow statement, a profit and loss statement, and a balance sheet for the business. It is crucial that the numbers presented be real numbers. Good funders will know if the writer has "pulled them out of the air." Although a new company does not have historical data, it can look to similar businesses in the industry to make assumptions, as discussed in Chapter 11. This section should also include a set of assumptions for the pro forma financials that are being presented. Lack of proper research in this section can close the door before it opens. It should be noted that most funders would want 3 years of financial statements, from the start-up point to the projected third year of operation. For purposes of this text, the financial statements for one year are presented.

1. Cash flow statement.
2. Assumptions.
3. Profit and loss statement.
4. Balance sheet.

Operating and Control Systems

The operating and control plan illustrates that the entrepreneur understands the important of administrative policies, procedures, and controls. It is used to show that all aspects of the business from an operation and control point of view have been addressed.

1. *Receiving orders.* What administrative policies, procedures, and controls will be used to receive merchandise? Explain how orders will be processed after they are received. Describe the type of database that will be used to track this information.

2. *Paying suppliers.* What administrative policies, procedures, and controls will be used for paying suppliers? Identify procedures for controlling due dates on bills. List accounting and bookkeeping controls that will be needed to pay the suppliers.

3. *Reporting to management.* What administrative policies, procedures, and controls will be used for reporting to management? Explain the communication process that employees will follow to report incidents to management. Describe the format and schedule to be used for management meetings, who will attend, and how often meetings will be held. List the types of reports to be used.

4. *Staff development.* What administrative policies, procedures, and controls will be used for staff development? Explain provisions made for employee training, promotions, and incentives. The entrepreneur may choose to use outside consultants or to provide in-house training.

5. *Inventory control.* What administrative policies, procedures, and controls will be used to control inventory? How often will physical inventories be taken?

6. *Handling returns.* How will returns be documented for proper credit? Identify a system for handling customer complaints. Also, identify how feedback from customers will be used to improve customer service and product development.

7. *Company budgets.* What administrative policies, procedures, and controls will be used to monitor the company budgets? Explain how often budget information will be updated for review. Set up budgetary controls for travel, phone usage, photocopies, supplies, and car allowances, if applicable.

8. *Security systems.* What administrative policies, procedures, and controls will be used for providing security for the business?

9. *Documents and paper flow.* What will be the flow of information throughout the system? What documents must be prepared for a transaction? Identify all things that should happen in a transaction. Include examples of such forms as invoices, sales tickets, and charge documents in the appendix.

10. *Planning chart: product availability.* When will the merchandise be in and ready for the store to open? List all the activities necessary to get the merchandise in the door. List the names of the persons that will be responsible for each activity, as well as completion dates. Outline the timing of events by month for a minimum of 12 months.

11. *Planning chart: financial requirements.* List the amount of money that will be needed to finance the project, who will provide the money, the date the money will be needed, and the proposed repayment plan.

12. *Planning chart: marketing flow chart.* When will the advertising be developed and implemented? List when marketing activities will be carried out, the persons responsible for each activity, and the completion dates. Outline the timing of events for a minimum of 12 months.

13. *Risk analysis.* What are the potential problems, risks, and other possible negative factors that the venture might face? Design innovative approaches to solve the following types of problems: incorrect sales projections, unfavorable industry trends, unexpected competition, unavoidable labor problems, inadequate capital, management or personnel concerns, unavailable merchandise.

14. *Salvaging assets.* What could be salvaged or recovered if any of the above risks would materialize and make the venture unsuccessful? This list may include inventory and fixtures.

Growth Plan

The growth plan is designed to forecast, as accurately as possible, what will be needed to help the business grow in the future. The growth plan is based on a set of assumptions. This section of the plan should be looked at to determine whether the entrepreneur has anticipated plans for expansion or growth. A business can grow too fast, fail to access the needed capital to grow, and end up closing its doors. Following are components of the growth plan section:

1. *New offerings to the target market.* What new merchandise, business locations, or channels of distribution will the business pursue in the future? What new marketplaces will each of the new product lines penetrate? What will be the projected revenues from the new product lines or store locations for the next 3 to 5 years?
2. *Capital requirements.* What are the financial requirements for pursuing a new product line or business location? How will the money be generated for future growth? Identify whether debt or equity will be used to raise the needed capital for future growth.
3. *Personnel requirements.* What management personnel and other employees will be needed to support the projected growth? List job titles, brief job descriptions, salaries, and benefits.
4. *Exit strategy.* How will the growth plan enable the owner to exit the business? Explain the intended strategy for selling the business or another exit strategy.

Appendix

The appendix is intended to include any documentation needed to support the plan. The appendix may include the following:

- Résumés of the management team and key personnel.
- Any employee contracts such as noncompete agreements.
- Personal financial statements for the principal(s) of the business.
- Copies of any contracts or documents needed by suppliers.
- Samples of advertising brochures or other forms of advertising.
- Copies of any logos that have been developed.
- Copies of any letters of reference.
- Copies of any documents needed to support data in the industry study or marketing plan.
- Photographs of the preferred business location.
- A map showing the location of the business.
- An outline of the layout of the store.

TIPS FOR WRITING A GOOD BUSINESS PLAN

Bankers, venture capitalists, and other investors look at hundreds of business plans in a year. As a result, the entrepreneur's ability to capture the funders' attention is most important. It does not take long for a funder to dismiss a plan. Following are some tips for preparing an eye-catching business plan.

- First, determine who the reader will be. In order for the document to be effective, the entrepreneur must take into account the reader's perspective. For example, a banker will look for the business's ability to generate positive cash flow. Additionally, the banker will want to know that the entrepreneur has sufficient collateral to support the loan request and that the management team is in place to provide the knowledge necessary to create a successful business. In contrast, suppliers may look only at the concept of the business and the ability of the business to attract customers.
- Second, prepare an outline for the plan. Taking the time to prepare an outline will help the writer stay focused and organized.
- Next, write the plan. The length of the plan will depend on what it takes to say what needs to be said. There is no magic number. The less complicated the business, the fewer pages it will take to describe. A typical plan ranges from 20 to 40 pages.
- Take the time to review the plan before it is distributed. Search for spelling, grammar, and sentence structure errors, as well as omissions and incorrect data. Errors within the plan send the message that the entrepreneur is not detailed or interested enough to make sure the plan is correct. The assumption becomes that this person may not have the discipline needed to run a business.
- The business plan is not meant to justify opening the business. Rather it is used to evaluate, objectively, whether or not the concept will work. Be careful that the plan is not written simply to confirm the entrepreneur's viewpoint. Conduct all the research necessary to find out the answer to the question, "Will this business really work in this market?"
- "Be careful with superlatives. Readers are naturally skeptical of overreaching self promotion. Avoid using words such as 'best,' 'terrific,' 'wonderful,' or even 'unmatched.'"[2]

PACKAGING THE BUSINESS PLAN

The plan should be presented well. It must send the message that time and care were taken in putting the plan together. Below are some suggestions for presenting the business plan:

- Make sure that the plan is printed on quality paper.
- Make sure to number the pages.
- Format the plan using headings and subheadings that correspond exactly to the table of contents. It will make it easier for the reader to find information.
- Use photographs and illustrations, as they are very effective in providing the reader with information about the merchandise or business location.

CONCLUSION

The importance of a sound business plan cannot be overemphasized. Many potentially successful businesses have failed because they lacked one, and many succeeded because of one. A well-written business plan will serve as an invaluable roadmap in ensuring that the company reaches its goals. It will be used as a tool in accessing capital and selling the company to potential investors and the management team.

The business plan contains the following components: cover letter, the cover page, table of contents, the executive summary, the management plan, the product/service plan, the marketing plan, the merchandising plan, the financial plan, operating and control systems plan, the growth plan, and the appendix. Each section or component should objectively address both the strengths and weaknesses of the business. It will become the tool for making a dream a reality.

REFERENCES

1. Arthur DeThomas, and William Fredenberger, *Writing a Convincing Business Plan* (Hauppauge, New York: Barron's Business Library, 1995, p. 47)
2. Rhonda M. Abrams, *The Successful Business Plan: Secrets and Strategies* (Palo Alto, California: Running 'R' Media, February, 1999, p. 32)

RESOURCES

FastTrac™ New Venture and FastTrac™ Planning are programs offered in many states throughout the country. Log on to www.fasttrac.org for more information. FastTrac™ is owned by the Kauffman Center for Entrepreneurial Leadership at the Ewing Marion Kauffman Foundation.

Industry-at-a-glance reports are industry studies conducted by the Small Business Research and Information Center at the University of Missouri-Rolla, 1999 (www.umr.edu/~tscsbdc/iagall.html).

SUGGESTED READINGS

Rhonda Abrams, *The Successful Business Plan: Secrets and Strategies* (Palo Alto, California: Running 'R' Media, February 1999, p. 32)
Stanley Rich and David Gumpert, *Business Plans that Win $$$* (New York, New York: Harper & Row, 1985)

Sample Business Plan

COVER LETTER

December 24, 20XX

Mr. Bill Eversharp, Vice President
Greatest Bank & Trust
983 Side Street
City, State 22222

Dear Mr. Eversharp:

As we agreed during our meeting on December 15, I am enclosing the business plan to support a loan request in the amount of $60,000 for start-up capital for my company BeTwixt, Inc. As we discussed, an additional line of credit is requested in the amount of $62,000 required in November for core inventory and start-up costs.

Thank you for your consideration. I look forward to your reply and to the prospect of a long-term relationship with your bank.

Sincerely,

Sally Rich
BeTwixt, Inc.
123 Retail Avenue
Diva City, State 55512
111-555-0101
betwixt@email.com

Encl.

of

BeTwixt, Inc.
123 Retail Avenue
Diva City, State 55512
111-555-0101
betwixt@email.com

Presented by:
Sally Rich
Larry LaChamp
December 24, 20XX

CONTENTS

EXECUTIVE SUMMARY

BeTwixt, Inc., was incorporated by Sally Rich in October 20XX and currently has s-corporation status. BeTwixt, Inc. will be a family-owned retailer of women's clothing, offering clothing to women sizes 12–20 who want a fashionable look at affordable prices. The product offering will consist of apparel suitable for business and casual dress. Prices will range from $25 to $89.

The store will be located at 123 Retail Avenue in downtown Diva City. It will be located on the corner opposite Anthony's Store and Cyndi's Company. The location offers shoppers the convenience of a centralized location and a variety of shopping opportunities that cannot be found elsewhere in the area. The location benefits BeTwixt, Inc., with its heavy foot traffic and easy parking. It will be located near the university and both Core and Charge colleges.

BeTwixt, Inc., will be managed by its owner, Sally Rich, who has employed Larry LaChamp to act as assistant manager. The management team has over 13 years of experience in the industry. Ms. Rich holds a bachelor of science degree in fashion merchandising with a minor in marketing. She has held positions as buyer, sales associate, and director of public relations. Mr. LaChamp holds a bachelor of science degree in business administration and a master of science degree in business administration with an emphasis in marketing. He has held positions in the field of marketing and advertising, operations, and customer service for a retail clothing store. BeTwixt, Inc. will also employ two part-time sales associates to help with the day-to-day operations of the business.

BeTwixt, Inc., recognizes its need for outside advisers to lend expertise in various areas. The company has associations with individuals who bring expertise needed to the success of the company. The list of these individuals is located in the Management Plan.

The demand for apparel in the size range noted above is growing. This size category has grown 20 percent since 1994 to approximately $23 billion in 1997. Plus-size women are the fastest growing segment of the U.S. population. Finding clothing in this size range can be difficult. BeTwixt, Inc. will fulfill a need in the immediate geographic area to serve this population. Approximately 25 percent of the population of Diva City falls within the age group of the target market. Other stores in the immediate area are not meeting the current needs of the market due to their current merchandise offerings.

Based on pro formas, BeTwixt, Inc. is requesting a loan in the amount of $60,000. A line of credit in the amount of $62,000 has also been requested. The funds from the loan will be used to purchase core inventory and cover start-up costs for opening the business.

PRODUCT PLAN

Purpose

BeTwixt, Inc., will be a family-owned retailer of women's clothing, offering clothing to women in sizes 12–20. The company was legally incorporated in 20XX and currently has s-corporation tax status. It will be owned and operated by its major stockholder, Sally Rich. BeTwixt's strength will stem from its adherence to its goal of providing excellent customer service and its belief that employees are the company's most valuable asset.

The Company was founded to meet market demand for larger-size women wanting a fashionable look at affordable prices. The product line will offer an extensive selection of larger-size women's apparel suitable for business and casual dress. Research indicates that six out of every ten women wear size 12 or larger and that half of all American women are size 14 or larger, with nearly a third size 16 or above, yet fashion retail stores have limited styles and selections for the larger-size woman (ABC Annual Report, November 20XX).

Unique Features

BeTwixt, Inc., will offer products ranging from sportswear to professional business wear. The products will be in the midprice range with clothing ranging from $25 to $89. Lines carried will cater to women ages 21 to 35.

Self-esteem can sometimes be an issue with consumers shopping in this size range. In an effort to combat this issue, BeTwixt, Inc., will "resize" its merchandise, changing labels from sizes 12, 14, 16, 18, and 20 to read sizes 2, 4, 6, 8, and 10. Research indicates that women feel better about themselves when they wear a smaller size in apparel (M. Smith, *What Women Wear*, January 20XX).

Stage of Development

BeTwixt, Inc., will sell established, brand-name women's apparel and accessories. The company has secured vendors such as Kenneth Cole, Elisabeth, and Positive Attitude. New product lines in this size range are continually being developed and sold at apparel markets. The company will be sensitive to new opportunities and to changing customer needs, attitudes, and preferences. It will be an ongoing goal of BeTwixt, Inc., to attend apparel markets and look for opportunities and ways in which the company can better meet the needs of its customers.

Location

The store will be located at 123 Retail Avenue in downtown Diva City. It will be located on the corner opposite Anthony's Store and Cyndi's Company. This centralized location, along with the unique downtown area shopping experience, offers shoppers convenience, variety, and shopping opportunities that cannot be found elsewhere in the area. The 123 Retail Avenue location allows the store to capture the marketing benefits of heavy foot-traffic during the entire year, easy parking, and customer access to a variety of other retail establishments and restaurants in the area. The retail customer mix already attracted to this location by the existing stores includes residents of approximately six adjoining counties, the university, and two colleges.

The 3,000-square-foot facility will host 2,500 square feet of sales floor space and 500 square feet of office storage space. Receiving facilities are accessible at the rear of the store, next to the office space. Leasehold improvements include painting, lighting, new floor coverings, the addition of two dressing rooms, and remodeling of the bathroom, all of which will cost $10,000. An additional $8,900 will be spent on furniture, display racks, tables, and office equipment.

The landlord, Butch Wall, has agreed to a 3-year lease and will accept a 2,500 deposit. Lease payments have been negotiated at $2,500 per month and will be reviewed at the end of year 2. Utilities are not included in the lease payments. Utilities are estimated between $50 and $300 per month (see attached cash-flow statement). See Location plan for further detail.

Legal and Regulatory

Federal Trade Commission (FTC) regulations require retailers and manufacturers to sell clothing that is accurately and completely labeled with information on where a product is made and the proportions of fibers present in the product. The rules apply to storefront operations, mail-order companies, and Internet sales. Although this company is not a manufacturer, it is aware that such regulations exist within the industry and will sell merchandise with such labeling.

Local Licenses and Permits

Diva City requires a city business license and an occupancy permit in order to conduct business in that city. All local licenses and permits will be obtained as required by local and state laws and regulations.

Product Limitations

The women' apparel industry changes as fashion changes each season. As this causes the inventory to be perishable, stale, unsold inventory must be discounted in an attempt to move it out of the store.

Markdowns on merchandise will be taken monthly. Merchandise will remain discounted until sold. If necessary markdowns will be taken on fall/winter merchandise during the month of January and on spring/summer merchandise during the month of July.

Related Products

In addition to clothing, BeTwixt, Inc., will carry 5 percent of its stock in accessories. Accessories will include jewelry, hair accessories, sunglasses, handbags, wallets, and gift items. The store will carry designs by Kenneth Cole, Fossil, and Nine West. Photographs of the proposed inventory can be found in the Appendix.

BeTwixt, Inc., will carry six primary product lines, five secondary product lines, and an assortment of accessories. Product will be purchased at market five times per year.

Positive Attitude
111 Center
New York NY
212-555-4342

Bechamel
333 Left
New York NY
212-555-8888

Tommy Hilfiger
888 North
Los Angeles CA
333-555-8766

Napa Valley
777 East
Los Angeles CA
310-555-4848

Fossil
98 Corner
Columbia MA
573-555-8787

Kenneth Cole
99 Program
New York NY
212-555-9796

Elisabeth
222 Right
New York NY
212-555-2345

Nine West
848 West
New York NY
212-555-3333

Onyx
999 South
Los Angeles CA
310-555-3456

Suppliers will provide payment terms, 8 percent due 30 days from the date of invoice. Products will typically be shipped 30 to 60 days from the date the orders are placed.

Management Philosophy

BeTwixt, Inc., will adhere to the philosophy that three groups are responsible for the company's success: its customers, the people in the company, and the management team that leads the organizational personnel. Owner Sally Rich believes that it is management's responsibility to create the atmosphere and establish the relationships that emphasize the importance of each member of the company and its appreciation of the contribution made by each to the company's success. She further believes that:

1. **BeTwixt, Inc., customers are its lifeblood.** Every customer must be treated by any BeTwixt, Inc., representative as if he or she were the company's best customer. At BeTwixt, Inc., the adage that the customer is always right means: The customer has the right to a quality product and quality service. BeTwixt, Inc., has the responsibility to see that these customer rights are addressed.

2. **BeTwixt, Inc., employees are the company's most important assets.** Employees are vital members of the organizational team, and what the company accomplishes is accomplished through them. It is the responsibility of the management team to treat subordinates with the same degree of dignity and respect that would be afforded Ms. Rich or any other employees hired by the company. A BeTwixt, Inc., manager has the responsibility to create an atmosphere and work environment that allows subordinates the opportunity to be contributing, respected members of the team and to perform to the best of their ability. This requires a manager, through word and deed, to be a leader. As a leader, a manager must positively influence the behavior of others. While a manager is ultimately responsible for the successful execution of his or her duties, that manager must act on the belief that these responsibilities cannot be met without the cooperation of motivated, productive employees.

3. **Employee performance must be fairly evaluated.** Employees have the right to expect that their job performance will be measured and evaluated by standards that are free from personal bias and reflect effort, results, attitude toward customers, and the degree to which the employee is a cooperative team player.

Management Team

As indicated by the organizational chart, located on page 352, BeTwixt, Inc.'s key personnel are the owner/president, assistant manager, and part-time sales representatives. A summary of the background and qualifications of each position-holder is provided, and complete résumés are included in the Appendix.

Owner/President

Sally Rich holds a bachelor of science degree in fashion merchandising from the University of State, with a minor in marketing. Her 8 years of experience in sales and customer service include positions as a buyer for Saks Fifth Avenue in New York, NY; a sales associate for Famous Barr; and a public relations assistant for Agnes B., a French designer. While employed at Saks Fifth Avenue, Ms. Rich was responsible for supervising employees in the absence of the assistant manager. Her work history and education will provide her with the experience needed to contribute to the success of the company. Ms. Rich will be responsible for purchasing inventory and working with manufacturers. She will be active in customer relations and quality control issues. She will also be responsible for entering daily receipts, checking invoices against inventory, marking goods, and determining markdowns.

Assistant Manager

Larry LaChamp holds a bachelor of science degree in business administration and a masters of science degree in business administration with an emphasis in marketing from Some University. He has over 5 years' experience in the field of marketing and advertising for a retail clothing store. Mr. LaChamp was also responsible for many of the daily operations of the store, including marking and placing goods for sale to the customer and receiving and verifying inventory. As assistant manager, he will assume the roles of floor manager and sales manager. He will be heavily involved with the company's marketing strategy. The assistant manager will work 30 hours per week.

Sales Associate

BeTwixt, Inc., will employ two part-time sales associates. These individuals will have 2 to 3 years' experience in fashion retail sales. Their responsibilities will include folding, steaming, and pressing incoming merchandise; and displaying merchandise on the floor. They will be responsible for assisting customers and following up on sales. They must demonstrate excellent skills in customer relations. Each sales associate will work 25 hours per week. Ads will be placed in local newspapers to advertise these positions.

Compensation and Ownership

BeTwixt, Inc., will be a closely held s-corporation. This company is owned solely by Sally Rich. The corporation charter authorizes 100 shares of common stock. These shares have an assigned par value of $1.00. One hundred shares will be issued to Sally Rich at the time of filing.

As of the date of this plan, BeTwixt, Inc., has the following compensation package and incentive program in place:

Owner	Assistant Manager	Sales Associate
Salary: $1,000 p/mo. Owner may take profit as additional draw at year end. Health insurance: 80/20 coverage	$25,000 p/yr. 30 hours per week Thirty percent (30%) discount on merchandise. Dollar amount cannot exceed 10% of annual salary. Discount may not be used for family and friends. If sales projections are exceeded, assistant manager will receive 5% of salary as bonus at year end (provided the company is profitable). Health insurance: 80/20 coverage	$8.00 p/hour. 25 hours per week Twenty percent (20%) discount on merchandise. Dollar amount cannot exceed 10% of annual salary. Discount may not be used for family and friends. If sales projections are exceeded, sales associate will receive 5% of salary as bonus at year end (provided the company is profitable).

Board of Directors/Advisory Council

At the time of this writing, BeTwixt, Inc., has no outside members on the board of directors; however, management recognizes the need for outside advisers to provide expertise in various areas. Each advisory council member will receive a $100 gift certificate one time per year. The company is pleased to have associations with the following persons:

Legal
Tom Lawyon
Lawyon, Lawyon, and Howell
3456 Almond Street
Some City, State 45444

Retail
John and Jane Marley
Some Sport Retail Clothing Store, Inc.
4879 Any Street
Some City, State 22222

Accountant
Sara Numberscruncher, CPA
Numberscruncher, Hitt, and Hitt
48987 Suite 100
Some City, State 22222

Insurance (medical)
Cindy Cure
Cure & Associates
5858 Walnut
Some City, State 22222

Insurance (general business and professional liability)
John Munch
Always There Insurance Co.
456587 Pine Street
Some City, State 22222

Marketing
Paula Principal
GoGettem, LLC
487 Cherry Street
Some City, State 22222

Banking
Bill Eversharp
Vice President
Greatest Bank & Trust
983 Side Street
Some City, State 22222

Contractual Agreements

The assistant manager will hold a noncompete agreement with BeTwixt, Inc. The agreement will stipulate that upon termination of employment, Larry LaChamp cannot open a store within a 50-mile radius for a period of not less that 3 years from the date of termination.

Insurance

BeTwixt, Inc., will maintain liability insurance and normal business coverage through Always There Insurance Co. The company was issued the following quote as of April 30, 20XX:

> $XXX Liability
> $XXX Theft
> $XXX Fire

Health Insurance will be provided through Cure & Associates. As of April 30, 20XX, BeTwixt, Inc., was issued the following quote:

$XXX

CURRENT ORGANIZATION CHART

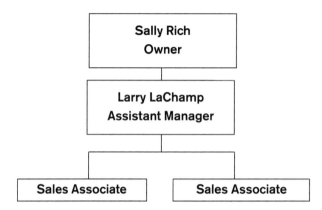

"Currently, in the U.S., 168,025 firms are apparel retailers having annual sales of about $162.4 billion," according to *Marketplace*. In addition to the 168,025 firms that are primarily apparel retailers, 21,948 additional firms sell apparel, but not as their primary business; however, these stores post significant annual apparel sales of about $90.2 billion.

Most apparel retailers in the United States have four or fewer employees. Of these firms, 13 percent employ 1 employee, 42 percent employ 2–4 employees, 10 percent employ 3–9 employees, 4 percent employ 20–24 employees, 1 percent employ 25 or more employees, the number of employees for 30 percent is unknown. Apparel retailers having annual sales of less than $200,000 make up a significant portion of the industry. Those with annual sales of over $500,000 represent 5 percent of the market or less. (Small Business Research & Information Center, *Industry-at-a-Glance,* Apparel Retailing SIC code 56, 1999, pp. 6–7.)

"In 1998, retail had a good year with all segments showing some growth. Men's wear sales grew the most, with an annual increase of seven percent (7%). The women's market gained 3.7 percent, boys' grew 5.6 percent, girls' increased 2.5 percent, and infants' and toddlers' increased by 2.2 percent." (Small Business Research & Information Center, *Industry-at-a-Glance,* Apparel Retailing SIC code 56, 1999, p. 6.)

Dollars ($ Billions)

	1996	**1997**	**1998**
Men's	49.3	50.8	54.3
Women's	85	89.2	92.6
Children's	27	29	30
Total	131.3	169	177

"The women's plus-size category had grown 20 percent since 1994, to approximately $23 billion in 1997. Plus-size women are somewhat older, and the fastest growing portion of the U.S. population is 55 years old and older. Also, a younger market segment has emerged because 22 percent of the teenage population is estimated to be overweight. Many catalogers and retailers see the plus-size segment as no different from mainstream women's clothing. The problem is that the plus-size woman has a difficult time finding items she wants in the manufacturer's normal size ranges. Lane Bryant, Roaman's, the catalog *Silouettes,* and other plus-size retailers have gone to the World Wide Web to reach more consumers." (Small Business Research & Information Center, *Industry-at-a-Glance,* Apparel Retailing SIC code 56, 1999, p. 6.)

"The inner cities seem to have room for more apparel retailers. Inner-city markets can account for $85 billion in annual retail spending, according to estimates found in a recent study by the Initiative for a Competitive Inner City (ICIC), a national nonprofit organization. Nevertheless, retailers are only taking $64 billion, due to the perception that inner cities are difficult and unprofitable markets. Many retailers think that a low-income area means there is no market. However, in an inner-city square mile, the number of retail dollars is two to six times higher than in an affluent, suburban square mile, according to the *ApparelNews.Net*. Other findings conclude that inner-city shoppers are more fashion conscious, buy at the beginning of the season at full price, have an orientation to brand and service, have a greater interest in credit, are attracted to specialty stores, and will seek out discount department stores." (Small Business Research & Information Center, *Industry-at-a-Glance,* Apparel Retailing SIC code 56, 1999, pp. 38–39.)

Industry Trends

Large-size teens and women in their twenties are craving more fashion conscious clothing. The large-size category is getting its boost from younger shoppers. The younger customer is the segment of the large-size population that is fueling the greatest leap in demand. The large-size woman wants to look like her misses- and junior-size counterparts.

Although the bricks-and-mortar store is wanted and needed, recent growth of apparel sales over the Internet warrants brief discussion. BeTwixt, Inc., does not have initial plans for selling merchandise on-line; however, it is an area that will be evaluated in the future.

Demographics. The table below highlights apparel sales for baby boomers and generation Xers (those born after 1979 and before 1994). The most prominent difference between baby boomers and generation Xers is the approach to shopping. Almost one-third of baby boomers buy on impulse; while nearly half of generation Xers do. In 1998, 49 percent of baby boomers enjoyed shopping, as did 47 percent of generation Xers. Both groups spent an average of an hour and a half in apparel stores on each shopping trip.

Age (Years)	Units	Dollars
Under 14	0.4%	0.4%
14 to 16	0.7%	0.8%
17 to 19	1.0%	0.9%
20 to 24	5.2%	5.0%
25 to 29	9.1%	8.3%
30 to 34	13.3%	10.9%
35 to 44	29.0%	26.8%
45 to 54	19.1%	21.9%
55 to 64	10.3%	11.7%
65 and over	10.5%	11.9%

Other similarities are that both generations form their apparel ideas from what they already own, with window and store displays as the number two source. One difference between the groups was the influence of peers, commercials, and celebrities: Generation X was more susceptible to these influences. However, when the baby boomers were the age that generation Xers are now, the same could be said of them. Only 7.4 percent of baby boomers choose specialty stores, while 18.6 percent of generation Xers prefer specialty stores.

Retailers have to either grow new customers from childhood or entice them from the competitors. The key to reaching members of this group is to understand them and then develop marketing and merchandising strategies to fit their needs. Price was the most important factor to apparel shoppers, with fiber content ranking second, and cleaning instructions ranking a very close third.

With today's busy lifestyles, wasting the customer's time is not acceptable. Advertising or making promises the business is unable to keep is lying, and consumers will not forgive and forget. Salespersons who do not know the products will be unable to do their job. Customers ignored by the staff will not come back. Consumers judge the business by the people working there. (Small Business Research & Information Center, *Industry-at-a-Glance,* Apparel Retailing SIC code 56, 1999, pp. 13–17.)

Seasonality Factors

Although variation will occur by manufacturer, most manufacturers of fashion merchandise develop five seasonal lines. They include the following: fall I, fall II, holiday, spring, and summer. Some manufacturers, particularly those catering to designer oriented customers, produce an additional line, cruise, which is delivered between holiday and spring seasons. Other manufacturers, especially those with lines that do not reflect a high level of seasonal changes, may present two lines per year; fall/winter and spring/summer.

Profit Characteristics

Profit characteristics for the fashion retail industry reflect a 50% markup on merchandise, with an average markdown of 18%. The table below lists several industry standard financial ratios for apparel and accessory store operations:

Ratio Type	Ratio for Businesses Having Medium Asset Levels
Current	2.8
Quick	0.9
Sales/Receivables	24.6
Debt/Tangible Net Worth	1.1
Sales/Total Assets	3.0

Source: Robert Morris Associates *Annual Statement Studies* component of *FISCAL*, ver. 6.13, 1996.

Basis of Competition

Price is an important factor to apparel shoppers. In a study published by *Lifestyle Monitor*, Spring 1999, p. 10, 57.8 percent of women felt price was very important. Although price is not the only basis for competition within the industry, it is a factor among consumers. Other factors that can influence the industry include convenience, accessibility, and fabrics.

Competition

The city of Diva has six businesses that carry women's apparel with combined sales of approximately $3 million. Competition in the area is based primarily on selection and quality of merchandise. BeTwixt, Inc., will compete on this basis. In an effort to address the issue of how women feel about themselves buying larger sizes, the store will change sizes from 12, 14, 16, 18, and 20 to read 2, 4, 6, 8, and 10. The six businesses located in Diva City do not offer a large selection of clothing for woman sizes 12–20. Two of the stores, Midvale and Only Yours offer higher-end clothing and do not offer sizes 12–20. The other three offer these sizes, but are limited in selection. Women in Diva City spend approximately $XX on clothing each year (site source). Many are traveling to other cities or ordering on-line to meet their needs.

Located in a university town, Diva City carries a large population of both baby boomers and generation Xers. Approximately 45 percent of the population of Diva City is made up of these groups. Twenty-five percent within this population are women ages 18 to 42.

The intention to market BeTwixt, Inc., in the mid-income level, medium quality and size niche will put the store in competition with the established stores in the area. The business will be located in the downtown area, thus providing easy access. Because this is a start-up company, management conservatively estimates that the company will capture 10 percent of its target market for the first year, and from 15 percent to 20 percent of this market by the end of year 3. BeTwixt, Inc., will be able to offer good quality merchandise to be sold at a retail price that is competitive with stores outside the immediate geographic area.

It is anticipated that competition will increase as the success of the store becomes evident. The window of opportunity to establish the customer base prior to seeing an increase in competition is approximately 3 years. This assumption is based on the time in which new competition typically enters this market.

Target Market/Customer Profile

Diva City has a population of XX of women ages 18 to 34. This age group comprises one-fourth of the large-size market population in this geographic area. Demographics also show a medium income level of $XXX, with X% being college students or working professionals. Their primary motivations for purchase are:

1. The desire to buy in their geographic area.
2. The need for quality clothing in sizes 12–20.
3. The ability to purchase quality clothing at reasonable prices.

In a survey conducted through the local chamber of commerce and the university, female consumers ages 18–34 who indicated they were a size 12–20 stated that they would purchase clothing in the area if the selection existed. They also indicated that they spend approximately $XX on clothing each year.

Pricing Profile

BeTwixt, Inc., will use the keystone method of retail pricing. This method means setting retail prices at double the cost of the merchandise at wholesale to obtain the original selling price. This type of pricing is standard for the industry and not typically questioned by consumers.

The Company intends to place the following opening orders at the corresponding wholesale prices:

Positive Attitude	$XXX	Napa Valley	$XXX
Elisabeth	$XXX	Nine West	$XXX
Bechamel	$XXX	Fossil	$XXX
Tommy Hilfiger	$XXX	Kenneth Cole	$XXX
Onyx	$XXX		

The lines and pricing of merchandise can be found in the merchandising section of this business plan.

Break-even Analysis

Based on projections, BeTwixt, Inc., will break even in December of 20XX.

Advertising and Promotion

Four of the Diva City stores have been in the market for over 6 years. They advertise through radio, television, and newspaper. As BeTwixt, Inc., must establish an image in the retail consumer market, the company's entry into the market will be accompanied by an intense 12-month promotion campaign consisting of a grand opening, and both radio and newspaper advertising. The total promotional budget for the first year of the business is $15,000. This amount will be reduced by 30 percent in the second and third years if market acceptance rates and sales targets are met.

The Company will create a circular to run in the local newspaper every Sunday for the first 4 months of operation. Two weeks prior to the opening of the store, a circular will be placed in the local newspaper and radio spots will announce the opening.

Radio spots will be run on stations 11.1 and 22.2. Advertising spots will run for 30 seconds and will be focused on prime drive home time, from 3:00 p.m. to 8:00 p.m. These stations and time slots have been selected based on statistics indicating that most female listeners between the ages of 18 and 34 listen to these stations at these times. (Media Market, 20XX)

Guarantees

Returns may be made within 30 days of purchase. Cash refunds will be given with attached sales receipts.

Future Markets

BeTwixt, Inc., recognizes the opportunity to create awareness of the store and expand sales with the strong customer base of Internet consumers. Apparel goods are typically the first level of items purchased on the Web and are among the leaders in online purchases. The business will continue to monitor sales and weigh options with regard to a Web presence.

Regional Location

The success of BeTwixt, Inc., relies a great deal on its location. BeTwixt, Inc., will be located at 123 Retail Avenue in downtown Dive City. Diva City, State, is located in the western region of the United States. The store will be located opposite Anthony's Store and Cyndi's Company. BeTwixt will be located in the inner-city area. Market research indicates that locating the business in an inner-city area provides a great deal of opportunity. In an inner-city square mile, the number of retail dollars is two to six times higher than in an affluent, suburban square mile. Buyers in inner-city areas are fashion-conscious, buy at the beginning of the season at full price, have an orientation to brand and service, have a greater interest in credit, and are attracted to specialty stores. BeTwixt, Inc., is targeting women, sizes 12–20, in the younger age group. Located near two colleges, this area of Diva City attracts a young, fashion conscious population.

This location provides easy access for the delivery of merchandise. BeTwixt has verified shipping methods, times of delivery, and accessibility with all its suppliers.

The location also provides BeTwixt, Inc., with the opportunity to seek qualified sales associates. College students are eager to seek employment in the downtown area, near the college campuses.

Demographic and Psychographic Characteristics

More than XXX people reside per square mile in Diva City (see the population density for Diva City in the Appendix). Demographics include a population of XXX, primary age group 25 to 44, an income level of $XXX. Most have received a secondary education and are holding professional positions. The colleges in the area bring a younger shopper to the area.

Individuals shopping in the Retail Avenue area are primarily age 25 to 44 with an income level of $XXX. They are fashion conscious professionals and students.

Competition

Six fashion retail businesses are located in Diva City that carry women's apparel. Combined, these stores boast sales of over $3 million. Competition in the area is based primarily on location and selection of merchandise. These six locations do not offer a large selection of clothing for the woman size 12–20. Two of the stores, Midvale and Only Yours offer higher-end clothing and do not offer sizes 12–20.

The six fashion retail businesses are located in the following areas:

Anthony's Store	142 Retail Avenue
Cyndi's Company	118 Retail Avenue
Midvale	4300 Suburban Street
Only Yours	Stadium Avenue
Clothing Is In	Broadway and Forrest
Dress Yourself Up	Park Avenue

Only Anthony's Store and Cyndi's Company are located within a 1 mile radius of Be-Twixt, Inc.

Due to the lack of selection based on size in this market, and the lack of stores carrying merchandise in this size range, in this geographic location, BeTwixt has the opportunity to capture a large share of the market for women seeking this size range. BeTwixt anticipates capturing over 60 percent of the market share.

Site

BeTwixt, Inc., located at 123 Retail Avenue, is within 2 blocks of a free municipal parking complex. Parking spaces are typically available in this garage.

Location Factors

Merchandise will be sold at a retail location. Customers will have the ability to select merchandise from a brick-and-mortar retail store. Sales associates will be available to help customers with their shopping and buying decisions.

Physical Visibility

Located on the corner of 123 Retail Avenue, BeTwixt is visible from all directions of a major downtown intersection. Retail Avenue runs directly to both colleges and is the street most used to reach these destinations. Because BeTwixt will rely to a large extent on foot traffic; this location provides the best possible scenario.

Location within the inner-city is not conducive to attracting a majority of shoppers from the suburbs. Stores located within this area indicate that most customers are shopping on lunch hours and as they go to and from school. Therefore, good visibility is necessary to be successful.

Finances and Locations

BeTwixt will lease space at 123 Retail Avenue. The leasor requires a deposit of $2,500 with rent at $2,500 each month. The initial lease is for a 3-year period with an option to renew for two additional 3-year periods. A rent increase will be reviewed at the end of 3 years. BeTwixt, Inc., will have a first right of refusal should the property be placed on the market for sale.

Shoppers and customers will have access to a variety of merchandise in over 2,500 feet of selling space. The additional 500 square feet will host fitting rooms, storage, and the cash desk.

An adjoining 1,500 feet of retail space would be available to lease within 2 years should BeTwixt decide to expand its facility.

Facilities

The facility features a brick façade with large display windows flanking a double door entry. Parking spaces are available directly in front of the store and in the adjacent parking lot. A large sign featuring the store name hangs over the entry and additional signing hangs from the canopy. The store has Berber carpeting throughout which is accented by large stone tiles in the entry way and around the cash desk. The décor is French country in neutral colors. Fixtures are primarily distressed and whitewashed pine. Mannequins consist of muslin-covered dress forms. A crystal chandelier provides a focal point in the center of the store. The lighting has been custom-designed to highlight merchandise offerings, provide a true reflection of color, and facilitate work areas, such as the cash desk. The cash desk, located at the front of the store, is constructed to hold the POS system, wrap equipment and supplies, credit card materials, and a telephone/fax machine. Fitting rooms are located toward the back of the store; they are comfortably yet minimally furnished and well lit. A three-way mirror and pedestal outside the fitting room allows the customer to view the back and front of a garment while facilitating alteration needs.

Layout

See attached layout plan in the Business Plan Appendix (page 371).

MERCHANDISING PLAN

Proposed Lines

BeTwixt, Inc., will carry the following lines of women's apparel:

Primary

Manufactuer	*Source*
Positive Attitude	New York
Elisabeth	New York
Bechamel	New York
Napa Valley	Los Angeles

Secondary

Fossil	Massachusetts
Kenneth Cole	New York
Nine West	New York
Onyx	Los Angeles

Assortment of Stock

Merchandise classification:

Activewear	15%	tops, bottoms
Sportswear	20%	tops, bottoms, denim
Accessories	5%	jewelry, sunglasses, handbags
Career wear	30%	tops, bottoms, skirts, pants, jackets, suits
Dresses	20%	career, casual, special occasion
Sleepwear	10%	pajamas, robes, gowns, loungewear

Market Trips

Where	When	Objective	Cost
Los Angeles	July	Purchase OS for opening	$XX
Dallas	September	Purchase stock for spring	$XX
Los Angeles	January	Purchase stock for summer	$XX
Los Angeles	March	Purchase stock for fall I	$XX
Dallas	June	Purchase stock for fall II	$XX

Markup Policies

BeTwixt, Inc., will use the keystone method of retail pricing. This method means setting retail prices at double the cost of the merchandise at wholesale to obtain the original selling price. The store will mark up merchandise 100 percent based on cost; 50 percent based on retail.

Markdown Timing and Percentage

Markdowns are taken on a monthly basis on 15 percent of merchandise.

Return Policy

BeTwixt, Inc., will accept returns within 30 days of the date of purchase. The receipt must accompany the merchandise in order for the consumer to receive a cash refund. Merchandise returned without a receipt will result in a store credit for the amount of the purchase.

FINANCIAL PLAN

Cash on Hand: Principal will inject gift from parents in the amount of $30,500.

Loan: A loan for start-up expenses is requested in the amount of $60,000. For projection purposes, the loan had been calculated at an interest rate of 10 percent for a period of 60 months. The loan injection will be used as follows:

$50,000—Core inventory
$3,000—Advertising
$3,500—Security system
$1,500—Grand opening expense
$2,000—Secure lease on building

Revolving Line of Credit: A line of credit in the amount of $62,000 has been requested. For projection purposes, interest accrues at the rate of 10 percent and will be paid monthly.

Rate: Landlord has agreed to a 1-month deposit of $2,500. The facility is 3,000 square feet. The facility has 2,500 square feet of sales floor space and 500 square feet of office/storage space.

Travel Expense: Travel includes buying trips to market five times per year plus an initial buying trip. Travel expenses include hotel, meals, and transportation.

Advertising: Management will advertise through local newspapers and radio ads. Advertising will increase in the months of November and December to promote the holiday season. Newspaper ads will run 2 times per month at a cost of $3,900 p/yr. Radio ads will run 2 times per week for 28 weeks for a cost of $9,100.

Accounting and Legal: Professional fees of $250 per month have been allocated for accounting services. Legal services will be engaged on an "as needed" basis. An allocation of $600 has been made for start-up and first-month legal expenses.

Leasehold Improvements: Leasehold improvements include painting, lighting, new floor covering, construction of two dressing rooms, and remodeling of the bathroom. The total for these will be $10,000. $8,900 will be spent on furniture, display racks, tables, and office equipment.

Direct Labor: BeTwixt, Inc., will employ 1 assistant manager at a salary of $25,000 per year and two part-time sales associates at $8.00 per hour/25 hours per week. Wages for part-time employees are based on 50 working weeks per year with rotation for time off.

Insurance: Insurance includes casualty, hazard, and liability insurance. Health insurance is calculated at $250 per month for both the owner and assistant manager.

Bank Charges: Bank charges are based on a 2.5 percent service charge for credit card transactions and standard account service fees of $60 per month.

Taxes/Licenses: These include the business license of $125 (start-up) and a $425 property tax on business assets.

Owner's Draw: The owner will receive a draw of $1,000 a month for the first 6 months with an increase to $2,000 per month beginning in month 7.

Inventory: BeTwixt, Inc., will have a core inventory of $50,000 and will maintain an inventory level of $50,000 (at cost).

BeTwixt, Inc.

Pro Forma Cash Flow
12 Months 2002

		Start-up	Jan.	Feb.	Mar.	Apr.	May	June	July	Aug.	Sept.	Oct.	Nov.	Dec.	Totals
1	Cash On Hand	30,500	900	274	348	7,117	583	2,449	9,338	3,137	886	11,253	525	464	
2	Loan Proceeds	60,000	0	24,000	1000	12,000	0	0	21,000	8,000	0	10,000	5,000	0	141,000
3		0	0	0	0	0	0	0	0	0	0	0	0	0	
4	Cash Sales		15,000	20,000	21,000	27,000	32,000	22,000	17,000	32,000	27,000	22,000	55,000	90,000	380,000
5		0	0	0	0	0	0	0	0	0	0	0	0	0	
6		0	0	0	0	0	0	0	0	0	0	0	0	0	
7	Total Cash	90,500	15,900	44,274	22,348	46,117	32,583	24,449	47,338	43,137	27,886	43,253	60,525	90,464	
8															
9	Expenses														
10	Rent	2,500	2,500	2,500	2,500	2,500	2,500	2,500	2,500	2,500	2,500	2,500	2,500	2,500	30,000
11	Direct Labor		3,000	3,000	3,000	3,000	3,000	3,000	3,000	3,000	3,000	3,000	3,000	4,000	37,000
12	Payroll Expense		690	690	690	690	690	690	690	690	690	690	690	920	8,510
13	Inventory	50,000	0	33,000	0	34,000	0	0	28,000	30,000	0	30,000	47,000		202,000
14	Repairs/Maintenance		25	25	25	25	25	25	25	25	25	25	25	25	300
15	Office Supplies	500	25	25	25	25	25	25	25	25	25	25	25	25	300
16	Travel Expense	3,750	3,750	0	3,750	0	0	3,750	3,750	0	3,750	0	0	0	18,750
17	Advertising	3,000	1,000	1,000	1,000	1,000	1,000	1,000	1,000	1,000	1,000	1,000	1,500	1,500	13,000
18	Bad Debts		50	50	50	50	50	50	50	50	50	50	50	50	600
19	Bank Charges		300	350	350	400	400	350	300	400	400	350	600	1,000	5,200
20	Contributions		0	0	250	0	0	250	0	0	250	0	0	250	1,000
21	Dues & Subscripts	175	0	0	0	0	0	0	0	0	175	0	0	0	175
22	Insurance		750	250	250	750	250	230	750	250	250	750	250	250	4,980
23	Meals & Entmnt		50	50	50	50	50	50	50	50	50	50	50	50	600
24	Office & Postage		50	0	180	0	0	180	0	0	180	0	0	180	770
25	Security	3,500	30	30	30	30	30	30	30	30	30	30	30	30	360
26	Accounting & Legal	250	600	250	250	250	250	250	250	250	250	250	250	250	3,350
27	Taxes & Licenses	125	0	0	0	0	0	0	0	0	0	0	0	425	425
28	Telephone/Comm.	1,000	231	231	231	231	231	231	231	231	231	231	231	231	2,772
29	Utilities	750	300	200	125	50	50	75	125	150	110	110	110	110	1,515
30	Interest & Principal		0	0	200	208	19,308	150	150	325	392	392	475	62,517	84,117
31	Amortizing Loan I & P	0	1,275	1,275	1,275	1,275	1,275	1,275	1,275	1,275	1,275	1,275	1,275	1,275	15,300
32	Leasehold Improve.	10,000	0	0	0	0	0	0	0	0	0	0	0	0	0
33	Furniture/Equip/Racks	8,950	0	0	0	0	0	0	0	0	0	0	0	0	0
34	Income Tax	0	0	0	0	0	0	0	0	0	0	0	0	7,150	7,150
35	Sign	3,600	0	0	0	0	0	0	0	0	0	0	0	0	0
36	Grand Opening	1,500	0	0	0	0	0	0	0	0	0	0	0	0	0
37	Total Expenses	89,600	14,626	42,926	14,231	44,534	29,134	14,111	42,201	40,251	14,633	40,728	58,061	82,738	438,174
38	Owners Draw	0	1,000	1,000	1,000	1,000	1,000	1,000	2,000	2,000	2,000	2,000	2,000	2,000	18,000
39	Total Cash Payments	89,600	15,626	43,926	15,231	45,534	30,134	15,111	44,201	42,251	16,633	42,728	60,061	84,738	456,174
40	Cash (End of Month)	900	274	348	7,117	583	2,449	9,338	3,137	886	11,253	525	464	5,726	
41															
42	Operating Line of Credit	0	0	24,000	25,000	37,000	18,000	18,000	39,000	47,000	47,000	57,000	62,000	0	
43	Amortizing Loan Bal.	60,000	0	0	0	0	0	0	0	0	0	0	0	0	
44															
45															

Profit and Loss Statement
For
Year ended December 31, 20XX

Revenue

1	Sales	$ 380,000
2	Cost of Goods Sold	202,000
3	**Gross Profit**	**178,000**

Expenses

Operating Expenses

4	Rent	$ 30,000
5	Direct Labor	37,000
6	Payroll Expense	8,510
7	Repair/Maintenance	300
8	Office Supplies	300
9	Travel Expense	18,750
10	Advertising	13,000
11	Bad Debts	600
12	Bank Charges	5,200
13	Contributions	1,000
14	Dues & Subscriptions	175
15	Insurance	4,980
16	Meals & Entertainment	600
17	Office & Postage	770
18	Security	360
19	Accounting & Legal	3,350
20	Taxes & License	425
21	Telephone/Communications	2,772
22	Utilities	1,515
23	Depreciation/Amortization	4,510
24	**Total Operating Expenses**	**$ 134,117**

Other Revenue and Expense

25	Miscellaneous Income	0
26	Interest Expense	8,679
27	Total Expenses	$ 142,796
28	Income Before Taxes	35,204
29	Income Tax	7,041
30	**Net Income**	**$ 28,163**

Balance Sheet
BeTwixt, Inc.
December 31, 20XX

ASSETS		LIABILITIES AND OWNER'S EQUITY	
Current Assets:		**Current Liabilities:**	
Cash & Marketable Securities	$ 5,726	Notes Payable–Bank	$ 0
Accounts Receivable	0	Notes Payable–Other	0
Inventory	50,000	Accounts Payable	397
Prepaid Expenses	0	Accruals	212
		Income Tax Payable	0
		Current Portion of LTD	9,736
		Other Current Liabilities	0
Total Current Assets	**$ 55,726**	**Total Current Liabilities**	**$ 10,345**
Fixed Assets:		**Long-Term Liabilities:**	
Fixed Assets	$ 22,550	Long-Term Debt	$ 39,508
Less Accumulated Depreciation	(4,510)	Subordinate Officer Debt	0
Notes Receivable	0	Total Liabilities	49,853
Intangibles	0	Common Stock	18,000
Deposits	4,250	Capital Surplus & Paid in Cap.	0
Other Assets	0	Retained Earnings	10,163*
Total Net Fixed Assets	22,290	(Less) Treasury Stock	0
		Total Net Worth	28,163
Total Assets	**$ 78,016**	**Total Liabilities & Net Worth**	**$ 78,016****

Note * = Net income ($28,163) minus owner's draw ($18,000)

** = Total Liabilities & Net Worth equal Total Liabilities ($49,853) plus common stock ($18,000) plus retained earnings ($10,163)

Ordering and Receiving Merchandise

Merchandise will be ordered at market.

Paying suppliers

Eight percent discount 30 days—RTW; net to 3 percent discount 30 days.

Reporting to Management

All sales associates will report to the assistant manager. The assistant manager then reports to the owner/manager. All incidents occurring within the store will be reported to the assistant manager who will in turn return report to the manager. An incident form is included in the Appendix. It is required that the form be completed and given to management within 24 hours of the incident. Weekly staff meetings have been scheduled prior to Saturday opening.

Staff Development

In order to stay informed of customer expectations and the degree of customer satisfaction achieved, BeTwixt, Inc., has established policies that include (a) conducting surveys of existing customers and (b) adopting a "customer is always right" attitude in responding to complaints about merchandise and/or service. Sales training meetings will be attended one time per year at the expense of BeTwixt. Although not indicated in the financials, BeTwixt can and will pay for such training. The market indicates training can be attended for approximately $100 per person for a two-day seminar.

Inventory Control

Physical inventory will be monitored in the following manner: two times per year (beginning of month, January and July) physical inventory.

Returns

Customers have 30 days in which to return items purchased within the store. Cash refunds will be given for merchandise returned with a sales receipt. For merchandise returned with no receipt, store credit will be given for the amount of purchase. Merchandise will then be returned to the floor for sale. Merchandise returned for defects will be returned to the manufacturer within 30 days of receipt.

Company Budgets

Budget meetings will be held with the advisory council every 6 months. The owner will monitor cash flow on a monthly basis during the first year of operation and every quarter during the second year of operation. Budgetary issues will be addressed with the advisory council at each quarterly meeting.

Security Systems

All packages belonging to employees must be checked during the day. Packages brought in from other stores must be left in an authorized location. Purchases made by employees during the day will be held in an authorized location. All employee packages will be subject to inspection. All merchandise will be tagged with a security device to reduce the risk of shoplifting.

Documentation

Documentation used to transact purchases and receive or ship merchandise is included in the Appendix. All orders must be verified by the manager or assistant manager.

Planning Chart/Product Availability

It will be the responsibility of management to ensure all merchandise is received in time for opening.

Marketing Flow Chart

Both the manger and assistant manager will be responsible for placing advertisements with the media. Initial ads have been developed and are included in the Appendix. Future advertisements, will be completed 3 months prior to the running of the ad.

Risk analysis

Risk is always a factor to be considered when opening a new store. BeTwixt researched the immediate area in terms of lease agreements and other businesses in the market in which BeTwixt will serve. Based on this information, it is not anticipated that competition will enter the market within the next 3 years.

Salvaging Assets

Should it become necessary to liquidate the business, BeTwixt will hold a liquidation sale and sell its remaining merchandise. Fixtures will be sold at auction.

BeTwixt, Inc., understands the importance of focusing on what the customer wants and the importance of staying on top of the latest fashions in the industry. It is anticipated that merchandise will remain relatively constant in terms of amount of inventory and the size of the store. It is the intent of the owner to keep the store at 2,500 square feet. Future merchandise such as hosiery, lingerie, and shoes may be added as the customer base grows.

By 2003, more than 40 million households are expected to shop on-line. Between 1998 and 2003, the amount of money spent on-line is expected to increase dramatically, according to a recent *Forrester Report* (Vol. 1, No. 8, November 1998). Consumers' anxiety over security and privacy is the largest external barrier that retailers face in selling on-line according to the Ernst & Young/National Retail Federation (E&Y/NRF) *Second Annual Internet Shopping Survey.* Insufficient resources and integration with existing business processes were the largest internal problems.

The *Second Annual Internet Shopping Survey* conducted by E&Y/NRF showed that 59 percent of retailers plan to sell through the Web, which is more than double the percentage for the previous year. If the numbers are realized, then two-thirds of those surveyed will be selling on-line by the end of 1999. (Small Business Research & Information Center, *Industry-at-a-Glance,* Apparel Retailing SIC code 56, 1999, pp. 24–30.)

In a recent survey conducted by Zona Research, data indicated that people shopped on-line to:

- save time (36 percent)
- save money (15 percent)
- avoid crowds, rude clerks, and raging drivers (11 percent)
- have a better selection (10 percent), and
- have fun (10 percent)

On-line apparel retailing is growing because more households are getting wired, more women are on-line, and an expanding list of fashion firms and retailers are on-line. Apparel had risen from one of the least-purchased categories to the sixth spot in 13 kinds of merchandise sold on the Web, according to *Women's Wear Daily.*

The on-line shopping population is roughly divided into thirds among buyers, non-shoppers, and browsers. Apparel made 23.2 percent of Web shopping purchases in the spring of 1998, according to *Women's Wear Daily.* Women now make up 39 percent of Web shoppers. The 30-to-54 age group does the most on-line shopping, according to *Women's Wear Daily.*

Capital Requirements

To increase inventory to include new merchandise classifications such as hosiery and shoes, an additional $XX in capital would be required. Based on projections, Be-Twixt, Inc., would inject $XX of company funds and request a loan in the amount of $XX to be repaid over a 5-year period.

To develop an on-line store, projections indicate $XX would be needed to take the company in this direction.

Personnel Requirements

It is anticipated that Web sales would necessitate two additional employees to take orders and ship merchandise to the customer.

Exit Strategy

It is the intent to grow the business to be sold 10 years from the date of opening.

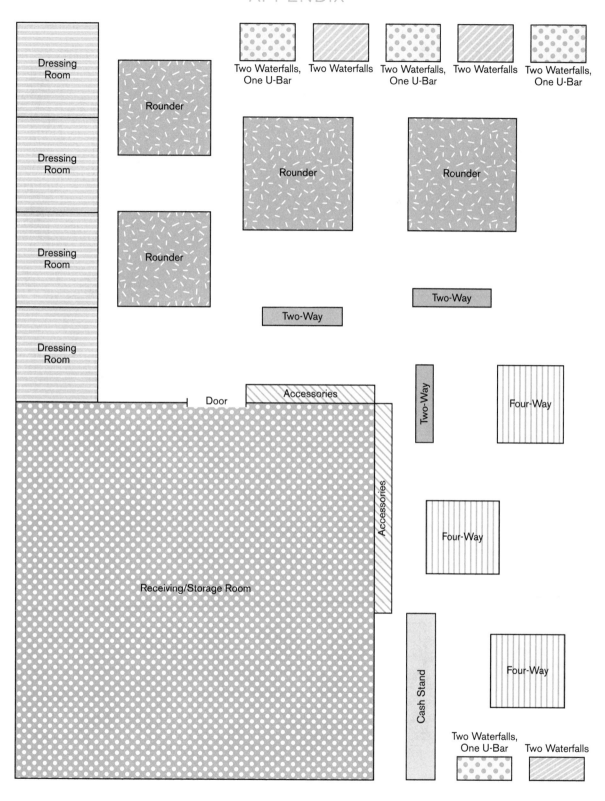

Dressing Room

Dressing Room

Dressing Room

Dressing Room

Rounder

Rounder

Rounder

Rounder

Rounder

Two Waterfalls, One U-Bar

Two Waterfalls

Two Waterfalls, One U-Bar

Two Waterfalls

Two Waterfalls, One U-Bar

Two-Way

Two-Way

Two-Way

Four-Way

Four-Way

Four-Way

Door

Accessories

Accessories

Receiving/Storage Room

Cash Stand

Two Waterfalls, One U-Bar

Two Waterfalls

Note to Student: Due to the space available in this text some attachments that would appear in the Business Plan Appendix have not been included. See chapters for attachment suggestions.

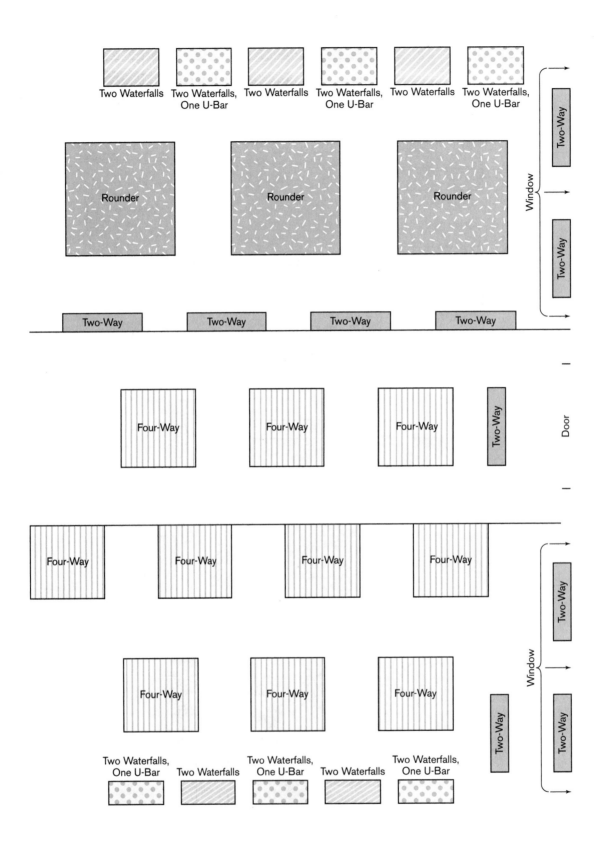

Appendix A

RESOURCES FOR
THE FASHION RETAIL ENTREPRENEUR

This listing features organizations, publications, and Web sites to support the retail entrepreneur in business planning.

American Demographics, Inc.
www.demographics.com
An organization that publishes *American Demographic Magazine*, which provides authoritative information about consumer and business trends, and *Marketing Tools*, which is a monthly magazine focusing on tactics and techniques for improving marketing effectiveness.

***Annual Statement Studies,* Robert Morris Associates**
A reference book that contains balance sheets, income statements, and 16 widely used ratios for industries in five categories: manufacturing, wholesaling, retailing, servicing, and contracting. Available through most banks.

Bureau of Labor Statistics
Division of Information Services
www.bls.gov
A federal agency that reports labor-related information such as wages, prices, and cost of living.

EntreWorld
www.entreworld.org
A Web site offered through the Kauffman Center for Entrepreneurial Leadership that provides information on various aspects of business.

Fairchild's Financial Manual of Retail Stores
www.fairchildpub.com
Fairchild Publications
Library resource book is an annual financial manual for general merchandising chains, discount chains, mail-order firms, drugstores, shoe stores, etc. It includes names of officers and directors, number of stores, sales and earnings, income accounts, and assets and liabilities.

Franchise Handbook
U.S. Government Printing Office
www.franchisehandbook.com
A book disclosing the annual survey of over 900 franchisors covering number of outlets, time in business, cost of a franchise, financial assistance, and training procedures.

The Franchise Annual Director
www.infonews.com/franchise
Information about franchising, franchisors, franchisees, and benefits of a franchise.

Internal Revenue Service (IRS)
www.irs.gov
Provides publications that address the tax issues of concern to the entrepreneur.

Library of Congress
lcweb.loc.gov/homepage/lchp.html
National repository of resources.

National Association of Small Business Investment Companies (NASBIC)
www.nasbic.org
A trade association sponsored by the Small Business Association to provide information about sources of loans for small businesses.

National Association for the Self-Employed (NASE)
www.nase.org
An association that provides members with access to a business consultant. Group health and disability insurance are also available.

SBA Publications
www.sba.gov
Small Business Association offers publications and booklets to help establish budgets, personnel policies, and business plans. A list of publications is available.

Service Corps of Retired Executives (SCORE)
www.score.org
Provides free individual counseling, courses, conferences, and workshops.

Small Business Administration (SBA)
www.sba.gov
A federal agency that assists with women's businesses, veterans' affairs, disasters, financial management, minority businesses, statistical data, export advice, and general business questions.

Small Business Development Centers
Usually university-affiliated advisory centers located across the United States that provide counseling to small businesses. A Web search of small business development centers will provide a directory.

Standard & Poors Corp.
Industry Surveys
www.standardpoor.com
A series that covers various segments of industry. Compares growth in sales and earnings of the leading companies in each industry as well as tracks the profit margins, dividends, price-earnings ratios, and other data for each company over a 5-year span.

U.S. Bureau of Census
U.S. Department of Commerce
www.census.gov
A federal department that provides material on geographic, population, and industry trends.

U.S. Chamber of Commerce
www.uschamber.com
Provides data on all types of businesses nationwide. Sources of state information and state industrial directories are available. Local chambers of commerce can supply information.

U.S. Office of Consumer Affairs
Consumer Information Catalog
Publications that identify and describe major federal agencies and U.S. corporations.

Glossary of Terms

6-month plan A half-year merchandise plan that reflects planned and actual sales, markdowns, purchases, and stock for each month. *Ch 9*

Accelerated depreciation Any depreciation method that produces depreciation at a greater rate in the early years of an asset's life. *Ch 4*

Accounts receivable Money that is owed to the business for merchandise sold on credit. *Ch 11*

Accounts payable Obligations owed to creditors. *Ch 11*

Accruals payable Obligations accrued by a business that have not yet been paid. *Ch 11*

Acid test See *quick ratio*. *Ch 11*

Advertising A paid, impersonal communication delivered through mass media. *Ch 7*

Advertising allowances Advertising purchased by the buyer that has been negotiated with the vendor and paid for through the dollars allocated by the buyer's company. *Ch 9*

Advisory team An outside team of advisors that provides the entrepreneur with knowledge and input in making good business decisions, particularly in the areas where the entrepreneur has limited knowledge and expertise. *Ch 8*

Affiliate A web site owner who places merchant promotions on his or her site and makes a commission when a sale is generated from the Web site. *Ch 6*

Agent intermediaries Those who sell the products of domestic companies in foreign markets without actually taking ownership of the merchandise. *Ch 13*

All-in-one pricing The setting of every item at the same price, resulting in some items at below-average markup while others may be above-average markup. *Ch 9*

Angels Individuals who invest in start-up companies in exchange for an equity position in the company. *Ch 11*

Apparel mart A building or group of buildings that houses showrooms in which sales representatives present apparel lines to retail buyers. *Ch 9*

Application of industry averages The most common method of determining annual sales volume. *Ch 5*

ARPANET Advanced Research Projects Agency Network, started in 1969 to link computer systems for the U.S. Department of Defense, scientists, and academics in a collaborative environment. *Ch 6*

Articles of incorporation Document filed with the secretary of state to form a corporation. *Ch 10*

Articles of organization Documents filed with a state to form a limited liability company. *Ch 10*

Assets What a company owns. Assets may include such items as equipment and inventory. *Ch 11*

Assumptions An explanation of the source and thought process behind the set of financial numbers. *Ch 11*

Augmented The final level of all products that refers to the extras offered by the product. *Ch 2*

Backstock Merchandise that is held off the sales floor until needed. *Ch 9*

Back-up orders Shipments planned for later deliveries. *Ch 9*

Balance sheet A "snapshot" of a business at a given point in time that will reflect what the business is worth. *Ch 11*

Banner advertising Promotional announcements that appear at the top or side of a Web page. *Ch 6*

Bartering The process of finding a business with complementary needs in order to exchange some goods and services for others. *Ch 13*

Below market pricing Pricing merchandise below prices competitors demand. *Ch 7*

Benchmark operations A business that reflects a vision similar to the one the entrepreneur has for his or her business, but is usually not in the same location. *Ch 9*

Blue sky (good will) assets An intangible asset such as a business's image, personality, customer base, or name that the owner of a business may charge for when selling the business. *Ch 4*

Board of directors A group of people elected by the stockholders of a corporation who will be responsible for overseeing the overall direction and policy of the corporation. *Ch 8*

Bonus A lump-sum payment based on performance over an extended period of time. *Ch 12*

Book inventory The financial record of the stock. *Ch 12*

Book value The value of an asset as reflected in the company's financial records books. *Ch 4*

Boutique layout A layout pattern that divides the store into a series of individual shopping areas, each with its own theme. *Ch 5*

Brand A name, term, sign, design, or combination of these that is intended to identify the goods or services of one seller or group of sellers and to differentiate them from those of competitors. *Ch 2*

Brand badge The perception that a brand reflects customers' inner selves, who they want to be or believe they are. *Ch 2*

Brand mark · The part of a brand that can be recognized, but cannot be spoken. *Ch 2*

Brand name The part of a brand that can be vocalized. *Ch 2*

Brand sponsorship The selection of a brand name to incorporate into the merchandise assortment. *Ch 2*

Brand value The worth of the brand in terms of customer recognition, image, and potential sales volume. *Ch 2*

Branding The process of attaching a name and a reputation to something or someone. *Ch 2*

Break-even point The point at which the company shows neither a profit nor a loss, but simply covers all its costs. *Ch 11*

Brick operation A retail operation where consumers can visit the facility in person. *Ch 2*

Bundling A term used for items that are grouped together and sold for less than if each item was purchased separately. *Ch 9*

Business license A license that enables a company to conduct business within a specific jurisdiction. *Ch 10*

Business location The site and facility where the business is physically situated, as well as where catalogs are mailed and/or the business's Web site or Internet links. *Ch 5*

Business plan A document that provides direction and focus for both operations and growth for the company. *Ch 1*

Buyers Individuals who determine the merchandise needs for departments, or, sometimes entire stores, and, ultimately, make the inventory purchases. *Ch 9*

Buying power index A report published in the Survey of Buying Power that identifies consumer purchasing patterns in different states and regions. *Ch 3*

Cash The money that flows through the business in a continuous cycle without being tied up in any other asset. *Ch 11*

Cash flow The amount of cash that flows in and out of the business during an accounting period. *Ch 11*

Cash flow statement A financial document that determines the cash needs of the business on a month-to-month basis. *Ch 11*

Cash on hand The amount of cash the entrepreneur has to inject into the company. *Ch 11*

Central business district The area where downtown businesses were established early in the development of the city. *Ch 5*

Certificate of good standing A document issued by the state that certifies the corporation has complied with all laws and regulations to remain a separate legal entity. *Ch 10*

Certified Development Company (CDC) A nonprofit organization designed to promote economic growth in a community. *Ch 11*

Channel of distribution The avenue selected for moving goods from producer to consumer. *Ch 7*

Chart of accounts A listing of the accounts used by a business to track its transactions. *Ch 11*

Click operation A retail operation that consumers can visit over the Internet. *Ch 2*

Click through The activity of continuing toward the purchase process on-line. *Ch 6*

Clientele file A file that contains a customer profile form and provides information about the customer, contact information, size, brand preferences, past purchases, and personal information. *Ch 12*

Closed competitive environment A situation that is saturated with a high level of competition. *Ch 3*

Closely held corporations Corporations whose shares are typically held by a small number of people. *Ch 10*

Closeout merchandise Merchandise that has been overproduced or returned by retailers due to a lack of sales or shipment past the cancellation dates as specified on orders. *Ch 9*

Communication The process of transferring information and ideas from one person to another, with consistent understanding of the meaning. *Ch 8*

Compensation The employee's payment for services rendered. *Ch 12*

Compensation package Monetary or other value an employee receives in exchange for services. *Ch 8*

Competitive pricing A strategy in which a retailer bases its prices on those of the competitors. *Ch 7*

Completion (cancellation) date The last day that the buyer has authorized the vendor to ship merchandise. *Chs 9, 12*

Connectiveness The ways in which Web sites and affiliates partner in meeting customers' needs and interests. *Ch 6*

Contribution margin A figure that impacts calculating a break-even point and is equal to sales less variable costs. *Ch 11*

Control The point in the strategic planning process where results are compared to the goals and objectives. *Ch 12*

Convenience goods Products that the customer purchases frequently and easily, usually with minimal comparison shopping and evaluating. *Ch 2*

Cookies Allow e-commerce sites to collect and record visitor information and identify customers that best fit the target customer profile. *Ch 6*

Cooperative A resident buying office that represents a group of stores and operates under a corporate ownership. *Ch 9*

Cooperative advertising A program in which the vendor shares the cost of advertising with the retail operation. *Ch 9*

Copyright The exclusive rights to reproduce, publish, or sell the trademark in the form of a literary, musical, or artistic work. *Ch 2*

Core One of the three levels of all products that refers to the main benefit or service of the true product. *Ch 2*

Core inventory The inventory on hand when the doors of the business open. *Ch 11*

Corporation A separate legal entity created under the authority granted by state law. *Ch 10*

Cost of goods sold The wholesale price of the merchandise sold. *Ch 11*

Cost of sales to inventory ratio A ratio that measures the number of times inventory is turned over during the year. *Ch 11*

Counter trade A transaction in which a company selling goods and services in a foreign country agrees to help promote investment and trade in that country. *Ch 13*

Crawlers (spiders) A method used by crawler-based search engines to peruse all Web pages including titles, contents, graphics, audioclips, animation, and other elements. *Ch 6*

Cross-filing A reference system in which information is listed by two or more categories. *Ch 12*

Current assets Those items that can be converted into cash within one year or within the normal operating cycle of the company. *Ch 11*

Current liabilities Those debts that must be paid within one year or within the normal operating cycle of the company. *Ch 11*

Current portion of long-term debt The portion of the loan that will be paid in one year. *Ch 11*

Current ratio A ratio that measures whether or not the company has enough liquidity from its current assets to pay its short-term obligations. *Ch 11*

Customer mobility The ease with which clients can find a parking place, enter the establishment, and move about the business. *Ch 12*

Customer traffic patterns A technique that retailers use to increase the customer's exposure to the merchandise assortment through a creative design of aisles or the placement of departments. *Ch 5*

Cyclical patterns Recurring swings in business activity that move the business—its sales, cash flow, and profits, from a downslide to an upswing and back again. *Ch 3*

Dating An additional amount of time in which the retailer can pay the vendor. *Ch 12*

Debt financing The process of securing funds by borrowing money that must be repaid. *Ch 11*

Debt ratio Measures the portion of total assets that are financed through debt. *Ch 11*

Debt to equity ratio Measures the proportion of assets that are financed by creditors to those assets that are contributed by the owners. *Ch 11*

Decline stage The final phase of the product life cycle when consumers lose interest in the product. *Ch 2*

Declining stage for markets A phase in the product life cycle when profits and cash flow are reduced due to a lack of demand for the product as a result of technological, social, economic, and demographic shifts in the external and internal environments. *Ch 3*

Demographics The characteristics of a population or population segment used to identify consumer markets. *Ch 3*

Depreciation The allocation of the cost of an asset over the term of the asset's useful life. *Ch 4*

Direct competition Those retailer's products or services that consumers treat as acceptable alternatives. *Ch 3*

Direct exporting Where selling goods to another country takes place through the parent company. *Ch 8*

Disclosure document A document that provides information on advertising costs that the entrepreneur must pay to the franchisor. *Ch 4*

Disintermediation Elimination of inventory and of intermediaries through the use of digital networks. *Ch 6*

Distribution channels The routes taken to move the product to the wholesale businesses, or to the ultimate consumer. *Ch 3*

Distribution practices The manufacturer's policies about which retail operations will be shipped. *Ch 9*

Domain name The title of each hierarchal level of an Internet system. *Ch 6*

Domain Naming System (DNS) The system that administers names by giving different group responsibility for subsets of names. *Ch 6*

Domestic state The state in which the corporation chooses to locate its business. *Ch 10*

Durable goods Products that normally survive many uses, such as apparel, shoes, and home accessories. *Ch 2*

E-commerce A form of trade that is transacted electronically. *Ch 1*

Embargo A form of non-tariff that is a ban on imports of specific products. *Ch 13*

Employee procedures manual A guide for employees that indicates business policies and procedures. *Ch 12*

Employee stock ownership plan A plan under federal law that allows employees to buy stock in the company with funds borrowed from a bank, with the principal repaid from an employee's profit-sharing plan . *Ch 4*

Entertailing A concept that combines an interesting retail environment with appealing activities and desirable merchandise. *Ch 5*

Environmental scan An overview of significant areas such as the economy, politics, and social trends. *Ch 3*

Equity financing A form of financing that involves sharing ownership of the business. *Ch 11*

E-tailing Internet-based retailing. *Ch 9*

Exclusive goods Merchandise that is limited in distribution to specific retail operations. *Ch 2*

Exclusivity The limited availability of merchandise. *Ch 9*

Expanding stage A phase in the product life cycle where markets are in a growth stage and have the advantage of a rapidly increasing consumer base. *Ch 3*

External environments Variables that affect the firm's performance, but are outside the direct control of management. *Ch 3*

External sources Sources the entrepreneur may employ outside the company such as resident buying offices, fashion forecasters, and reporting services. *Ch 9*

Fair market value The value as the price at which the property would change hands between a willing buyer and a willing seller when the seller is not under any compulsion to sell, and both parties have reasonable knowledge of the relevant facts. *Ch 4*

Fashion goods Items that are popular for a given period of time. *Ch 2*

Fashion items Items that are frequently available in a wide range of styles and have a life expectancy that is relatively brief. *Ch 9*

Fashion seasons Collections of fashion merchandise developed by the manufacturer for varying time periods (e.g., fall I, fall II, holiday, spring, and summer). *Ch 9*

Fictitious name registration A person operating a business under a fictitious name files a certificate with the secretary of state disclosing the true name of the owners of the business for the purpose of protecting creditors from fraud and deceit. A fictitious name is any assumed name, style, or designation other than the proper name of the entity. Any business not required to file a document disclosing its name to the secretary of state's office must file a fictitious name registration. *Ch 11*

FIFO (First in, First out) A method for valuing and recording inventory that applies a higher value to goods according to the order in which they are received. *Ch 12*

Financial patterns The standards and norms used to determine pricing, to evaluate merchandise performance, and to specify billing terms within the fashion industry. *Ch 3*

Fixed assets Those assets that were acquired for long-term use in the business. *Ch 11*

Fixed costs Those costs that will be incurred whether a sale is made or not. *Ch 11*

Fixed-rate compensation Hourly, weekly, or monthly pay that is not tied exclusively to performance. *Ch 12*

Flexible markup policy A plan that allows the entrepreneur to apply different levels of markup to varying merchandise classifications. *Ch 7*

Focus groups A primary source of information that uses a group of persons in an interview situation to gain customer insight and to identify the future wants and needs of potential customers. *Ch 3*

Forecasting The art of estimating what is likely to happen given an assumed set of conditions. *Ch 3*

Foreign corporation A corporation that conducts business in a state other than its domestic state. *Ch 10*

Foreign licensing agreement An agreement that may occur when small companies enter markets abroad by licensing businesses in other nations to use their patents, trademarks, copyrights, products, or processes. *Ch 13*

Formal One of the three levels of all products that includes packaging, quality, styling, and any other tangible features of the product. *Ch 2*

Four Ps of marketing The elements needed to determine the marketing strategy: product, place, price, and promotion. *Ch 7*

Franchise Refers to an agreement granted to a dealer by a franchisor to sell products or services in a specified manner. *Ch 4*

Franchise fee A sum of money the franchisee must pay to the franchisor to operate a business. *Ch 4*

Franchisee The purchaser of a franchise. *Ch 4*

Franchisor The company that gives the investor the right to operate a business for a fee. *Ch 4*

Free-form layout An interior layout pattern that utilizes displays of varying shapes and sizes. *Ch 5*

Front-end costs See *start-up costs*. *Ch 4*

Funders Individuals or institutions and organizations that loan or grant money to the business. *Ch 1*

General agreement on tariffs and trade (GATT) An agreement established to encourage world trade. *Ch 3*

General line A wide variety of merchandise, one that has great breadth. *Ch 2*

Grid layout An interior layout pattern in which displays are arranged in a rectangular fashion so that the aisles are parallel to one another. *Ch 5*

Gross margin ratio A ratio that measures the amount of profit after direct costs are deducted. *Ch 11*

Gross profit The profit a company will generate before deducting operating expenses and other expenses, including interest. *Ch 11*

Growth capital The money needed to help a business grow and expand. *Ch 11*

Growth stage The second phase of the product life cycle that occurs when a larger number of consumers begin to accept and purchase the product. *Ch 2*

Growth strategies Plans that enable the entrepreneur to build and expand upon the initial business. *Ch 13*

Hard goods Non-apparel products such as appliances, furniture, and electronics. *Ch 2*

High-end goods A term used by retailers that refers to merchandise at the top of the pricing spectrum. *Ch 2*

Hourly plus commission (base plus commission) A payment alternative through which the salesperson earns a set amount for each hour, week, or month worked, as well as a percent of his or her sales volume. *Ch 12*

Hypertext link Connects the shopper to a new page or site on the Internet. *Ch 6*

Incentives Rewards given to employees to help motivate them in their work. *Ch 12*

Incidental costs Those costs in a business that may occur sporadically. *Ch 7*

Income statement A comparison of expenses against revenue over a certain period of time, usually one year. *Ch 11*

Independent A type of resident buying office that has no affiliation with any specific company or group of companies; rather it represents retailers who are willing to pay a fee for its services. *Ch 9*

Index of retail saturation (IRS) A method of estimating income and expenses for a location by measuring the number of customers in a specified area, their purchasing power, and the level of competition. *Ch 5*

Indirect competition Those retailer's products or services that can be easily substituted for one another. *Ch 3*

Indirect exporting When companies sell products internationally through a intermediary company in the entrepreneur's home country. *Ch 13*

Industry All companies supplying similar or related products/services. *Ch 3*

Initial markup The first markup added to the cost of merchandise to determine a selling price. *Ch 9*

Initial public offering (IPO) A company's first sale of stock to the public. *Ch 4*

Intangible products Goods that cannot be touched or held, such as a service or an idea. *Ch 2*

Intellectual property Any product, service, or retail operation that is the result of a creative process and that has commercial value. *Ch 2*

Internal markets Those activities in the business that are under the direct control of management. *Ch 3*

Internal sources Resources within the operation that an entrepreneur may investigate to gain information that may benefit the business. *Ch 9*

Interorganizational system (IOS) Electronic links that facilitate the flow of organizations, information, and communication. *Ch 6*

Intranet Electronic links for in-house communication. *Ch 6*

Intrapreneurship An organizational culture in which employees are encouraged to think as entrepreneurs. *Ch 10*

Introductory pricing A strategy that uses lower-than-competition pricing to gain entry into a market. *Ch 9*

Introductory stage The first stage of the product life cycle when innovative goods that appeal to fashion leaders, or trendsetters, are first offered. *Ch 2*

Inventory The merchandise selection a business has available to sell. *Ch 11*

Inventory turnover ratio Measures the number of times the company's inventory is sold during a year. *Ch 11*

Invoice The vendor's detailed payment listing with prices. *Ch 12*

Job analysis The process of evaluating the tasks needed to be accomplished. *Ch 8*

Job description An outline of the tasks, duties, and responsibilities of a position. *Ch 8*

Jobber A person who is paid a flat fee and/or a percentage of the liquidation sale to sell off inventory and dispose of the remaining stock. *Ch 4*

Joint ventures When two or more U.S. businesses form an association for the purpose of exporting their goods and services abroad. *Ch 13*

Just-in-time inventory control A method of inventory that calls for inventory to be shipped as it is sold. *Ch 12*

Key vendors The lines carried in depth by a retail organization. *Ch 9*

Layaway A service in which the customer can hold an item by making a deposit, then making weekly or monthly payments on the merchandise until the merchandise is paid off. *Ch 12*

Layout The arrangement of the equipment, fixtures, and inventory in a business. *Ch 5*

Lead time The amount of time needed between placing an order and receiving the goods in the retail operation. *Ch 9*

Leadership The ability to create an environment in which others feel empowered to work together to achieve a common goal. *Ch 8*

Legal entity An individual or organization that is legally permitted to enter into a contract or be sued if it fails to meet its contractual obligations. *Ch 10*

Letter of intent A letter addressed to a company stating the desire to conduct business. *Ch 4*

Leveraged buyout A takeover of a company or purchase of the controlling interest of the company using a significant amount of borrowed money. As a result, the public corporation becomes a privately held one. *Ch 4*

Liabilities A claim a creditor has against the company's assets. *Ch 11*

Licensing The practice of buying or selling the use of a brand name from one company to another. *Ch 2*

LIFO (Last in, First out) A method for valuing and recording inventory that places a higher value on most recently received merchandise. *Ch 12*

Limited liability company (LLC) An entity that offers the advantages of a corporation in terms of limited liability and the pass-through tax advantages of a partnership. *Ch 10*

Limited line A particular product category with depth of selection. *Ch 2*

Limited partnership A partnership composed of at least one general partner and one or more limited partners. *Ch 10*

Line of credit A short-term loan that provides cash flow for the day-to-day operations of the business. *Ch 11*

Liquid OTB Unspent funds that allow merchandise to be bought to update inventories and to replenish items that have sold out. *Ch 9*

Liquidation The process of converting assets into cash. *Ch 4*

Liquidation value The value of assets when sold. *Ch 4*

Liquidity ratio A ratio that measures the ability of the business to pay its current obligations as they come due. *Ch 11*

Long-term liabilities Those debts that will come due beyond a 1-year period. *Ch 11*

Loss leader The selling of one or a few items at or below cost price in order to attract customers, to generate traffic. *Ch 9*

Low-end goods A term used by retailers that refers to merchandise representing the budget price points. *Ch 2*

Maintained markup The amount a garment had to be reduced before it would be purchased by the consumer. *Ch 9*

Management succession A change in management. *Ch 4*

Manufacturer's brand The most traditional brand type of brand sponsorship, often referred to as a national brand. Examples of manufacturer's brands are Liz Claiborne, Donna Karan, and Adidas. See also *national brand. Ch 2*

Markdown   A decrease in the selling price of an item.   *Chs 9, 12*

Market analysis   The process of analyzing data to create useful information to guide the entrepreneur in determining the ability of the business to generate sales and create a positive cash flow.   *Ch 3*

Market factor method   A forecasting approach that is made by identifying the relationship between sales behavior and the behavior of a factor or a set of factors that is highly correlated with sales.   *Ch 3*

Market leader   A business that has the largest market share as it enters a growth stage.   *Ch 13*

Market penetration   Refers to the strategies used to reach the company's target market.   *Ch 3*

Market research   A systematic, objective collection and analysis of data of both internal and external environments.   *Ch 3*

Market weeks   A traditional purchase period when buyers begin to make selections for the next season.   *Ch 9*

Markup   The amount added to the cost of the product to establish the selling price.   *Ch 7*

Maturity   The third stage in the product life cycle that occurs when the product reaches a peak or plateau and is mass-produced and mass-marketed.   *Ch 2*

Members   A name that refers to the owners of a limited liability company.   *Ch 10*

Merchandise assortments   The selection of inventory a retailer carries or a manufacturer produces.   *Chs 2, 9*

Merchandise classifications   Related groups of items found in a department of the retail operation.   *Ch 9*

Merchandise discounts   A form of incentive that the majority of fashion retailers use to recruit and reward employees.   *Ch 12*

Merchandise fulfillment   The process of providing merchandise as requested by the consumer.   *Ch 12*

Merchandising   The buying and selling of goods.   *Ch 9*

Merchandising and operating results (MOR)   Information on national retail sales published by the National Retail Federation.   *Ch 3*

Merchant   A retailer who has products or services for sale.   *Ch 6*

Merchant intermediaries   Those who actually purchase the goods at a discount from domestic companies and resell it abroad.   *Ch 13*

Minimum orders   The dollar or unit amount that the vendor requires before accepting an order.   *Ch 9*

Mission statement   A statement that addresses what business the company is in, its primary purpose, strategies, and values.   *Ch 1*

Model stock   An inventory that includes an appropriate assortment of merchandise in terms of price points, styles, size ranges, colors, and fabrics.   *Ch 9*

Motivation   The willingness to exert high levels of effort toward organizational goals, conditioned by the effort's ability to satisfy some individual need.   *Ch 8*

Mystery shopper   Refers to a person employed to shop at specific stores and report on findings related to customer service, merchandise assortments, store layouts, and other topics.   *Ch 3*

Name search   A search of the names of corporations that are registered with a state's secretary of state's office.   *Ch 10*

National brand   The most traditional type of brand sponsorship. See also *manufacturer's brand*.   *Ch 2*

National Retail Traffic Index (NRTI)   A report that provides information about shopper traffic in a specific area.   *Ch 5*

Near cash assets   Those assets that can easily be converted to cash.   *Ch 11*

Net profit on sales ratio   A measure of a company's profit per dollar of sales.   *Ch 11*

Net sales   The dollar amount of sales made during a specific time period excluding sales tax and any returns or allowances on merchandise.   *Ch 11*

New stage   A phase in the product life cycle that provides excellent opportunities for entrepreneurial businesses in the formative stage.   *Ch 3*

Niche retailing   A form of retailing that refers to identifying and fulfilling the specific merchandise needs of a specific customer group.   *Ch 13*

Nondurable goods   Products that are normally consumed in one or a few uses, such as shampoo.   *Ch 2*

Non-selling space The amount of square footage not being used as selling space. *Ch 12*

Nonstore retail operations Operations that do not have a physical environment, though which the customer can see, touch, and try on the merchandise. *Ch 9*

Nontariff A form of regulation imposed on products brought into a country to protect their internal businesses and to regulate trade. *Ch 13*

Nonverbal communication A form of communication that relates to how one acts. *Ch 8*

Notes payable The obligations due to creditors that have loaned the company money. *Ch 11*

North American Free Trade Agreement (NAFTA) Created a free trade area among the United States, Canada, and Mexico. *Ch 13*

North American Industry Classification System (NAICS) Classifies U.S. industries by type and then further divides the classification into subcomponents. *Ch 2*

Objective and Task Method A method of determining an advertising budget by linking the advertising expenditures to specific objectives. *Ch 7*

Odd pricing The technique of setting prices that end in odd numbers. *Ch 7*

Off-balance sheet valuations The values within a business that do not appear in the firm's financial reports. *Ch 4*

Offering memorandum A document that is often prepared by a business broker that contains comprehensive information about the company and will serve as a basis for the buyer's preliminary evaluation of the company. *Ch 4*

Off-price merchandise Goods that the buyer has been able to purchase from the manufacturer at less than the wholesale price. *Ch 9*

On-hand stock The amount of inventory the retailer needs to reach sales goals less the merchandise that is currently available. *Ch 9*

On-order Orders that have been placed with the vendor, but have not been shipped. *Ch 9*

Open book management The sharing of all company information with all employees, including financial data. *Ch 8*

Open competitive environment A situation in which the entrepreneur finds very little competition for the business. *Ch 3*

Open-to-buy (OTB) The amount of funds the buyer should be spending in each merchandise classification for each month of the business. *Ch 9*

Operating agreement A contract that dictates an LLC's organizational structure, describes internal policies, and specifies how the profits will be shared. *Ch 10*

Operating costs The day to day expenses incurred in running a business. *Ch 7*

Operating expenses Those costs that are related to maintaining the operations of the business such as rent, telephone, meals and entertainment, and office supplies. *Ch 11*

Operating ratios Ratios that measure how effectively a company utilizes its resources. *Ch 11*

Operations The procedures put in place to actually run the business. *Ch 12*

Organizational chart A chart that defines how the business is organized and illustrates the relationship between the positions. *Ch 8*

Organizational culture The personality of the business, its attitudes, values, and communication style. *Ch 8*

Original retail price The initial selling price established for an item. *Ch 7*

Organizational structure The way in which the organization defines job tasks, how these tasks are divided and grouped, and how they are coordinated. *Ch 8*

Outsourcing Contracting with individuals or other businesses outside the company. *Ch 1*

Overage The dollar amount when the physical inventory is greater than book inventory. *Ch 12*

Overbought A term used when the buyer has purchased more than allocated and/or when sales are lower than planned. *Ch 9*

Owner's draw The amount of money the owner is taking out of the company. *Ch 11*

Owner's equity The owner's claim to the assets of the business after all obligations have been accounted for and satisfied. *Ch 11*

Packing slip The vendor's listing of merchandise in a particular carton or container. *Ch 12*

Participative management   A management style that allows employees at all levels of the organization to be trusted and empowered to make decisions and to take the actions necessary to get the job done.   *Ch 8*

Partnership   A business that is formed when two or more individuals join together to make a profit.   *Ch 10*

Partnership agreement   A document that dictates in writing the details of operating the partnership.   *Ch 10*

Percentage of sales (or profits) method   A method used to establish a working advertising budget by taking budgeted costs as a percentage of sales.   *Ch 7*

Performance appraisals   A tool used to measure an employee's actual performance against the performance desired by an employer.   *Ch 8*

Perpetual markdown policy   A policy that occurs when retailers reduce the prices on merchandise each month for a variety of reasons.   *Ch 9*

Physical inventory count   A formal, item-by-item analysis of the operation's stock on hand.   *Ch 12*

Planned obsolescence   A concept that occurs when the customer makes an emotional decision to buy something new and fashionable.   *Ch 9*

Point-of-sale (POS)   A computerized cash register that generates a customer receipt while adjusting the retail dollar inventory value.   *Ch 12*

Population density   The number of people per square mile residing in a given area.   *Ch 5*

Power centers   A concept that combines the drawing potential of a large regional mall with the convenience of a neighborhood shopping center.   *Ch 5*

Prepaid expenses   Payments in advance for services that will benefit the business in the future.   *Ch 11*

Price ceiling   The maximum price a consumer is willing to pay for a product or service.   *Ch 7*

Price floor   The minimum price that can be charged for a good or service based on costs.   *Ch 7*

Price lining   A marketing strategy based on maintaining a consistent pricing philosophy for all products.   *Ch 7*

Price skimming   The technique that can be offered by retailers selling a product that is new to the market, or to an elite group of buyers not sensitive to price.   *Ch 7*

Primary sources   Information resources that include the use of focus groups, current customers, employees, suppliers, and consultants.   *Ch 3*

Prime selling space   A location with the highest level of customer traffic.   *Ch 5*

Principal payment   The portion of a note or loan excluding interest.   *Ch 11*

Privacy statement   Informs consumers that appropriate security measures are implemented.   *Ch 6*

Private brand   This may be referred to as the agent, distributor, or dealer brand.   *Ch 2*

Private label   Represents a brand name exclusive to a retailer.   *Ch 2*

Privately owned   A type of resident buying office that is owned by the retailer.   *Ch 9*

Product   Any item or service offered to a market for attention, acquisition, use, or consumption.   *Ch 7*

Product life cycle   A model designed to identify the maturation stage of a particular product by approximating its level of consumer acceptance.   *Ch 2*

Profit   The difference between a company's total revenue and its total expenses.   *Ch 11*

Profitability ratio   Measures how efficiently a business is managed.   *Ch 11*

Pro forma   A term that is used in the business and accounting industry to indicate projected data.   *Ch 11*

Promotion   The activities needed to inform the potential consumer about the product.   *Ch 7*

Proprietary brands   A brand owned by a retailer and often represented by celebrity partners who add prestige and familiarity to the brand image.   *Ch 2*

Protected class   A class such as race, color, national origin, sex, age, religion, and disability.   *Ch 8*

Psychographics   The use of data to study and measure attitudes, values, lifestyles, and opinions for marketing purposes.   *Ch 3*

Publicly held corporations   Corporations that have a large number of shareholders and are traded on one of the large stock exchanges. *Ch 10*

Purchase agreement A document that is used when purchasing property that states the purchase price, terms of payment, and related issues involved in the sale. *Ch 4*

Purchase journal A log of all purchase orders placed and not received. *Ch 9*

Qualitative data Informed estimates used to forecast sales for a new business. *Ch 3*

Quantitative data Mathematical information used to analyze historical or estimated data to forecast sales for a new business. *Ch 9*

Quick ratio A ratio that calculates whether or not the company has enough liquid assets, or cash, to cover its short-term obligations. *Ch 11*

Quota A government-regulated limit on the amount of a product imported into a country. *Ch 13*

Quota plus commission A form of sales commission where the salesperson is assigned a sales goal and receives a specified percent of sales generated above the goal. *Ch 12*

Ratio analysis An analysis that allows the entrepreneur to examine the relationship between one financial value and another. *Ch 11*

Reintermediation Occurs when new intermediaries use electronic networks to add value to the intermediation process and replace traditional intermediaries. *Ch 6*

Relationship selling A form of selling that uses relationships to attract and maintain a loyal customer base. *Ch 7*

Research and development An on-going analysis of trends and issues that will impact the products, services, operations, promotional efforts, competitors, and customers of the business. *Ch 12*

Resident buying office A company that performs advisory tasks and assists the entrepreneur and/or buyer by providing a significant number of services. *Ch 9*

Retail layout The arrangement of merchandise and methods of display of merchandise in a store. *Ch 5*

Retained earnings Net income kept within the business. *Ch 11*

Return authorization label A label requested by the buyer from the vendor that

assures a shipment being returned will be accepted at the receiving dock of the manufacturer. *Ch 12*

Risk ratio Measures the extent of a company's debt. It shows the level to which the entrepreneur relies on debt to finance the operations of the business. *Ch 11*

RTM (RTV) Merchandise sent back to the manufacturer or vendor. *Ch 12*

Sale for cash plus a note A business transaction option that occurs when the seller of property holds on to a promissory note for a portion of the business until the entrepreneur has paid the note. *Ch 4*

Sales compensation A method of variable compensation. *Ch 12*

Sales forecast An informed estimate based on a given set of assumptions about the future sales volume for a specific target market and a specific merchandise classification. *Ch 9*

Sales tax bond A deposit held by the state to offset any unpaid sales tax incurred by the business. *Ch 1*

Salvage investments See *turnaround* *Ch 4*

Sample A group randomly selected from the target population. *Ch 3*

S-corporation A corporation that differs from a c-corporation in terms of its federal tax issues. *Ch 10*

Seasonal patterns Distinct changes in activity within a calendar year that affect sales, cash flow, and profits. *Ch 3*

Secondary sources Information already available for use such as government census reports, information from news organizations, the Internet, commercial on-line services, and trade associations. *Ch 3*

Secure Electronic Transactions (SET) On-line security system developed by Visa and Master Card. *Ch 6*

Secure Socket Layers (SSL) A security system that encrypts on-line communications to make Web site transactions private. *Ch 6*

Seed capital (start-up capital) The amount of money the business needs to open its doors. *Ch 11*

Selling space The amount of square footage to be allocated for displaying merchandise to be sold. *Ch 12*

Service products Activities, benefits, or satisfactions that are offered for sale.

Shareholder   A person who owns stock in the company, but has a right to very little participation in the management of the corporation.   *Ch 10*

Shopping-cart technology   Software that allows consumers to select items and to accumulate them in their electronic shopping baskets before proceeding to payment options.   *Ch 6*

Shopping goods   Products that the customer often compares on the basis of price, quality, style, and related factors.   *Ch 2*

Shortage   The difference when there is less physical inventory than book inventory. *Ch 12*

Shrinkage   The industry term for inventory losses resulting from employee theft, shoplifting, and/or clerical errors.   *Ch 12*

Skimming   A strategy in which the retailer sets a high initial price, usually through high markup, and then gradually lowers it. *Ch 9*

Soft goods   Fabrics and home textiles.   *Ch 2*

Sole proprietorship   A business that is owned and operated by one individual. *Ch 10*

Space value   The value of each square foot of space in the store in terms of generating sales revenue.   *Ch 5*

Spamming   The use of mass e-mailing to people who have not expressed interest in receiving the information.   *Ch 6*

Specialty goods   Products that a significant group of buyers is habitually willing to make a special purchase of; this merchandise has unique characteristics and/or special brand identification. *Ch 9*

Spreadsheet   An electronic chart that simplifies data and increases accuracy when dealing with business analyses.   *Ch 12*

Stable market   A phase in the product life cycle where customer sales have leveled off.   *Ch 3*

Standard industrial classification (SIC)   A system that classifies U.S. industries by type, then further divides the classification into subcomponents.   *Ch 3*

Staples   Goods that are in demand for an extended period of time and not subject to rapid style changes.   *Ch 9*

Start-up costs   Costs that are incurred by the entrepreneur to begin the operation of a business.   *Ch 4*

Stickiness   The use of informative content on a Web site to keep shoppers on the site or to encourage them to return for more information later.   *Ch 6*

Stock-keeping unit (SKU)   The identification numbers given to an item of merchandise.   *Ch 12*

Stock-to-sales ratio   A measurement of sales and inventory performance that works in alignment with stockturn to see if the stockturn goal is in reach.   *Ch 9*

Stockturn   A measurement of inventory performance that guides the entrepreneur in assessing the productivity of inventory. *Ch 9*

Straight commission   A form of remuneration through which the salesperson is paid a percent of his or her sales volume.   *Ch 12*

Style   The specific looks within the subclassification.   *Ch 9*

Subclassifications   A detailed breakdown of the merchandise classification based on the variables of price, color, size, and style. *Ch 9*

Supply chain management   A trend in merchandise fulfillment that enables the entrepreneur to provide the customer with merchandise in a timely manner.   *Ch 12*

Supply channels   The companies that provide materials and equipment needed to manufacture the product, as well as companies that actually sell the goods.   *Ch 3*

SWOT analysis   A method of business analysis that focuses on the strengths, weaknesses, opportunities, and threats of a business idea.   *Ch 1*

Tangible products   Products that can be touched. See also *durable goods* and *non-durable goods*.   *Ch 2*

Target demographics   The specific consumer subgroups in a given population that a retail business aims to attract.   *Ch 5*

Tariff   A tax or duty that a government imposes on goods and services imported into that country.   *Ch 13*

Title search   A search that may be done when purchasing property to make certain that the seller has clear title and that there are no recorded claims or liens against the property.   *Ch 4*

Tracking merchandise   Monitoring the performance of items in the inventory. *Ch 12*

Tracking plan A plotted pattern that is created from observing the movements of random samples of shoppers. *Ch 5*

Trade dress The combined visual components of a trademark. *Ch 2*

Trade intermediaries A business that serves as a distributor in foreign countries for domestic companies of all sizes. *Ch 13*

Trademark A brand or part of a brand that is given legal protection because it is capable of securing legal rights. *Ch 2*

Transaction A cash or credit sale, an exchange, or a return. *Ch 12*

Trunk shows An event that features a designer or company representative who brings the line to the retailer's operation for the customer to see and learn about first hand. *Ch 9*

Turnaround A business that is failing, but for which there are obvious changes that, when implemented, would make the business successful *Ch 4*

Turnkey operation A business that is completely assembled or set up to begin operation and is then leased or sold to an individual to manage . *Ch 4*

U.S. Small Business Administration (SBA) A federal agency designed to help obtain financing for both start-up and existing small companies that do not qualify for traditional loans because of the risk of failure or lack of a good asset base. *Ch 11*

Uniform Partnership Act (UPA) An act that governs the operations of a partnership in the absence of a partnership agreement. *Ch 10*

Uniform resource locator (URL) A string of characters that identifies the location of every page, graphic image, and title on the World Wide Web. *Ch 6*

Unique selling proposition (USP) A key benefit of the product or service to the consumer, that sets the product or service apart from its competition. *Ch 7*

Unsought goods Merchandise the customers, did not seek out and didn't know they needed until it found them. *Ch 2*

User characteristics An aspect of the regional market feasibility study that categorizes the traits of the user. *Ch 3*

Variable costs Expenses that vary in proportion to changes in the level of activity or in proportion to sales. *Ch 11*

Variable-rate (merit) compensation Payment tied directly to the performance of the individual or group. *Ch 12*

Vendor analysis An analysis that summarizes sales, markdowns, and returns for each manufacturer and can guide buyers after the opening season.

Venture capitalists Private persons or organizations that purchase an equity position in the company in exchange for a return on their investment. *Ch 11*

Venture managers An individual who works to grow a business to the point that it can be taken public once its size and profitability allow. *Ch 4*

Verbal communication A form of communication that relates to what is said. *Ch 8*

Vision statement A statement that addresses what the owner or business stands for, believes in, and intends to accomplish. *Ch 1*

Working capital The money needed to operate the business on a short-term basis. *Ch 11*

Index ✕✕✕✕✕✕✕✕✕

Many entrepreneurs spend a great deal of time setting up and establishing a functional format to effectively express their entrepreneurial vision in print. By using the proven FastTrac™ planning processes on The Business Mentor™, you will save time and get a jump-start in developing successful plans. Throughout this planning process, the FastTrac mentors will point you in the right direction, challenge your thinking, provide tips and ideas, and direct you to resources and solutions. It's almost like having your own personal mentor who inspire you, motivate you and support you in your business venture.

INSTALLING THE BUSINESS MENTOR

Insert The Business Mentor CD-ROM into your CD-ROM drive. The installation routine begins automatically. If installation does not begin, then choose Run from the Start taskbar and type "D:SETUP." If using another CD-ROM drive letter, substitute it for "D:". Confirm or change the installation directory.

RUNNING THE BUSINESS MENTOR

After The Business Mentor has been installed, you can run the program automatically by inserting the CD-ROM into your computer's CD-ROM drive. If the CD-ROM is already in the drive, click on the Windows Start button and select The Business Mentor from the list of available Programs.

The Business Mentor Minimum System Requirements
- Windows 95/98, Windows NT 4.0 or Windows 2000 or higher
- Pentium II processor or higher
- 64 MB RAM or higher
- 10 MB available hard disk space
- 16-bit graphics card or higher
- Microsoft Word 97 or higher (or other word processing software capable of opening text-based documents in RTF format)
- Microsoft Excel 97 or higher (if you do not have Excel, all spreadsheet templates are available in Adobe PDF format for viewing and printing)
- Microsoft Internet Explorer 5.0 or Netscape Navigator 4.7 or higher (or other Internet browser software such as AOL)
- Adobe Acrobat Reader 4.05 or higher (version included on CD-ROM)
- QuickTime 4.1.2 or higher (version of 5.0 included on CD-ROM)

THE FASTTRAC PLANNING TEMPLATES

The Business Mentor CD-ROM provides a collection of helpful information and resources for working on two important planning documents, the Feasibility Plan and the Business Plan. In this course you will be working on a Business Plan. Each Planning Template is organized into sections of the plan. Each section of the plan contains a series of questions and supporting information. The plan sections are easy to navigate and are tied directly to the key sections of the corresponding Business Plan.

The FastTrac Business Planning Template
The FastTrac Business Planning Template guides you through the writing of a business plan. Simply answer the detailed questions to populate each section of the plan. Included in the Business Planning template is a Microsoft Excel-based Financial Plan Template. The key sections covered in creating the Business Plan include: Executive Summary, Management and Organization Plan, Product/Service Plan, Marketing Plan, Financial Plan, Operating and Control Systems Plan and the Growth Plan.

PRODUCT SUPPORT

E-mail and Fax Support
E-mail and fax support are available seven days a week. Send e-mail to support@fasttrac.org or fax your question to (816) 235-6216. FastTrac typically can respond to your questions within 48 hours.

FOR A FULL DESCRIPTION OF HOW TO USE THE BUSINESS MENTOR, PLEASE SELECT THE TECHNICAL HELP ICON LOCATED IN THE MENTOR'S OFFICE ON THE CD-ROM.